AF179473

ENHANCED TRANSITION THROUGH OUTWARD INTERNATIONALIZATION

Transition and Development

Series Editor: Professor Ken Morita
Faculty of Economics, Hiroshima University, Japan

The Transition and Development series aims to provide high quality research books that examine transition and development societies in a broad sense – including countries that have made a decisive break with central planning as well as those in which governments are introducing elements of a market approach to promote development. Books examining countries moving in the opposite direction will also be included. Titles in the series will encompass a range of social science disciplines. As a whole the series will add up to a truly global academic endeavour to grapple with the questions transition and development economies pose.

Also in the series:

Institutional Change in Transition Economies
Edited by Michael Cuddy and Ruvin Gekker
ISBN 0 7546 1977 X

The Social Impact of Informal Economies in Eastern Europe
Edited by Rainer Neef and Manuela Stănculescu
ISBN 0 7546 1950 8

Small Firms and Economic Development in Developed and Transition Economies: A Reader
Edited by David A. Kirby and Anna Watson
ISBN 0 7546 3060 9

Modeling Russia's Economy in Transition
Peter Wehrheim
ISBN 0 7546 3299 7

Foreign Direct Investment in Central and Eastern Europe
Edited by Svetla Trifonova Marinova and Marin Alexandrov Marinov
ISBN 0 7546 3026 9

Facilitating Transition by Internationalization
Outward Direct Investment from Central European Economies
Edited by Marjan Svetličič and Matija Rojec
ISBN 0 7546 3133 8

Enhanced Transition Through Outward Internationalization

Outward FDI by Slovenian firms

ANDREJA JAKLIČ and MARJAN SVETLIČIČ
Faculty of Social Sciences,
University of Ljubljana, Slovenia

ASHGATE

© Andreja Jaklič and Marjan Svetličič 2003

All rights reserved. No part of this publication may be reproduced, stored in a retrieval system or transmitted in any form or by any means, electronic, mechanical, photocopying, recording or otherwise without the prior permission of the publisher.

Andreja Jaklič and Marjan Svetličič have asserted their right under the Copyright, Designs and Patents Act, 1988, to be identified as the Authors of this Work.

This book is a revised version of documents presented by the authors in the context of the European Commission's Phare ACE Programme. Its content does not, however, express the Commission's official views. Responsibility for the information and views set out in the book lies entirely with the authors. Original documents © European Communities, 2001.

Published by
Ashgate Publishing Limited
Gower House
Croft Road
Aldershot
Hampshire GU11 3HR
England

Ashgate Publishing Company
Suite 420
101 Cherry Street
Burlington, VT 05401-4405
USA

Ashgate website: http://www.ashgate.com

British Library Cataloguing in Publication Data
Jaklič, Andreja
Enhanced transition through outward internationalization : outward FDI by Slovenian firms. - (Transition and development)
1.Investments, Slovak 2.Slovenia - Economic policy
I.Title II. Svetličič, Marjan
332.6'734973

Library of Congress Cataloging-in-Publication Data
Jaklič, Andreja.
Enhanced transition through outward internationalization : outward FDI by Slovenian firms / Andreja Jaklič, and Marjan Svetličič.
p. cm. -- (Transition and development)
Includes bibliographical references and index.
ISBN 0-7546-3134-6
1. Investments, Foreign--Slovenia. 2. Corporations--Slovenia. 3. Slovenia--Economic conditions. I. Svetličič, Marjan II. Title. III. Series.

HG5687.A3 J35 2002
332.67'34973--dc21

2002074549

ISBN 0 7546 3134 6

Printed and bound in Great Britain by MPG Books Ltd, Bodmin, Cornwall

Contents

PART III INVESTING ABROAD: FROM IDEA TO RESULTS

PART IV CASE STUDIES

PART V LESSONS FROM SLOVENIA

List of Figures

List of Tables

List of Boxes

About the Authors

Andreja Jaklič is a young researcher and teaching assistant in the field of International Economics and International Finance working in the Centre for International Relations at the Faculty of Social Sciences, University of Ljubljana. She is a member of European International Business Academy (EIBA) and Central and Eastern European International Studies Association (CEEISA). Her papers presented at several international conferences – EIBA, CEEISA and European Association for Comparative Economic Studies (EACES) – were included in the related proceedings. She is the author of articles published in *Eastern European Economics*, *Transnational Corporations*, *Economic and Business Review for Central and Eastern Europe* and some chapters in books published by Elsevier, Ashgate, Lappeenranta University of Technology and Union of Economists of Slovenia.

Marjan Svetličič is Professor of International Economics and former Dean at the Faculty of Social Sciences, University of Ljubljana. He is a member of the European Academy of International Business Board and has been a consultant to a number of international organizations. He is also a member of the editorial boards of several academic journals and author and editor of many books and articles, including *Foreign Investment in Central and Eastern Europe* (with P. Artisien and M. Rojec, Macmillan Press Ltd., Basingstoke, 1993), *The World Economy: Challenges of Globalization and Regionalization* (editor with H. Singer, Macmillan Press Ltd., Basingstoke, 1996), and *Small Countries in a Global Economy* (editor with D. Salvatore and J.P. Damijan, Palgrave, Basingstoke, 2001).

Preface

In 1991 Peter Drucker claimed in an interview with Forbes magazine 'you'll see more Slovenias' (p. 74). What he meant was that the emergence of small countries is a trend of the future and not unique to Slovenia. Otherwise, 'among those countries seeking membership in the European Union, Slovenia's position seems to be unique. It is the most developed among them, with a physical infrastructure suggesting an economic potential for economic expansion; it has a very favourable geographical location and its economy has suffered less from socialist mis-development than the others' (World Bank, 1999; p. 45).

Is it possible to say that we are also going to see more Slovenias involved in the internationalization of firms' activities, which is the topic of this book? Will other transition countries follow the intensive investing abroad undertaken by Slovenian firms? Kalotay claims that Russia and Hungary are becoming important investors abroad. Nevertheless, the expectations of a very strong upswing in outward foreign direct investment (FDI) by Slovenian firms failed to materialize (in the period before 1998, authors' note). With the end of the transition, firms no longer needed their system-escape footholds to carry out business in major markets. They could decide to return to trade at arm's length. Hence, some decided to discontinue outward FDI or even to go as far as to divest (Kalotay, 2002; p. 275). The situation has changed substantially since then; Slovenian firms have started to invest very strongly in the former republics of Yugoslavia and other Central and Eastern European countries (CEECs).

This increased internationalization in recent years of Slovenian firms and those from transition economies in general is one reason we decided to look into outward internationalization through FDI more closely. Another reason is that it has been an almost completely neglected issue. The literature on transition economies has so far concentrated almost exclusively on inward FDI, forgetting that inward and outward investments are merely two sides of the same coin.

The expected strengthening of internationalization was perhaps the most important reason leading to this book on outward investment by Slovenian firms. In fact, this intensification has already happened; in the last three years outward FDI by transition countries has grown very quickly, even faster than inward investment (see UNCTAD, 2001). Firms are realizing that, without internationalization, they can no longer maintain their market shares. Internationalization is also their response to the threats of globalization and a way for firms to adapt to the challenges posed by integration into the European Union (EU).

What also stimulated research in the area of outward FDI was the neglect of the internationalization issue, even ignorance, apparent not only in Slovenia but also in other transition economies. The internationalization of firms from transition economies was only a few years ago considered an 'exotic' activity, yet it is now gaining in importance under the pressures of globalization. At a conference in 1996 in Ljubljana, when one of the authors was explaining the theoretical necessity to invest abroad (Svetličič, 1996a), the following question was put to him: 'are you serious, we need capital at home, therefore we must import it and not export it'. This is the best illustration of how skeptical even professionals were. The same was true when advocating the establishment of Slovenian multinationals in the context of preparing a long-term strategy for the international economic co-operation of Slovenia (Svetličič, 1995). Some foreign experts even claimed this was not a serious proposal. Firms have a different opinion and have already been doing it for decades without any top-down support. Today's blooming multinationals from transition economies are the best proof of how wrong they were. Almost simultaneously, we applied for a Phare Action for Cooperation in the field of Economics (ACE) project on the outward foreign direct investment undertaken by three candidate-countries. That proposal was turned down, basically due to its 'low policy relevance'. The same project was accepted two years later. In 2001, research in the field of investment by Slovenian firms in former Yugoslavia, the most dynamic part of outward internationalization, was booming. The climate has changed dramatically. Those who saw outward FDI a few years ago as an almost unpatriotic activity are now advocating it. Amongst those, you can also find some who are unenthusiastic about the inflow of foreign capital. 'Ideologically-based' fears of dependency resulting from inward FDI are quickly forgotten when it comes to the potential of profit for one's own firm as an investor abroad. In other words, capitalism is all right when it comes to 'exporting it' but this is not so when it is imported from abroad through FDI, when foreigners come to your 'playground' and make decisions instead of or together with you. Those proposing such internationalization back then are now warning that only investing in former Yugoslavia is not the optimal long-term policy. In order to be competitive world-wide, internationalization should not stop on the borders of the former common state, while investing in the EU is one way of adapting to anticipated membership in the EU.

The first challenge the authors have to address is whether such trends are exceptional, limited to Slovenia or a few other transition economies, or whether this is only the start of a long-term trend. Are other transition economies following Slovenia, or is this a very specific case? We are convinced that transition economies will ride internationalization and globalization waves very quickly and that we will soon see the 'honeymoon' of their multinationals, which are in any case no longer such a 'rare bird'. UNCTAD (2001) collected data for the 25 largest of these multinationals, including five from Slovenia. What a change that is compared to just 20 years ago when, while discussing the Code of Conduct on Transnationals in the United Nations Commission on Transnational Companies, officials from socialist countries bitterly opposed the proposal of a group of Western countries that the Code and the United Nations Centre on Transnationals should include these enterprises if they complied with other criteria such as an international spread of their activities (for more on this, see Hamilton, 1986; pp. 4 and 5).

Why is Slovenia such an interesting case to study? First, it is the most advanced transition economy in terms of gross domestic product (GDP) per capita and, according to theory, outward FDI is supposed to follow a country's level of development. At the same time, Slovenia is a small country and the theory also predicts that small countries are supposed to be more internationalized than large ones. Slovenia is also a country where outward investment did not start with transition, with the system's change. The earliest outward FDI started back in the 1950s, firmly in socialist times when Slovenia was still part of Yugoslavia. Therefore, it is no surprise that some Slovenian firms are truly multinational and account for important market shares in industrial countries rather than just in 'fellow' transition economies.

Although small, the experiences of Slovenian companies in internationalization seem to be relevant not only for other small transition economies, but also from a theoretical point of view. Namely, their internationalization started even before inward investment which somewhat contradicts the prevailing contention of the investment development path paradigm that a country first imports FDI and, only later after having reached a certain development level, starts exporting capital. Does this mean a departure from the traditional explanation of sequential growth involving first inward and only then outward FDI? We will try to demonstrate that the internationalization of Slovenian firms generally does follow the accepted explanation of internationalization as a sequential process, although the stages seem to be ever shorter now and the need to jump over stages seems to be increasing. There are even many similarities with the internationalization of certain other small economies. Portugal is one case in point, where the first stage of its internationalization was directed to former colonies (see Simoes, 2001). Clearly, previous political and economic ties play a significant role and can facilitate outward FDI.

However, those who claim that outward FDI still only has a marginal importance are right to a certain extent. FDI is still very modest in volume, although it is growing fast and, we predict, will accelerate greatly in the future. Therefore, it is surely high time that research is undertaken early enough so that other firms and authorities can learn from others' experiences and mistakes, rather than merely brilliantly explaining what happened in the past. This book is a modest attempt in this direction. We hope it proves to be useful not only for academics, but also for politicians when designing policies, businessmen in facing the challenges of internationalization in increasingly more dramatic and urgent ways and, lastly, the general public. Fears that outward FDI means the exporting of jobs and exports of much needed capital at home are still very strong, while a broader understanding of the restructuring role of investing abroad deserves more attention. FDI can only develop smoothly if attitudinal barriers are gradually dismantled. This could also be one of the main objectives of the book.

Last but not least, does Slovenia as 'one among the most successful transition economies of Central and Eastern Europe' and one which 'has already achieved significant economic convergence with the European Union, and has built an impressive record of sustained, broad-based growth, reflecting strong competitiveness' (IMF, 2001; p. 2) have some lessons to tell to other countries? Are these lessons relevant to them? Has outward FDI contributed to Slovenia's success story and its growing competitiveness?

The key novelty of the book is its concentration on outward internationalization through direct investment abroad. So far, the literature has only concentrated on inward FDI and its development role while it is obvious from the theory that inward and outward FDI are only two sides of the same coin of the internationalization of firms' activities. In summary, this book's objectives are:

- to evaluate the process of outward internationalization and its significance in the transition from a planned to a market economy;
- to evaluate the role of transnational companies from transition economies for the national economy and the development implications of outward internationalization;
- to put Slovenia's experience in internationalization into the framework of existing internationalization theories, to detect the differences, if any, compared to that involving similar firms from transition economies or those from Organization for Economic Cooperation and Development (OECD) countries;
- to examine the determinants and barriers to the outward internationalization process; and
- to identify whether the internationalization of Slovenian firms is transition-specific, given its different systemic background.

Acknowledgements

While in this book we have tried to pay due credit to various authors through citations, it is only appropriate to acknowledge here that many of the findings presented have their roots in research started four years ago within the framework of two PHARE ACE projects[1]. Clearly, the book would not have been possible without these projects being financed by the EU Commission. The authors have also benefited from the continuous financial support of the Ministry of Education, Science, Sports and Technology of the Republic of Slovenia over many years.

The germination and initial fleshing out of ideas however drew heavily on the ideas of our partners in these projects: Katalin Antaloczy, Marie Bohata, Wilfred Altzinger, Christian Bellak, Maja Bučar, Andrea Éltető, Reijo Luostarinen, Matej More, Andras Oszlay, Matija Rojec, Lojze Sočan, Dariusz Rosati, Vitor Simoes, Metka Stare, Urmas Varblane and Alena Zemplinerova. Several workshops, collegial discussions and other comments are reflected here as well. Particular thanks goes to Matej More whose work was the basis for the chapter on the legal framework for outward FDI by Slovenian firms and Matija Rojec who prepared a comprehensive evaluation of Yugoslav legislation on investments abroad.

The book is about firms which invest abroad, explaining how they do it, what problems they face and what are ultimately the results. Although the roots of our research were nourished in the intellectual humus of the research and academic community, the real inspiration came from the managers of companies doing real work, investing abroad and in doing so facing many problems and overcoming so many barriers in the home and host countries. It is about the results and achievements of their undertakings. In seeking to reflect what has really been going on in firms we have had to rely heavily on several discussions with the managers of companies and other experts. It is almost impossible to mention all of them. Let us indicate in particular those who provided insights for the preparation of the case studies included in the book: Zoran Jankovič, Mateja Jesenek and Jana Bergant (Mercator), Jože Kozmus and Monika Žvikart (Prevent), Metod Dragonja, Dragan Kesič and Branka Jerše (Lek), Stojan Petrič and Anica Uršič-Vončina (Kolektor), Jože Colarič, Mihael Japelj and Simona Kastelic (Krka), Franjo Bobinac, Ivan Viteznik and Bojana Rojc (Gorenje), Nikolaj Bevk, Boris Stemberger and Mitja Tavčar (Iskraemeco).

They shared with us their experiences, concerns and ideas and, if the cases are useful reading for those still thinking of internationalizing their activities, we should all be thankful to them. We have also benefited from discussions and contributions of all participants at the Workshop on Outward FDI, which we organized in Ljubljana together with the Chamber of Commerce and Industry of Slovenia in 2000.

The chief data source for the book was of course our surveys. We all know how annoying they are if you are a manager facing so many day-to-day challenges. Yet, the managers were kind enough to respond to them allowing us to make some of the generalizations we set out in this book. Special thanks also go to the Slovenian Export Corporation, particularly Miran Jus, which is not only doing a good job in facilitating outward internationalization, but which also proved to be very helpful in collecting our second survey. In addition, this book would not be possible without the data collected by the Bank of Slovenia and the Ministry of Finance. Whenever we needed additional explanations or other help in interpreting the results of their databases, we received friendly and abundant support from them, which is not always the case when dealing with official institutions.

Production of this book would also have been impossible without the excellent work of Murray Bales who has valiantly sought to manipulate our translated English into a more correct form. Finally, the book had to be prepared for printing. Here, two important people came into play. We cannot imagine preparing the book without the efficient services of Marjana Jevšenak, the secretary at the Centre of International Relations of the Faculty of Social Sciences, throughout our research and without Karmen Zahariaš, who prepared the manuscript for publication in book form in, as usual, a very short time.

Note

1 Phare ACE project no. P97-8073-R, 'Outward internationalization facilitating transformation and EU Accession; The case of Czech Republic, Hungary and Slovenia', and no. P98-1162-R, 'EU-integration-driven investment networking: outward foreign direct investment of candidate-countries'.

List of Abbreviations

ACE	Action for Cooperation in the field of Economics
AP	Agency of the Republic of Slovenia for Payment Transactions
BiH	Bosnia and Herzegovina
BIT	Bilateral Investment Treaty
CEE	Central and Eastern Europe
CEECs	Central and Eastern Europe Countries
CEFTA	Central European Free Trade Association
CIR	Centre of International Relations
CIS	Commonwealth of Independent States
CMEA	Council for Mutual Economic Assistance
CSFR	Czechoslovakia
CZ	Czech Republic
DM	Deutsche Marks
EBRD	European Bank for Reconstruction and Development
EEC	European Economic Community
EFTA	European Free Trade Association
EU	European Union
FDA	Food and Drug Administration
FDI	Foreign Direct Investment
FRY	Federal Republic of Yugoslavia
FYR	Former Yugoslav Republic
GATT	General Agreement on Tariffs and Trade
GDP	Gross Domestic Product
HDR	Human Development Report
ILO	International Labour Organization
IMAD	Institute of Macroeconomic Analysis and Development
IMF	International Monetary Fund
M&A	Mergers and Acquisitions
Mfr	Manufacturing
MNCs	Multinational Corporations
MNEs	Multinational Enterprises
NACE	Nomenclature statistique des activités économiques dans la Communauté européenne (classification comparable to International Standard Industrial Classification = ISIC Rev. 3)

NAFTA	North American Free Trade Association
OECD	Organization for Economic Cooperation and Development
OLI	Ownership, Location and Internalization
OPT	Outward Processing Traffic
pc	per capita
PPP	Purchasing Power Parity
R&D	Research and Development
SAA	Stabilizing Association Agreements
SEC	Slovenian Export Corporation
SFRY	Socialist Federal Republic of Yugoslavia
SMEs	Small and Medium Enterprises
TNC	Transnational Corporation
TQM	Total Quality Management
UN	United Nations
UNCTAD	United Nations Conference on Trade and Development
USA	United States of America
WDR	World Development Report
WIIW	Vienna Institute for International Economic Studies
WWII	World War II
WTO	World Trade Organization

PART I
ORIGINS OF SLOVENIA AND ITS OUTWARD INTERNATIONALIZATION

Chapter 1

Introduction

In facing the many challenges when starting to prepare this book, the authors agreed that the vitality of outward FDI as an entry mode to the global economy should first be discussed in the context of a development strategy and the transition process. The Slovenian experience of internationalization must be compared with the experiences of other transition economies in order to see to what extent it is unique. Analysis should be based on in-depth evaluations of the size, trends, geographical distribution, and sectoral allocation of such outward FDI as well as the chief motives, barriers and problems. Third, the book should provide empirical insights into issues like the development impact of such outbound internationalization, and the extent to which outward FDI is instrumental in development/transition, EU accession and competitiveness strengthening. In short, the link between internationalization and transition has to be explained.

The book's theoretical framework is a set of theories proven to have the strongest power in explaining outward FDI by Slovenian firms and firms from other transition economies for that matter. They comprise: (i) the investment development path paradigm (Dunning, 1981, 1993; and Dunning and Narula, 1996); (ii) the Scandinavian sequential internationalization pattern that reflects increasing international involvement in terms of entry mode, product and market diversification (Welch, Luostarinen, 1988; Johanson, Vahlne, 1977); (iii) the eclectic paradigm (Dunning, 1993) that synthesizes the three necessary conditions (ownership, location and internalization advantages – OLI) for firms to undertake outward FDI; (iv) life cycle theory (Vernon, 1966); and (v) Ozawa's dynamic paradigm of transnational corporations assisted development (1992).

Despite their claims to be generally relevant, we should in addition consider whether these theories can also explain outward FDI by transition economies or whether their explanatory power is limited. There are so many specific, system-based characteristics that make applying theories based on the market economy tradition very difficult, at least to the initial stage of development of such investments. Industry and firm-specific characteristics and the stage of their development (previous experience) are very important explanatory variables that vary from case to case. Any generalizing of the experiences of outward FDI by Slovenian companies or even by other investors from transition economies has to be undertaken with caution.

In line with the rationale, we decided to divide the book up into five parts. The first is devoted to Slovenia's origins, its economy, history and the beginning of outward internationalization. The second part discloses the development of the outward investing in the nineties at the macroeconomic level by introducing the evolution of legal framework, analysing outward FDI trends, their geographical and sectoral distribution, particularities of outward FDI in the successors to the SFRY and the importance of outward investors in the Slovenian economy in general. The third part focuses on the firm-level perspective of outward direct investing; it analyzes the characteristics of investing companies and their affiliates, the motivations for investment, the barriers they are facing in internationalising their business and, finally, the impacts of such activities abroad. In the fourth part, selected cases of Slovenian multinational companies are evaluated. The last, fifth, part of the book concentrates on the lessons the Slovenian case could hold for other transition economies. It examines what the response of governments should be in regulating or promoting this new type of international activities of firms from transition economies and assesses the relevance of the Slovenian case.

When preparing the empirical part of the book in particular, the real problem was the availability of data. In transition economies, the statistical base on outward FDI is very poor, in some cases it did not exist until recently. If data is available, problems remain of their reliability, short time series, non-comprehensiveness etc. The only way around such limitations was to employ various data sources. Our empirical analysis is therefore based on secondary data available on outward FDI and primary data collected through surveys. Interviews of managers and case studies support the interpretation of results.

Table 1.1 Data sources for the study

Secondary data	Primary data
• Bank of Slovenia • Ministry of Finance • Media, business press	• Survey among companies investing abroad, June to September 1999 • Survey among the biggest exporters and the fastest growing firms, June to August 1999 • Survey among leading investors, June 2000 • Survey among companies investing abroad, June to September 2001 • Interviews

The main source of secondary data on outward FDI (and FDI in general) is official data from the Bank of Slovenia. It provides a set of aggregate data (such as time series data on the volume of outward FDI, stocks and flows of investments, geographical distribution, breakdowns by activity, ...) published in a specialized annual publication entitled Direct Investment. Another secondary data source of outward FDI statistics is the Ministry of Finance that runs a register of announced investments abroad[1]. For the purpose of firm-level analysis, data from the Bank of Slovenia were combined with the database of the Agency of the Republic of Slovenia for Payment Transactions (AP) that provides financial data (balance sheets, income statements) on companies.

The lack of qualitative information led us to collect primary data on outward FDI. We aimed to provide additional information on outward FDI within firms through structured questionnaires. Four surveys were launched for this purpose.

1. Survey on outward FDI of Slovenian companies (Survey 1999), carried out from June to October 1999 on a sample of companies that involve outward direct investment. As a sample framework, we used the sample of all non-financial sector companies registered in 1997 and analyzed at the aggregate level[2]. The Survey 1999 sample included 32 companies or 7.7 per cent of Slovenian companies with outward FDI. The sample companies had a 15.9 per cent share in the total value of capital of Slovenian companies abroad and 17.4 per cent of all Slovenian outward FDI (in terms of number). Since the financial sector has about 30 per cent of all Slovenian outward FDI stock, the sample companies represent 22.7 per cent of the outward FDI of the non-financial corporate sector. The questionnaire gathered elementary data on an investing company and its foreign affiliate(s), as well as the main determinants of outward FDI such as the motivation for, effects of and barriers to outward FDI. Since this was the most extensive survey, it represents the main data source for this country study.
2. Survey on potential outward FDI of Slovenian companies, carried out from June to October 1999 on a sample of potential investors. Lists of the biggest exporters and the fastest growing firms in Slovenia, which had not yet been registered as direct investors abroad, were used as the sample framework. The questionnaire was very similar to the former one, but shorter. The analyzed sample included 32 companies.
3. Survey on managers on internationalization through outward FDI, carried out on 1 June 2000 on a sample of the leading direct investors abroad. Top managers responded to the questionnaire at a workshop on 'Slovenian Investments Abroad; Why, How and Where?' held at the Chamber of Commerce and Industry in Ljubljana. This survey aimed to analyze

attitudes, experiences and knowledge about internationalization. Again, the sample included 32 companies (a 64 per cent response rate).

4. A second survey on outward FDI of Slovenian companies (Survey 2001) was carried out from June to September 2001. As a sample framework, we used a list of companies registered as direct investors abroad in 1999. The questionnaire was sent by post to 407 companies. Up until September 2001, 52 questionnaires had been returned; meaning a 13 per cent response rate however, of those, 10 questionnaires were not sufficiently completed and consequently only 37 (9 per cent) were included in the sample for analysis. To a large extent, the sample in Survey 2001 matched the sample in Survey 1999. Eighty per cent of the sample companies included in the first survey repeated the questionnaire again and panel data are available.

In spite of all of these efforts, the many data and statistical problems did limit the scope of our research. A very important one is the short histories of both Slovenia as an independent state and this phenomenon (outward FDI as an internationalization mode) and, consequently, the shortness of time series that prevents us conducting trend and time-series analysis. Initially, before transition they followed a different rationale and were not considered an important issue deserving regular statistical coverage. The obvious result is the non-developed and incomplete statistical coverage. Consistent time series only begin in 1993 when the Bank of Slovenia started the required reporting on direct investment. The data on previous outward FDI differ in their comprehensiveness due to methodological changes. The 'youthfulness of outward FDI' itself causes most of the data difficulties presented below.

Data is also very limited in terms of scope which narrows the possibilities of qualitatively evaluating this phenomenon. Aggregate data on outward FDI flows and stocks and the number of outward FDI is available, as are stock breakdowns by country and activity (of investing firms not affiliations). Coverage is still incomplete. As a result, differences may occur when comparing different statistical sources.

Missing categories especially involve foreign affiliates, as to which the official statistics keep few records. With the exception of the total number of foreign affiliates established (or acquired) by Slovenian companies and a breakdown by country, there is also no data on the activity or product specialization of foreign affiliates, their performance or legal status to allow any more complete picture of intra-firm relations (such as intra-firm trade).

To overcome the barriers to a qualitative analysis, we had to rely on surveys, interviews and even media reports which raises the question of representativeness. Sample companies may not be typical or representative of all the companies investing abroad. Since the total number of investors is unknown in several aspects, an assessment of representativeness is often impossible. When gathering primary data, the authors also confronted the confidentiality of outward FDI data. Firms are generally very reluctant to report information on outward FDI since they often treat it as a business secret. Consequently, the sample in any of the surveys is small. Due to the low response rate it cannot be taken to be fully representative, which is its main limitation. The samples are representative in terms of the sectoral structure, as well as the geographical allocation. However, as in the case of most surveys, the results are biased in favour of large and successful companies. The well-chosen sampling framework, however, puts the sample near to a random selection. Dynamic (and not only static) records of company data, since the sample companies reported certain items of information for two or three time sections, also reduced some of these limitations. Since the samples differ by time periods, this represents another limitation in method selection.

The book is the outcome of more than four years' research within Phare ACE projects. The first project only included three countries, Czech Republic, Hungary and Slovenia, whereas the second one also covered Estonia and Poland. We are thereby in a position to put Slovenia's outward FDI story into a comparative perspective with other transition economies. Luckily, we did not start from zero. We were able to build on ongoing research on Yugoslav investments in developing countries that started back in 1972 and went on for about fifteen years. In such a way, we are able to see the early roots of the internationalization of the then socialist enterprises, which is important since most of today's investors abroad are the same, albeit transformed, firms.

We hope this is a book with a message. However, it is also a collection of interesting stories about international business and companies. Our hope is that reading this book will help convince at least some readers that the ideas contained in it are not only theoretical but can guide one towards better business in the future.

Notes

1 For more on data availability, see Jaklič et al., 2001.

2 The questionnaire was sent by post to a group of direct investors in 1997. 17.7 per cent of the questionnaires were returned; of those 10 per cent were not properly completed and only 32 (7.7 per cent) were included in the analysis.

Chapter 2

Slovenia – A New State in the World

Legend says that God, when creating the World, completely forgot Slovenia. Feeling guilty once realizing this, he gave the Slovenians a piece of everything: mountains, sea, forests, caves, plains, etc. While little, Slovenia is rich in everything in small quantities. With 20,000 square kilometres, it is about half the size of Denmark and almost the same size as Israel. Only five countries out of 132 included in the World Bank's 1999/2000 World Development Report (WDR) are smaller in size terms. Its population constitutes just 0.03 per cent of the world population, 0.06 per cent of gross world product, yet already 0.16 per cent of world exports in 1998 which demonstrates its above-average integration into the global economy[1].

Figure 2.1 Map of Slovenia in Europe

It is a parliamentary democracy with approximately two million people who are mostly of Slovenian nationality (88 per cent) and are Roman Catholic. Only one country is smaller while five included in the WDR 1999/2000 have the same population size as Slovenia. With GDP per capita of US$ 9,105 in 2000, it is well above the average level of medium-income countries.

Slovenia is the most developed transition country of Central and Eastern Europe (CEE). Its nominal GDP per capita in 1999 was 2.1 times more than that of Hungary (in purchasing power parity (PPP) 40 per cent less) and almost 6.6 times more than that of Romania (in PPP only 2.6 times)[2]. Per capita GDP is close to that of Greece and Portugal (in PPP it already exceeds that in Greece), but 1.4 times lower than that of Ireland[3]. Thirteen candidate-countries had 35 per cent of the EU 15 average GDP per capita in 2000, while Slovenia with 71 per cent had already overtaken Greece at 69 per cent. Czech Republic is the next closest candidate (60 per cent), followed by Hungary with 52 per cent (see Brandsma et al., 2001; p. 14).

In spite of the transition recession all transition economies faced, the Slovenian economy's real growth rate in the 1989-2000 period with an index rate of 114 (1989 = 100) is only slower than Poland with its 127 index score (EBRD, 2001; p. 59).

Slovenia used to be a much more outward-oriented economy than most former socialist countries, which traded mostly among themselves[4]. During transition, a reorientation to the West also happened quite rapidly there. The comparatively strong export orientation is also demonstrated by the relatively high level of exports per capita (pc).

Table 2.1 Per capita merchandise exports of selected countries in 1998 in US$

Country	Export pc	Country	Export pc
Belgium	17,170	Czech Rep.	2,636
Ireland	15,813	Hungary	2,294
Finland	8,472	Portugal	2,350
Slovenia	4,560	Spain	2,796

Source: Calculations based on the 1999/2000 World Development Report.

Slovenia lags behind highly developed small countries, yet it is running ahead of many developed and all former socialist countries in terms of export orientation. Recently, however, its export openness measured as a share of exports in GDP has fallen (from 63 per cent in 1992 to 59 per cent in 2000), although general openness (exports and imports together in GDP) increased from 102 per cent in 1992 to 104 per cent in 2000 (see Table 2.4).

Although a small country, it is not so small in terms of import levels which in 1995 were almost the same as those of Romania with a population more than 10 times the size, and only 1.5 times smaller than those of Hungary with its five-times greater population. Slovenian imports lagged behind Russia only seven-fold even though the Russian population is 73 times larger.

Table 2.2 Merchandise imports by selected countries 1990-1998, billion US$

Country	Population (million)	Merchandise imports 1990	1998
Poland	39	15	52
Slovenia	2	7	11
Czech Rep.	10	-	35
Romania	22	10	13
Russia	147	49	74
Hungary	10	11	27

Source: 2000/2001 World Development Report.

Although salaries are much higher compared to other transition economies[5], this is offset by higher labour productivity[6] which was in 1998 71 per cent of EU level (EU is 100) compared to 58 per cent in the case of Hungary and Czech Republic or 38 per cent in the case of Poland and already higher than in Portugal (55 per cent of EU level) (see Eurostat, May 2001).

According to the Global Competitiveness Report of the World Economic Forum (Porter et al., 2001), Slovenia lags behind some other transition economies in terms of competitiveness.

Table 2.3 Competitiveness ranking by selected transition economies[i]

Country	Current competitiveness[ii] rank	Growth competitiveness[iii] rank
Hungary	26	28
Estonia	27	29
Slovenia	32	31
Czech Rep.	35	37
Poland	41	41

Source: Porter et al., 2001, p. 15.

Notes:

i 75 countries are evaluated in total.

ii It focuses more on microeconomic competitiveness.

iii Growth competitiveness measures macroeconomic development potential in the next five years.

Slovenia's performance relative to current competitiveness can in particular be explained by technology factors, the underperformance of public institutions and the lower quality of the national business environment. In terms of the technology index[7], Slovenia lags behind Estonia by 22 places and Hungary by nine places, while for instance in the quality of the business environment it is nine places behind Estonia and ten places behind Hungary. Notable competitive disadvantages of Slovenia lie in its poor cluster development (rank 69), foreign access to local capital markets (rank 69), lower levels of FDI and technology imports (rank 68), inflexible hiring and firing practices (rank 66), fewer possibilities for foreign banks' entry (rank 59) (Porter et al., 2001, pp. 20 and 301). By removing such barriers or disadvantages, which evaluators obviously foresee, competitiveness can be substantially improved. This explains why, in spite of the present lagging behind some other transition economies, the growth competitiveness potential measuring more macroeconomic development potential in the next five years is actually improving only for Slovenia while other countries are moving down the scale.

Short history

Slovenia is one of the youngest European countries, having become independent on 25 June 1991 after the collapse of the Socialist Federal Republic of Yugoslavia (SFRY). The route to independence was not simple. The world powers wanted to prevent the disintegration of Yugoslavia fearing that it could stimulate the disintegration of the Soviet Union. History has shown this was wrong, given that the Soviet Union was about to disintegrate in any case.

Nevertheless, aspirations for independence have a much older origin. Already in 1848 the first Programme for an Independent Slovenia was published by Slovenian intellectuals then living under the first Hapsburg monarchy (later the Austro-Hungarian empire) which for the first time, beginning with the 14th century, included all of the Slovenian regions in one state[8]. After World War I, Slovenia joined the newly formed state 'the Kingdom of Serbs, Croats and Slovenians', which in 1918 was renamed Yugoslavia. In 1941, as part of Yugoslavia Slovenia was occupied and divided among the allies of the Third Reich. Slovenia was divided among three invaders; Germans, Italians and Hungarians (see more in Prunk, 1996; p. 103). After strong resistance by communist-dominated partisans, the independence of Yugoslavia of which Slovenia was part was regained in 1945. From liberation onwards, development in Slovenia proceeded according to laws passed by the central communist government in Belgrade, which initially almost entirely copied the Bolshevist system of the Soviet Union. After the conflict with Stalin in

1948 the system gradually started to change. In 1951, self-management was declared as the guiding principle of the economy. So-called market socialism was emerging and differentiated the SFRY from other socialist countries. The system had its own ups and downs; periods of liberalization and decentralization were followed by retreats to greater centralization and domination by the leading communist party. With the crises of self-management and mounting ethnic problems following the 'death of the historical leaders of the revolution and socialist development (Tito, Kardelj, Bakarić) who had succeeded in controlling the political situation in Yugoslavia with instruments of party policies, a very important subjective factor was lost. In the first half of the 1980s, sharp interethnic and inter-republic conflicts appeared, aggravated by economic crises' (Prunk, 1996; p. 124). Finally, such mounting ethnic-based conflicts coupled by economic crises and the emerging Serb nationalism led to the disintegration of Yugoslavia in 1991.

Slovenia's independence has its origin in a referendum for independence held on 23 December 1990 at which 88.5 per cent of the population voted for independence. Prior to that the first free elections had already taken place within the SFRY in April 1990. Following the Declaration of Independence on 25 June 1991[9], the first Constitution was accepted on 23 December 1991. The EU recognized Slovenia on 15 January 1992. On 22 May 1992, Slovenia became the 167th member of the United Nations (UN) and soon after, in 1993, it also became a member of all major international financial organizations. A year later (1994) it joined the General Agreement on Tariffs and Trade (GATT) and thus became a founding member of the World Trade Organization (WTO). In 1996 the European Agreement was signed and Slovenia became a member of the Central European Free Trade Association (CEFTA). Slovenia also concluded free-trade agreements with the European Free Trade Association (EFTA) and with Croatia, Macedonia, Estonia, Latvia, Lithuania, Israel and Turkey. However, it is not a member of the OECD even though it has applied for membership. When the first transition economies were accepted the status of Yugoslavia had still not been fully resolved, which created some formal barriers to Slovenia's membership in this international organization. When these barriers were eliminated, OECD policy reflected consolidation and not the broadening of its membership.

Slovenia used to be the most developed republic of the SFRY

Within Yugoslavia, Slovenia was the most developed and outward-oriented republic. Per capita social product was in 1990 two times higher than the average for Yugoslavia (see Potočnik et al., 1995; pp. 12-15). Slovenia accounted in 1990 for 29 per cent of Yugoslav exports and 20 per cent of its

GDP despite having just eight per cent of its population (Pleskovič and Sachs, 1992; p. 2). This gap even widened after gaining independence and during the transition. In 1990, the GDP pc of Slovenia was US$ 6,100, of Yugoslavia US$ 3,060, while the average of the non-Slovenian part of Yugoslavia was US$ 2,800 (Pleskovič and Sachs, 1992; p. 5). Today, Slovenian GDP pc is nearly ten times the level achieved in the Federal Republic of Yugoslavia (FRY) of US$ 940[10].

Already in 1980 developed countries accounted for 58 per cent of all Slovenian exports. In 1996 that share increased to 68 per cent[11]. The growth rate of the Slovenian economy in the 1952-1990 period exceeded the average of Yugoslavia (5.1 per cent compared to 4.9 per cent).

Foreign direct investment started in Slovenia in 1967 when a quasi-equity joint ventures law was passed in Yugoslavia, the first in any socialist country after the Second World War. In addition, several Slovenian firms already started to internationalize their operations in the early sixties, in most cases first by establishing representative offices and later by setting up trade and production firms abroad as well.

It is within this historical context that Slovenia has developed certain starting advantages over other former socialist countries. Firstly, due to its much more liberal international orientation, Slovenians together with other citizens of former Yugoslavia were able to travel abroad with fewer limitations than citizens of other socialist countries even before the major market-oriented economic reform of 1965. In 1968 visas for foreigners were eliminated, in 1973 no visas for Yugoslav citizens were necessary for all European countries, with the exceptions of Albania and Greece. The distinctive economic system, frequently called market socialism, featuring the almost autonomous status of firms[12], a more developed banking sector involving commercial banks and, last but not least, strong economic co-operation with the West are factors that made the SFRY different. Slovenian firms started to be at least partly exposed to competition from industrial countries already in the 1960s, at a time other socialist countries mostly traded among themselves. The starting point of Slovenian companies was somewhat better, since at least some managerial knowledge had been accumulated before the transition started.

Slovenia also possessed some disadvantages compared to other transition economies. The first one is that its political independence was gained so late, and the second one involves the transition from a regional to a national economy. The state apparatus was supposed to be built largely from scratch. Other countries in transition already had such state institutions, albeit in a different system. Therefore, gaining independence and international recognition was no easy task for Slovenia. All of these factors complicated Slovenia's transition. Another disadvantage was its inherited advantages since they somehow slowed down the process of transition, in particular privatization.

The national economy's profile

The Slovenian economy is well on the road to structuring its economy like the OECD countries. Services already accounted for 59 per cent of GDP in 2000, manufacturing 27 per cent and agriculture 3.2 per cent. The structure of manufacturing industry in Slovenia is like that in Czech Republic, Hungary, Poland and Slovakia, fairly close to that seen in the EU member-states and, in particular, in Spain, Portugal and Greece (Brandsma et al., 2001; p. 69).

Its own currency, the tolar, was introduced in October 1991. On 8 October 1991, the Bank of Slovenia effectively became an independent central bank although preparations for monetary independence had started in September 1990 as a response to the deepening economic and political crisis in Yugoslavia (see Kranjec, 1993; p. 204). External convertibility was achieved in 1993. On 1 September 1995, Slovenia accepted Article 8 of the Statute of the International Monetary Fund (IMF), thus proclaiming full convertibility of the tolar (Mencinger and Suppan, 1995; p. 237). In spite of many suggestions by the IMF and other foreign experts to introduce a fixed exchange rate, currency board or to peg the tolar, a managed flexible exchange rate was introduced. This was not such an easy and stand-alone step. Several preparatory steps were taken before[13] which, together with the decision for a managed float, decisively contributed to the successful transition of the Slovenian economy[14].

Slovenia has since the decline in 1991-1992 (largely due to the loss of the former Yugoslav market which had accounted for almost 25 per cent of all sales of Slovenian firms[15]) 'made remarkable economic progress in the period 1993-2001, i.e. after the so-called transition depression. Slovenia moved quickly to establish macroeconomic stability, to launch the systemic transformation of the economy. This was achieved despite disruption of trade flows and despite regional instability associated with the break-up of the SFRY… Slovenia's stabilisation was the backbone of fast recovery' (World Bank, 1999; p. 1). The growth rate enjoyed in the 1996-2000 period was, at 4.2 per cent, much higher compared to the average 3.5 per cent for all 13 candidate-countries (Brandsma et al., 2001; p. 14).

In its ten years of existence, Slovenia has stabilized its economy, reduced its inflation rate from the inherited average annual rate of 1,306 per cent suffered in the last quarter of 1989, to 201.3 per cent in 1992 gradually through to upper single digits (World Bank, 1999; p. 2). Since 1995, the inflation rate has remained unchanged for a long period of time at a level of eight to ten per cent, primarily due to the policy of relative price adjustments in the administratively controlled sector. In 1998 and 1999 the pace of inflation slowed substantially. After the initial transitional recession, reflected in decreasing GDP growth rates, Slovenia obviously quickly succeeded in regaining economic growth. After reaching a peak of 9.1 per cent in 1993, the rate of unemployment measured by ILO standards was reduced to seven per cent in 2000. Economic progress was obviously achieved with less social tension than in other transition economies thanks to gradualism being harnessed as a dominant approach to reforms and the declared social welfare state. The Human Development Report 2000 (HDR) ranked Slovenia 29th in the world[16].

Stabilization of the economy was achieved parallel to the more complex transition experienced by most other economies in transition. Apart from the transition from a socialist economy with social ownership[17] to a market economy with predominantly private ownership, basically composed of macroeconomic stabilization, internal and external liberalization, and privatization, Slovenia also experienced a transition from a regional to a national economy. In its double transition, Slovenia had also been exposed to the so-called 'Gulliver effect' as far as its economic development is concerned (see Senjur, 1993; and Bleyer and Szapay, 1991). This means that Slovenia had been forced to follow the development patterns of the state as a whole. Even today, the Slovenian economy lacks specialization due to its inherited overall economic structure (see Simoneti et al., 2001).

In addition, in Slovenia transition towards a well-performing market economy has been carried out simultaneously with the process of its accession to the EU. In order to become a full member of the EU in the near future, the country has to design and implement all the essential reforms and transformations that will facilitate faster economic growth and catching up with developed European countries as well as the Slovenian economy's increased competitiveness (Potočnik, Senjur and Štiblar, 1995). In spite of a general belief that such reforms are necessary for adapting to the EU, they are in fact more transition- than EU-specific.

Due to its inflationary implications, liberalization of administered prices did not rank very high among economic policy priorities in the period after independence. Prices of fuel and gas, public utilities, communal services, basic food products remained for a long time a relevant impediment to the efficient allocation of resources through price signals, which has hampered any faster economic restructuring. In 1996, the Government started an active price liberalization policy and allowed the higher growth of administered prices. As a result, price distortions were lowered and the share of controlled prices in the consumer price index was reduced from 22.4 per cent in 1996 to 14.5 per cent in May 1999 (see Institute of Macroeconomic Analysis and Development – IMAD, 1999).

High interest rates were another concern of monetary policy. Although they have declined in nominal and real terms, they continue to be high. Any further fall in real interest rates can only result from strengthened competition among banks including foreign ones, which have already entered the local market, although the privatization of the main banks has only just started.

Closely linked with the problem of high real interest rates is the issue of deindexation. In spite of gradually increasing the use of nominal rates for monetary policy instruments by the Bank of Slovenia, the voluntary deindexation process has been very slowly picked up by other economic agents.

Slovenia's economy still suffers from persistent structural weaknesses. The process of restructuring the Slovenian enterprise sector has been relatively slow. Restructuring has been manifested by insolvencies of loss-making companies and recently by increased operating profits in privatized companies. Value added per employee is rising in all categories of companies involved in commercial activities, yet it still lags well behind European averages. Formerly socially-owned, now privatized companies are still in the phase of defensive restructuring and downsizing. Economic policy related to the enterprise sector has concentrated on defensive restructuring and the rehabilitation of enterprises in trouble. The pace of enterprise creation in Slovenia has been slow. The time has come to reorient enterprise sector economic policy into a pro-active policy which seeks to eliminate administrative barriers, support new entries of domestic and foreign companies, and develop growing and prospective companies and activities. In the enterprise sector, most privatized companies are still to establish corporate governance and to undertake offensive restructuring (see Mrak, Rojec and Potočnik, 2002; pp. 37-62). Internationalizing their activities is one way to facilitate restructuring.

The Slovenian banking sector has changed significantly since independence in 1991, but it is still far away from being internationally competitive either in terms of soundness, efficiency, costs or product variety. On one hand, some of these changes like adjustment to a market economy and the management of bad debts are the result of shocks common to all transition economies. On the other hand, however, the Slovenian banking sector is also and has been characterized by some country-specific features. First, banks within the former Yugoslavia were founded and owned by social enterprises. Second, prior to independence some degree of competition and market behaviour already existed in the Slovenian banking system. The most pressing problem of the Slovenian banking sector in early transition was the high share of non-performing loans. At the time of the country's independence, some 30 to 40 per cent of the banks' loans were non-performing and, consequently, the banks operated with excessively high intermediation spreads and real lending rates. Like the banks, the insurance sector has also not yet been privatized. Before 1990, the sector was dominated by one insurance company with a 95 per cent market share. This social ownership, exceeding 50 per cent of the total capital in two cases, is expected to be transferred to state ownership. Foreign entities are allowed to operate in the insurance market although their actual participation is limited to a few insurance companies with a small market share. The biggest problems of the Slovenian insurance sector are its relatively poor financial health, especially of smaller insurance companies and, until recently, the unresolved conflict between the Government and the management (and owners) of the largest insurance company (see Mrak, Rojec and Potoènik, 2002; pp. 53-57).

Table 2.4 Slovenia 1992-2000 in numbers (US$, current prices and in per cent)

	1992	1994	2000
GDP US$ million	12,523	14,368	18,122[i]
GDP pc	6,275	7,233	9,105
Exports and imports (US$ million)	12,822	14,132	18,846
Exports of goods and services (US$ million)	7,900	8,637	10,617
Share of merchandise exports in GDP (%)	53	48	48
Share of exports and imports of goods in GDP (%)	102	98	104
Share of exports of goods and services in GDP (%)	63	60	59
Inward FDI, stock (US$ million)	954[ii]	1,326	2,809
Share of FDI in GDP (%)	7.6	9.2	15
Outward FDI, stock (US$ million)	281[ii]	354	794

Sources: Monthly Bulletin, Bank of Slovenia, October 1993, December 1995 and March and December 2001, plus revised data of the Statistical Office of Slovenia. The source for FDI was Direct Investment 1994-1999, Bank of Slovenia.

Notes:

i GDP fell in US$ from 1999 because of the rise in the dollar's exchange rate. In 1999 GDP was US$ 20,071 million, and in per capita terms US$ 10,109.

ii 1993.

For political reasons, quite some time passed before the Ownership Transformation Act was finally adopted in 1992 and amended in 1993, when privatization in fact started. Slovenia's privatization concept involved a mixture of free distribution, internal buy-outs with discounts and commercial privatization. The Privatization Law provided several methods of transformation. First, the free transfer of 40 per cent of ordinary shares to financial institutions. Citizens received ownership certificates according to age in a nominal value ranging from DM 4,000 to DM 6,000. The second mode was the internal distribution of shares to employees in exchange for ownership certificates. Internal buy-outs of shares as a third method was limited to 40 per cent of the shares of the social capital at a discount of 50 per cent. The scheme favoured internal buy-outs. The privatization of trade and manufacturing has now been completed, while that of the major banks and public utilities has only started. This is also one of the key explanations as to why there has been a more modest inflow of FDI compared to other transition economies.

We start the comparison with 1992, which is the first full year of the independent Slovenia, while 1994 is the first statistically normal year[18]. Progress in almost all areas is obvious although the expectations were even higher. GDP increased in real terms by 40 per cent (compared to 1994 by 29 per cent). What is disappointing is the stagnation of openness measured by the share of exports in GDP, particularly compared to 1992. The current account position also deteriorated. The current account balance was positive up until 1998 when a deficit started, amounting to US$ 594 million at the end of 2000. Services can no longer finance the deficit in the trade balance.

The direction of trade has not changed substantially; exports to the EU increased slower than total exports, although Slovenian firms have maintained their market share in EU markets.

Table 2.5 Regional structure of Slovenian exports 1992-2000 (in US$ million, current prices, shares in per cent)

Regional structure of exports (US$ million and per cent)	1992	1994	2000
Exports total	6,681	6,828	8,731
Share of EU in total exports	61	66	64
Share of exports to USA in total exports	2.9	3.7	3.1
Share of CEFTA in total exports	3.9	4.9	7.9
Share of former Yugoslavia in total exports	23	15	16
Imports total	6.141	7.304	10.115
Share of EU in total imports	60	69	68
Share of USA in total imports	2.7	2.7	2.9
Share of CEFTA in total imports	3.3	2.7	2.9
Share of former Yugoslavia in total imports	19.7	8.0	5.9

Sources: Monthly Bulletin, Bank of Slovenia, October 1993, December 1995 and March 2001, plus revised data of the Statistical Office of Slovenia.

Most exports are destined for the EU, with Germany accounting in 2000 for 27 per cent of Slovenian exports and Italy for 14 per cent. Increasing foreign competition in the Slovenian market (effective tariff rates of protection were reduced from 53.0 per cent in 1986 to 7.03 per cent in 1993) and the collapse of the former Yugoslav market urged Slovenian enterprises to reorient themselves to exports, predominantly to EU markets.

The structure of trade is prevailingly intra-industrial and not that different from the average intra-EU trade structure. It has changed, although competitiveness compared to other CEFTA countries has deteriorated since some of them, particularly Hungary, have substantially increased their market shares. The share of goods for reproduction increased from 46 per cent in 1992 to 48 per cent in 2000, similarly with investment products (from 10 to 13 per cent). Simultaneously, the share of final products dropped from 45 per cent to 38 per cent in the same period. Most exports were concentrated in products for which demand was increasing in the world market, meaning that the export growth was not a result of increased competitiveness but influenced by the growth of the world economy (see Strojan-Kastelec, 2001; p. 5). 'Slovenian export expansion between 1992-1995 has not been pulled by unskilled labour intensive products but more on those technology and human capital intensive ones. Their share in exports has increased from 50 per cent in 1992 to 58 per cent in 1997. The share of only technology intensive products has increased from 17 in 1992 to 20 per cent in 1995, that of human capital intensive ones from 33 per cent to 38 per cent over the same period. Nonetheless the pace of change declined significantly over 1995-1997' (see World Bank, 1999; p. 51). Today, motor cars are a major export item (8.5 per cent in 2000, seats 4.4 per cent, pharmaceuticals 4.2 per cent, steel and steel products 3.4 per cent).

The biggest task ahead for the Slovenian economy is to restructure in the direction of higher value added activities. So far, value added per employee has been 2.9 times lower than in the EU 15 (Rojec et al., 2001; p. 20). Present trends are not too encouraging as the export structure is not changing enough in this direction. FDI, which facilitated such transformation in Hungary, has been too modest to serve this end. Therefore, Hungary is ahead of Slovenia in a second group of countries driven by investments according to the World Competitiveness Report. 'Cheap and low qualified labour is no longer of much use for economies like Slovenia and Hungary,' concluded G. Sachs and M. Porter. 'Their competitiveness will rather depend on their ability to assimilate technologies' (see Boillot, 2001).

In terms of attracting inward FDI, Slovenia lags well behind other transition economies. Even in per capita terms it is among those transition economies which have attracted the least FDI, whereby the ratio of FDI inflows to GDP is small both in terms of stock, flows or share in GDP (see EBRD, 2001; p. 68). FDI stock in Slovenia at the end of 2000 amounted to US$ 2,809 million (see Rojec et al., 2001; p. 6). The year 2001 brought about an important positive change; flows of FDI already amounted to US$ 441,8 million. These higher inflows are predominantly the consequence of a limited number of foreign acquisitions triggered off by the beginning of privatization in sectors like public utilities and banks. Therefore, it is expected that such a trend will continue in the years to come.

In spite of the modest share in GDP seen so far, foreign-owned firms already seem to play an important role. At the end of 1999, foreign-owned firms holding 11.4 per cent of total equity, 12.1 per cent of all assets and 8.8 per cent of all employees of the Slovenian corporate sector generated 15.0 per cent of the total sales, as much as 19.7 per cent of the total operating profit and 11.6 per cent of total operating losses. Foreign-owned firms were the most successful in exports, where they realized no less than 26.1 per cent of the entire exports of the Slovenian non-financial corporate sector (see Rojec et al., 2001; p. 6). Exports and sales seem to be the areas where foreign-owned firms show the most favourable trends in comparison with domestic companies. It would therefore be interesting to see whether foreign firms are also important investors abroad, as has been demonstrated in Hungary for instance (see Éltető, 2002).

Slovenia and the EU

European Economic Community (EEC) membership became the strategic goal of Slovenian foreign policy as early as in March 1991 (see Svetličič, 1998). Negotiations on an association agreement with the EU officially started by the mandate of the Council of Ministers given on 6 March 1995, which was then signed in June 1996 and came into effect on 1 February 1999. By the end of 2001, Slovenia was the only one of the Luxembourg group of EU candidate-countries to have closed 26 of the 29 chapters of the acquis communitaire opened for negotiations[19] and had proved itself to be one of the most qualified candidates for EU accession. Although it signed the Association Agreement with EU much later than other associate members of the EU[20], it is on the right path to conclude accession negotiations by the end of 2002 and to thereby be part of the first enlargement group.

To a large extent this can be attributed to its better starting position inherited from the past. Slovenia began to be strongly integrated with the EEC much earlier than any other former socialist country. Slovenians pressed for closer ties first with EFTA and later with the EU already within Yugoslavia. Before the Europe 1992 programme was adopted, studies were made in 1989 on how to prepare for the New Europe. A special Co-ordinating Commission for Europe 1992 was established in Slovenia, then still part of Yugoslavia, to co-ordinate all adjustment activities. In the Federal Parliament, Slovenia pushed for the adoption of a special unilateral declaration on approaching EFTA, which was in fact passed much later. In spring 1990, the Government of

Slovenia adopted special directives on how to adjust to Europe 1992. Approximation of legislation was a constituent part of this programme. All new laws were supposed to be verified from their adjustment aspect with European legislation/directives. But all of these decisions remained dead letters to a large extent. Internal politics, political parties' disputes about the privatization concept, and disputes about responsibility for past political developments and similar issues were then more important.

It is also possible to say that the issue of EU membership was one of the prominent reasons for the disintegration of Yugoslavia. As the most developed part of Yugoslavia, Slovenia wanted to start negotiating an Association Agreement with the EEC, whereas such a move was still too early for many other republics. The less-developed republics would have faced much stronger economic problems as a result of joining the EEC than the more developed Slovenia. Apart from that, ideological barriers were much stronger in the other republics than in Slovenia.

Summary

What is really important to know before studying the internationalization of activities of Slovenian firms is that the Slovenian economy was somehow different to other former socialist countries. It was more open, its liberalization started earlier, and its more autonomous firms accumulated some market experiences while already in the socialist system. This particularly applies to the strong export orientation to the West.

Historically, Slovenia was always part of Western culture and has more in common with other Western European countries than, for instance, with Kosovo in spite of the fact that both were once part of the same country. Although the reasons for Yugoslavia's disintegration were mostly political, economic factors, which are usually not taken into consideration, should not be omitted from the picture. This includes the aspiration to join European integrations faster than other republics wanted. Slovenians desired faster reforms in the direction of a market economy. In contrast to all other former Yugoslav republics, the way to independence was almost without violence, although the day after independence was declared the Yugoslav armed forces attacked Slovenia with the aim of regaining control and overthrowing the Slovenian Government.

The transition process, which started before independence, was accelerated once an independent state was achieved. However, according to the declared social philosophy Slovenians decided to undertake a gradual transition and avoid any shock therapy. In Slovenia the transition concept was somehow unique, more gradual than elsewhere and based from the beginning on a managed floating exchange rate contrary to the 'recipes' so strongly prescribed for all transition economies by foreign experts, including those from the IMF without any consideration of the country's specific situation. Later, even they accepted that the right decision had been taken. Privatization has been much slower than in other former socialist countries. Among other things, this partly explains the much more modest inflow of FDI.

The fact that Slovenia's starting position was better than for other Yugoslav republics and other transition economies did facilitate its transition but, at the same time, this slowed down the reforms. Some tradition in a market economy, and the autonomy of firms and relatively early start to doing business in Western markets made Slovenian companies ready for internationalization sooner than others.

Notes

1 Calculated on the basis of 1999/2000 WDR.

2 The gap has increased slightly from 1990 in the case of Hungary and substantially in comparison to Romania.

3 If not otherwise indicated, the figures are from 'Slovenia 2001 in Figures'.

4 The share of socialist countries in exports of Hungary in 1989 was 47 per cent, Poland 41 per cent, Czechoslovakia (CSFR) 62 per cent, while Slovenia's share was only 27 per cent (see Svetlièiè, 1993; p. 158).

5 The average gross monthly wages in Slovenia was US$ 870 (July 2000), while in Czech Republic it was US$ 345 (August 2000), in Hungary US$ 269 (September 2000), in Poland US$ 465 (September 2000), while in Macedonia it was just US$ 130 (August 2000).

6 Labour productivity is calculated by dividing gross value added at basic prices by the number of persons employed including self-employed.

7 Two factors can explain such lagging behind. Firstly, the lower innovation capacity index as 'country's potentials – as both a political and economic entity – to produce a stream of commercially relevant innovations' (Porter et al. 2002, p. 105). Czech Republic ranked 26th, Estonia 27th, Hungary 28th, while Slovenia was 31st (Porter et al., 2002, p. 104) and, secondly, the lower economic creativity index which 'attempts to gauge economies' involvement in new technologies, combining pure innovations with transfer of technology and startups' (Hungary ranked 21st, Estonia 29th, Czech Republic 40th and Slovenia 41st) (Porter et al., 2002, p. 121).

8 Going back further in history the present day territory of Slovenia was settled back in Roman times. In the 6th century Lombards came to the territory of Slovenia. After their departure, Slavic people settled between 580 and 590. Slavic society developed in a Slav province called Karantanija with its own dukes. By the second half of the 14th century, the Hapsburgs ruled over nearly all the Slovenian territory. After his victory over Austria in 1809, Napoleon created the Illyrian Provinces from several Slovenian and Croatian regions for four years. The Slovenian language gained importance in public use. After Napoleon's

defeat, the Austrians authorities returned. The Spring of Nations gave birth to the Programme of the United Slovenia (for details, see Prunk, 1996).

9 Constitutional Manifest on the Sovereignty and Independence of the Republic of Slovenia.

10 World Bank and WIIW databases incorporating national and international statistics.

11 The shares are not completely comparable since exports now also include trade with other parts of former Yugoslavia.

12 The former Yugoslavia had neither an open economy nor a state monopoly over foreign trade. Yugoslav market socialism was based on self-management; firms had considerable autonomy in conducting business transactions, although they were closely monitored by the state (World Bank, 1999; p. 54).

13 The printing of 'banknotes' in October 1990 was the first act of creating an independent monetary system. It was followed by the introduction of a flexible exchange rate of the (still) Yugoslav Dinar in March 1991.

14 See more in Mencinger, 1995.

15 In the 1990-1995 period, sales to other republics of the former Yugoslavia dropped from US$ 6,662 million to US$ 1,209 million, while exports to other countries rose from US$ 4,118 million to US$ 7,107 million (see Mrak, Rojec and Potoènik; 2002, p. 60).

16 The first transition economy to follow was Czech Republic in 34th, Slovakia in 40th and Hungary in 43rd places (p. 157).

17 This specific ownership structure meant that most enterprises were *de facto* but not *de jure* owned by employees (World Bank, 1999; p. 85).

18 If we take 1994 as the base year, we eliminate the impact of the 'abnormal' export increase in 1992-1993 (forced exports according to Bole, 2001; pp. 55-59).

19 In addition, there are two other chapters – *institutions* and *other* – whose contents have not yet been defined.

20 Slovenia signed the Association Agreement with the EU in 1996, while Hungary and Poland already did so in 1991 and Czech Republic, Bulgaria, Romania and Slovakia in 1993.

Chapter 3

The History[1] of Outward Investing

Introduction

The internationalization of Slovenian firms cannot be understood without knowing at least briefly how and when the Slovenian economy's internationalization actually started. Namely, this has a very important bearing on the current path of internationalization. Firstly, because most leading multinational firms from Slovenia were established several decades ago. Some emerged even in the late 1950s immediately after the first touches of liberalization of then Yugoslav socialist economy, when the state monopoly over foreign trade started to be relaxed. The legal environment and the whole system was so important for outward FDI that an explanation is necessary of the main characteristics of Slovenia's legal and policy frameworks for outward FDI in the contexts of the former Yugoslavia, the changes brought about by the transition from a socialist to a market economy and, finally, of the independent Slovenia.

Genesis

Traditionally, the primary motive of Slovenian firms going international was to expand exports to Western markets and facilitate imports, yet this was too frequently hampered by changes in foreign trade and exchange regulations. Going abroad to earn hard currency was a system-determined motive. By going abroad, firms escaped the systemic barriers and achieved a certain freedom in business operations and in non-interrupted imports of parts, while they were also permitted to keep some of the foreign exchange earned freely in then socialist system (see also Svetličič et al., 1994).

The substantial legal and policy changes seen in the last forty years have had an important impact on the determinants and patterns of Slovenian outward FDI. The key issues are firstly whether, when investing abroad, socialist firms followed a similar or different rationale compared to market economy firms. Secondly, what were the determinants of socialist firms investing abroad, which factors were more important, system- (investing country) or firm-specific, i.e. were the firm's characteristics those which pushed FDI outward, or were certain external (system) pull factors more important? Thirdly, is the emerging outward FDI of firms from transition countries a continuation of the earlier internationalization of socialist firms, or does it represent a more or less completely new phenomenon? Fourthly, can the existing internationalization theories be applied to the outward FDI of socialist firms?

If it were the predominantly socialist system characteristics that urged socialist firms to invest abroad[2], then the existing internationalization theories cannot really be applied to the early investments of socialist firms, and the emerging internationalization of firms after the beginning of the transition process would have nothing to do with the outward FDI of former socialist firms.

If, on the other hand, the outward FDI of socialist firms were determined by a similar pattern of determinants as for market economy firms, it would be possible to apply international production theories to the case of the internationalization of former socialist firms, and one could treat the emerging outward FDI of firms from transition countries like a continuation of the internationalization process that started in the socialist period.

Perhaps the most important issue to be addressed involves the answer to the question why outward FDI in Slovenia started before inward FDI. This would suggest that the investment development path model (see Dunning, 1981; Dunning and Narula, 1996) is not valid in Slovenia. Our hypothesis, however, is that the outward FDI of socialist firms was to an important extent motivated by system characteristics or, better put, deficiencies. To the extent that outward FDI was the system-escape type[3] it cannot be treated as the *normal* path of internationalization of market economy firms. Today's emerging outward FDI of Slovenian firms is, therefore, to that extent a new phenomenon with origins in the outward FDI of former Slovenian socialist firms.

Legal and policy framework for outward FDI in former Yugoslavia

At the beginning, the reason for the initial push to set up trading companies abroad involved finding ways and means to penetrate Western markets from initially mostly Eastern-oriented Slovenian international trade. Too frequent changes and other sorts of volatility in the systemic environment for international trade forced firms to look for ways to isolate themselves from such changes. The most important issue was how to secure the necessary raw materials, intermediate products, machinery and equipment from abroad. Later on, outward FDI increasingly became an instrument of export promotion since chronic shortages of foreign exchange increasingly characterized the economy of former Yugoslavia, based on an import-substitution development strategy.

Formally, the possibilities for outward FDI were opened up by elimination of the state monopoly in international economic relations, by increasing the autonomy of enterprises and by the introduction of certain market elements to the economic system.

Periods of outward FDI by firms from Slovenia as part of former Yugoslavia

In terms of the characteristics of outward FDI and particularly the legal regulations and strategies in this field, we can distinguish four stages in the outward FDI of former Yugoslavia, which Slovenia was then part of:

1. *Infant stage*, between the early 1950s and 1964;
2. *Liberal stage*, between 1965 and 1972/73;
3. *Harshening regulations stage*, 1972/73 until the end of 1988;
4. *Political transition stage*, 1989 to 1991.

The data for initial stages are very limited. Since initially there were no real laws regulating such firms' activities, any more comprehensive evidence also failed to exist. Nevertheless, soma data is available and is presented later (see 2.3). A similar situation was also seen in other former socialist countries, although their internationalization was much more modest.

There were two key reasons for starting outward FDI in the first infant stage period. The first was the economic blockade of the then Yugoslavia applied by the Soviet Union after the 1948 dispute, which called for total reorientation of the country's international economic relations towards the West. At first, securing the necessary inputs and machinery from the West was the primary determinant in the context of an ideological reorientation of the former major orientation of international economic co-operation with then socialist countries. It was politically and economically motivated. Politically, because Stalin had applied economic sanctions to Yugoslavia after the 1948 dispute. The result was the Foreign Exchange Reform of 1961 which changed the basic perception of the role of international economic relations, which were no longer 'only the instrument of maintaining the external financial balance but should enable the linking of the Yugoslav economy to the economies of other countries'. Companies started to urge the government to regulate these activities. The 'Decree on certain activities of domestic enterprises abroad' (Official Gazette of the Socialist Federal Republic of Yugoslavia - OG SFRY, 26/60) was passed in 1960. It was short and liberal enough to stimulate the establishment of companies abroad.

The second *liberal stage*, between 1965 and 1972/73, was the period of the fastest growth of Yugoslav production and trading companies abroad.

Table 3.1 Historical overview of legal and policy frameworks for outward FDI of former Yugoslavia as reflected in the respective legislation

	1960	1972/73	1977/78/82	1985	1989
Respective law	Decree on activities abroad	Law on companies abroad	Law on economic activities abroad	Law on economic activities abroad	Foreign Trade Law
Type of outward FDI allowed	- new companies - investing in foreign companies	- new companies - investing in foreign companies - branches	- new companies (including banks, insurance) - investing in foreign companies - branches/representative offices	- new companies (including banks, insurance) - investing in foreign companies - acquisition of foreign companies - holding companies (more than 50% Yugoslav share required) - branches/representative offices	- companies (including banks, insurance) - investing in foreign companies - holding companies (more than 50% Yugoslav share required) - branches/representative offices
Firms allowed to invest abroad	- involved in production - registration for foreign trade transactions	- registered for foreign trade transactions - bank authorized for foreign transactions	- registered for foreign trade transactions - banks authorized for foreign transactions	- firms (including banks, insurance companies) - holding companies abroad (more than 50% holding companies share required)	- legal persons - holding companies abroad (more than 50% holding companies share required)
Legally-defined objectives of investing firm	-	-	- to increase/promote exports - to ensure supply of raw materials - to intensify international integration of Yugoslav economy - to develop production/productivity	- to increase/promote exports/foreign exchange earnings - to acquire new markets - to ensure supply of raw materials - to intensify international integration of Yugoslav economy - to develop production/productivity	-
Activity of company abroad	-	-	- activity of the investing firm	- activity of the investing firm - supporting the basic activity	-
Specific approval requirements	- repatriation of profits and capital is legally possible - disposing with adequate staff for company abroad - feasibility study - investing firm liable only up to invested capital - inspection of books	- repatriation of profits and capital is legally possible - repatriation of a defined share of profit - inspection of books - feasibility study - information on foreign partner - investing firm liable only up to invested capital	- repatriation of profits and capital is legally possible - repatriation of a defined share of profit - for trading entities: exports from Yugoslavia to be biggest part of turnover - inspection of books - feasibility study - information on foreign partner - disposing with adequate staff for company abroad - investing firm liable only up to invested capital	- repatriation of profits and capital is legally possible - repatriation of defined share of profit - for trading entities: exports from Yugoslavia to be significant part of turnover - inspection of books - control of operations - disposing with adequate staff for company abroad - feasibility study - information on foreign partner - investing firm liable only up to invested capital	- regular financial control of company abroad - investing firm liable only up to invested capital

Book-keeping reporting necessary	- delivery of business reports/balance sheets - investing firm's books to reflect relations with company abroad	- delivery of business reports/balance sheets to National Bank - special account for transactions with company abroad	- reports to the National Bank - special book-keeping for company abroad	- special book-keeping for company abroad	- annual reports to the Social Accountancy Service
Profit repatriation	- Ministry of Finance can request part of the profit to be exchanged for dinars	-	- a predetermined share of profit to be repatriated within 30 days	- a predetermined share of profit to be repatriated within 60 days	- in case of balance-of-payments problems, the government can determine a share of profit to be repatriated
Use of profit	- to invest abroad - to put into foreign exchange account in Yugoslavia	- to invest abroad - to give loan to companies abroad - to put into foreign exchange account in Yugoslavia or abroad	- to invest abroad - to give loan to companies abroad - to repay credits taken for establishing company abroad	- to invest abroad - to give loan to companies abroad	- to invest abroad - to give loan to companies abroad
Termination/ dissolution of company abroad	-	-	- profit/capital repatriation is no longer possible - investing firm cannot ensure insight/control any more - no more confidence in foreign partner - loss in 3 consecutive years - for trading companies: exports from Yugoslavia are not the biggest part of turnover	- profit capital repatriation is no longer possible - Foreign Trade Ministry does not have access to books - objectives of investment are not realized - problem of losses is not resolved - for trading companies: if exports from Yugoslavia is not significant part of exports	- profit/capital repatriation is no longer possible - profit has not been repatriated for more than 2 years
Repatriation of capital	-	- within 90 days of termination/dissolution	- within 90 days of termination/dissolution	- within 90 days of termination/dissolution	- within 90 days of termination/dissolution
Incentives for investing abroad	-	-	-	-	-

Sources: 1960: Decree on certain activities of domestic firms abroad (OG SFRY, 26/60).
1972/73: Law on establishing companies abroad (OG SFRY, 39/72, 13/73).
1977/78/82: Law on performing economic activities abroad (OG SFRY, 15/1977, 17/78, 5/82).
1985: Law on performing economic activities abroad (OG SFRY, 71/85).

The first complex market-oriented Economic Reform of 1965 represented a crucial turning point which implicitly involved a strong stimulus for outward FDI. Foreign economic relations were seen as one of the main vehicles for realization of the reform's objectives. Enterprises got a relatively high level of autonomy and the state further reduced its role in foreign economic relations. This period can be regarded as the take-off period of many affiliations abroad.

The third stage, from 1972/73 until the end of 1988, can be labelled the *harshening regulations stage*. At the beginning of the 1970s, it became clear that the Economic Reform of 1965 had failed to produce the expected results. The transition from extensive to a more qualitative model of development had as a side-effect deterioration of the foreign trade balance. Some kinds of agreements among firms started to replace the previously planned strengthening of market relations. This opened the door widely up to the interference of politics in the economy. For outward FDI, the consequence was more restrictive legislation and the relatively close administrative monitoring of companies established abroad.

In 1972, the first law on foreign companies introduced strict criteria for establishing companies abroad. The assumption was that affiliations abroad had escaped the control of the Yugoslav authorities. Therefore, a kind of campaign was launched at the beginning of the 1970s to put them under stricter control. All companies established abroad had to pre-register their operations. New criteria were introduced in monitoring these operations. Their number therefore dropped.

The law on book-keeping from 1976 (OG 38/76) introduced the need for special book-keeping for all those companies abroad that had more than 51% of a Yugoslav equity share. Practice showed that this involved the sending every month of approximately 2,000 copies of different documents. Such a provision was not only against international law (extraterritorial application of national law), but also very expensive and, according to the domicile law, illegal.

In the mid-1970s, the so-called higher forms of international co-operation (basically everything except for exports and imports) became the preferred forms of international co-operation, particularly in economic relations with developing countries. Yugoslavia as a non-aligned country paid special attention to its economic co-operation with developing countries. Nevertheless, such co-operation mostly grew as a result of special preferential treatment received in certain periods. This included the preferential loans and even financing of equity capital for firms established in developing and CMEA countries provided by the Yugoslav Bank for International Economic Co-operation, established in 1987 (initially as a Fund for financing exports of capital goods and for insuring risks, and later also the Solidarity Fund with

Non-aligned and Developing Countries of 1975). In Slovenia, for instance, a special fund for financing pre-investment studies for the establishment of companies in developing countries had already been founded in 1974 (see Vezjak et al., 1980; p. 250), by firms themselves along with the participation and administration of the then Chamber of Economy and Ljubljanska Banka.

The next two laws on outward FDI (from 1977, amended in 1978 and 1982, and from 1985) showed similar trends. Although the types of affiliates allowed to be established or acquired abroad were broadening all the time, the general spirit was to more strictly regulate their activities. The key legally-defined objective for investing abroad was to increase exports from Yugoslavia. An investing firm had to repatriate a certain share of profits of its company abroad and to realize the larger part of its turnover through exports from Yugoslavia. Investing firms were liable only up to the amount of capital invested.

The fourth, *political transition stage* lasted from 1989 to 1991 when Yugoslavia began to disintegrate. The comprehensive market-oriented economic reforms introduced at the end of 1988 brought this 'foreign-exchange-generating' attitude to outward FDI with a lot of administrative interference to an end. In 1989, outward FDI started to be treated as a normal part of foreign economic relations. It was regulated in the framework of the Foreign Trade Law.

Main features and determinants of former Yugoslavia's outward FDI policy

Trends in the outward FDI legislation and policy of former Yugoslavia were determined by: (i) developments in the economic system, especially the understanding of the role of international economic relations and the development concept; (ii) frequent changes in the economic development of the country, especially in its international economic relations; (iii) trends in the world economy; and (iv) by the evolving attitudes/strategies to outward FDI.

Yugoslav outward FDI had the following characteristics:

1. *Outward FDI as a residual, a spin-off of developments in the Yugoslav economic system and the role of international economic relations in that system.* In spite of the early start of outward FDI from Yugoslavia, relatively exceptional for a socialist economy of that time, one can hardly say that an official policy of outward FDI existed at any time in former Yugoslavia. The laws of 1977 and 1985 in fact defined what were supposed to be the objectives of an investing firm (see Table 3.1). The overall Yugoslav understanding of outward FDI was not as a self-induced autonomous

process of internationalization, but more as exports supporting spin-offs of the gradual liberalization of the socialist economic system.

2. *Outward FDI as a reflection of macroeconomic, especially foreign trade trends.* Outward FDI policy reflected the development cycle of Yugoslavia. At first, the primary motive was to enable imports and, later, with opening up of the economy and parallel to the deteriorating balance of payments situation (particularly after the 1973/74 oil crises) exports became the most important macroeconomic push factor. The legal framework for outward FDI oscillated accordingly; periods of more liberal regulation were followed by the introduction of greater restrictions and more regulation.
3. *Outward FDI as a trade (export) supporting and balance of payments deficit induced phenomenon.* Since balance of payments difficulties were almost a hallmark of former Yugoslavia, the main determinant of outward FDI policy was to increase exports (also a legally prescribed objective) and foreign exchange earnings (see Table 3.1). From the government perspective, outward FDI was not only trade/export-supporting but also induced by the balance of payments deficit. This is most obviously demonstrated by the prescription that a certain share of the profits of companies abroad should be transferred to home. In 1987, wholly- (Yugoslav-) owned trading companies abroad had to repatriate 30 per cent of their profits, 15 per cent if they were established in developing countries and 7.5 per cent if they were in the least developed developing countries. The shares for wholly- (Yugoslav-) owned production companies were lower (15 per cent, 7.5 per cent and three per cent, respectively), while banks had to repatriate 40 per cent if they were involved in developed countries and five per cent in developing ones.
4. *Outward FDI as a temporary problem-resolving, policy-supporting activity.* At the macro level, outward FDI always seems to be seen as a kind of temporary phenomenon. With a solution to balance of payments difficulties, there would not be a need for FDI any more. Investing firms were required to define the time period in which the invested capital would be repatriated. This was based on the concept that the invested capital should be repatriated in the foreseeable future.
5. *Outward FDI began to be regulated only by an adequate legal framework with a time lag.* The logical consequence of this 'reactive' attitude to outward FDI was that it was always regulated ex post, after Yugoslav enterprises had already developed a certain pattern of activities abroad. Yugoslav outward FDI policy was therefore more of a reactionary policy, a tight hand on the reins in a period of deteriorating economic conditions (particularly the balance of payments), and liberalizing when the general economic situation improved.

6. *Outward FDI as a system-escape mechanism for enterprises.* It would be too strong to claim that enterprises applied consistent outward FDI strategies. Enterprises saw the establishing of companies abroad as an export promoting mechanism, as well as for securing the necessary imported machinery and inputs on a preferential basis. Enterprises very rarely invested abroad on the basis of firm- and location-specific advantages. In addition, very few companies used outward FDI as an instrument to strengthen their competitive position in the international market by relocating some labour-intensive activities in developing countries. If they did, such operations mostly failed[4].
7. *Inconsistent 'official' Yugoslav attitude to outward FDI.* Although enterprises were allowed to start operations abroad, the general legal and policy climate for their establishment and operations was not very stimulating. In spite of gradual liberalization, there were constant ups and downs. Attitudinal barriers persisted. The deterioration of the economic situation bolstered the position of advocates of import-substitutive development strategies and of restricted and controlled international economic relations. The first signs of the failure of the Economic Reform of 1965 involving negative balance of payments trends at the beginning of the 1970s led to the introduction of very strict control mechanisms for companies abroad (including a double-bookkeeping system[5]), which were semi-officially often regarded as 'law avoiding operations'. Companies abroad started to 'escape' from the control of Yugoslav authorities, and a kind of campaign was launched to keep them under stricter control. All companies established abroad had to pre-register their operations. More 'social' criteria were introduced in monitoring these operations. As a consequence, there were fewer of them.

The only kind of outward FDI always officially treated as welcome was FDI in developing, non-aligned countries. Yugoslav enterprises, however, did not really follow the declarations. They invested in developing countries only as far as this was stimulated by specific incentives given to them in a certain period. These incentives included preferential loans and even the financing of equity capital for companies established in developing countries provided by the Yugoslav Bank for International Economic Co-operation.

Evolution of outward FDI by socialist firms

Socialist firms were thus not complete newcomers when it came to investing abroad. The total number of affiliations abroad that McMillan was able to detect at the end of 1983 was 635. Most of them were established in the West

(484) and only 151 in developing countries. This reveals their primary trade orientation. Only 15 per cent of the total number of their investments in the West and five per cent in developing countries date to before 1965. The rate of investment really accelerated in the 1970s. By the early 1980s, these investments had spread on a global scale across a broad spectrum of countries and activities (McMillan, 1987; pp. 29, 34 and 161-163).

Yugoslavia was not a member of CMEA and therefore data on the internationalization of their firms was not included in his data bank. Limited evidence however indicates that Yugoslav firms were the most active in their activities abroad among all firms from socialist countries. By 1974, all together Yugoslav firms had 336 companies abroad[6], mostly in Western countries[7].

Table 3.2 Number of enterprises abroad affiliated to Yugoslav firms in the 1974-1978 period (situation at end of year)

Region	1974	1978
Western industrialized countries	305	272
Developing countries	31	46
Socialist countries	-	-
Total	336	318

Source: Based on companies' reports to the Social Accounting Office of Yugoslavia in 1978; quoted from Svetličič 1979; p. 7.

Of those, trade companies dominated, followed by production, construction, transport and tourism and, finally, banks. Most firms in Western countries were concentrated in 19 countries[8] (Svetličič, 1975; p. 16 and Svetličič 1979; p. 7) which is not a negligible number for such an early internationalization process.

The number of subsidiaries abroad obviously dropped from 1972 to 1974 due to the tightening up of the regulatory framework. Many companies therefore ceased to exist in this period. After this period of consolidation, the number again increased to almost 2,000 by the end of 1986 and thus clearly exceeded the total number for CMEA countries. With few exceptions[9], their scale of operation was relatively limited. Yugoslav enterprises abroad employed 10,684 people at the end of 1983, of whom 55 per cent were in developing countries, reflecting the predominance of labour-intensive manufacturing industries (Artisien et al., 1991; p. 230).

Slovenian firms played a prominent role in such business activities of firms abroad particularly if one puts aside the number of so-called federal trading companies established in the capital of then Yugoslavia[10]. In 1979 Slovenian companies accounted for 25 per cent of 349 hundred-per cent-owned and mixed companies abroad. Eight years later, this share had increased to 32 per cent (Vezjak et al. 1988; p. 219). The first Slovenian outward FDI after WWII we were able to trace took place back in 1959 when the trading company Intertrade set up a subsidiary in India. Gorenje established its first affiliate abroad in 1965 in France. Slovenian electronics conglomerate Iskra set up its first trading firms in 1967 in London (Guest Ltd.) and Stuttgart (Iskra Elektronik Stuttgart)[11]. The trading company Intertrade set up a subsidiary Intraco in India.

In the second liberal period from 1966 to 1972/73, many companies were established. Among them, Tomos started to produce scooters in Komasi, Ghana (Tomos Ghana). The trading company Slovenijales started tropical wood exploitation and processing (Slovenia Bois) in the Central African Republic in 1970[12]. It was one of the largest projects there.

In spite of tougher regulations in the third period of outward FDI, a number of companies were established abroad[13]. This type of international economic co-operation was not negligible since, according to the Federal Statistical Office, through this form 5 per cent of exports was directed abroad and 9 per cent of imports; in developing countries the shares were even higher (14 per cent in exports and 29 per cent in imports). Such companies abroad all together employed 2,383 people in 1978, 1,759 from the SFRY (Svetličič, 1979; pp. 71, 122 and 145). By 1984, the shares increased to 27 per cent of Yugoslav exports and 12.5 per cent of imports[14] (Svetličič and Rojec, 1985; p. 10). In terms of invested capital, industrial countries were much more important since they attracted 72 per cent of all capital invested abroad in 1982 (Svetličič and Rojec, 1985; p. 18).

In terms of activity, there was an important difference between affiliations in industrial and developing countries. In developing countries, manufacturing units played quite an important role while in industrial countries the facilitating of trade by sales units was their most important activity (226 out of 318 in 1978).

After the changes, involving first pre-registration and then a broadening of the scope of international activities, internationalization was boosted. The number of affiliations of all different kinds increased from 1986-1988 to 2,225 in 1992. If only equity ventures are calculated (excluding units for construction works), then the figure moves from 670 to 744.

Three tendencies are particularly evident. First, developing countries became, thanks to substantial construction activities, the most important regional destination of internationalization. Western countries followed, but were leading in terms of all kinds of subsidiaries, particularly wholly-owned ones. In the East, firms only undertook construction works. The balanced distribution of representative offices demonstrates that their primary function was the promotion of trade with respective markets.

Table 3.3 Number of Yugoslav economic entities abroad, end of 1986 and 1988

	Developed market-economy countries		Eastern European socialist[i] countries		Less-developed countries		Total	
	1986	1988	1986	1988	1986	1988	1986	1988
Number of countries	24	25	11	12	62	60	97	97
Number of entities - Total	555	623	443	558	994	1,044	1,992	2,225
1. Subsidiaries	271	308	1	-	63	64	335	372
a) Wholly- (Yugoslav-) owned	193	224	1	-	25	27	219	251
b) Majority- (Yugoslav-) owned	27	30	-	-	4	3	31	33
c) Minority- (Yugoslav-) owned	51	54	-	-	34	34	85	88
2. Entities for construction works[ii]	71	103	167	244	697	754	935	1,101
3. Representative offices	220	194	253	275	198	195	653	664

Source: Artisien et al., 1991; p. 227 (for 1986) and Artisien et al., 1992; p. 33 (for 1988).

Notes:

i Includes China and Mongolia.

ii Entities for construction works and business entities were both set up to undertake construction projects abroad. Business entities (88, but not included in the table), however, were not legally bound to draw up their balance sheet reports for the Yugoslav authorities.

By 1988, Slovenian companies were involved in 87 firms abroad (60 being wholly-owned), 266 entities for investment projects abroad, 89 representative offices, while in 28 foreign companies and five banks Slovenian firms acted as minority shareholders. Large Slovenian firms like Iskra, Gorenje, Elan, and Slovenijales had by the end of 1988 established a number of companies abroad. Iskra had 12 companies and six representative offices in the West, three representative offices in CEE countries. Slovenijales had 12 companies abroad, Industrija motornih vozil (IMV) eight, Gorenje seven, Elan six, Jugotekstil five, Lesnina four, Emona four etc (see Svetlièiè et al., 1994; p. 366). The share of Slovenian firms in all Yugoslav subsidiaries abroad was obviously important (28 per cent by the number of entities). More detailed information on such investments is now only available for the period after 1993. Regionally speaking, Germany assumed the most important role, followed by Italy, Switzerland and France. Over 60 per cent of entities abroad were involved in trading. The share of manufacturing was relatively more important than it was for the CMEA member-countries.

Although the number of companies established abroad is impressive and some good results were achieved, rates of divestment were, not surprisingly, also quite high. Yugoslav firms were generally newcomers in this form of international activities. Many failures were the result of inadequate preparations, insufficient pre-feasibility studies and a lack of information. In short, the lack of knowledge was responsible for most failures. Nevertheless, many managers involved in such operations today claim that was the necessary price for learning by doing and a good basis for today's internationalization and avoidance of past mistakes which were, given the modest ventures, not so expensive.

System-escape determinants of outward FDI by Slovenian firms

There are basically two explanations for this early internationalization of companies from Slovenia. The first relates to the economic sanctions imposed on Yugoslavia by Stalin in 1948. Firms started to seek goods and technology from the West also by establishing affiliates in the West. The second push for internationalization was the Economic Reform of 1965. Many market elements were brought into the then planned economy and companies acquired a relatively autonomous status. They started to be fully responsible for the sales and marketing of their products. The position of managers became very different to that in other CEE countries. To the extent that a number of decisions were being taken by the companies themselves, they became agents of the market and managers were forced to adopt many market-driven practices. The Reform also changed the foreign trade system. Foreign trade ceased to be a state monopoly, enterprises became 'independent' foreign trade operators which opened up possibilities to also consider investment operations abroad.

The economy started to become increasingly import dependent but also ever more export oriented to Western markets. The establishment of representative offices or branches and later affiliations abroad became a way of facilitating imports to Yugoslavia and later promoting own exports.

Having a direct presence abroad gradually became a *conditio sine qua non* for a relatively 'open' socialist economy as Yugoslavia was, at least for the largest companies. By investing abroad, firms attempted to acquire the marketing, technological and managerial skills necessary for their foreign trade operations so as to expand exports to Western markets and to facilitate imports. Later on a new motive started to dominate, namely the achievement of a privileged foreign trade and foreign exchange position. This privileged position was explicitly and implicitly the consequence of the contemporaneous foreign trade and foreign exchange regime. Under this regime, exporters had to sell foreign exchange at the official overvalued exchange rate of the Yugoslav currency dinar and when they needed foreign exchange for their own imports they had to wait in the 'administrative queue', or to buy the 'rights to foreign exchange' in the inter-firm market at a higher rate. According to a 1973 Federal Assembly Resolution[15], firms with an affiliation abroad started to be excluded from this regime. This resolution:

1. Explicitly allowed firms to use part of the foreign exchange earnings from these companies' operations for their own imports and to keep foreign exchange proceeds longer than other firms[16].
2. Implicitly enabled firms to keep the foreign exchange in these companies instead of transferring it to home. This helped them avoid the problems of selling foreign exchange at the overvalued official dinar exchange rate, i.e. to avoid losses from the margin between the official (selling of foreign exchange) and the black/grey market exchange rate (buying of foreign exchange). Instead, they could make substantial earnings from the difference between the official and black market exchange rates.

This assisted companies in becoming somewhat 'foreign exchange' independent, able to fund necessary intermediate products regularly, unlike other firms. In a situation of permanent foreign exchange shortages and overvaluation of the dinar, this system-escape motivation for outward FDI became increasingly important. Imports by firms with companies abroad were much less dependent on changes in foreign trade and the foreign exchange regime. They were in a position to import intermediate products, spare parts etc., without interruption, even in periods of the most drastic import restrictions and foreign exchange shortages, which kept escalating with the ever increasing external debt problems of the Yugoslav economy. In view of the frequent changes in the Yugoslav legal environment, outward internationalization became a 'stability-seeking' or 'shock-absorbing' operation. 'To a certain degree, internationalization was a way of escaping from uncertainty and unpredictability. By establishing companies abroad Slovenian firms got a certain freedom of operation and became at least partly immune from frequent changes to the regulatory and policy framework at home. By establishing companies abroad they increased their competitive edge in terms of regular access to foreign exchange without losing the margin between the market and official exchange rate' (Svetličič, Rojec and Lebar, 1994; p. 365).

Emerging pre-transition outward FDI and the investment development path theory

Outward FDI in the Yugoslav case was, therefore, to a great extent a system-escape operation and did not follow a 'normal' investment development path which starts with inward and only later with outward FDI. Contrary to the theoretical predictions, outward FDI by Yugoslav firms started back in the 1950s. The first legal document regulating outward FDI dated back to 1960, while the first inward foreign investment law (allowing a specific type of contractual joint venture) was introduced in 1967. The inward-outward FDI sequence seems to be reversed in the case of Slovenia. Firm- specific, location-specific or internalization advantages in the traditional sense did not play a major role in outward FDI. Location-specific advantages played an important role in quite a specific sense; i.e. the location abroad gave the investing firms a special legal status. This enabled them to strengthen their competitiveness and develop a kind of firm-specific advantage in terms of being able to import regularly and to collect agio between the official and black market exchange rates. This was only possible through internalization within the firm, by having one's own companies abroad or other types of long-term co-operation with foreign partners.

This non-fitting of Slovenia's pre-transition inward-outward FDI sequence into the investment development path model does not indicate a deficiency in the investment development path model but the irregularity of the pre-transition outward FDI of Slovenian enterprises. This outward FDI was to a great extent not driven by genuine firm-specific advantages, but by the socialist economic system's deficiencies which motivated firms to avoid them – in a sense such FDI was more the result of defensive motives. 'Most companies abroad (predominantly only trade subsidiaries) were export (market) seeking and intermediate goods import seeking. What happened in Slovenia should also be distinguished from the pattern of Third World multinationals that initially, according to Cantwell and Tolentino (1987), concentrated on resource-based industries' (see Svetlièiè et al., 1994; p. 367). When one tries to test the validity of the investment development path model for Slovenia, the path to be monitored mostly began only with the establishment of a real market economy that is with the beginning of the transition process. Only then, did an appropriate system framework which makes firms behave like real market actors, including the domination of the firm-specific determinants of internationalization, begin to prevail. There are two convincing facts proving this. Many pre-transition foreign affiliates of Slovenian firms disappeared. Secondly, a number of new affiliates abroad that have appeared recently are based on very different motivating factors and have different geographical locations. The newly emerging outward FDI of Slovenian firms can therefore be partly regarded as a new and partly an inherited phenomenon. A proportion of outward FDI in the past was also initiated by genuine firm-specific determinants. Early internationalization positively contributed to the development of investing firms' capabilities and is instrumental for today's internationalization.

Summary

Since late 1950 when Slovenian firms first began investing abroad, there have been a lot of changes which have radically changed the environment and, thus, also the determinants and motivation for outward FDI. Up until recently, the motivation for investing abroad was determined more by system and macroeconomic factors than by business, firm-specific and company-competitiveness-driven considerations. Systemic factors, which could explain the lion's share of such operations, at least in industrial countries, could be an argument that challenges what appears as a 'reverse investment development path' model, meaning that outward FDI started before the inward type. Specifically, the system-escape dimension may explain such a departure from the paradigm. With the introduction of a market economy following Slovenia's independence, system-escape investment lost its importance, while other motives gained in significance. Slovenia's 1991 regime of outward FDI fully liberalized outward FDI both from the aspects of currency restrictions and restrictions on underlying transactions. Slovenia in this respect already fully complies with EU standards. These legal changes, accompanied by mounting economic policy awareness of the increasing necessity to invest abroad, have brought firm-determined considerations for outward FDI to the fore. 'Normal' (in terms of theory) outward FDI began to emerge. The reverse sequence was so strongly system-based that the predictions of the theory are applicable, particularly since recent outward FDI developments do support the investment development path model. Although a cumulative learning process started with the early beginning of outward FDI, the 'real' outward FDI by private firms basically started only with the transition process.

Notes

1 This chapter is based mostly on a background study prepared by Rojec and Svetlièiè for the World Investment Report 1995.

2 The question arises whether firms in socialism are really *normal* firms, which follow profit or growth maximisation as a bottom line. If they are state-owned and follow decisions taken by the state, the answer is no. But firms in Yugoslavia became much more autonomous and exposed to market forces. 'The specific ownership structure meant that most enterprises were *de-facto but not de-jure owned by employees*' (*World Bank*, 1999, p. 85). They came closer to normal market agents. With the major Economic Reform of 1965 in the former Yugoslavia, state ownership was abolished, a self-management system was introduced and companies received a certain degree of autonomy within so-called 'market socialism'. Due to these changes, the International Finance Corporation started to grant loans to Yugoslav enterprises implicitly, considering them as having the characteristics of private firms.

3 See the later explanation of such outward FDI.

4 For instance, the Jugotekstil shirt factory in Kenya.
5 The Law on Bookkeeping from 1976 (OG SFRY 38/76) introduced the obligation of special book-keeping for all companies abroad with a more than 51 per cent Yugoslav share.
6 They were established predominantly as wholly-owned firms (65 per cent) and 30 per cent as mixed companies (Svetličič, 1975; p. 15).
7 Unfortunately, data for affiliations in OECD countries is more limited than for those in developing countries since after 1972 a special project on evaluating co-operation with developing countries also included a regular study of the activities of the affiliations there. No similar study was undertaken for their activities in OECD countries. Nevertheless, it is possible to note that most of such affiliations in the West were trade-related and very few were in production. Many construction firms also established affiliations for undertaking construction works abroad on a regular and long-term basis. Establishing a company in such markets was a way of facilitating such activities.
8 Western Germany was leading with 98 companies, followed by Italy with 53 companies, Austria 36, USA 30 and Switzerland 29 (Svetličič, 1975, p. 47).
9 Slovenia's Bois, a tropical wood exploitation and processing joint venture established in the Central African Republic, was one of the largest projects in that country and its major source of FDI. DAWA, Krka's pharmaceutical firm in Kenya, was (according to *The Standard*, Nairobi, 18 January 1984) the largest pharmaceutical factory in sub-Saharan Africa, contributing five per cent to Kenya's gross domestic product and employing approximately three per cent of its workforce (Svetličič and Rojec, 1985, pp. 91, 107, 137).
10 The most active were certain major trading companies like General-export, Progres, Centrotextil, Interexport, the engineering firm Energoprojekt, and Jugobanka among banks.
11 It became the largest Iskra trading company abroad with annual turnover of DEM 80 million. Later, in 1979, Iskra established Afericon in Caracas Venezuela and Televias, which was soon liquidated while Eurocomerce in Caracas, Venezuela has been operating also in 1980s. In order to supply the Andean market with electrical hand-machine tools Iskra also established Iskraemec in Ecuador. It represented 15 per cent of the ANDEAN market for these products in 1978 (Margan, 1882; pp. 217 and 218) quoted from Svetličič and Rojec (1985; p. 101).
12 In 1978 they also started the production of plywood.
13 Among them, in 1977 Krka established Dawa Pharmaceuticals in Nairobi Kenya that had a turnover of USD 5 million in 1984 (The Standard, City Edition, Nairobi, 18 January 1984). Emona established the trading company Aprimex in Kenya and in 1974 it acquired a concession for a coffee plantation in the Central African Republic; Tehnoimpex established the trading firm Jugoniger in Lagos (Nigeria). Comet established Coflex in Malta for the production of grinding wheels in 1979, in 1975 Gorenje set up a company in Austria which is now its major afiliation abroad, and Intertrade set up Bokyo-Tanneries Ltd. in 1976 in India.
14 The figures are not completely comparable due to the different sources involved.
15 It stipulated that in case there were any changes in foreign trade and the foreign exchange system, enterprises that entered into long-term agreements should be sure that the regulations in force on the day of the contract's registration would apply to such long-term contracts if this was more favourable to the contracting parties, or unless they decided to settle a particular question in some other way by mutual agreement (Svetličič and Rojec, 1985; p. 8).
16 'A typical example of such a strategy was the car trailer producer IMV. It established a network of subsidiaries in Western Europe for marketing and assembling trailers. With

foreign exchange earned by these subsidiaries, IMV was importing cars (co-operation with Renault) and selling them at a high profit, arising from a high margin of the market over the official exchange rate in the home market. In such a way, firms were trying to reduce the transaction costs related to uncertainties and risks involved with the irregular supply of parts etc.' (Svetlièiè et al., 1994; p. 365).

PART II
OUTWARD FOREIGN DIRECT INVESTMENT IN THE 1990s

Chapter 4

Legal Framework and Trends

Introduction

With the start of transition, further internationalization was not only a challenge but also necessary to succeed in the economic transformation process. Due to the many years of export experience, openness and, relatively early start and accumulated experiences in outward FDI (especially compared to other socialist economies), greater FDI outflows were expected after Slovenia's independence in 1991 and after a fully-fledged market economy started to be introduced. Accelerated investing abroad was also expected because of the increasing globalization and intensification of EU integration.

The rapid internationalization of Slovenian firms runs contrary to both the prevailing pattern described in evolutionary internationalization models and the experiences of more developed industrial countries. The push internationalization factors of those economies were: small size (small domestic markets that do not allow economies of scale and scope), limited domestic resources, good geo-strategic positions and openness. The same factors also played a decisive role in Slovenia. In addition, domestic (Slovenian) companies are small by international standards, which makes the gradual approach more suitable.

The fact that outward FDI started in Slovenia before inward FDI does indeed conflict with the sequential internationalization process (Luostarinen, 1994; Welch and Luostarinen, 1988), Ozawa's dynamic paradigm of TNC-assisted development (Ozawa, 1992) and the investment development path pattern (Dunning, 1993; Dunning and Narula, 1996). The difference in the timing of FDI flows that oppose these models has been explained by system-specific characteristics (Chapter 3). Thus, initial trends in Slovenia's internationalization pattern do not contradict the relationship between multinational activity and the level of economic development, which is the essence of the above-mentioned theories. Soon after foreigners were allowed to invest in Slovenia (or more accurately in the then Yugoslavia) outward FDI started to lag behind the inward type. In the years of transition from a planned to a market economy, Slovenian outward FDI began to follow the Scandinavian pattern or that of other small European countries like Portugal (see Buckley and Castro, 1998 and 1999; Simoes, 2000), Finland (see Luostarinen, 1979 and 1994) and Sweden (see Johanson and Wiedersheim-Paul, 1975), despite their much longer history of internationalization through outward investments. Slovenian companies are today following an accelerated sequential internationalization approach, which can be explained by the traditional internationalization theories. The process is faster, with the stages getting shorter and sometimes even being leaped over as Dunning and Narula predicted (1996).

Transition introduced fundamental changes. Three stages of the internationalization process can be identified in the nineties, predominantly characterized by institutional/legal and political developments, mostly privatization and accession to the EU:

1. Early transition stage (1990-1993) – the first wave of internationalization – marked by a rapid increase of outward investment on one hand, and divestments and restructuring on the other.
2. Consolidation phase in the mid-nineties (1994-1998) characterized by slow progress in outward investment activity that was mostly carried out by existing multinational companies, which consolidated and strengthened their foreign affiliates' network.
3. A new wave of internationalization at the end of decade (from 1999 onwards) – that speeded up the outward investments of existing multinationals and newcomers in terms of broadening and strengthening their foreign affiliate networks and rapid expansion to the former Yugoslav markets.

The dynamics of outward FDI in the past decade were determined by changes and developments in the domestic macroeconomic situation and competitiveness of domestic firms, the process of privatization and changes in laws concerning outward investment, the integration process of Slovenia and other transition economies into the EU and trends in world trade. This chapter presents general trends and the pattern of Slovenian outward FDI in the 1990s. We begin with the evolution of the legal framework and proceed by examining the development of outward FDI from the early years of transition up until recently.

Evolution of the legal framework[1]

The legal framework has significantly influenced the internationalization stages. Generally, three stages of outward FDI policies can be distinguished in post-1991 Slovenia:

1. Inherited liberal regime, or better put the virtual absence of any specific

regulations (a kind of legal vacuum) related to capital exports (1991 through to early 1993). At this stage, the first Slovenian Foreign Trade Law was passed.
2. 'Monitoring' stage, mostly as a response to certain negative aspects of outward FDI in the privatization process (end 1993-1994).
3. Gradual application of international standards in the field of outward FDI with full liberalization (New Foreign Exchange Law, 1999).

At first, Slovenia simply took over the Yugoslav legislation according to which legal entities were allowed to establish companies abroad with a permit from and upon registration with the federal authorities. The permit was confined just to legal entities, while private individuals were not allowed to establish companies abroad.

Foreign Trade Law of 1993

In 1993, the Slovenian Parliament passed a new Foreign Trade Law (subsequently amended in 1993, 1994 and 1995), which was more liberal. Among other provisions, Articles 22 to 24 of the Law regulated the outward investments of domestic legal and natural persons and foreign natural persons with a permanent residence in the Republic of Slovenia. The Law did not use the internationally recognized term 'direct investment' and was not very precise in its definitions. Pursuant to the Law (Article 22), domestic and foreign natural persons were allowed:

- to establish a company, bank, insurance and reinsurance company and financial organization abroad;
- to purchase or increase stakes in a commercial company abroad; and
- to invest in foreign commercial companies abroad.

Despite the lack of a definition of 'direct investment' (the somewhat vague expression 'purchase or increase stakes in ...' which could be misleading in the case of portfolio investment), the Law dealt with outward direct investment in a basic way.

Unlike the former law, natural persons were also allowed to invest abroad. Further, the provisions on financing were not as strict. Eligible persons were allowed to use whatever resources they had at their disposal, either their own or borrowed resources. This meant the base of investors was substantially broadened relative to the earlier legislation.

On the other hand, since Slovenia was in a transition period with its privatization process still in progress, the Law introduced some new restrictions for legal entities. The permission of the Ministry of Finance, which was the competent authority, for investing abroad could only be obtained if:

- all taxes had been paid by the proposed investing company;
- the investing company had made a profit in the previous year; and
- the investing company had already completed a privatization programme or had its privatization plan approved.

The above-mentioned conditions being met, the Ministry of Finance would then grant its permission for an investment to be made abroad. The Ministry of Finance also ran a register for all investments made by legal entities abroad. On the basis of an application for permission and after such permission had been granted, the Ministry of Finance would register the company. The investor – a legal entity – was thereafter obliged to register any changes to the investment. To reinvest the profits of a company abroad no permission was needed. However, like with all other changes to the investment this transaction had to be registered at the Ministry of Finance. Although the regulations seemed restrictive, it has to be said that there were almost no cases of application refusals. The regulations aimed more to monitor business activities abroad.

As for natural persons, they were free to invest abroad. They did not need the permission of the Ministry of Finance, nor were they constrained by the above conditions. They only had to report their investment to the tax authorities after it had been made.

Foreign Trade Law of 1999

After initiating negotiations with the EU to sign the Europe Agreement, the process of harmonization of financial and foreign trade legislation got underway. Liberalization was therefore initially very Europe-Agreement-driven and not so much the result of specific industrial policy. Such reasons came to the fore only later. In the framework of liberalizing capital account transactions, in April 1999 Slovenia adopted a new Foreign Exchange Law. The Law regulates operations between residents and non-residents and thereby also regulates issues related to capital movements. It is a major step towards full liberalization of the flow of capital. A number of restrictions on foreign investments in Slovenia were phased out, at the same time very few restrictions remain as to residents' investments abroad. Phasing out of the remaining restrictions is left to the implementing regulations which fall within the jurisdiction of the Bank of Slovenia and the Ministry of Finance. In this way, the conditions have been provided for smooth and speedy further liberalization, towards full capital account convertibility, without any complex amending procedures.

The Law introduces a clear internationally recognized definition of the term 'direct investment', secondly, it adopts a domicile approach and, thirdly, it phases out all restrictions on outward FDI. The definition of 'direct investment' is based on the EU's definition taken from the Fourth EU Directive 1988 (88/361 EEC) and harmonized with the OECD's definition from the OECD Code of Liberalization of Capital Movements[2]. The Law defines direct investments as all investments by an investor aimed at establishing lasting economic links and gaining the possibility of exercising effective influence over the management of a company or other legal entity.

The distinction between domestic and foreign entities has been eliminated. Instead, the Law introduces a domicile approach. This means it distinguishes between persons not on the basis of nationality or citizenship, but on the basis of residency. Accordingly, the legislation speaks of residents and non-residents, where residents are all companies and other legal entities with a registered office in the Republic of Slovenia. All other persons and entities are deemed non-resident. Consequently, when one speaks of outward FDI one speaks of direct investments of residents abroad.

As concerns residents' investments abroad, the Foreign Exchange Law no longer demands a permit for investments abroad. Residents, both legal and natural persons, are completely free to make a direct investment abroad. The Foreign Exchange Law also lifts restrictions on residents' purchases of real estate abroad.

The Law, however, retains the obligation of the former legislation to report and register outward FDI. Residents have to report to the Ministry of Finance within 30 days, and the Ministry of Finance continues to run its register. What is new is that the obligation to register extends to both legal and natural persons. Residents are also obliged to report changes regarding an investment to the Ministry of Finance. Data is collected for statistical and tax purposes.

Should capital movements cause or threaten to cause serious problems to the functioning of monetary and foreign exchange policy, the Bank of Slovenia can introduce safeguard measures which, however, cannot be taken for a period exceeding six months. Such measures can be directed only to capital transactions of a mostly short- and medium-term nature and must not directly affect long-term capital flows as direct investment and some other transactions. This also means that in any period of a currency crisis the Law does not authorize the Bank of Slovenia or any other authority to take any measures against direct investments.

Trends in outward FDI

Early transition stage

The beginning of the 1990s was accompanied by substantial economic and political changes. Independence crucially changed Slovenia's economic position. It began with economic and political transformation and the transition from a regional to a national economy. Slovenia gradually started changing all its legislation regulating international economic relations. Faced with many fundamental problems, outward FDI was not considered a true priority issue. In the pre-privatization situation, any investment abroad by non-privatized companies would be treated as an attempt to transfer capital abroad in order to reduce the value of the investing company before privatization. Thus, macroeconomic considerations and the economic system's turnaround played a decisive role in developing Slovenian attitudes to outward FDI in the early 1990s. Business considerations were pushed aside, although it was actually companies abroad that made the transition from domestic to foreign markets easier. They were very instrumental in compensating for the loss of the Yugoslav market through foreign markets and in helping to stabilize international business operations. The transformation process along with Slovenia's disintegration from Yugoslavia initially brought about two allegedly contradictory outward FDI tendencies.

On one hand, there was a boom in the establishing of small 'postbox' companies abroad. Surveys demonstrated that a great deal of foreign affiliates was established at the beginning of the nineties (Figure 4.1). There were at least five reasons for the first (transition) internationalization wave:

1. Pioneering tide of freed entrepreneurial spirit by establishing companies by natural persons at home and on that basis also abroad.
2. The transformation of previous entities in other parts of former Yugoslavia into companies where possible[3]. After the disintegration of Yugoslavia, many Slovenian firms found themselves in possession of a number of representative offices and affiliates in other parts of former Yugoslavia. These affiliates became international operations overnight and firms had to adapt to such new situations of 'forced' or induced internationalization. Such 'inherited investments' (Svetličič et al., 1994) represented an important share of Slovenian outward investments in the early years of transition. Although firms were familiar with the environment in legal terms, many things had changed. It might be that such forced internationalization acted as a stimulus for the future internationalization of these firms, allowing them to acquire experience and confidence in their internationalization capabilities.

3. Maintaining companies abroad was seen as a way to keep economic co-operation going with the former Yugoslav republics when they formally banned such economic co-operation with Slovenia or when the very shaky political and economic situation made direct business contacts less certain[4]. Affiliations abroad became a way of losing the Slovenian legal identity and keeping previous close business co-operation going at least on a limited scale in the interest of both business sides. Such 'window dressing' firms were mostly established in Austria, Italy and Hungary and enabled Slovenian firms to continue to do business with Serbia.
4. In the conditions of radical economic system changes and the high political and market uncertainties of the initial transition period, a number of firms began to look upon companies abroad as a mechanism to increase the stability of their business operations, and for export promotion.
5. For some firms, establishing companies abroad was also a mechanism to transfer financial sources and certain profitable parts of business activities abroad before the privatization process in an investing firm was to begin.

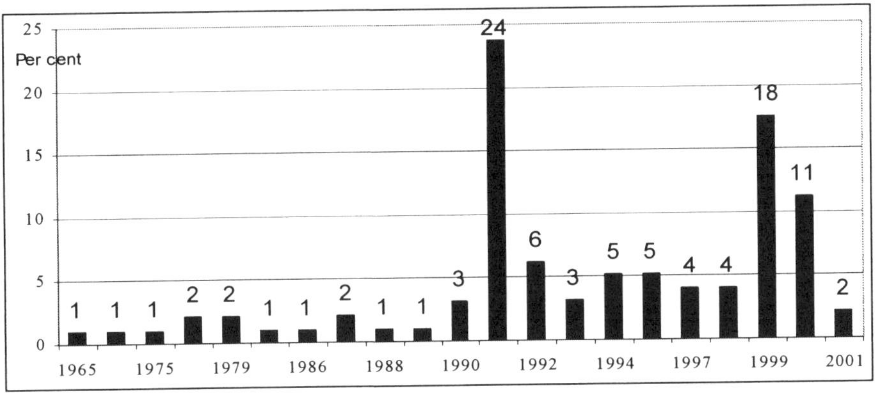

Figure 4.1 Number of foreign affiliates by year of establishment

Source: Survey 2001.

Note: N=156.

On the other hand, and as a response to transition and economic recession in general[5], a process of reorganizing the existing network of companies abroad has begun. Firms have had to scale down their foreign operations, close them or divest. Many large Slovenian investors also underwent a disintegration process or found themselves in crises that forced them to close their foreign operations down. Many of the small companies that emerged were unable to internationalize fast due to the lack of knowledge and capital. For a number of affiliations abroad, that had been established as a mostly system-escape operation, the reasons for their existence disappeared.

These tendencies that stimulated and de-stimulated the establishing of affiliations abroad had a common denominator. They characterize Slovenian outward FDI as a phenomenon induced by the transition process and disintegration from former Yugoslavia, while firm-specific reasons have only played a secondary role. Many representative offices established by Slovenian firms well before transition started were transformed into different kinds of affiliations. Wholesale operations by local companies were frequently substituted by own affiliates.

Uncertainties regarding formal recognition of the new state of Slovenia and how the rights and obligations, financial and other succession matters would be resolved posed a serious barrier to strengthening and upgrading the international economic expansion of Slovenian firms. Wars in Croatia, BiH and, finally, the Kosovo crisis also played a role in deterring Slovenian outward FDI from these countries.

Another factor with the same effect in Slovenia was the relatively negative political and public opinion of establishing companies abroad. It discouraged managers from embarking on developing long-term international investment plans. Outward FDI was frequently regarded as representative of the old nomenklatura while firms/managers' exports of capital were considered almost unpatriotic. In such a negative climate managers were unwilling to initiate or expand existing entities abroad. Their usual response was to 'wait and see'. The legislation itself prevented firms from investing abroad before their privatization had been completed, or at least before they had permission to invest abroad from the privatization agency.

By the end of 1992, when the Slovenian privatization law was adopted, privatization transactions were possible in accordance with the inherited Yugoslav privatization law, bringing about a lack of any control over the privatization process. There were cases of so-called 'wild privatization', which in most cases took the form of establishing 'by-pass' companies. In the case of by-pass companies, assets and goodwill (above all clients) of non-privatized companies were transferred to newly-established private by-pass companies (owned by individuals previously employed by the non-privatized company), while the non-privatized company was left with liabilities. Companies abroad offered obvious possibilities for by-pass operations. Suspicions grew that large amounts of money were transferred abroad and then used at home in the privatization process. The issue of outward FDI frequently became labelled as criminal, as the flight of capital. A public opinion poll in 1994 was more pragmatic, albeit quite undecided.

Table 4.1 How do you view the possibility of Slovenian companies investing abroad?

• Investments abroad should be unrestricted	19%
• Investments abroad should be controlled	30%
• Investments should be limited	15%
• Any outflow of capital should be stopped	19%
• Don't know	18%

Source: Svetličič, 1994; p. 1375.

The change in attitudes to outward FDI came about relatively soon, partly as a consequence of the country's economic recovery after 1993. With the improving situation in the economy, economic growth and a surplus in the current account of the balance of payments created a sterilization problem for the Central Bank. Outward FDI began to be considered as one way of reducing such pressures.

Mid-nineties consolidation stage

After 1994 the Slovenian economy grew and strengthened in the context of growing industrial production, gross fixed capital formation and lower inflation. The more accepting public opinion and government approach to outward FDI after 1993 and legislative changes also led to a rise in total outward FDI stock (see Table 4.2). The growth of Slovenian outward FDI stock from 1994 to 1997 was constant but gradual (see Figure 4.2). The increase in the value of total outward FDI stocks (consisting of equity and reinvested profits, plus net claims on foreign affiliates) was more a result of growing claims on companies abroad that easily exceeded liabilities to foreign investors than any changes in equity capital. The value of equity capital and reinvested earnings remained quite stable in this period, though their share in total stock value fell from 97 per cent in 1994 to 61 per cent in 1998. Annual FDI outflows in 1994 and 1995 were negative, indicating divestments still took place. The outward FDI stock amounted to 29 per cent of inward FDI stock in 1993 and the outward/inward FDI stock ratio was falling up until 1997 (Figure 4.3).

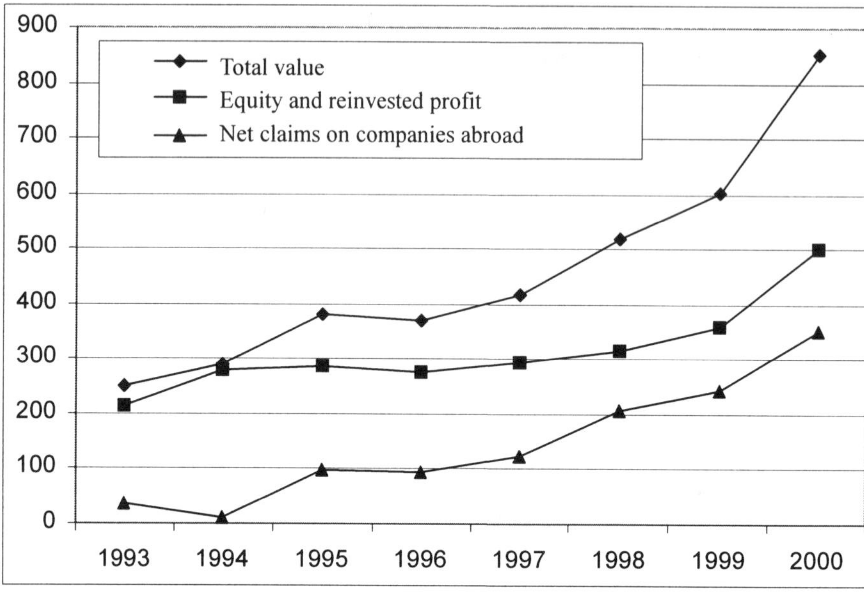

Figure 4.2 Trends in outward FDI stocks 1993-2000 (€ million)

Note: Total outward FDI stocks = equity and reinvested earnings plus net claims on companies abroad.

Source: The Bank of Slovenia's data.

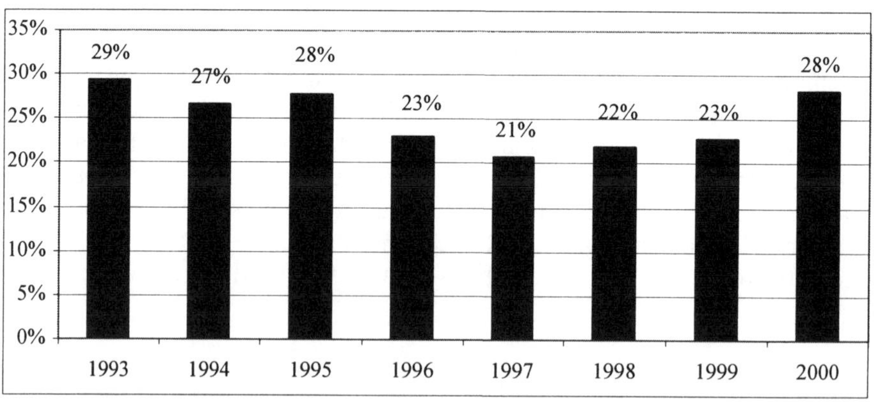

Figure 4.3 Outward/Inward FDI stock ratio (%)

Source: Calculations using the Bank of Slovenia's data.

The mid-nineties coincided with the most intense phase of the privatization process. The slow privatization process involving an undefined and diversified ownership structure of firms is probably the main reason preventing any more decisive steps towards internationalization. Managers' initial preoccupation with the privatization process also prevented any bolder steps in developing new outward FDI strategies.

Table 4.2 FDI[i] stocks and flows 1993-2000 (€ million)

	1993	1994	1995	1996	1997	1998	1999	2000	2001
INWARD FDI									
a. Year-end stock									
Total value	851	1.081	1.376	1.612	2.000	2.360	2.650	3.020	n.a.
Equity and reinvested profits	633	788	940	1.028	1.412	1.717	1.889	2.024	n.a.
Net liabilities to foreign investors	218	293	437	583	587	643	761	994	n.a.
Liabilities to foreign investors	310	388	544	724	757	738	872	1.126	n.a.
Claims on foreign investors	91	95	108	141	169	95	111	130	n.a.
b. Annual inflow	97	108	137	155	332	221	170	191	442
OUTWARD FDI									
a. Year-end stock									
Total value	251	289	382	371	416	519	603	854	n.a.
Equity and reinvested profit	216	279	286	277	294	314	359	501	n.a.
Net claims on companies abroad	35	10	97	94	122	206	244	353	n.a.
Claims on companies abroad	227	216	275	280	365	355	401	526	n.a.
Liabilities to companies abroad	192	207	178	186	243	149	157	174	n.a.
b. Annual outflow	0.9	-2.5	-3.9	4.8	31.9	-1.8	35.7	71.7	113.2
c. Growth rates year-end stock total in %	n.a.	15.1	32.5	-3.0	12.1	24.7	16.3	41.5	n.a.

Notes:

i FDI is defined as where an investor holds a 10% or higher share in a company. A negative outflow value means a divestment.

n.a. = not available.

Source: The Bank of Slovenia.

The level of outward FDI increased mostly due to the rise in investments made by firms that already had investments abroad. Key players in internationalization through outward FDI were usually the most successful companies which also had relatively rich export experience (or experience with other internationalization modes such as licences, franchising agreements, long-term contracts or inward processing). In Slovenia, outward FDI in the mid-nineties was thus far more the result of expanding the international network of the most successful and established multinational companies than of newly entering investing firms. In any case, investing abroad usually followed exports. In the 1994-1998 period, equity and reinvested earnings increased by € 35 million (12 per cent), while net claims on companies abroad in the same period increased by € 19 million. The 1994-1998 period was a consolidation phase since the aggregate number of investors and investments registered stabilized and did not fluctuate substantially. In the nineties, the share of companies with outward FDI in the total Slovenian corporate sector was modest, at about 1 per cent. The aggregate number of companies investing abroad was, according to the Bank of Slovenia, ranging from 420-440 in the mid-nineties. This is also confirmed by our surveys. According to Survey 1999, foreign affiliates' growth in the nineties was higher than the growth of companies investing abroad. A stronger increase in the number of foreign affiliates began at the end of the nineties.

Table 4.3 Number of investing companies (investors) and their foreign affiliates 1992-1998

	1992	1995	1998	Index 95-92	Index 98-95
No. of investors (current year)	25	29	32	116.0	110.3
No. of foreign affiliates	67	91	137	135.8	150.5
Average no. of foreign affiliates	2.1	2.8	4.3	133.3	153.6

Source: Survey 1999.

The enhanced growth in outward investing at the beginning of the nineties represented the first stronger internationalization wave; partly of those companies that were 'born multinationals overnight' in the territory of former Yugoslavia after Slovenia's independence and partly a reflection of the strengthened outward investment activity of companies that completely lost their former markets and had to enter new ones. As the growth of foreign affiliates shows (Table 4.3), companies that started directly investing abroad permanently expanded their international networks of foreign affiliates. On the other hand, new entrants to the outward FDI internationalization process emerged slowly.

The mid-nineties was therefore above all a phase of gradual growth and positioning of existing multinational companies. Consolidation of the foreign affiliate network took place especially in the developed neighbouring countries such as Italy, Austria and Germany as major export markets. The sales promotion activities of affiliates there became centralized. The deepening, and as regards Austria also widening, of the EU integration process, of the single market, caused a sort of 'investment diversion effect' since the European market can be efficiently served by a smaller number of foreign affiliates. The spread of foreign affiliate networks was oriented to Eastern and Southern European markets, where Slovenian firms were also more competitive.

A new wave of internationalization – end of the nineties

Many new FDI projects abroad were initiated by the end of the nineties (see Figures 4.1, 4.2, and Table 4.1), not only by existing multinational companies but also by newcomers. To a large extent, these activities were directed to the successor countries to former Yugoslavia. After a take-off in 1997, outflows increased again in 1999 and 2000. According to the register at the Ministry of Finance, an increase was expected especially in 2001, when it recorded a 1.6-fold increase in terms of the number of investments and a 2.1-fold rise in terms of the value of investments flows. In 2001, Slovenia registered a record FDI outflow of € 113.2 million, which was over 50 per cent of the average annual FDI inflow in the 1995-2000 period.

In 2000, the stock of Slovenian outward investment increased by € 251 million which was more the result of increased equity and reinvested earnings (an increase of € 142 million) and less due to increased net claims on companies abroad (an increase of € 108 million). Similar movements were seen in 1999. In fact, 1999 and 2000 were the first years since 1994 to see a considerable increase in equity and reinvested earnings. The second wave of internationalization also brought an increase in the number of foreign affiliates.

The substantial increase of outward FDI at the end of the nineties was thus partly a result of investments by newcomers, and partly of the growth of the existing multinational companies. Foreign affiliates generally increased in number and size terms. Survey 1999 demonstrated an expansion in the average affiliate number per investor from 2.8 to 4.3 in the 1995-1998 period (Table 4.3), while Survey 2001 shows an increase from 3.6 to 4.4 in the 1997-2000 period (Table 4.4). Slower growth of the average number of foreign affiliates per investor in Survey 2001 can be explained by the less intensive level of internationalization of companies that started investing abroad only at the end of the nineties. 'New entrants' that only began investing abroad mostly have just one or two foreign affiliates (the modus value was one), while the 'early transition multinational birds' are rapidly expanding their foreign affiliate networks, not just in terms of number, but also size. The most internationalized firms owned up to 24 foreign affiliates in 2000. On average, foreign affiliates grew by all business indicators (equity, assets, turnover, number of employees, exports)[6].

Table 4.4 Number of investing companies and their foreign affiliates 1997-2000

	1997	2000
No. of investors included in the survey	25	35
No. of foreign affiliates	84	154
Minimum no. of foreign affiliates	0	1
Maximum no. of foreign affiliates	20	24
Average foreign affiliate number	3.4	4.4

Source: Survey 2001.

Slovenian outward investments at the end of the past decade also grew when measured as a percentage of GDP. Outward FDI stock as a percentage of GDP doubled from 1993 to 2000 and reached 4.4 per cent (Table 4.5). The share of inward FDI in GDP also doubled in that period. In 2000 outward FDI represented 28 per cent of inward FDI (Figure 4.3). Still, these figures are very low compared to developed countries or the average of European Union countries where in 1999 the share of outward and inward FDI in GDP reached 29.6 and 22.2 per cent, respectively (UNCTAD, 2001; p. 325)[7]. On the other hand, some of its members, for example Portugal, had very similar ratios in the mid-nineties.

Table 4.5 Inward and outward FDI stock as a per cent of GDP, GDP growth rates and FDI inflows and outflows as a per cent of gross fixed capital formation

	1993	1994	1995	1996	1997	1998	1999	2000
Inward FDI as a % of GDP	7.5	9.2	9.4	10.6	12.1	14.1	13.3	15.5
Outward FDI as a % of GDP	2.2	2.5	2.6	2.4	2.5	3.1	3.0	4.4
Annual growth rates of GDP	2.8	5.5	4.1	3.5	4.6	3.8	5.2	4.8
FDI inflows as a % of gross fixed capital formation	4.7	4.4	4.4	4.4	7.5	3.5	3.4	3.6
FDI outflows as a % of gross fixed capital formation	0.04	-0.1	-0.1	0.2	0.7	-0.2	0.6	1.3

Source: The Bank of Slovenia.

Of all first-wave EU candidates (or EU countries in general), Slovenia is among the last in terms of inward FDI stock in absolute terms and in terms of share in GDP. The lagging behind other candidate-countries is slightly less pronounced in terms of FDI per capita. Nevertheless, it is among the first as regards outward FDI[8]. Although the short time series makes it difficult to undertake a reliable trend analysis, estimates show that Slovenia is moving from the second towards the third stage of the investment development path, yet the pattern is not exactly as predicted (Svetličič and Bellak, 2001). Slovenia is still a net FDI receiver, but the gap between inward and outward FDI stock is narrowing as Dunning predicts in the investment development path model. According to him, the national income level is the most important determinant of outward FDI, while for Ozawa it is changing competitive and comparative advantages that are at the forefront. Due to it having the highest per capita GDP, the development path model would predict that Slovenia should be the leading CEEC to invest abroad. The leading position in the share of outward FDI stock in GDP is also a result of the relatively longer tradition in investing abroad compared to other CEECs and more 'inherited' investments abroad[9].

By co-operating with foreign multinational corporations, firms enhance their capabilities and thus become able to invest abroad later. In some countries, foreign-owned firms are the major investors abroad. The influence of inward FDI on outward internationalization as predicted in the evolutionary models (the inward-outward linkages explained in Ozawa's dynamic paradigm and in the investment development path) is not so strong in Slovenia. On the contrary, major investors abroad are indigenous Slovenian firms, although inward FDI started to assist substantially in restructuring the corporate sector. The study of foreign-owned companies showed that inward FDI, i.e. foreign – owned companies increased allocation efficiency by concentrating in activities with above-average profitability, value added and capital intensity as well as improved technical efficiency by increasing productivity and competitiveness (Rojec, 1998 and Rojec, 2000a, 2000c). Nevertheless, the Slovenian industrial structure has not changed essentially.

This partly explains why foreign-owned companies that invest abroad – so-called indirect investors – have represented a small share of companies that invest abroad. In 1999 only 11 per cent of companies that invest abroad were foreign owned. The capabilities to undertake outward FDI are not only the result of inward FDI, but also of other forms of inward internationalization (such as inward-processing traffic, long-term co-production, licences, strategic alliances), which played a more important role in strengthening the ability of Slovenian firms to undertake investments abroad. They stimulate firms to follow their customers or competitors. The emergence of multinational companies in Slovenia is on the whole more a result of the liberalization, privatization and revived growth in the period of transition than any interaction with inward FDI. The transition triggered the process of changing the configuration of OLI advantages and stimulated outward FDI.

Outward FDI flows also gained compared to gross fixed capital formation[10] (Table 4.5) especially at the end of the nineties. From the negligible (0.04 per cent) share at the beginning of the 1990s, outward FDI amounted to 1.3 per cent of gross fixed capital formation in 2000, which is still negligible in comparison to developed countries[11] but close to the average of Central and Eastern Europe (1.7 per cent in 1999). Since gross fixed capital formation growth slowed down in 2000 and 2001, while FDI flows increased, further growth in that indicator is expected.

Our analysis also showed that outward FDI does not crowd out domestic investments (see Chapter 11). The correlation analysis[12] confirmed that outward FDI complements, rather than substitutes, home investments within firms. An outward FDI increase would therefore not reduce domestic investment, although according to financial doctrines the cost of capital increases along with the amount of capital borrowed. Consequently, home and outward foreign investments are regarded as substitutes. The decision to undertake outward FDI would, according to financial doctrines, reduce the possibilities to invest at home and vice versa (Blomström and Kokko, 1994; p. 346). But when becoming multinational, companies increase their access to capital, reduce their related costs due to improved ratings, create more funds within the company and gain opportunities for internal sourcing. Further, vertically integrated firms establish units abroad to be complementary to units at home.

Plans and further strategies

Today, increasing numbers of companies are becoming aware of international growth opportunities, particularly if they come from small countries. This is true for companies at all different levels of internationalization; those already investing abroad, those exporting and those yet to enter foreign markets. It is therefore not surprising that the surveys demonstrated the quite ambitious outward FDI plans of Slovenian companies. The 1999 survey of the largest exporters and fastest growing firms revealed that 53 per cent of them intended to upgrade internationalization and invest abroad in the next three years[13]. Only 12.5 per cent saw no need for affiliates abroad. Some of these plans came to fruition already in the 2000-2001 period when record outflows and many new outward FDIs were registered.

Also ambitious are the plans of existing Slovenian multinational companies. Most of those already investing abroad plan to expand their existing foreign affiliates or establish new ones. The closing of existing affiliates is rarely planned. In the 2001 survey eighty-seven per cent of sample companies provided information on future plans for outward foreign investments. Future ambitions of the sample companies differed, some companies might have several parallel plans for future outward FDI activity (expanding existing and establishing new units within the next two and the next five years), while others only plan to undertake one type of expansion (Table 4.6).

Table 4.6 Further plans for outward FDI (per cent of companies of the total that mentioned any of the selected plans)

	Expanding existing affiliates	Establishing new affiliates	Closing existing affiliates
Within the next 2 years	40.5	21.6	2.7
Within the next 5 years	27.0	32.4	5.4
Within the next 10 years	59	43.8	15.6

Source: Survey 2001 and Survey 2000.

After large FDI outflows in 2001, investment activity within the next two years will predominantly be realized through the expansion of existing affiliates (40 per cent). In the five-year investment plans of existing multinational companies, the establishing of new affiliates was prioritized over the expansion of existing affiliates. On average, the sample companies plan to establish 3.25 new foreign affiliates in the next five years (Survey 2001). The values of planned outward investments also tend to increase but vary according to the industry and period. In the short run, the investments planned vary from € 100,000 to € 5 million in manufacturing, and from € 50,000 to € 80 million in services, while in the medium term five-year plans they vary from € 50,000 to € 10 million in manufacturing, and from € 50,000 to € 150 million in services. In the long run - over the next ten years - the leading Slovenian investor had even more intensive investment plans. Strategies are expected to become more complex since many firms plan to simultaneously expand and close existing affiliates and to establish new ones. In spite of usually overly optimistic scenarios being included in future investment strategies in order to create a positive corporate image, we can nevertheless expect more and more companies to enter foreign markets directly as well as the further internationalization of existing companies. The international dimension of a company's operations and strategy is growing.

Summary

By intensifying the market economy the period of transition has accelerated the process of outward internationalization. The legal framework has liberalized and removed restrictions and introduced an institutional framework harmonized with OECD and EU standards. While transition triggered off outward FDI on the one hand, on the other it has hampered the speed of internationalization. Several transition-specific barriers stemming from unfinished economic transformation and a lack of relevant experience make internationalization through outward FDI a major challenge. In particular, because the success of transition also significantly depends on the success of internationalization.

Trends in Slovenian outward FDI going through three stages (see p. 46) also demonstrate the relevance of stage development or evolutionary models (Welch and Luostarinen, 1988; Vernon, 1966; Johanson and Wiedersheim-Paul, 1975; Johanson and Vahlne, 1977). Previous exporting experiences have proved to be very important. Those Slovenian firms that were once major exporters (or direct investors) in the socialist era were among the first to start internationalizing their activities after transition started. Firms firstly enter foreign markets through exports and then continue with outward FDI, initially mostly by establishing trading units abroad and later production ones.

Exceptions to this rule are clearly the new SMEs established after the transition which started their operations abroad in this new period. At first glance, some of these firms may appear to be 'born global' although their level of internationalization is still very limited (in terms of the geographical direction of their activities and level of related investments). However, managers of many of these newly established firms came from large (previously socialist) companies where they acquired basic knowledge of internationalization. After transition started, they created their own enterprises and later started their own operations abroad, largely based on the experiences and networks established when they worked in socially-owned enterprises. Companies may be 'born multinational' but that does not apply to their management. 'Natural born globals' are very rare. Most of the investing firms abroad are what we call "leapfrogging globals", i.e. they became global in a very short time and jumping over some stages predicted by evolutionary models.

The value of outward FDI stock increased 3.4 times from 1993 to 2000 and amounted to 4.4 per cent of GDP in 2000, putting Slovenia among the top transition economies. According to plans and further strategies, outward FDI is expected to increase in the near future. Clearly companies are aware of the need for further internationalization but they lack the capacity to realize such plans. The ambitious plans may suggest they underestimate the complexity of making a first entry through outward FDI, which has in practice proved to be more difficult than expected by managers. Foreign operations are particularly difficult tasks for the smaller companies that dominate the Slovenian corporate sector and which have only limited resources.

Notes

1 This chapter is based substantially on M. More, 1999.
2 Slovenia became the first transition country and non-OECD member to adhere to the OECD Declaration on MNEs on January 21, 2002.
3 In the Federal Republic of Yugoslavia it was impossible since such entities were in fact nationalized. Since the change of regime in Belgrade, a bilateral investment treaty has already been initialled (February 2002) and is expected to be signed in the next few months in order to stimulate investments by Slovenian companies in FRY which has been declared to be in the interests of both sides.
4 Trade with some other parts of former Yugoslavia became relatively insecure. Before the disintegration of the SFRY, the Serbian government bound its companies by law to cease business co-operation with Slovenian companies. Claims of Slovenian companies in Serbia were unpaid and premises confiscated. Managers became very innovative in searching for new forms of trade and payment arrangements based on international standards.
5 In early transition depression growth rates were negative and industrial output was falling. Growth resumed in 1994.
6 For more on foreign affiliates, see Chapter 9.
7 While in the developed economies the share of outward FDI in GDP is higher than the share of inward FDI in GDP, the opposite applies in transition economies.
8 The outward FDI stock per capita in 2000 was US$ 401 in Slovenia, US$ 199 in Hungary, US$ 173 in Estonia, US$ 163 in Czech Republic, while in Slovakia and Poland it was just US$ 59 and US$ 39, respectively (see Chapter 21).
9 The only comparable country in transition in this regard is the Czech Republic with its 'inherited' investment in Slovakia, although here a different – territory principle – for dividing up assets was applied (see Bohata, 2000; p. 19).
10 The average annual growth of gross fixed capital formation in the 1995-1999 period was 13.5 per cent (the record year was 1999 with 19 per cent growth and a 28 per cent share in GDP), considerably more than average annual growth of GDP (4.2 per cent).
11 The outward GDP flow as a per cent of gross fixed capital formation in 1998 amounted to 26 per cent for the European Union, 2.2 per cent for Hungary and 1.4 per cent for Czech Republic.
12 Performed on a sample of 416 companies investing abroad (Trtnik, 2000; p.62). The correlation coefficient was positive and statistically significant, but low (0.2).
13 A similar result came from a comparable study in 1995; more than 50 per cent of firms planned to invest abroad (see Krašovec, 1996). Obviously, actual realization of such plans in the mid-nineties lagged behind; there were less 'newcomers' among companies with direct investments abroad than expected. Companies were either too optimistic in their plans or were unable to bring such plans to fruition.

Chapter 5

Geographical and Industrial Distribution

Introduction

This chapter analyzes which countries in the past decade have attracted the most Slovenian investment, which industries were the most important investors abroad. It also analyzes changes in the dynamics of the geographical and sectoral distribution of outward FDI. Are outward investments concentrated or spread around the world, and how has the diversification of target markets changed? Are host markets for outward FDI the same as export markets? What is the proportion of Slovenian outward investment stock in high versus low- and middle-income countries? What are the most internationalized industries? Are manufacturing firms more important investors than services firms?

All of these questions are addressed to assess whether Slovenia is following the pattern predicted in evolutionary models. Companies display a basic tendency, particularly in the early stages of internationalization, to approach markets that are physically, historically and culturally closer, more familiar and not so demanding before they consider countries that are further away and with which they have fewer business and political ties. The gradual process also predicts the stepwise internationalization of activities from manufacturing (secondary) industry to the services (tertiary) sector (Luostarinen, 1994; p. 6)[1]. The significant diversification of host markets and the variety of industries involved in outward investing could, therefore, indicate the greater maturity of a country's internationalization process.

Geographical allocation

Defining internationalization as a process of increasing involvement in international operations requires seeing outward FDI as a step following exports, which largely influences the choice of a host location. In the most intense transition period (1989-1995), the trade and FDI patterns of CEE experienced significant changes. The most obvious trend was the strong expansion of trade with OECD countries, in particular with the EU, whereas CMEA intra-regional trade collapsed (Guerrieri, 1998). Trade liberalization and economic reforms have had an impact on the trade patterns and investment relations of the transition economies. The massive geographical reorientation of trade has also brought about the dispersion of trade and influenced the geographical spread of FDI. In Slovenia, unlike in other transition economies, the changes were less intensive. Foreign trade was to a large extent concentrated on the EU region even before transition started[2]. Transition further enhanced exports to industrial countries, largely due to the collapse of the Yugoslav market.

Outward FDI has not followed this intensification of trade with industrial countries. On the contrary, some outward FDI in industrial countries has been divested (see Chapter 4), while it has substantially increased in less developed countries, mostly CEECs, particularly in the successor states to the SFRY. In 2000, 80 per cent of Slovenian outward FDI stock, was located in lower-income countries. The geographical allocation of Slovenian outward FDI confirms the relevance of at least three theoretical concepts: Ozawa's dynamic paradigm of TNC-assisted development (Ozawa, 1997), the 'flying geese' model (Akamatsu, 1961; pp. 205-208 and Kojima, 1977; p. 150), and the sequential internationalization pattern, already supported by many small European countries[3].

According to *Ozawa's dynamic paradigm*, a greater volume of inward FDI and loss of export competitiveness at the start of transition should be followed by increased outward FDI flows to countries with lower labour costs. However, the early nineties lent only weak support for this pattern since FDI outflows were initially not predominantly directed to low-cost locations and not in manufacturing where low labour costs are crucial[4]. Affiliations abroad were established mostly as sales units in more developed countries, most often in Austria, Italy, Germany and Hungary[5].

Gradually, less developed countries have increased their weight by recently (re)establishing manufacturing and marketing units in successor states to the SFRY. However, the most important explanations include not merely labour-cost differences but, above all, previous business ties, together with knowledge of the market and language. In the late nineties, labour costs and production units abroad played increasingly important roles. Such investment patterns can be explained by both the Ozawa model and network theory (Johanson and Mattsson, 1986).

If the importance of subsidiaries' exports and operating costs were to rise, the geographical concentration of Slovenian outward FDI would reflect the relevance of the 'flying geese' model that has been used to describe the pattern of dynamic expansion of trade and FDI in the Asian region, especially in the East Asian rapid-growth years from about 1987-1996[6]. With higher growth rates, Slovenia might appear as leading the flight pattern, with traders and investors of the CEECs flying together in an inverted 'Y' towards economic development. Initial product exports by Slovenia (or other advanced countries) are becoming uncompetitive due to increasing wages and the eroding of comparative advantages. Therefore, relocating production to low-cost countries is one way of enhancing competitiveness and offering new export platforms. In spite of such advantages of relocating production to low-cost countries, this was not found to be a major motive for existing Slovenian outward FDI (see Chapter 8). In fact, the surveys revealed a much higher share of affiliates in trade than in production where lower wages were not the prime motive (see Chapter 9). In the future, it is expected the relevance of this model will grow.

The *sequential internationalization pattern* has a stronger explanatory power in describing Slovenia's outward FDI. The geographical concentration of export and outward FDI confirms that minimum physical and cultural distance, historical ties and past experience are the most important determinants of internationalization conducted by Slovenian firms. The concentration of value is even higher in outward FDI than in exports. The top three export markets accounted for 48.5 per cent of total exports (the top five for 63 per cent[7]), whereas the top three host countries received 62.2 per cent (the top five 69 per cent) of total outward FDI stock in 2000. While investing Slovenian companies mostly serve Western European countries through traditional exports supported sometimes by trade affiliations there, entering via direct investments is more significant for Southern and Eastern European markets (Figure 5.1 and Table 5.1).

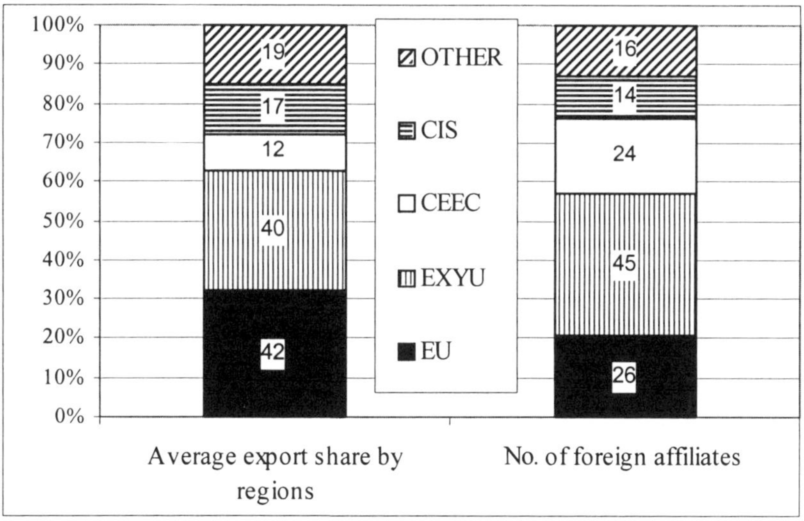

Figure 5.1 Exports versus foreign affiliates by region

Source: Survey 2001.

The strategy of location choice and decisions for first-market entry using outward investment correspond to the sequential internationalization pattern. The export and host FDI markets do overlap. For every sample company, the number of its export markets is bigger than the number of markets in which they have established foreign affiliates. Most commonly, the first (and second) foreign market entered via outward FDI was Croatia. More than half of the sample companies (56 per cent) established their first or second foreign affiliate in Croatia. Italy, Germany and Austria follow in terms of frequency as the first outward FDI entry destination. These countries have for years been the most important trading partners of Slovenia and therefore Slovenian companies have a relatively rich experience and knowledge of these markets. The next group of countries attracting Slovenian outward FDI includes Yugoslavia, BiH and Russia.

The sample companies did not enter more than one foreign market with outward FDI in a one-year period, nevertheless there were some cases where the sample companies did establish two or even three foreign affiliates in different markets within a single year. While bigger companies with some investing experience started to diversify their market portfolios, smaller investors' choice was based above all on their limited abilities to penetrate. Earlier investing abroad and greater geographical diversification increased the flexibility of firms and cut their dependence on business cycles[8].

In spite of high concentration, outward direct investments are also dispersed over a number of countries[9]. The network spread index[10] for Slovenia exceeds 22 per cent[11], which is an extremely high value compared to other developed countries. A similar network spread index value is held by the USA (21.8 per cent), while Japan has a lower one (18.4 per cent), although these two countries are the world's biggest foreign direct investors (UNCTAD, 1998; p. 324)[12]. The biggest and most successful Slovenian investors abroad do have subsidiaries around the world, they have really become multinational corporations[13]. According to our surveys, the average investing company has foreign affiliates in four different countries. A quarter of the sample companies has a foreign affiliate in only one country. One-eighth of them have affiliates in at least ten countries, meaning that only a few firms are truly global.

The high network spread index implies higher (transaction) costs of managing distant operations, but may also indicate risk dispersion and high levels of ownership advantages (and their transferability) including the knowledge of market conditions in many countries, or a combination of ownership and internalization advantages. Slovenia's high network spread index value is consistent with the expectation that companies from small, open economies should be more internationalized and have a broader foreign affiliate network spread. Increasing internationalization could be a substitute for the limited expansion potential, slower growth rates and opportunities to achieve efficiency in the home market alone.

Host countries for outward FDI

In the 1993-2000 period, the former Yugoslav markets received 50 per cent to 70 per cent of total outward FDI stock (see Figure 5.2, Table 5.1). A very similar picture of concentration emerges if we consider the number of Slovenian companies with outward investments (see Table 5.2), or the number of outward investments by country[14]. In 2000, former SFRY countries attracted 65 per cent in terms of value, or 910 out of a total of 1281 outward FDI cases.

The second most important country grouping involves other CEECs, which are increasingly attracting Slovenian investors, due to its market size, particularly Poland. Outward FDI amounted by 2000 to seven per cent of the aggregate stock[15]. Czech Republic and Hungary follow. The most important receiver in Eastern Europe is Russia, with two per cent of outward stock. In Southern Europe, Romania is the leading partner.

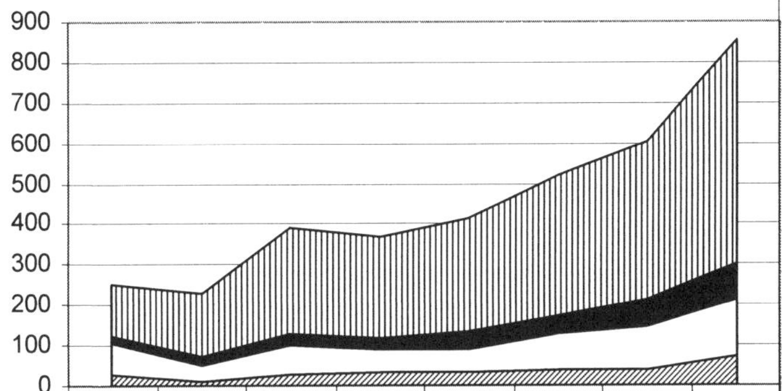

	1993	1994	1995	1996	1997	1998	1999	2000
Successors to the SFRY[i]	128	155	260	251	282	344	390	551
Other CEECs and CIS[ii]	18	24	33	31	44	45	67	89
EU and Switzerland	78	39	68	54	57	90	105	144
Other	25	10	30	35	33	40	41	70

Figure 5.2 Regional location of Slovenian outward FDI; end-year stock in € million

Source: The Bank of Slovenia.

Notes:

i Successors to the SFRY: Croatia, BiH, FYR Macedonia, FR of Yugoslavia.

ii CEECs and CIS: Albania, Bulgaria, Czech Republic, Estonia, Hungary, Latvia, Lithuania, Poland, Romania, Slovakia, Armenia, Azerbaijan, Belarus, Georgia, Kazakhstan, Kyrgyzstan, Moldova, Russia, Tajikistan, Turkmenistan, Ukraine, Uzbekistan.

These two groups of countries were gaining in importance in terms of the invested value and number of investing firms (Table 5.2) while EU countries were, to our initial surprise, losing their attractiveness in the mid-nineties. This reorientation to less developed markets suggests that the knowledge, experience and especially the firm- and ownership-specific advantages of Slovenian companies have generally been sufficient in less demanding markets, but less so in industrial countries compared to the strong firm-specific advantages possessed by large Western multinationals.

For those firms that only succeeded in the mid-nineties to substitute exports to ex-CMEA and ex-Yugoslav markets with EU markets, another barrier to outward FDI might be a lack of knowledge of Western European markets (see Chapter 10) and, consequently, excessive risk when directly investing there. The standardized products exported there do not call for a close proximity to customers as with high-tech products where the producer also has to provide related services. Although investing in the EU has been regarded as very effective *ex ante* adaptation to integration by becoming local producers, such oncoming integration may also de-stimulate investment in the EU. Trade liberalization and a single market make exports by would-be members an efficient enough entry mode. As a result, outward FDI seems to have become a less attractive entry mode for EU markets. Some former affiliates located in the EU have also lost their previous system-escape rationale after the change of system.

Despite the falling number of investors in the EU, outward FDI stock in the majority of EU countries increased in the 1996-2000 period. Germany, along with neighbouring Austria and Italy, dominate in terms of both the outward FDI location and as trading partners. All three countries are (besides France) also the most important inward investors to Slovenia[16]. The importance of Austria as a location for Slovenian outward FDI can be explained not only by traditional internationalization patterns (neighbouring country with strong historical ties), but also by the 'origin covering' or 'window dressing' reason[17]. In the mid-nineties this motive lost importance. Since 1996 the number of companies investing in Austria and Germany has been falling, yet the investment value in these two countries has grown since 1998. EU countries in general became more important again at the end of the nineties (their share in total outward FDI stock rose by six per cent from 1994 to 2000), and also as a planned host location in the near future.

Table 5.1 Slovenian outward FDI stock by countries 1996-2000 (€ million)[i]

	1996	1997	1998	1999	2000
Croatia[ii]	190.5	219.6	271.1	291.3	384.5
Germany	45.0	31.1	37.0	45.1	75.8
TFYR Macedonia[ii]	18.5	17.5	21.2	39.0	71.1
Bosnia and Herzegovina[ii]	14.0	17.8	21.5	31.8	66.5
Poland	16,9	29.4	33.3	48.0	59.9
Austria	-4.8	14.6	28.5	24.6	29.8
FR Yugoslavia[ii]	27.7	26.7	29.7	28.3	28.6
Liberia	22.3	26.0	15.5	22.6	25.5
USA	18.2	20.6	15.6	20.7	23.8
Russian Federation	8.8	8.4	7.5	8.3	17.0
United Kingdom	3.5	5.7	6.1	10.9	11.2
Czech Rep.	9.4	8.1	3.7	4.3	11.2
Switzerland	11.8	13.8	12.6	8.8	9.0
Denmark	-0.3	-1.0	3.1	4.8	8.9
Italy	6.6	-1.0	6.2	15.4	8.8
France	1.9	3.4	4.3	3.9	8.6
Ukraine	1.0	2.6	7.0	8.1	8.0
Romania	0.4	2.2	3.8	4.5	5.9
Slovakia	0.2	0.3	0.3	5.0	5.6
Hungary	3.4	4.1	3.5	4.4	4.8
Malaysia	0.5	1.4	1.4	2.0	2.4
Ecuador	0.5	0.6	1.7	1.2	1.6
Belarus	0.2	0.3	0.5	0.6	1.3
Sweden	1.1	1.0	1.1	0.9	1.3
Bulgaria	0.7	0.4	0.5	0.7	1.2
Spain	-0.1	0.4	0.3	0.3	1.1
TOTAL	370.6	416.2	519.0	603.3	853.6

Source: The Bank of Slovenia.

Notes:

i Only host countries that received above € 1 million are included in the table.

ii Data concerning real estate owned by Slovenian households abroad (mainly real estate in Croatia) are excluded. Subjects of negotiations on succession, expropriated assets in these territories, and other assets transferred to the Slovenian government during the process of privatization are also excluded.

Table 5.2 Number of Slovenian companies with outward FDI by countries 1996-2000

	1996	1997	1998	1999	2000
Croatia	293	319	336	332	346
Bosnia and Herzegovina	63	73	85	99	123
Yugoslavia	68	70	71	67	68
Germany	75	68	66	64	54
Macedonia	62	60	61	56	53
Austria	59	55	55	51	47
Italy	46	40	38	34	34
USA	21	20	22	26	28
Czech Rep.	26	26	27	25	26
Hungary	23	21	24	24	24
Russian Federation	18	20	22	24	24
Poland	10	13	14	14	18
Slovakia	6	6	7	9	9
United Kingdom	8	7	7	8	9
France	10	10	11	10	8
Ukraine	4	8	8	9	8
Switzerland	9	8	8	7	7
Netherlands	5	5	6	4	5
Canada	4	4	4	4	4
Cyprus	5	4	5	4	4
Other	37	31	39	45	53
TOTAL[i]	440	466	493	497	525

Source: The Bank of Slovenia.

Note:

i Since a single company may have investments in several countries, the data on the aggregate number does not coincide with the overall sum of data distribution by country.

According to the surveyed companies' plans for investing abroad, this geographical allocation of outward FDI will not change significantly in the near future. The sample companies (Survey 2001) pointed to the countries of Central, Eastern and Southern Europe as the most common locations for new foreign affiliates, followed by the CIS and the EU, which is obviously regaining its old position. Among planned locations, we can also find many distant countries (such as Japan, the USA, Brazil, Malaysia, Iraq, and Korea).

Table 5.3 Number of affiliates planned abroad by country groups

	EU	CEEC	CIS	Other	Total	Average
No. of affiliates planned	22	46	27	9	104	3.25

Source: Survey 2001 (2-year plans).

Ex-Yugoslav markets are expected to remain the most attractive host location for Slovenian outward FDI, especially BiH, where more than one-fifth of the interviewed companies intend to establish a foreign affiliate before 2003. With the start of the privatization process in the countries of former Yugoslavia, their firms are becoming more attractive to Slovenian investors as acquisition targets.

Host-country determinants

What are the factors affecting a locational decision? Market determinants play the main role, followed by cost determinants and, lastly, institutional factors. As stated by our sample companies with outward direct investment, recent foreign affiliates' locations were mostly chosen to serve the local market and not to provide a springboard to third markets (see Chapter 9). Through mere exports companies cannot keep, let alone increase, their foreign market shares.

Market determinants. In terms of the importance of individual factors underlying locational decisions, as the most important economic determinant of a host country the sample companies indicated its market potential; namely the size and growth of the market and purchasing power (see Figure 5.3).

Cost determinants. A country's proximity was the third most important determinant in a locational decision, showing that transport and communication costs between the parent company and the foreign affiliate are still important considerations. Low operating costs were also seen as an important variable for foreign affiliates' locations.

Institutional determinants. Relatively less significant than economic determinants but still important in a host-country decision were those factors involving the policy framework for FDI and business facilitation (an FDI-friendly environment) such as low country risk, the tax environment and FDI regulation, administrative procedures and incentives. This is in line with the general trend that a friendly FDI policy framework is a necessary but not a sufficient condition for attracting FDI. It is also becoming relatively less important alongside the liberalization and harmonization of policies around the world.

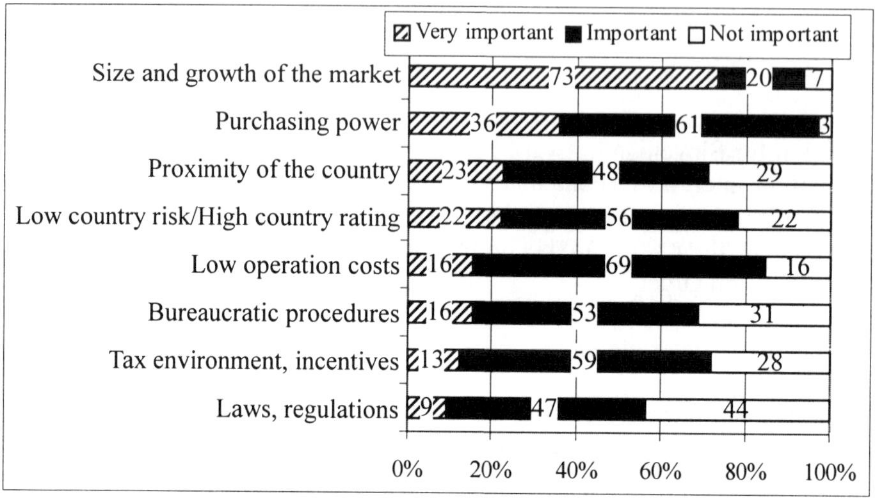

Figure 5.3 The importance of factors influencing an investment location decision

Source: Survey 1999.

The host countries where the lion's share of Slovenian outward investment is concentrated satisfy many of the stated determinants (big and growing markets with rising purchasing power, geographical proximity and low operating costs), except for country risks which are high. For firms with a good knowledge of these markets it is easier to tolerate higher risks due to expectations of high returns within a short time.

Industrial distribution[18]

According to the stock of outward FDI by activity, the same sectors retained importance throughout the whole of the nineties. Companies in the manufacturing sector accounted for about one-half of outward FDI stock at the end of 2000 (54.4 per cent, 12.7 per cent more than in 1994). This indicates the increasing necessity and ability of Slovenian manufacturing enterprises to internationalize.

Table 5.4 Slovenian outward FDI by activity[i]

code			1994	1995	1996	1997	1998	1999	2000
			As a % of total						
D	15	Mfr. of food products & beverages	13.9	9.7	7.3	7.0	14.4	11.0	8.0
D	16	Manufacture of tobacco products	2.8	2.2	2.4	2.2	0.3	2.5	-
D	18	Mfr. clothing apparel; dressing fur	1.0	0.8	1.5	1.5	1.2	1.6	1.2
D	19	Leather tanning; mfr. luggage etc.	8.8	4.0	3.3	2.4	1.8	1.5	1.3
D	20	Mfr. of wood & wood, cork etc. goods	3.9	7.0	3.8	2.8	2.2	1.9	1.1
D	22	Publishing, printing & record media	1.5	1.9	2.3	2.0	2.1	1.2	0.8
D	24	Mfr. chemicals & chemical products	15.2	11.8	11.4	12.6	12.8	20.8	15.4
D	28	Mfr. fabricated metal, excl. machines	2.8	2.1	2.5	2.2	1.8	1.5	5.9
D	29	Mfr. of machinery & equipment nec.	5.0	4.6	7.6	9.5	1.5	6.9	10.2
D	31	Mfr. of electrical machinery etc. nec.	0.0	0.8	0.3	0.7	1.7	1.6	2.3
D	33	Mfr. medical & precision instruments	2.2	2.0	1.5	1.6	1.9	1.8	1.4
D	34	Mfr. of motor vehicles, trailers etc.	-4.8	0.0	1.8	0.6	3.7	1.4	2.1
E	40	Electricity, gas, steam & hot water	0.0	10.8	12.0	10.8	8.3	7.5	5.3
F	45	Construction	2.8	2.9	2.4	1.9	3.8	1.1	2.0
G	50	Sale, repair etc. motors; fuel	-12.6	-5.5	-10.0	-9.5	-1.1	-2.7	-2.5
G	51	Wholesale, commission, excl. motors	20.2	13.0	11.2	10.5	7.2	3.7	3.3
G	52	Retail trade, excl. motors; repairs	3.6	1.9	-0.1	-2.9	1.2	1.9	7.8
I	61	Water transport	6.1	4.3	6.6	6.7	3.1	2.9	-
I	63	Support transport; travel agencies	2.0	1.2	1.6	1.7	1.2	1.9	2.4
J	65	Financial intermediation, excl. insur.	7.9	11.5	17.5	18.3	32.8	12.1	11.9
J	66	Insurance, pension excl. comp. soc. sec.	1.4	1.5	1.5	1.3	-18.4	1.0	3.1
K	74	Other business activities	5.4	4.1	4.6	6.1	10.7	10.6	5.1
		Total	100	100	100	100	100	100	100

Source: Bank of Slovenia.

Note:
i Based on stock data; activities attracting more than 1% of total outward FDI stock are included.

The manufacturing sector was the first to start internationalization and also has the highest export propensity[19]. Chemicals and chemical products, machinery and equipment, food products and beverages, fabricated metal are the most outward oriented (Table 5.4)[20]. These capital-intensive sectors started internationalization through traditional exports and contribute the biggest share of Slovenian exports even today. The industries that were the first to start internationalization using traditional exports were also the first to use advanced modes of doing business abroad. These industries are in addition more advanced in inward internationalization, especially as regards experiences with subcontracting, licensing, outward processing and inward FDI. In the nineties, the manufacturing sector was the foremost recipient of FDI in

Slovenia with 43.1 per cent of total FDI stock at the end of 2000[21]. This helped boost the capacity to undertake outward internationalization.

The internationalization of services is much less developed, mainly due to weak competitiveness and the lack of internationalization experiences, but has been rising since 1993. Service sector firms rarely engaged in investment abroad, except for some banks and trading companies (trade-promoting services), which followed the large manufacturing firms in their foreign operations (Stare, 2001). Exceptions to this include construction services that also have a rich experience dating to the pre-transition period. In the 1994-1999 period, the share of the service sector in total outward FDI stock fell from 43.5 per cent to 34 per cent. One explanation is the fact that privatization has not yet concluded in the service sector (banking, insurance).

Industrial allocation in the nineties reveals the strong concentration of outward FDI in a few activities (Table 5.4). Since these main activities are the most internationalized, they can be identified as the most competitive ones. Chemicals and chemical products, the most important outward FDI activity in manufacturing, represent 15 per cent of all outward FDI stock (see Box 5.1). The level of outward FDI from this activity has tripled since 1994.

Box 5.1 The pharmaceutical industry's export growth due to outward FDI internationalization

The pharmaceutical industry is known for its strong internationalization and concentration. Strong ownership-specific advantages (mostly in the form of intellectual property), motivate it to internalize activities while significant trade barriers stimulate a local presence. Slovenian pharmaceutical companies are important outward investors and are among the most internationalized (the industry as a whole realizes 74 per cent of operating revenues through sales made abroad, their intangible assets on average represent 37 per cent of total assets). The three most important players that determine the dynamics and development of the Slovenian pharmaceutical industry are Krka, Lek (see case studies) and Bayer Pharma Ljubljana. Krka was ranked 11th among the top 25 non-financial MNCs based in Central Europe[22]. On a global scale, Krka and Lek rank among the most dynamic mid-sized pharmaceutical companies. Although they are domestic market leaders in medicines (each holding about a 17 per cent market share, while Bayer Pharma held about 4.5 per cent in 2000) foreign competition in the domestic market is getting tougher. Despite high and constant growth in the pharmaceutical market, the share of domestic producers fell from about 53 per cent in 1994 to below 40 per cent in 2001. This drop in domestic sales was largely compensated for through sales abroad (see Figure 5.4). Specific features of the industry and many administrative barriers to trade are forcing firms to arrange a direct presence in foreign markets. The widespread network of foreign affiliates assists in export promotion, while production facilities have enabled them to acquire domestic producer status. In 1994, the key market for Slovenia's pharmaceutical industry was the domestic market (56 per cent of sales). Intensive internationalization during the nineties reversed this situation with foreign sales becoming 2.8-times more important than domestic sales.

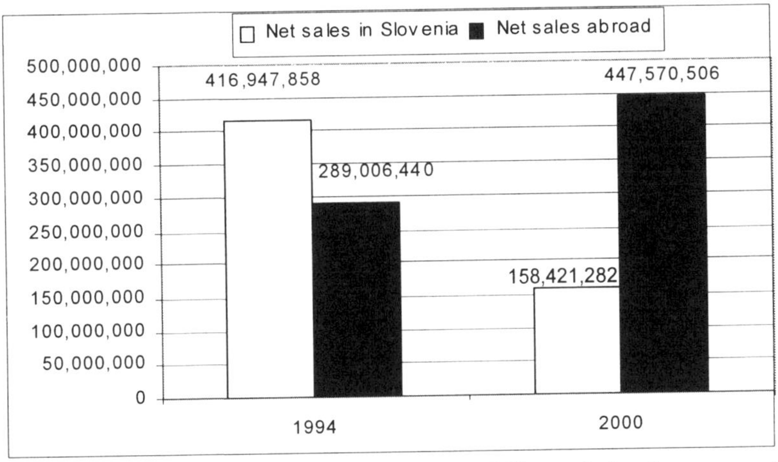

Figure 5.4 Changes in the sales structure of Slovenia's pharmaceutical industry from 1994 to 2000 (in €)

Source: Gospodarski Vestnik information database.

Manufacturers of food and beverages also emerged as important outward investors. The stock of outward FDI in this activity has more than doubled since 1994 to reach about 11 per cent of total stock. Firms in this industry expanded their operations especially in the territory of ex-Yugoslavia and this provides them access to low-priced resources (raw materials, agricultural products as well as cheaper labour). A further increase of foreign operations in the manufacturing of food and beverages is foreseen.

The manufacturing of machinery and equipment also almost doubled its outward FDI stock value in the 1994-2000 period. For an industry that is very sensitive to economies of scale, quality and cost competitiveness, relocation and efficiency-seeking investment is needed to further expand and sustain competitiveness.

A fall in relative and absolute terms (divestments) in outward FDI was experienced by wholesale trade during the nineties (in 1994-2000 the outward stock halved, while the share in the total shrank by 13 per cent). The domination of large trading chains makes the entry of Slovenian wholesale traders into international markets difficult.

Falls in the share in total outward FDI stock along with diminishing stock values were also recorded by leather and leather products, wood and wood products and publishing and printing sectors. This indicates that firms in such sectors are not thinking of relocating their activities to lower-cost countries despite their lower competitiveness.

Financial intermediation kept its share in total outward FDI stock. Conventionally, the most important investors within this group are the banks that support Slovenian exporters. As exports are primarily oriented to EU markets, the foreign affiliates of Slovenian banks are also concentrated in EU markets. Only recently have banks started to follow clients that also invest elsewhere abroad. Banking investments have in addition been accompanied by other financial intermediaries, especially investment funds that started investing in the former Yugoslav region parallel to the intensification of privatization in 1998 (see Chapter 6).

The end of the nineties also saw the growing role of other services, especially services relating to retail trade, insurance[23] and other business services. The extraordinary growth of retail trade in 2000 is above all a result of investments made by the Mercator Group that started a rapid expansion of mega market stores in the region of former Yugoslavia (see Chapter 19). Other business activities recorded the fastest growth since 1993. On one hand, this may indicate a trend of a gradual shift to higher value services (Stare, 2001). On the other hand, services companies have started to follow their customers in stepping up internationalization. Besides, companies classified within this activity are very prone to tax minimizing and transfer pricing. Manufacturing companies often establish a company in this activity by themselves to reduce taxes and duties.

In the future, service firms are expected to launch greater investments. According to Survey 2001, future investments in terms of the number of foreign affiliates will be similar in both services and manufacturing, while differences in value will remain. Since multinational services companies are a facilitator of trade and investment flows and often build up the necessary infrastructure, the enhanced internationalization of services could provide an incentive for the internationalization of other sectors. They have facilitated the faster dissemination of information which has in turn allowed firms to undertake direct investments abroad.

Summary

Despite high diversification in terms of number of host countries, in value terms outward FDI is concentrated in countries that are less developed than Slovenia. While Slovenian exports are concentrated in developed EU markets, outward investment is mostly located in low- and middle-income countries (mostly in former Yugoslavia and CEE). Developed markets are therefore mostly served by traditional exports, whereas a combination of market penetration methods is increasingly being used in less developed markets.

The industrial distribution of outward FDI is significantly determined by a handful of large investors (by Slovenian standards). Since manufacturing has always largely depended on exports, while services suppliers have concentrated on the domestic market with its high level of protection, the manufacturing sector is far more active in outward investment activity than the services sector. The most important services investors are financial intermediaries, retail trade and suppliers of other business services. Except for pharmaceutical firms, the most important manufacturing firms are those involved in intermediary products.

The last decade did not bring any significant changes in either the industrial nor geographical distribution of outward FDI. The leading and successful companies from manufacturing have broadened their international networks of foreign affiliates around the world, while less experienced companies have become regional multinationals.

The geographical and industrial distribution confirms the relevance of internationalization as a gradual learning process in terms of entry modes, market choice and the outward orientation of industries. Outward FDI follows exports, the most important trading partners are important host locations for outward investments, while those activities experiencing the most intense competition are among the first to invest abroad.

Notes

1 The holistic internationalization pattern predicts a sales product strategy pursuing the following steps: goods, services, systems, know-how (Luostarinen, 1994; p. 6).
2 Also see Chapter 2.
3 For example, small European countries, i.e. Finland (Luostarinen, 1979 and 1994), Sweden (Johanson and Wiedersheim-Paul, 1975), Portugal (Buckley and Castro, 1998 and 1999; Simoes, 2000).
4 Inherited investments were exceptions in this regard but did not originate from FDI outflows (see Chapter 4).
5 Some of them had a 'window dressing' purpose (see Chapter 4).

6 The 'flying geese' model can characterize the changing industrial structure within a given country, or the international shift of a given industry from advanced to less-advanced countries. An example of the former might be the changing competitiveness in a country over time from a labour-intensive industry, such as textiles, to a capital-intensive industry, such as chemicals. One example of the latter international sequence is the shifting of the textiles industry from Japan to the Asian newly-industrializing countries of Hong Kong, Singapore, South Korea, and Taiwan. The 'flying geese' then move on, relocating the textiles industry in Asean countries such as Indonesia, Malaysia, and Thailand; then on to China and, finally to India, Vietnam or other emerging lower-cost competitors. The flying geese model of a shifting comparative advantage reflects how factor endowments such as labour and capital change with economic development. FDI transfers factor endowments to host countries and necessitates industrial restructuring in the source countries, thus improving both the source's and the host's positions in the international division of labour.

7 Germany (27.1 per cent) is followed by Italy (13.6 per cent), Croatia (7.8 per cent), Austria (7.5 per cent) and France (7 per cent).

8 A good example of a well-diversified foreign affiliate network is Gorenje d.d. (see Chapter 13). Its rich market portfolio has helped it survive dramatic political and economic changes, the loss of markets and allowed stable operations.

9 Similarly, Slovenian exports are very dispersed (Trošt, 1993).

10 As a measure of transnationality, the network spread index of a country reflects the number of host countries in which foreign affiliates are established (N). The index is derived as a percentage of the number of foreign countries in which the companies could have potentially located affiliates (N = 178, on the basis of UNCTAD, 1998; p. 44). The network spread index is only a partial measure of internationalization, neglecting the magnitude of business activity in a host country and counting each host country only once, independent of the levels of assets, sales, production or employment located in it.

11 Only countries with a positive stock value are taken into account. If all countries are included, the index would exceed 28 per cent.

12 Figures for the highest number of host countries (according to 1996 Dunn & Bradstreet data) show: the Netherlands (40.3 per cent), Great Britain (38 per cent), Switzerland (38 per cent), Sweden (31 per cent), Germany (29 per cent), Norway (27 per cent), Australia (26 per cent), Republic of Korea (24 per cent), France (23 per cent), Italy (22 per cent), and Belgium (21 per cent).

13 Gorenje d.d., the largest Slovenian multinational company, for example, has foreign affiliations in 25 different countries (2000), while Lek d.d., one of the two largest pharmaceutical companies in Slovenia, has companies in 13 different countries and representative offices in 11 different countries (see the Case Studies).

14 The concentration in successor states to the SFRY is partly a reflection of inherited investments and partly the result of new FDI flows into this region (see Chapter 6).

15 The most representative investments in Poland are in the pharmaceutical industry. Well-known investors there are the biggest Slovenian pharmaceutical companies Krka and Lek (see Chapters 15 and 16).

16 Although a typical foreign investor in Slovenia is a small- to medium-sized company from one of the nearby EU countries, especially Austria, FDI in Slovenia is heavily concentrated in a relatively small number of the largest FDI projects, mostly involving European multinational enterprises (Rojec et al., 2001).

17 By investing in Austria, Slovenian firms tried to disguise the address of their headquarters

or the origin of goods to be exported to Serbia since it started to ban 'imports' from Slovenia even within the integrated Yugoslavia, and after the disintegration of Yugoslavia (see Chapter 4). Austria was always among the top countries as to profits realised by outward FDI. In 1998 it dropped to second place.

18 The Bank of Slovenia only records the activity of an investing company and not of foreign affiliates. The activity of an investing company may be a guideline for assessing a foreign affiliate's activity, although they may differ. A foreign affiliate breakdown will be examined on the basis of survey data in Chapter 9.

19 In manufacturing, 39.4 per cent of companies are exporters and 58.6 of sales revenues are realized by exports.

20 53, 41 and 57 per cent of the total number of companies within an industry are exporters. Their share of export revenues in total sales revenues in 2000 was 12.4, 12.5 and 14.4 per cent, respectively.

21 In manufacturing, FDI is heavily concentrated in paper and paper products, chemicals and chemical products, machinery and equipment, rubber and plastic products, and motor vehicles and trailers. Outside manufacturing, FDI is concentrated in trade, financial intermediation and other business services.

22 Ranked by foreign assets in 1998. In addition, it was nominated the most successful Slovenian company in 2000 by the Business Central Europe magazine.

23 The most important investor in this activity is Triglav d.d., the leading Slovenian insurance company.

Chapter 6

Investment in the Successors to the SFRY

Introduction

In spite of the wars and horrors witnessed after the disintegration of the SFRY, economic ties in the 'Balkan powder keg' were never completely broken off. By 1993 trade had only dropped to 14 per cent of the 1990 level, but since then it has been on a constant rise. In 2001, Slovenia realized 17 per cent of total exports in these markets. Political and diplomatic relations among successor countries are not yet at a satisfactory level and several safety, political and economic problems remain open. Still, business ties have been reinforced, especially at the end of the last decade.

Outward investments have seen impressive growth, particularly following stabilization at the end of the nineties. Sixty-five per cent of Slovenian outward investment stock in the successor states to the SFRY means such a dominant geographical concentration that it raises questions as to Slovenian companies' abilities to sustain such outward internationalization also elsewhere and whether this 'putting all eggs in one basket' strategy is too risky. The geographical concentration of Slovenian outward FDI is not only strong in terms of stocks, but also in terms of the number of investments and affiliates there (see Tables 5.1 and 5.2). Two-thirds of investing companies choose at least one successor state to the SFRY. Although several successful cases and rapid growth are evident, several questions remain. Are the frontiers of former Yugoslavia also the frontiers of the expansion of many Slovenian multinational companies, or are they on the path from a multi-domestic to a global strategy? Has the pattern of trade and organization of production from socialist times returned? Can regional multinationals grow into global multinationals? Can they remain sustainable regional leaders? Are the companies that invest there different to companies investing elsewhere?

This chapter discloses the reasons underlying the concentration of Slovenian investments, examines the dynamics and extent of outward investment in successors to the SFRY, plus particularities by countries and finally analyzes whether the companies investing in this region are in any way different to companies that invest elsewhere.

Why precisely successors to the SFRY?

Before independence, the SFRY market was the most important one for Slovenian companies. In the former common market, Slovenian companies' investments 'served for trade promotion and for a vertically organized production process with large intra-firm trade, as typical for vertical multinational companies' (Markusen, 1995). Slovenian firms mostly carried out lower stages of the production process in other republics, imported raw or intermediary products and remade them into final products before exporting or (re)selling them in other republics. Intra- and inter-firm trade was strongly interrupted by Slovenia gaining its independence. In the 1990-1993 period, Slovenian sales to the successor states of the SFRY fell from USD 6,662 million to USD 965 million (Damijan and Majcen, 2000). Exports were redirected to Western markets but the majority of Slovenian companies wanted to (re)establish and (re)gain market shares there. Liberalization of trade in this region only began in the second half of the nineties. Trade relations were also very unbalanced with a large trade surplus in Slovenia's favour with each former republic (see Mrak et al., 2001). Outward FDI is therefore an especially appropriate entry mode for gaining domestic producer status and easing pressures on reducing exports. FDI ties have reduced information gaps and economic distrust and have been an effective long-term way of linking countries economically, socially and politically.

Chapter 5 confirmed that the location pattern and geographical concentration of Slovenian outward FDI is in line with most common theoretical concepts of internationalization such as Uppsala School, the dynamic paradigm of TNC-assisted development (Ozawa, 1997), the 'flying geese' model (Akamatsu, 1961) and product life cycle (Vernon, 1966). While the former stress geographical, historical and cultural proximity and consequently accumulated knowledge in foreign markets, the latter focus on differences in the development level and possibilities for prolonging product life, increasing market shares but also increasing efficiency in the production process. The rapid expansion of Slovenian investments in the former SFRY was therefore no theoretical surprise.

Reasons for the rapid rise in the direct investment of Slovenian firms in successors to the SFRY can be classified into two push factors and one pull factor. The two push factors are the existing OLI advantages of Slovenian firms pushing on their internationalization, coupled by the limited opportunities to increase market shares in existing markets of industrialized countries. On the other hand, ongoing privatization and other developmental disadvantages of successor countries to the SFRY are pulling Slovenian firms to grasp the new opportunities emerging there that are also location-based due to having once lived together in the same country.

Ownership- or *firm-specific advantages of Slovenian firms* in these markets are particularly strong. According to interviews and surveys, Slovenian firms feel strong competitive advantages over local firms in several areas; technological know-how, organizational know-how and the strongest ones in marketing know-how (see Chapter 8). Slovenian companies are able to put them into effect in the states of the former SFRY better than anywhere else. Slovenian products are well known and generally have a very good image. Coming from the most developed republic of the former SFRY, Slovenian companies and their brand names are very well recognized and appreciated and do not need significant additional investments to achieve market recognition[1]. Buying Slovenian products also has the status of buying commodities with a reputation and legally, unlike products in the widely used black market in the FRY and BiH.

These markets are also relatively convenient because they have not been divided up by foreign competitors yet. Since many Slovenian firms possess rich experience and knowledge about the former SFRY markets, they want to ensure their market shares before their competitors enter. They seek to achieve a *first-mover advantage* already in the rebuilding phase of these countries, which has been treated as the best method for gaining a considerable market share in the long run. Early entrance through outward FDI is expected to be rewarded in these markets. Especially since Slovenian firms are not treated as 'ordinary' foreigners but, due to historical experience and their rich knowledge of culture, languages, customs and the business environment, as quasi locals. Due to historical ties, many Slovenian enterprises or their management also perceive successors to the SFRY as a quasi-domestic market. Slovenian managers also have very strong personal and business contacts that reduce risk and enable successful operations, even for smaller companies. This knowledge was and is the most important firm-specific advantage of Slovenian firms when entering successors to the SFRY. Foreign investors from the rest of Europe act in this area with caution, yet they have clearly noticed the breakthrough of Slovenian firms in the Balkans[2].

Increasing investments in the region are also the result of a 'gregarious instinct' among Slovenian firms, as companies tend to *follow the leading competitors* into other markets (Knickerbocker, 1973). Several firms speeded up investment activity in this region as a response to the 'fashion' set by the leading companies that first detected an opportunity. Domestic market leaders have rapidly adjusted their strategy and aimed to become regional market leaders. The most active sector in outward investments was the manufacturing sector. Services companies started to *follow their customers* later.

While previously firms entered individually, the tougher struggle for these markets led to co-operation and joint entering, or at least to a 'follow the leader' strategy. Some firms made a joint strategy of entering through outward

FDI after considerable difficulties in trade relations. This is particularly true in services. In a similar way to how Mercator has linked the food-processing industry and the retail trade together, the Ljubljana Stock Exchange and Kmeèka družba have encouraged some financial intermediaries, investment funds and brokers.

The revival of the former SFRY markets also took place as a consequence of the small domestic market with increasing competition and the slowdown in demand in Slovenian firms' prevailing export markets experienced in the nineties. In the EU market, Slovenian firms faced strong competition from other transition economies struggling for market shares. Besides, in successors to the SFRY the financial aspect of export sales has been much better since Slovenian firms are able to realize there much higher prices than in developed industrial markets (Damijan, 2001; pp. 108-109).

Most investment to the former SFRY has been market-seeking (see more in Chapter 8). The key motive has been keeping and/or enlarging market shares, albeit sometimes accompanied by other motives specific to a location such as resource-seeking in FYR Macedonia and in BiH; for example in the food and tobacco industries (like Droga d.d., Kolinska d.d., Tobaèna d.d., see case boxes in Chapter 8), and some strategic asset-seeking investments as in the case of Hermes Soft Lab in Bosnia and Herzegovina (see Box 8.2).

Internalization advantages were also very important in determining decisions on entry mode and the relation between outward FDI and export (as well as other entry modes). While direct investments in these countries involve additional risks compared to exports, internalization advantages seem quite high at the moment. The first incentive is to achieve better protection of intellectual property, which is still very poor there. Companies have an easier time controlling their intellectual property and defending their original products against imitations when they have a direct presence[3]. Poor legal protection also limits the use of several other entry modes such as licensing, franchising and contracts. Companies state that it has been very difficult to find a reliable and suitable business partner. The inadequately upheld rule of law makes any other form of business co-operation quite risky. Therefore, outward investing has often become the most appropriate penetration mode. The second incentive for internalization comes from the current condition of the markets. Local firms recently involved in the privatization process have generally been underpriced, which has stimulated their acquisition. Most frequently Slovenian firms are total or majority owners of foreign affiliates.

The strategy of entering markets emerging from the SFRY at the end of the nineties changed in comparison to the first half. The greenfield investment strategy that dominated in the early and mid-nineties was, after privatization started, combined with a M&A strategy. The increase in acquisitions after

1998 was also easier because some experiences were gained by M&A in the domestic market (see also the case study of Mercator). Privatization and the favourable prices of available companies stimulated leapfrogging in terms of the 'normal' gradualism of internationalization. Most frequently companies in successors to the SFRY follow a sort of combined strategy of greenfield investments and M&A.

Location advantages of successor SFRY states that are the most attractive to Slovenian firms were mostly market related. Since Slovenia is a very small market, the approximately ten times greater population of that territory already represents a locational advantage. Besides, these markets have lower competition and higher growth potential. According to Survey 1999, the growth and market potential outweighs any other location determinant (see Chapter 5). Also attractive is potential access to neighbouring markets or the markets of their most important trading partners, like the possibilities of using the Serbian market as a springboard to the vast Russian market (due to bilateral trade agreements) or the Romanian market.

What is similar is the potential effect of the expected trade liberalization of this area – planned integration of bilateral agreements of successors to the SFRY into a free-trade area – a Balkan Union – before 2003. Slovenia might enjoy such benefits only for a very short period, since EU membership would change its position. Another location-specific advantage of that region arises with stabilization of the region and the signing of special agreements with the EU, the so-called stabilizing association agreements (SAA). These agreements (planned to be signed by all countries by 2002) offer countries of the Balkan Union tariff-free exports to the EU. Gaining this asymmetrical status in trade could motivate FDI. Other southern successor countries which have not concluded SAAs, like Macedonia, have also gained investors' attention by offering production locations outside the EU but still geographically close (for example the tobacco company Tobačna d.d.). The next most significant location factors are physical vicinity, logistical advantages due to know-how and the variety of modes available (despite the obsolete infrastructure) and the similarity of legal systems (noting their common origin).

The most important *disadvantages* of successor countries to the SFRY are the high country risk of these countries due to: (i) ongoing political instability and institutional weakness; and (ii) the very slow process of economic recovery and transition towards a market economy, which has led to moderate purchasing power and insolvency. Institutions that regularly assess the country risk of individual countries rank the successors to the SFRY as either highly risky (BiH, FYR Macedonia, FRY) or as moderate risk countries (Croatia). Such ratings limit the countries' access to the international financial market and act as a barrier to attracting FDI (Mrak et al., 2001; pp. 132-133).

These disadvantages exist in each successor country, yet their relative importance differs from one country to another. In BiH, the FRY and Macedonia political and institutional weakness dominate, while in Croatia economic and financial risks are more important. Most successors to the SFRY are far from their pre-1990 economic performance levels, while their positions relative to other countries in CEE have also deteriorated. In 2000 the estimated level of GDP in Croatia, FYR Macedonia, BiH and FRY was 80 per cent, 77 per cent, 70 per cent and only 48 per cent of the 1989 levels, respectively (EBRD, 2001; p. 15). However, with greater political and economic stability and introduction of economic reforms, direct investors expect continuing high rates of economic growth.

Nevertheless, Slovenian investors were very active even though no investment protection agreements were in place before 1996 and diplomatic relations were not established (for example with Serbia). Analysis revealed that most Slovenian investments went into successor states before bilateral treaties to promote trade and investment were concluded (see the detailed data on bilateral investment treaties and double taxation treaties in Chapter 20). The institutional framework has only recently been taking shape more quickly, as a response to growing economic co-operation.

The extent and dynamics of investments in successor states to the SFRY

Historical ties have influenced geographical concentration more than cultural or geographical proximity. Today's concentration has been partly influenced by so-called *inherited investments* (Svetličič, 1994), i.e. investments that belonged to Slovenian companies after the disintegration of Yugoslavia (see Chapter 3), but also to a large extent by the increasing FDI outflows seen in the second half of the nineties. A substantial increase has been recorded since 1998. At the end of 2000, the total stock of Slovenian FDI in the former SFRY amounted to € 550 million, which represented 65 per cent of total Slovenian outward FDI stock (Table 6.1). The most important receiver was Croatia with € 384.5 million, followed by FRY Macedonia and BiH with € 71.1 million and € 66.5 million, and the FRY with € 28.6 million. The total sum of investment in the former SFRY realized by Slovenian firms is even higher, since some firms invest in the successor states also through their units located abroad (transactions of non-residents are not included)[4].

Since 1997 Slovenian FDI outflows to the former SFRY have continuously exceeded FDI inflows made by investors from these countries. The structure of outward FDI stock[5] shows that net claims on companies abroad are higher than equity capital. Claims on companies exceed the value of liabilities in each successor state. The growth of total outward FDI stock was more a result of growing net claims than of growing equity. The increase in equity capital was more significant only in 2000. The high share of net claims is a consequence of the fact that most foreign affiliates in these countries are trade oriented.

Table 6.1 Slovenian FDI stock in successors to the SFRY in 1994-2000 (end year, € million)

	1994	1995	1996	1997	1998	1999	2000
Slovenia's FDI in the SFRY's successors	205.1	249.5	250.8	281.6	343.5	390.4	550.7
Equity investment	154.4	159.6	150.3	155.7	184.1	208.9	290.1
Claims	62.0	96.6	105.2	136.6	165.8	186.0	273.7
Liabilities	11.3	6.6	4.7	10.8	6.3	4.5	13.1
FDI from SFRY's successors in Slovenia	338.1	325.8	292.0	276.7	94.1	86.9	61.8
Balance	133.0	76.3	41.2	-4.9	-249.4	-303.5	-488.9

Source: The Bank of Slovenia.

FDI outflows and entry to these markets have largely been dependent on the schedule of privatization. In Croatia, privatization has recently almost finished. A similar position is seen in Macedonia, while BiH, Serbia, and Montenegro have only started their privatization processes. A strong increase was noted in 1998 when privatization started in Bosnia and Herzegovina. Slovenian privatization funds were some of the most successful groups to collect vouchers.

Table 6.2 Outward FDI stock in successors to the SFRY as a share of the total

	1994	1995	1996	1997	1998	1999	2000
Croatia	54.5	46.6	51.4	52.8	52.2	48.3	45.1
FYR Macedonia	4.5	4.3	5.0	4.2	4.1	6.5	8.3
Bosnia and Herzegovina	4.2	3.3	3.8	4.3	4.1	5.3	7,8
FR Yugoslavia	7.9	11.0	7.5	6.4	5.7	4.7	3.4

Source: Bank of Slovenia.

Slovenian companies are important investors in the successor states, but their significance varies from country to country. While the most important receiver is Croatia with 45 per cent of total outward investment stock, Slovenia is ranked only in tenth spot among the top inward investors[6]. The low share of

Slovenian firms in total inward FDI stock is a consequence of non-participation in telecommunications and banking, where Croatia has attracted its largest FDI inflows. One explanation is that the privatization of the main Slovenian banks has not yet concluded and the unresolved problem of deposits of Ljubljanska banka d.d. gained in the former SFRY.

The industrial structure of investors is similar for the whole region of former Yugoslavia. Five industries provided almost half of Slovenian outward FDI stock in Croatia; chemicals and chemical products, food and beverages processing industry, electricity, gas and hot water, other business activities and retail trade (except for investors from electricity, gas and water, investments from these sectors rose strongly between 1994 and 2000). The industrial distribution is largely influenced by particular individual investors (see Table 6.3).

Table 6.3 Top Slovenian investors in successors to the SFRY

Croatia	FYR Macedonia	BiH	FRY
Perutnina Ptuj	Era	Prevent	Mercator
Prevent	Tobačna	Mercator	Planika
Mercator	Lek	Terme Čatež	Gorenje
Pivovarna Laško	Fructal	Zavarovalnica Triglav	Planika, Mura, Polzela, Lisca, Labod
		Droga	(Centrotekstil)
		NLB	
		Intereuropa	

Source: Chamber of Commerce and Industry.

Croatia is the most frequently selected country for the first and second foreign affiliate. As much as 37.5 per cent of sample companies in Survey 1999 cited Croatia as the first foreign market entered by outward FDI. More than half of the sample companies established their first or second foreign affiliate (or both) in Croatia. Croatia has also proven to be the most profitable market for outward FDI.

Slovenian companies hold the greatest relative importance in BiH, where they are the number one investor (with a 20-30 per cent share in total Bosnian inward FDI stock). The most significant are investments by companies from the retail trade, food and beverages processing industries, manufacturing of machinery and equipment, wholesale trade and financial intermediaries. Slovenia's share in total Macedonian inward FDI stock exceeds seven per cent. Financial intermediaries, chemicals and chemical products, and the tobacco industry are the most important investors in this country. The position of Slovenian investors in the FRY has also become increasingly important. Recently, they became the second biggest foreign investor. The largest amounts have been invested by firms from trade, food processing, wood manufacturing, and insurance.

Do the companies that invest in the successor countries differ from other investors?

The strong concentration of Slovenian outward investment in successors to the SFRY creates fears that such an orientation to less demanding markets might lead to the deterioration and de-stimulation of ambitions to move towards more demanding markets. Yet, such fears appear to be unwarranted.

First, because in general Slovenian firms' prevailing foreign entry method is through exports which are concentrated in more developed and demanding EU markets. Investing abroad is still much less important. Secondly, exports and outward investing are complementary (see Chapters 7 and 11). Companies employ them simultaneously in order to optimize their market position and results. After all, further technological development and growth of a company is only possible on the basis of keeping market shares and improving results. Thirdly, the concentration of Slovenian outward investments is no surprise according to prevailing theoretical internationalization models or the praxis of many small countries (see Chapter 5). It reflects a stage of development and the composition of competitive advantages, which are not different for other investors in successors to the SFRY or those investing in other countries.

To identify any differences in investing in this region compared to other areas, the authors divided companies up into three categories: i) those investing exclusively in the states of former Yugoslavia; ii) those that also undertake outward FDI in other states; and iii) those that make outward FDI exclusively in other markets and do not invest in the region of former Yugoslavia at all. The structure of investors from the 2001 sample by selected groups shows that the share of investors exclusively investing in the states of former Yugoslavia is the smallest (28 per cent of sample companies), the largest share (37 per cent) belongs to those investing in the states of former Yugoslavia and elsewhere, while those investing exclusively elsewhere represent 35 per cent. This reveals that investors are not only focused on the region of former Yugoslavia but have a relatively dispersed location choice. The large share of investors with affiliations within and beyond the states of former Yugoslavia suggests the diversification, strategy and long-term orientation of their outward investments (sequential broadening). The surveys and interviews revealed that former Yugoslav markets were often used as an outward investment starting point and/or a springboard to other markets.

With regard to the abovementioned investment location groups, we studied the motivation, competitive advantages, barriers and effects of outward investment (see Tables 6.4 and 6.5). Since these characteristics are discussed in detail in part three, we focus here on differences by location group only. Surprisingly, the analysis found no large significant differences among the abovementioned groups. Irrespective of where an investment is intended, the motives for investment are substantially alike.

Competitive advantages are also very similar regardless of the investment location. Companies not investing in the region (but exclusively elsewhere), however, ranked competitive advantage in technological, marketing and organizational know-how higher, the largest differences being in technological knowledge. Smaller differences were also found in R&D expenditures and in the share of university-educated employees. Although not significantly, the share of R&D expenditures of companies investing exclusively in the former SFRY was lower than the two other groups (but especially compared to companies investing in the former SFRY and elsewhere). Penetrating the former Yugoslav market might be possible with relatively weaker comparative advantages. However, companies that invest only in the area of the former SFRY on average doubled their investment in R&D between 1997 and 2000, which means significant progress. Curiously, the share of employees with a university education was highest for companies investing only in the successors to the SFRY, suggesting a relatively high-skilled labour intensity.

Few significant differences were discovered solely among barriers to outward investing. The host-country environment is namely a much larger barrier to investors involved exclusively in the former SFRY (this barrier differs significantly, especially between those investing only in the former SFRY and those also investing elsewhere). The situation is similar in the case of financing problems (but not significantly different). Significant differences were also seen in the evaluation of home-country circumstances. Interestingly, these were ranked as the least problematic by those investors investing in both the former SFRY and elsewhere (i.e. investors with the most diverse network of affiliations abroad, which have substantially more experience as well as possibilities of avoiding the negative effects of a particular environment precisely because of their dispersed network). Also in line with expectations is the personnel and knowledge problem; for those investing only in the former SFRY the lack of human resources (knowledge) is a relatively less important barrier than for others (non-significantly).

Table 6.4 Motives and competitive advantages of investors by the location of investment[i]

		N	Mean	St. Dev.	St. Err.	Min.	Max
MOTIVATION							
Market-related	Exclusively succ. SFRY[ii]	12	4.6	0.8	0.2	3	5
	SFRY + elsewhere[iii]	14	4.6	0.6	0.2	3	5
	Exclus. elsewhere[iv]	12	4.6	0.9	0.3	2	5
	Total[v]	38	4.6	0.8	0.1	2	5
Labour costs	Exclusively succ. SFRY	12	3.0	1.0	0.3	1	4
	SFRY + elsewhere	14	2.5	1.2	0.3	1	5
	Exclus. elsewhere	11	3.1	1.3	0.4	1	5
	Total	37	2.8	1.2	0.2	1	5
Other cost-related motives	Exclusively succ. SFRY	12	3.1	1.2	0.3	1	5
	SFRY + elsewhere	14	2.8	1.3	0.3	1	5
	Exclus. elsewhere	11	3.7	0.6	0.2	3	5
	Total	37	3.2	1.1	0.2	1	5
Acquisition of strategic assets	Exclusively succ. SFRY	12	3.6	0.9	0.3	2	5
	SFRY + elsewhere	14	3.0	1.4	0.4	1	5
	Exclus. elsewhere	11	3.0	0.4	0.1	2	4
	Total	37	3.2	1.0	0.2	1	5
COMPETITIVE ADVANTAGES							
Technological know-how	Exclusively succ. SFRY	11	3.7	1.2	0.4	1	5
	SFRY + elsewhere	13	3.8	0.8	0.2	3	5
	Exclus. elsewhere	8	4.4	0.5	0.2	4	5
	Total	32	3.9	0.9	0.2	1	5
Organizational know-how	Exclusively succ. SFRY	11	4.0	1.2	0.4	1	5
	SFRY + elsewhere	13	3.6	1.0	0.3	2	5
	Exclus. elsewhere	8	4.1	1.0	0.4	3	5
	Total	32	3.9	1.0	0.2	1	5
Marketing knowledge	Exclusively succ. SFRY	11	4.3	0.8	0.2	3	5
	SFRY + elsewhere	13	4.0	1.2	0.3	1	5
	Exclus. elsewhere	9	4.3	0.7	0.2	3	5
	Total	33	4.2	1.0	0.2	1	5
R&D expenditure 1997	Exclusively succ. SFRY	5	1.7	2.4	1.1	0.5	6
	SFRY + elsewhere	8	4.7	4.7	1.7	0.8	13.4
	Exclus. elsewhere	10	3.6	3.1	1.0	0	10
	Total	23	3.6	3.7	0.8	0	13.4
R&D expenditure 2000	Exclusively succ. SFRY	6	2.1	2.5	1.0	0.4	7
	SFRY + elsewhere	10	4.6	4.6	1.5	0.5	13.9
	Exclus. elsewhere	10	4.6	3.4	1.1	0	10
	Total	26	4.0	3.8	0.7	0	13.9
% of university-educated employees	Exclusively succ. SFRY	10	17.0	20.1	6.4	0	51.5
	SFRY + elsewhere	11	13.5	14.5	4.4	1.6	51
	Exclus. elsewhere	11	13.1	10.0	3.0	1	36
	Total	32	14.4	14.9	2.6	0	51.5

Source: Survey 2001.

Notes:

i 1 - not important, 5 - very important. The Post Hoc Test, Bonferroni method was used for the comparison of means. No statistically significant differences were found.

ii Exclusively succ. SFRY: investors investing exclusively in the markets of successors to the SFRY.

iii SFRY+ elsewhere: investors directly investing in the markets of successors to the SFRY and elsewhere.

iv Exclus. elsewhere: investors that do not directly invest in the states of former Yugoslavia, but exclusively elsewhere.

v Total: all investors regardless of the investment location.

Table 6.5 Barriers and effects of outward FDI by the location of investments

		N	Mean	St. Dev.	St. Err.	Min.	Max.
BARRIERS to outward FDI							
Lack of financial resources	Exclusively FYM	11	3.4	1.5	0.5	1	5
	FYM + elsewhere	14	2.8	1.3	0.4	1	5
	Exclus. elsewhere	12	3.0	1.0	0.3	1	5
	Total	37	3.0	1.3	0.2	1	5
Lack of personnel (knowledge)	Exclusively FYM	11	3.2	1.3	0.4	1	5
	FYM + elsewhere	14	3.5	1.0	0.3	2	5
	Exclus. elsewhere	12	3.9	0.9	0.3	2	5
	Total	37	3.5	1.1	0.2	1	5
Lack of information	Exclusively FYM	11	2.9	0.9	0.3	1	4
	FYM + elsewhere	14	3.1	1.1	0.3	1	5
	Exclus. elsewhere	12	3.2	0.9	0.3	2	5
	Total	37	3.1	1.0	0.2	1	5
Host-country specific factors	*Exclusively FYM*	*11*	*4.3*	*0.9*	*0.3*	*3*	*5*
	FYM + elsewhere	*14*	*3.1*	*1.2*	*0.3*	*1*	*5*
	Exclus. elsewhere	*11*	*4.0*	*1.1*	*0.3*	*2*	*5*
	Total	*36*	*3.8*	*1.2*	*0.2*	*1*	*5*
Home-country specific factors	*Exclusively FYM*	*11*	*3.2*	*0.9*	*0.3*	*2*	*4*
	FYM + elsewhere	*14*	*2.2*	*0.6*	*0.2*	*1*	*3*
	Exclus. elsewhere	*12*	*3.2*	*0.9*	*0.3*	*2*	*5*
	Total	*37*	*2.8*	*0.9*	*0.1*	*1*	*5*
EFFECTS							
Additional market shares abroad	Exclusively FYM	11	3.9	0.8	0.3	3	5
	FYM + elsewhere	14	4.1	0.7	0.2	3	5
	Exclus. elsewhere	9	4.2	0.4	0.1	4	5
	Total	34	4.1	0.7	0.1	3	5
Employment of parent company	Exclusively FYM	11	2.8	0.9	0.3	1	4
	FYM + elsewhere	14	3.3	0.6	0.2	2	4
	Exclus. elsewhere	9	2.8	0.8	0.3	1	4
	Total	34	3.0	0.8	0.1	1	4
Exports of parent company	*Exclusively FYM*	*11*	*3.5*	*0.5*	*0.2*	*3*	*4*
	FYM + elsewhere	*14*	*4.1*	*0.3*	*0.1*	*4*	*5*
	Exclus. elsewhere	*8*	*4.1*	*0.6*	*0.2*	*3*	*5*
	Total	33	3.9	0.5	0.1	3	5
Imports of parent company	Exclusively FYM	11	2.8	1.0	0.3	1	4
	FYM + elsewhere	14	3.1	0.9	0.2	1	4
	Exclus. elsewhere	8	3.0	0.9	0.3	1	4
	Total	33	3.0	0.9	0.2	1	4
Production volume of parent	Exclusively FYM	11	3.6	0.5	0.2	3	4
	FYM + elsewhere	13	4.0	0.4	0.1	3	5
	Exclus. elsewhere	9	4.0	0.7	0.2	3	5
	Total	33	3.9	0.5	0.1	3	5

Source: Survey 2001.

Legend: see Table 6.4. Statistically significant differences among groups of investors are in italics. (Bonferroni's Post Hoc Test was used to evaluate differences between groups.)

The effects of outward investments do not differ due to the different locations of outward FDI. The most visible differences are growth in market shares, growth in exports, and production volumes. The establishment of an affiliation exclusively in the area of former Yugoslavia stimulates exports significantly less (according to the post-hoc test, Bonferroni method), which could reflect the lower purchasing power of these markets. It might also suggest that exporting to affiliations (intra-firm trade) might be supplemented by local production.

Summary

Slovenian outward FDI experienced an increase and diversification in the nineties, but remained strongly concentrated in the successor states to the SFRY not only due to inherited investments but also to new FDI outflows. The former Yugoslav states offer a special challenge for the greater outward orientation of Slovenian firms and an opportunity to gradually learn about outward internationalization. As the theory suggests, outward FDI is a preferential entry mode in closer and more familiar markets, but also in the case of market failures (Moon, 1997). The markets of the former Yugoslav states – currently experiencing a slow transition – have more market failures[7] than developed market economies[8]. Investing is a strategic response.

Although history explains a lot, today's geographical concentration of Slovenian outward FDI cannot be regarded as a return to the past. Many firms investing exclusively in the former SFRY subsequently expand their activities to at least the region of CEE. Investing in the former SFRY therefore often reflects a strategy of becoming a regional leader or the first step towards broader internationalization. Therefore, it can be seen as a long-term reaction to the changing business environment and not only as an instrument of regaining what was formerly the one domestic market. If the only competitive advantages were know-how to do business and marketing knowledge, these advantages would evaporate as soon as the first-mover advantage disappears. Both the marketing competitive advantage and first-mover advantage are unsustainable if not upgraded in other fields. For regional multinationals remaining a sustainable regional leader or growing into global multinationals, owner-specific advantages should be upheld before the foreign competition enters. Above-average R&D expenditures promise that the so far prevailing location-driven advantages will gradually be replaced by ownership-advantage-driven internationalization. Internationalization is strengthening firm-specific advantages which can in the future gradually enable the more aggressive internationalization to encompass other markets.

Direct investment in most cases seems sustainable and is not a whim provided that the resulting profit is used creatively to strengthen one's own capabilities, and not only to defend achieved market positions. Increasing

R&D expenditures, more highly educated staff, a strong export orientation, the beneficial effects of outward FDI on strengthening investors' competitiveness, as well as the growing share of intra-firm trade are all signs that outward FDI in former Yugoslavia is forming part of a long-term internationalization strategy and is not a defensive response (Jaklič A. et al., 2002).

Notes

1 A recent study by the Partner Marketing Agency in Serbia demonstrated that Gorenje, for example, performs better than many globally famous trademarks (e.g. Marlboro, Milka, Panasonic or Levi's) in the category of spontaneous associations made by Serbian consumers. Gorenje was among the trademarks that consumers were confronted with daily in third position, immediately after Coca-Cola and Orbit (Bojčić, 2001). Fructal and Iskra were not far behind.

2 See Financial Times, 9 July 2001.

3 Local firms are very flexible and rapid imitators. Several Slovenian products have found their imitated products there. One of the most famous cases was poultry salami with the brand name Poli, produced by Perutnina Ptuj, d.d. The local fake product was named Doli and completely imitated the Slovenian (the same packaging, promotion tools, distribution channels) and caused a substantial loss in sales for the Slovenian producer.

4 Such is the example of the investment of LBH Bank in Tutonska Bank in FYR Macedonia.

5 Total outward FDI stock is composed of equity capital and net claims on companies abroad.

6 Among successor countries, Croatia has attracted the largest inflow of FDI and is becoming a regional headquarters for the Balkan region. Investments there are hence important not only because of the Croatian market, but for the whole Balkan region. As trade barriers in the region are eased and regional linkages grow, the significance of the frontiers of particular national markets falls away.

7 I.e. information asymmetry, governmental intervention, consumers and producers who do not behave competitively etc.

8 The same applies to several other developing countries' markets in which Slovenian firms are competitive.

Chapter 7

The Importance of Investing Companies

Introduction

The role of multinational companies is increasing across the world, not only in terms of international economic relations (since multinational sales exceed exports), but also as regards domestic employment, production, sales, value added and profit. Small economies are even more dependent on highly internationalized companies. Exporting alone does not ensure access to foreign markets and global sales of goods and services. Gaining and/or increasing foreign market shares often calls for a direct presence. Direct investment and exports are frequently complementary modes of international operation and firms must harness both to optimize their competitive positions. Outward FDI is an investment in growth and possibilities of enterprises serving the world market. Countries excluded from the integrated international production system are deprived of growth and development possibilities in the long run (Lall, 1996, 2000).

Compared to developed economies, Slovenia's 4.4 per cent share of outward FDI in GDP or 1.3 per cent FDI outflows in gross fixed capital formation does appear relatively low. But the facts that exports constitute about sixty percent of Slovenian GDP and that Slovenian companies investing abroad represent almost forty percent of total corporate sector exports show that outward FDI plays a much more important role in the national economy.

In order to assess development potential, this chapter examines how important Slovenian companies involved in outward FDI are for the Slovenian economy, what is their contribution to exports, employment and value added, how they perform, how investing companies compare to non-investing companies and the average Slovenian company, and what are the types of and differences among investing companies themselves[1]. Outward FDI is not only important for growth at the firm level (analyzed in greater detail in Chapter 11), but also at the country level.

The importance of investing companies for the entire corporate sector

Although in numerical terms companies investing abroad in the 1994-1999 period represented a very modest share in the entire corporate sector – slightly above 1 percent – and this proportion was very constant, they still have a substantial influence on the total corporate sector (Tables 7.1 and 7.2).

Table 7.1 Selected income statements/balance sheet items of companies with outward FDI[i] in the 1994-1999 period (values in SIT billion, except for no. of employees)

	1994	1995	1996	1997	1998	1999
Equity	1,151.3	1,298.2	1,386.7	1,505.5	1,607.9	1,860.4
Assets	1,811.5	2,062.4	2,253.2	2,466.7	2,605.4	2,646.4
No. of employees	138,915	138,883	136,746	129,694	124,605	135,958
Net sales	1,095.6	1,244.5	1,484.4	1,632.6	1,685.4	1,929.6
Exports	420.1	469.6	530.3	603.4	629.7	700.9
Value added[ii]	309.1	340.4	404.6	467.3	479.6	572.2
Operating profit	36.1	34.9	49.1	62.4	65.9	71.0
Operating loss	19.2	28.9	26.4	21.4	28.1	30.7
Net profit/loss	17.0	6.0	22.8	41.0	37.7	40.2
Investment outlays[iii]	n.a.	277.8	218.3	251.4	279.8	189.0

Source: Calculations based on Centre of International Relations (CIR) database and Agency for Payment Transactions (AP) data.

Notes:
i Enterprises with a 10% or higher equity share abroad.
ii Calculated as the difference between net sales and 'costs of merchandise, materials and services'.
iii Calculated as the difference between the value of fixed assets in the current and previous year, increased by depreciation in the current year.
n.a. = not available.

Table 7.2 Selected income statements/balance sheet items of companies with outward FDI in total non-financial corporate sector (in per cent) in 1994-1998 and change of shares[i]

	1994	1995	1996	1997	1998	1999	Change of share 1999-1994
No. of companies	1.3	1.21	1.15	1.13	1.09	1.3	n.s.
Equity	30.21	41.77	40.84	39.51	38.18	39.4	9.2
Assets	24.54	36.94	36.2	33.42	31.9	28.3	3.8
No. of employees	30.17	30.54	29.27	28.17	27.14	29.3	-0.9
Net sales	18.31	27.15	28.38	27.29	25.77	26.6	8.3
Exports	27.11	41.89	41.76	38.94	36.69	39.2	12.1
Value added[ii]	21.72	32.2	33.6	32.84	30.85	38.1	16.4
Operating profit	18.7	29.45	32.93	32.31	30.56	27.7	9.0
Operating loss	13.43	21.56	16.72	15	18.85	19.4	6.0
Net profit/loss	33.57	-38.05	-269.11	81.22	56.9	41.2	7.6
Investment outlays[iii]	n.a.	39.26	29.69	24.96	28.14	24.6	n.a.

Source: Calculations based on CIR database and AP data.

Notes:
i Enterprises with a 10% or higher equity share abroad.
ii Calculated as the difference between net sales and 'costs of merchandise, materials and services'.
iii Calculated as the difference between the value of fixed assets in the current and previous year, increased by depreciation in the current year.
n.a. = not available.
n.s. = no sense.

Companies with a direct investment abroad had an impressive 39.4 per cent of equity and 32 per cent of assets in 1999. They employed 29 per cent of employees and realized 26 per cent of sales and up to 39 per cent of all exports of the total corporate sector. The picture is similar with value added and operating profit, where investors realized 38 per cent and 27.7 per cent of the total corporate sector's figures. The net profit share of investors in the total corporate sector is even higher (41.2 per cent), so the relatively high share in investment outlays is not surprising (Table 7.2). Such high shares in selected balance sheets and income statements prove that, albeit small in number, companies with a direct investment abroad were significantly influencing and improving the performance of the entire Slovenian business sector and economy in general.

While the number of companies with outward FDI within the total corporate sector was constant over the 1994-1999 period, the value of outward investments and the importance of investors in the domestic economy were increasing. Highest growth was recorded in exports and value added. The only exception to this trend is the slightly falling share in the number of employees in companies with outward FDI. Such dynamics reflect restructuring and qualitative changes.

If we take for comparison the whole group of exporting companies, the extraordinary importance of investing companies becomes even more evident. Exporters in numerical terms represented 22.5 per cent of the entire corporate sector in 1999, but provided 68.9 per cent of employment in the total business sector, 75.2 per cent of sales, 72.5 per cent of value added and 95.4 per cent of profit. Companies with outward investment have obviously made a significant contribution to these shares, although not all investors abroad are exporters. Indeed, many Slovenian exporters have a low export propensity (measured as a share of export revenues in total sales revenues)[2] and hardly compete in foreign markets. Direct investments abroad help increase export propensity (see Table 7.5 and also Chapter 11 on the effects of outward investment).

Only competitive and successful companies are capable to internationalize through outward FDI. On the other hand, successful business indicators are also the effect of internationalization, albeit not the sole one. The next section analyzes differences between investing and non-investing companies, although they are not explained by outward FDI alone. Changes and differences in the period studied might be a significant consequence of the different access to market(s), access to resources, knowledge and information and competitive pressures that come with investing abroad.

Investing companies versus companies not investing[3]

The first important and enormous difference between companies investing abroad and non-investing companies (investors vis-à-vis non-investors) is the size of a company. The high share in the total business sector is significantly influenced by the size of these companies. It has a significant explanatory power in analyzing business indicators as well as the importance of companies with outward FDI in the total corporate sector (Table 7.3). A firm that grows within national borders can never be as big as a firm that also grows outside of them. Generally speaking, micro, small and medium-sized firms dominate among Slovenian investors abroad. Only some 15 per cent of them are large yet they exert a considerable influence. The average company with outward FDI is medium in size, while the average non-investing firm is small. The average investor in 1998 was (by number of employees) almost 37-times bigger than the average non-investor, it had 59-times higher equity value and 36-times greater assets. The average investor also had 33 times bigger sales. A big company has a greater likelihood of possessing ownership-specific advantages and the ability to acquire further advantages through internationalization. The size of a company influences its economies of scale and scope, efficiency and therefore its competitiveness.

Companies investing abroad are very export-oriented; exports of the average investor are 58-times greater than the exports of the average non-investor. Exports generally represent their first stage of outward internationalization. As regards value added, the average investor realized 56-times higher value added in 1999 than the average non-investor. In 1999 the differences in all selected indicators were much bigger than in 1994, suggesting investing firms had higher growth rates. The main performance indicators reveal that the performances of companies investing abroad outdo the performance of non-investing companies (see Tables 7.4 and 7.5). They are the Slovenian economy's engine of growth. Also revealed is the improving performance of companies with outward FDI from 1994 to 1999. Operating profit as a share of net sales, net sales per assets and net profit per equity and value added per employee are all higher for the average company investing abroad than for the average non-investing company. The average investor is also much more successful than the average Slovenian company (Table 7.4).

Companies with a direct investment abroad are more capital-intensive than non-investing ones. The capital intensity of the investor, despite the higher initial level, also increased faster. While assets per employee increased 1.6-times in 1994-1998 for the average investor, this indicator fell slightly for the non-investing firm. As to asset structure, investors also had a higher share of machinery and equipment than non-investors.

Focusing on efficiency and competitiveness, we found a significant difference in value added. On average, investors have much higher value added as a share of sales revenues (Table 7.5). Also higher is value added per employee. Remarkable growth in value added was realized in 1999 (also see Table 7.2), when average value added per employee in investing firms amounted to SIT 6.2 million (€ 32,000). The average exporting company, for example, realized SIT 4.9 million per employee (€ 23,900).

Competitiveness in value added is more the result of the lower costs of intermediary goods and services than of lower labour costs (Table 7.5). Internationalization and foreign affiliates allow investors more possibilities for cost minimizing. Costs of intermediary goods and services in sales revenues are namely lower for investors, while labour costs as a share of sales revenues are lower for non-investors. The higher labour costs per employee for investors most probably results from the more skilled and educated labour that is employed by investing companies relative to non-investors, which significantly increases value added. The skilled labour intensity of investors is also higher than the average Slovenian company.

Investors also have a better financial structure than non-investors. For the former, equity as a share of total equity and liabilities is higher, current liabilities as a share of total equity and liabilities are lower and the ratio between financial revenues and expenses is greater.

Comparing these two groups of companies and their business indicators confirms that companies directly investing abroad are a vital part of the Slovenian economy and much more successful than companies without outward FDI. Generally, differences in selected indicators increased slightly from 1994 to 1998, suggesting that companies without a direct investment abroad are lagging behind. The Slovenian economy's development and growth potential is therefore largely based on companies investing abroad.

Table 7.3 Selected income statements/balance sheet items for the average company with outward FDI,[i] the average non-investing company, and the average Slovenian company (in SIT million) in 1994-1999

	Average investor						Average non-investor						Average Company
All industries	1994	1995	1996	1997	1998	1999	1994	1995	1996	1997	1998	1999	1999
Equity	2,829	3,174	3,374	3,619	3,931	4,571	86	54	57	63	70	77	126
Assets	4,451	5,043	5,482	5,930	6,370	6,502	180	106	113	135	150	181	249
No. of employees	341	340	333	312	305	334	10	9	9	9	9	9	12
Net sales	2,692	3,043	3,612	3,924	4,121	4,741	158	100	106	120	131	144	193
Exports	1,032	1,148	1,290	1,451	1,540	1,722	37	20	21	26	29	. 29	48
Value added[ii]	759	832	984	1,123	1,173	1,406	36	22	23	26	29	25	40
Operating profit	88.8	85.2	119.6	150.1	161.1	174.4	5.1	2.5	2.8	3.6	4.0	5.0	6.8
Operating loss	47.1	70.7	64.1	51.5	68.8	75.5	4.0	3.2	3.7	3.3	3.3	3.4	4.2
Net profit/loss	41.7	14.6	55.4	98.6	92.3	98.9	1.1	-0.7	-0.9	0.3	0.8	1.5	2.6
Investment outlays[iii]	n. a.	679.2	531.3	604.4	684.1	464.3	32.6	12.9	14.7	20.8	19.2	15.6	20.4

Source: Calculations based on data from the Bank of Slovenia and the AP.

Notes:

i Enterprises with a 10% or higher equity share abroad.

ii Calculated as the difference between net sales and 'costs of merchandise, materials and services'.

iii Calculated as the difference between the value of fixed assets in the current and previous year, increased by depreciation in the current year.

Table 7.4 Key performance indicators of companies, with and without outward FDI, in the 1994-1998 period (all industries)

	Investors					Non-investors					Average Company				
	1994	1995	1996	1997	1998	1994	1995	1996	1997	1998	1994	1995	1996	1997	1998
Return or equity (ROE) (%)	3.1	2.7	3.5	4.2	4.1	5.9	4.6	5.0	5.7	5.8	3.6	3.8	8.3	10.4	4.8
Operating profit as a share of net sales (%)	3.3	2.8	3.3	3.8	3.9	3.2	2.5	2.7	3.0	3.1	2.7	2.6	4.7	5.3	3.3
Net sales per assets (total assets turnover ratio) (%)	60.5	60.3	65.9	66.2	64.7	87.8	94.8	94.4	88.5	87.3	77.3	77.8	96.0	93.6	80.1
Assets per equity (%)	157.3	158.9	162.5	163.9	162.0	209.5	194.6	197.7	213.2	213.6	175.1	186.4	182.8	211.3	182.7
Net profit/loss per equity (%)	1.5	0.5	1.6	2.7	2.4	1.3	-1.2	-1.6	0.4	1.1	-0.5	-0.5	-3.0	0.3	1.5
Value added per employee (in SIT billion)	2.22	2.45	2.95	3.60	3.85	3.46	2.27	2.42	2.89	3.21	1.90	2.18	2.46	2.99	3.39

Source: Calculations based on data from the Bank of Slovenia and the AP.

Table 7.5 Performance indicators of investing and non-investing companies by group in the 1994-1998 period

INDICATORS OF:	INVESTORS					NON-INVESTORS				
	1994	1995	1996	1997	1998	1994	1995	1996	1997	1998
A. SIZE										
1. Assets per company (SIT billion)	4,451	5,043	5,482	5,930	6,370	180	106	113	135	150
2. No. of employees per company	341	340	334	312	305	10	9	9	9	9
3. Net sales per company (SIT billion)	2,692	3,043	3,612	3,924	4,121	158	100	106	120	131
B. CAPITAL INTENSITY										
4. Assets per employee (SIT billion)	13.0	14.9	16.5	19.0	20.9	17.3	11.1	12.0	14.9	16.6
5. Machinery/equipment per employee (SIT billion)	1.7	2.0	2.2	2.5	2.7	2.8	1.8	2.0	2.4	2.6
C. ASSET STRUCTURE AND INVESTMENT										
6. Fixed assets as a share of assets (%)	68	69	69	68	69	65	67	62	64	64
7. Machinery/equip. as a share of fixed assets (%)	19	19	19	19	19	16	16	17	16	16
8. Investment outlays per assets (%)		13	10	10	11	18	12	13	15	13
D. VALUE ADDED										
9. Value added as a share of sales revenue (%)	28.2	27.4	27.3	28.6	28.5	22.8	21.5	21.3	22.0	22.1
10. Costs of commercial goods, materials and services per sales revenue (%)	71.8	72.6	72.7	71.8	71.6	77.2	78.5	78.7	78.0	77.9
11. Labour costs as a share of net sales (%)	21.5	21.4	19.8	19.2	19.5	15.7	17.1	16.4	15.9	15.7
E. SALES AND EXPORT ORIENTATION										
12. Net sales per employee (SIT billion)	7.89	8.96	10.85	12.59	13.53	15.20	10.57	11.34	13.15	14.52
13. Exports as a share of net sales (%)	38.3	37.7	35.7	37.0	37.4	23.1	19.5	19.7	21.8	22.4
F. LABOUR COSTS										
14. Labour costs per employee (SIT mill.)	1693	1915	2148	2413	2642	2387	1804	1854	2085	2285
G. FINANCIAL STRUCTURE										
15. Equity as a share of total equity & liabilities (%)	63.6	63.0	61.5	61.0	61.7	47.8	47.3	50.6	46.9	46.8
16. Current liabilities as a share of total equity & liabilities (%)	24.0	23.8	24.0	23.8	23.6	30.5	33.9	33.4	31.5	30.7
17. Ratio between financial revenues and expenses (%)	87.6	106.2	92.6	104.8	109.3	90.8	82.5	78.3	82.3	81.7
H. SOLVENCY										
18. Ratio between net sales and long-term & current operating receivables (%)	384.0	392.1	425.8	406.7	413.0	482.1	345.4	486.0	484.7	484.7

Source: Centre for International Relations; calculations based on data from the Bank of Slovenia and the APs.

Types of investing companies

Patterns of internationalization as regards foreign entry mode are similar, yet not all companies with outward FDI are alike. Not every investing company can be treated as a true multinational company. The common pattern so far revealed at the macro level has somewhat blurred the details and differences within the group of outward FDI companies. Chapter 4 described three stages of the outward internationalization process, reflecting some differences in the internationalization level of investing companies. The examination of surveys and case studies presented in parts III and IV offered more evidence of differentiation. This section tries to reveal the diversity seen among individual companies with outward FDI. Classifying companies by their company-specific characteristics might therefore help in identifying the stages and the typical characteristics of a particular internationalization stage in terms of a company's size, activity and business performance. The aim is to evaluate the developmental potential of particular investor types for the home economy and whether, from the macro aspect, prospective or non-prospective investors dominate.

The characteristics of companies with outward FDI were gathered from their financial reports that are limited since they do not contain several qualitative data. Identifying types of companies relative to internationalization stages would be more successful by using variables on firm-specific advantages like accumulated human resource capital (knowledge, internationalization experience etc.) or technological capability (innovation capability). The lack of data prevented us forming any such variables.

The method applied

Cluster Analysis was used for type identification. Starting with Hierarchical Cluster Analysis, we identified a number of groups[4]. A company investing abroad is used as a case. Distance or similarity measures are generated by the Proximities procedure. Statistics are displayed at each stage to help select the best solution[5]. The classification is displayed in a dendrogram (see Figure 7.1) to assess the cohesiveness of the clusters formed and provide information on the appropriate number of clusters to keep.

In the next step, after identifying a suitable number of groups we used a K-Means Cluster Analysis. This procedure attempts to identify relatively homogeneous groups of cases based on selected characteristics, using an algorithm that can handle large numbers of cases. However, the algorithm requires the number of clusters to be specified. We included cluster centres out of the hierarchical cluster analysis[6], which proved optimal. Statistics used in these methods for each case were cluster information and distance from the cluster centre.

Clusters of companies with outward FDI

We tried to answer the question of whether there are identifiable groups of companies investing abroad according to some general characteristics or business indicators. On the basis of Hierarchical Cluster Analysis and a dendrogram plot that applied Ward's method (see Figure 7.1), we selected five groups of comparable companies with outward investments abroad.

The main features of company groups are summarized in Table 7.6. The K-Means Cluster Analysis did not give very firm results; only two clusters, that are the smallest in number, proved to be more homogeneous. The most numerous clusters remained quite heterogeneous in terms of the size and activity of a company, as well as business indicators.

Table 7.6 Clusters of companies with outward FDI; frequency statistics and summary characteristics of types of investors

	Frequency	%	Cluster name	Business indicators of an average company with outward FDI[i]	Size and activity of the cluster's companies
1.	133	32.5	Promising ascenders	Below-average sales revenues and exports. Less equipped, more fixed assets. Lower costs of goods and materials, but above-average value added, above-average profit, outward FDI a little under the average.	*Heterogeneous in activity* (35% manufacturing, 18% trade, 25% real estate). *Heterogeneous in size* (12% big, 34% medium, 36% small, 18% micro).
2.	142	34.7	Internationalization laggards	Below-average exports, above-average domestic sales. Less equipped, less fixed assets. Slightly lower costs of goods and materials, lower labour costs. Outward FDI a little below the average. Other average.	*Heterogeneous in activity* (services dominate, 50% trade, 20% real estate). *Heterogeneous in size* (6.3% big, 21% medium, 45% small, 27% micro).
3.	109	26.7	Internationalization winners	Above-average exports. Below-average domestic sales. More equipped, more fixed assets. Above-average value added, outward FDI a little above the average.	*Manufacturing dominant* (80%). Mostly medium and big (35% big, 50% medium, 9% small, 5% micro).
4.	20	4.9	Slow adjusters	Well-above-average exports. Above-average labour costs. Less fixed assets, less equipped, well below-average value added, outward FDI below the average.	*Trade dominant* (65%). Manufacturing only 15%, 10% transport etc., 10% real estate. *Mostly micro and small companies* (0 big, 10% medium, 35% small, 55% micro).
5.	5	1.2	'Losers'	Below-average exports, below-average domestic sales, above-average costs of materials and labour. Less equipped, profit well under the average, often an operating loss, outward FDI above the average.	Real estate (60%), 20% transport. 20% manufacturing *only micro and small companies* (20% small, 80% micro).

Source: Own analysis.

Note:

i See the indicators for an average company with outward FDI in Tables 7.3, 7.4 and 7.5.

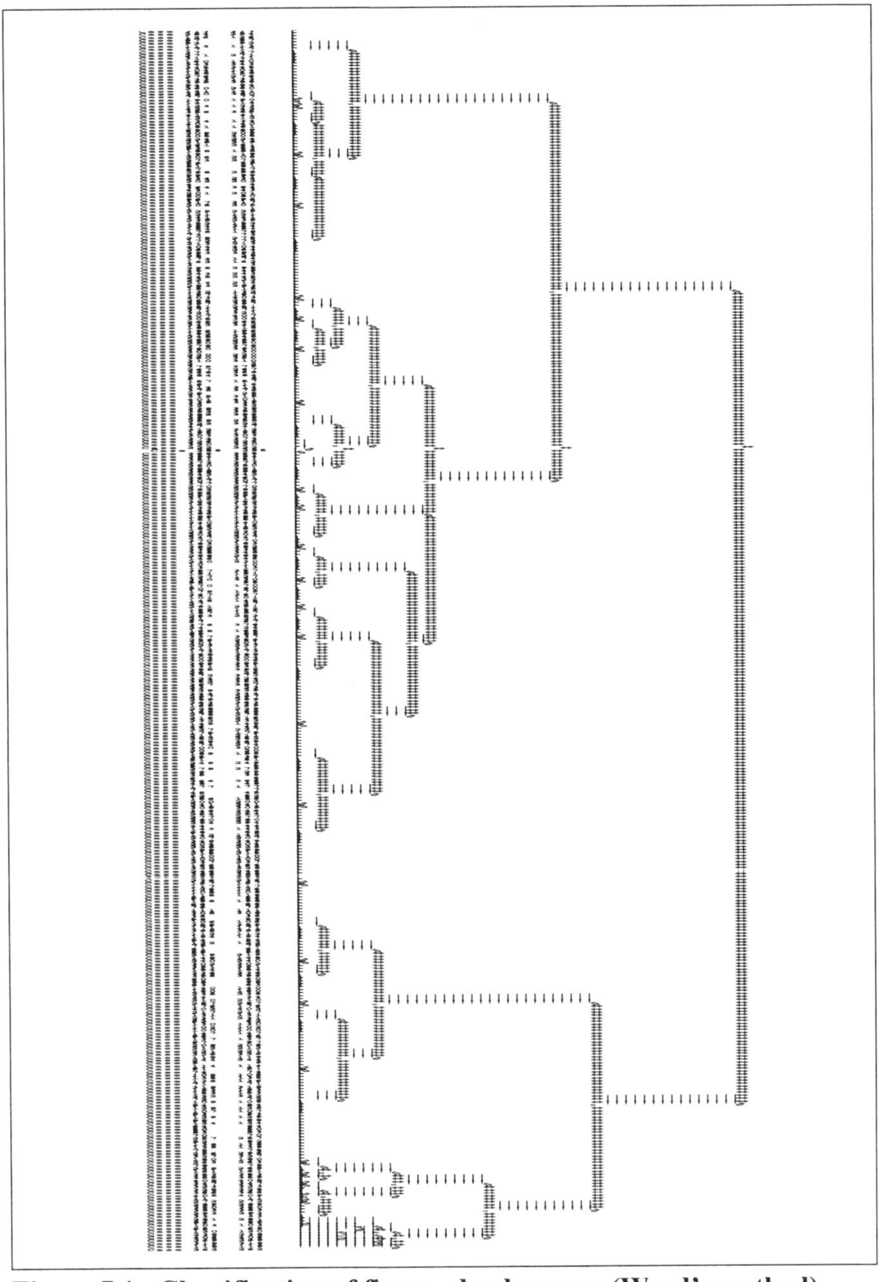

Figure 7.1 Classification of firms - dendrogram (Ward's method)

Source: Own analysis.

Although limited, Cluster Analysis revealed some general types of investors abroad and proved that companies investing abroad do differ in their internationalization stages and patterns. Cluster names (column four, Table 7.6) were given to describe their internationalization intensity, while the next two columns describe their most significant characteristics.

The first two groups, promising ascenders and laggards, are the largest and very heterogeneous in terms of size and activity and are quite close to the average investor according to selected business indicators. Yet business indicators by themselves suggest the first group (cluster) includes the most promising companies with above-average value added and above-average profit and below-average costs. They are often leapfroggers that skip over some internationalization phases (or have, for example, a very short export phase). The group of promising ascenders includes companies of every size, suggesting that size does not determine the success of outward internationalization and performance indicators.

The second cluster, the laggards, prevailingly includes services companies that are most similar to the average company investing abroad (see Tables 7.4 and 7.5). With export and outward FDI below the average and above-average domestic sales, the analysis confirmed the services sector's much lower outward internationalization as already revealed in Chapter 5. Lower labour costs suggest lower skilled labour intensity, which is otherwise an important facilitator of internationalization.

The third group, the winners, comprises important or leading Slovenian exporters, mostly strong, capital-intensive, manufacturing companies with a relatively stronger international network (well-above-average outward FDI) and less dependence on the domestic market. This group includes the highest share of large and medium-sized companies and can be treated as the most internationalized.

In the fourth group, micro and small trading companies dominate among the slow adapters. Beside indigenous trading companies that have only slowly adjusted to changes in their competitive environment, companies in this group are often established by bigger manufacturing firms and serve as trade facilitators. Despite below-average value added, they show good business indicators in general (above-average exports, average performance).

Finally, the fifth cluster, the losers, is the smallest and least promising. Small and micro companies, mostly in the services sector, with low or practically no assets, low (or no) sales, high costs and below-average operating performance (mostly operating losses) dominate. These firms have poor operating indicators as well as low developmental potential. Outward FDI (though above average) in this case does not seem prospective or development-oriented, but more an abortive experiment or a capital flight.

Summary

Despite the low share of outward FDI stock in GDP and small number of investing firms in the entire corporate sector, investors abroad represent a vital part of Slovenia's economy. Their contribution is especially significant as far as exports, employment, value added and profits are concerned. The Slovenian economy largely depends on the one per cent of companies with outward FDI responsible for 40 per cent of exports, 27 per cent of employment and 38 per cent of value added realized in the total corporate sector. International growth provides much better development opportunities than growth limited only to the domestic setting.

Companies investing abroad perform much better than non-investing companies, and compared to the average Slovenian company. The differences between investing and non-investing firms were identified in six key areas that, apart from ownership-specific advantages, could improve performance: company size, capital intensity, value added, export intensity, skilled labour intensity and financial structure. Companies investing abroad are larger, more capital-intensive, have a better asset structure and are more export-oriented. Investing firms performed better than non-investing firms and also improved in the second half of the nineties. The growth of investing companies was much faster than of non-investing firms. Investing abroad considerably speeded up companies' restructuring, especially as regards value added and export propensity.

Companies with outward investment also differ amongst themselves. Cluster Analysis identified five different types, the majority of which have had a very positive impact on Slovenia's economy since their export and/or value added has been above the average. Some have long experience in outward internationalization ('winners'), some have good operating results and promising growth prospects ('promising ascenders', including 'leapfroggers'), while some are at least able to adjust slowly to competitive pressures ('slow adjusters'). Many services companies that under-performed in terms of internationalization level ('internationalization laggards'), also play an important role in the domestic economy but their ability to further internationalize (transformation to the tradable sector) is essential for retaining that role. Investing 'losers', which do not show any development potential for the domestic economy, luckily represent the smallest group. All these results confirm the relevance of internationalization through outward FDI for development of the Slovenian economy.

Notes

1 For evaluating the role of companies investing abroad in the total corporate sector, standard descriptive analysis was employed. Selected items out of balance sheets and income statements were used to calculate some business indicators and examine the performance of selected firms. A secondary data source from the Bank of Slovenia was combined with the database of the AP. The non-financial corporate sector was taken into account.

2 About 40 per cent of exporters realize less than 10 percent of total revenues through their exports.

3 The comparison is based on mean values of selected indicators. The average value might always be strongly influenced by extreme values, but remains a reasonable indicator of comparison. Non-consolidated financial statements are taken for investing firms (statements for the investing parent only).

4 This procedure attempts to identify relatively homogeneous groups of cases based on selected characteristics. An algorithm is used that starts with each case in a separate cluster and combines clusters until only one is left. We analyzed raw variables as well as some standardizing transformations.

5 Statistics used in this method were: agglomeration schedule, distance (or similarity) matrix, and cluster membership for a single solution or range of solutions.

6 We selected two methods for classifying cases, firstly by updating cluster centres iteratively and secondly by only classifying. Use of the cluster centres out of the hierarchical cluster analysis proved to be the optimal solution (the lowest value of the criteria function).

PART III
INVESTING ABROAD: FROM IDEA TO RESULTS

Chapter 8

Motivations for Outward Investment

Introduction

Which incentives lead firms to engage in direct investment rather than using other internationalization modes? We have seen in the previous chapters that outward investment usually follows exports and is a result of gradually developing internationalization. International experiences enable firms to find new ways of increasing their rate of return. A common motive for the existence of firms and their activities can, according to neoclassical theory, be reduced to profit maximization – expressed in the rate of return – yet there are plenty of ways of achieving that final goal (for example, maximizing sales or market share, reducing costs etc.). Investing abroad is one way of addressing such challenges.

Motives for directly investing abroad can be very heterogeneous and also intertwined. Dunning distinguishes four main groups of motives: resource-seeking, market-seeking, efficiency-seeking and strategic-asset-seeking (1993; pp. 56-63). These groups of motives also determine the type of outward investment. Although overlapping, these groups of motives reflect historical developments in a country as well as with a firm's capabilities. The economic development of a country and a firm's growth and strategy influence the reasons underlying outward investments. The motives and their rankings change with a company's international experiences. Factors that determine the motives for outward investment are ownership/firm-specific advantages and the company's strategic goals. However, many multinational companies pursue a number of different motives that combine of each of the above groups.

Outward investing may be a result of an aggressive/offensive reaction, when a company pro-actively exercises its strategic objective(s), or a defensive reaction where the outward investment of a company is a response to actions taken by its competitors and is oriented to self-protection.

The next few paragraphs examine why Slovenian firms seek to become multinational companies. The analysis is based on two surveys carried out among Slovenian multinational companies. In 1999, since it was the first study of its kind, the motives were studied in detail. Several indicators were tested and later merged into four groups of motives. In the 2001 survey, we tested some of the main motives in order to trace potential changes in the major groups, but we also broadened the research to firms' competitive advantages. According to the OLI framework, ownership-specific advantages are a precondition for outward investments. Companies invest only if they have specific advantages, if there are better locations for them than at home and if internalization is the best way to maximize returns on such specific advantages. They are a necessary but not a sufficient precondition for outward FDI.

Why invest abroad[1]?

The most important motives were market-seeking, followed by strategic-asset-seeking, increasing efficiency and, lastly, resource-seeking ones (Figure 8.1). The small domestic market effect[2], the loss of the former Yugoslav market at the beginning of the nineties, increased competitive pressures from foreign companies in the domestic market and the development of internationalization have all influenced the intensity of the market-seeking motives group. According to Dunning (1993), this kind of motivation is strongest in the second stage of the investment development path. An evaluation of Slovenia's investment development path found that Slovenia is somewhere between the second and third stages (Svetlièiè, Bellak, 2001).

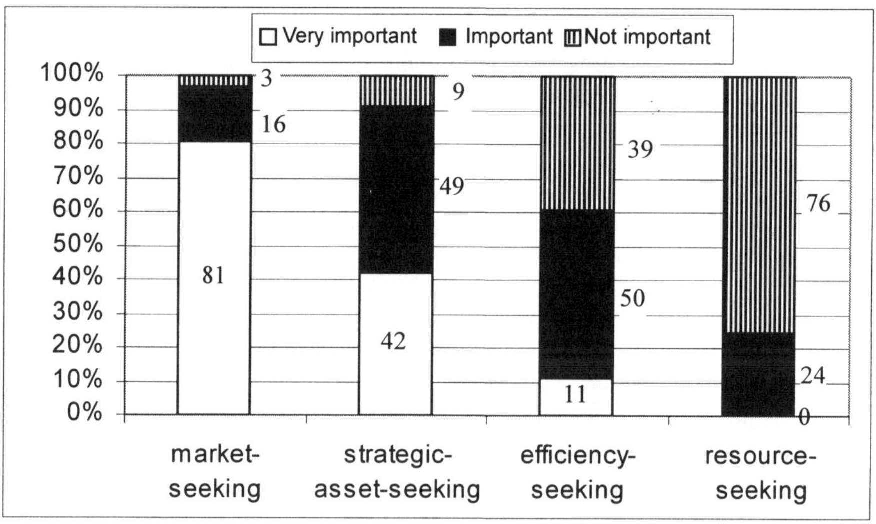

Figure 8.1 The importance of a particular group of motives (in per cent)

Source: Survey 1999.

The explanatory power of differences in factor abundance seems to be weak in making sense of the observed patterns of outward FDI. Although Slovenia is small and therefore, in terms of factor endowments, a relatively poor country with high labour costs, resource-seeking incentives surprisingly proved to be the least important (Figure 8.2). Regardless of the type of production factor, production factor costs were assessed as an unimportant motive for most of the sample companies. The low importance of natural resource-seeking motives may on the other hand be a result of their poor availability in the domestic economy. Resource availability provides domestic firms with skills and might be an important source for ownership-specific advantages in manufacturing that could be exploited abroad[3]. Slovenia had few natural resources and consequently could not develop such a type of competitive advantage.

Box 8.1 Resource-seekers

Droga Portorož d.d., and Fructal d.d.[i] are two large Slovenian food producers that could be used as rare examples of a resource-seeking outward investment.

The strengths and advantages of both companies were not only their tradition and experience since the fifties, developed production facilities and technological know-how, but also marketing know-how and very well established brands that are still famous in the former Yugoslav markets, along with substantial export experience (net sales abroad in 2000 represented about 28 per cent of the operating revenues of Droga and 47 per cent of Fructal, d.d.). Fructal has concentrated on fruit products, nectars and juices, while Droga's production range is more diversified (tea and coffee, spices, cereals and other foodstuffs).

The expansion to former Yugoslav markets began immediately after independence in 1991 was not only market-related (this motive was partly achieved by exports – the region represents about 76 per cent of the export revenues of Droga and about 85 per cent of Fructal's), but also involved access to raw materials. The location of its outward FDI was therefore determined by access to natural resources and secondly by the market potential of local and neighbouring markets. Due to good agricultural conditions, they established foreign affiliates in Macedonia and BiH.

Sources: Business press, www.fructal.si, www.droga.si.

Note:

i In 2000 Fructal was taken over by the Union d.d. brewery, but it retains the same production programme.

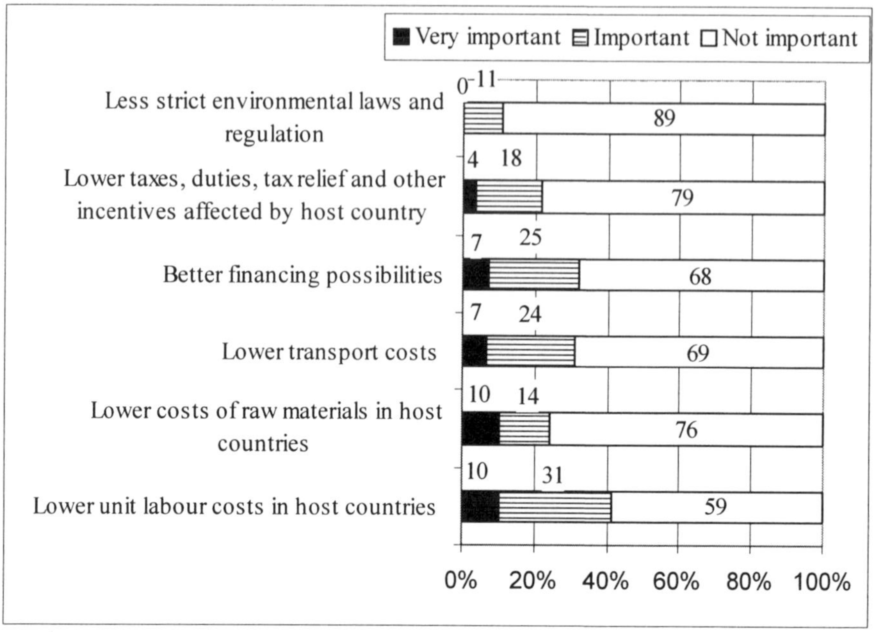

Figure 8.2 The importance of resource-seeking motivating factors (in per cent)

Source: Survey 1999.

Note:
Valid percentage of investors evaluating a particular motivation factor as very important, important or not important.

Unit labour costs were only slightly more important than other factors. That is surprising especially in view of Ozawa's paradigm and the general opinion that Slovenian labour costs are relatively high. Average labour costs in Slovenia are namely the highest among transition economies[4]. Countries that appear to be the main destination of Slovenian outward investments (see Chapter 5) have much lower labour costs, but also lower productivity. The biggest consequence of the low importance of resource-seeking motives is the fact that 90 per cent of Slovenian affiliates abroad are trading affiliations and only 10 per cent are production oriented. The other explanation for the smaller role of lower labour costs could be the lack of knowledge of what a global combination of factors (globalization) can offer in terms of strengthening competitiveness, together with the lack of capacity to achieve such globalization.

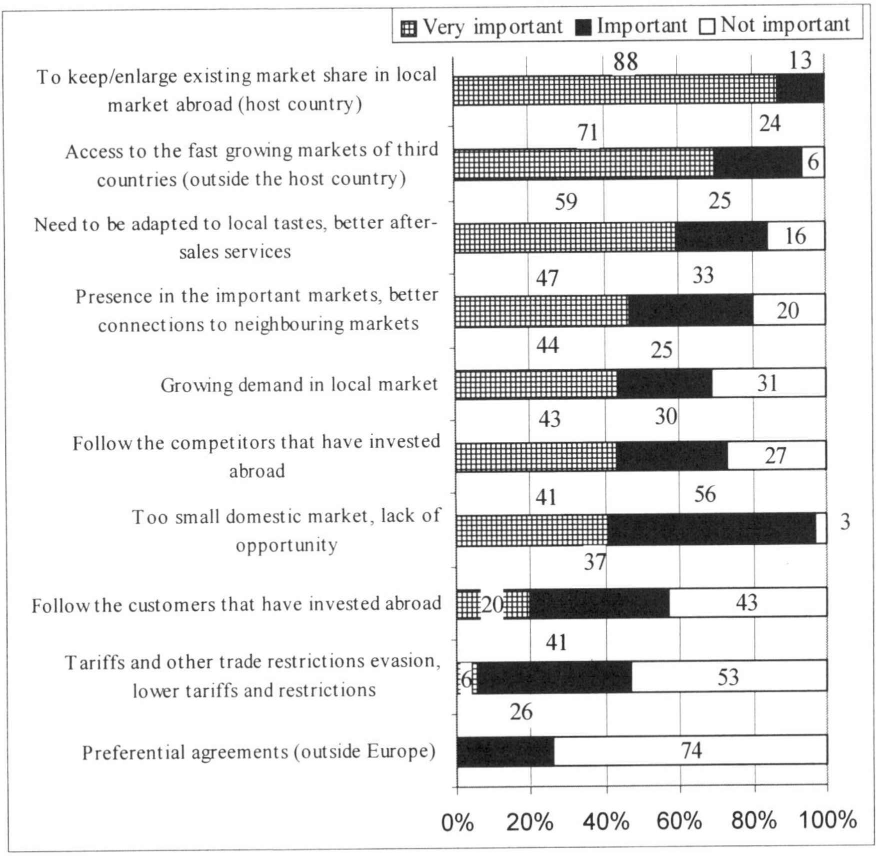

Figure 8.3 The importance of market-seeking motivating factors (in per cent)

Source: Survey 1999.

Note:
Valid percentage of investors evaluating a particular motivation factor as very important, important or not important.

The fact that market potential outweighs factor price differences (or labour cost, natural resources) suggests that firms realized that exports by themselves are no longer sufficient to retain the existing market shares abroad, let alone increasing them. It also demonstrates that Slovenian multinational enterprises are more of a horizontal than a vertical type. Vertical multinationals dominate when countries are very different in relative factor endowments (e.g. capital/labour, skilled/unskilled labour), while horizontal FDI predominates between similarly endowed, similar-size countries in the presence of relatively high trading costs (Markusen, 1997). The major locations of Slovenian outward FDI are not very different in factor endowments and production costs, except for labour costs.

The high importance of market-seeking motives (Figure 8.3) should initially be examined in the context of declining export competitiveness. The share of standardized and labour-intensive products is high, such exports are very sensitive to competitive pressures (commodity composition of exports is concentrated in those commodity groups for which foreign demand, which is the most important variable of export results, grows less than on average). Additionally, the commodity structure of exports has not changed much in the last few years (Strojan Kastelec, 2001). Although Slovenian companies succeeded in keeping their market shares in the EU almost unchanged, they have lost competitiveness with respect to CEFTA countries. The export growth of CEECs seen in the 1990s primarily depended on the initial level and structure of exports. This was much higher in Slovenia compared to other CEECs. The next important stimulus to exports could be inward FDI, which was much lower in Slovenia than in other CEECs. Inward FDI in Slovenia did not influence the change of production structure while FDI inflows to other CEECs significantly upgraded the production structure. Losses of export competitiveness force Slovenian companies to employ a new entry mode so they can try to at least keep their existing market shares. Outward FDI is therefore primarily a means of export promotion and keeping market shares. Tariff avoidance was a less important motive since the trade barriers with the main host countries and importers of Slovenian goods are low.

Slovenian firms also followed their competitors that invested abroad. They needed local presence to adapt their product to local tastes and to improve after-sales services. Some outward FDI also follows Vernon's life cycle (1966). Companies seek to capitalize their not very new technology but that which is suited to the needs of local factor configuration. A number of Slovenian firms are investing abroad in kind, transferring to their affiliations their own technology while, at the same time, starting to upgrade their own. Adapted technology and adapted products are together with organizational know-how their firm-specific advantages rather than very new products and very recent technology.

Strategic-asset-seeking motives proved to be the second most important incentive. Growth of a company and strengthening its overall competitive position were assessed as particularly important incentives for outward FDI (Figure 9.4). The strategic-asset-seeking investment orientation is a reflection of a long-term and internationally-oriented strategy (growth, strong competitive position, high profits) which is encouraging, although strong demand for strategic assets could also be stimulated by the unavailability of other resources. One explanation for the unexpected significant weight of the strategic-assets-seeking motive could also involve the fact that this answer sounds 'modern' and respondents might have been attracted to it without really knowing what it means.

Strategic-asset-seeking-motivated investments are frequently manifested through M&A, which have recently been the most important form of FDI growth in the world. Although M&A save time in the processes of a firm's growth and asset creation and offer quick technology and knowledge transfers, companies at the beginning of the internationalization process (like transition economies' firms) are often unable to cope with mergers and acquisitions. The surveys proved that M&A indeed were quite rare in the case of Slovenian outward FDI. Instead, greenfield investments predominated[5].

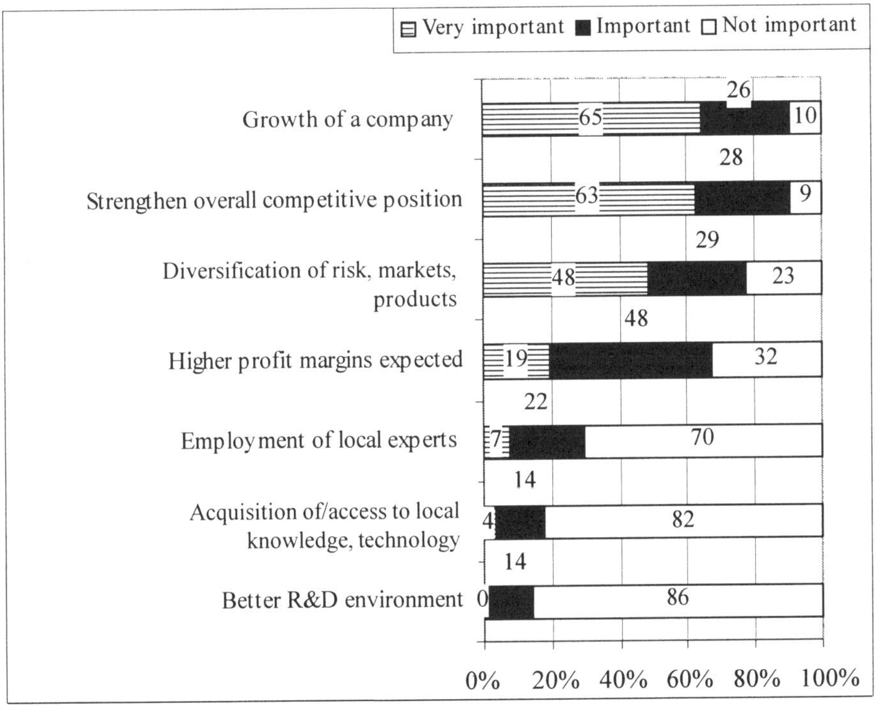

Figure 8.4 The importance of strategic-assets-seeking motivating factors (in per cent)

Source: Survey 1999.

Note:
Valid percentage of investors evaluating a particular motivating factor as very important, important or not important.

Box 8.2 Strategic-asset-seeker

Hermes Soft Lab, d.d. is a leading company in the field of innovative software solutions. In 1993 its CEO was voted European Entrepreneur of the Year and in 1997 the World Economic Forum proclaimed Hermes Soft Lab the fastest growing firm in Europe. Knowledge-intensive product/service, a continually growing market as well as good and ambitious management offered excellent future prospects that could be seriously hampered by the shortage of (domestic) experts. Although its most important markets are highly developed countries, their foreign affiliates are located in developing ones. The main aim of the first two affiliates abroad, namely in Sarajevo (BiH) and in Budapest (Hungary) were established to get access to the computer engineers available there.

The countries chosen are not really abundant in these 'created resources', but the advantage at that time was low competition among 'head hunters' – a lack of domestic firms – and consequently the low price of computer engineers. While Sarajevo was attractive due to its high unemployment, Budapest was abundant with young educated emigrants, including those from former Yugoslavia.

The collection of 'all available' computer-engineers in the region combined with long-term relationships with leading enterprises (Hewlett-Packard, Agilent Technologies, Erricson etc.) was a strategic asset that helped in creating an innovative global player in e-banking, telecommunications, storage and data management, network and systems management and web services.

Recently, the company has been seeking strategic assets through strategic alliances. StorScape, a joint-venture company established together with the Irish company Eurologic Systems, will pool their knowledge and offer services on storage and data management under their own brand name.

Sources: Business press, http://www.hermes-softlab.com/company

The firm-specific strategic advantages of Slovenian firms are specific products/services adapted and already well known in markets of penetration and know-how for doing business there. Less developed markets also offer the opportunity to exploit a first-mover advantage. After strengthening the market position and acquiring market knowledge, we can expect that the group of investors mainly motivated by strategic reasons will expand. For improving international competitiveness, this type of investment requires firm-specific advantages but, on the other hand, it also offers first-time foreign direct investors the opportunity to gain competitive strength in an unfamiliar market.

Strategically, outward FDI goes hand in hand as firms restructure their assets to meet their objectives (Dunning, 1993; 60).

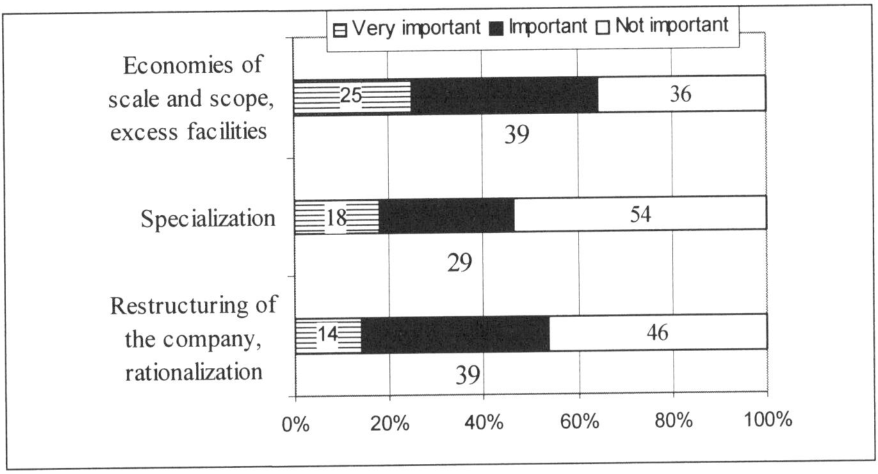

Figure 8.5 The importance of efficiency-seeking motivating factors (in per cent)

Source: Survey 1999.

Note:
Valid percentage of investors evaluating a particular motivating factor as very important, important or not important.

The efficiency-seeking incentive for outward FDI as the third most important group of motives is common (Figure 8.5) for investors already established abroad. It is less important for new investors abroad. The sequential internationalization pattern suggests that the efficiency-seeking motive will gain in importance by enhancing investments abroad. Such investments facilitate the continuing relocation of resources (by using differences and similarities of factor endowments and economic systems and institutional agreements in different countries) in pursuit of the maximum-efficiency objective. With centralized supervision of geographically spread activities, efficiency-seeking investment aims to increase yields through specialization, economies of scale and scope and risk diversification. Although the affiliate network of the average company in the sample is expanding, there are only a few *star companies* in a position to invest abroad for this reason. The important explanatory variable in this respect is the size and international experience of a company. Although Slovenian multinational companies are on average bigger and more experienced than companies not involved in a direct investment abroad (see Chapter 7) they are still relatively small and inexperienced compared to Western multinationals. The overall size of a home economy influences international business. Mass consumption enables economies of scale, low costs, standardized mass-market products. The domestic market does not offer such possibilities to Slovenian firms due to its small size and high labour costs, therefore achieving the economies of scale and scope and exploiting excessive production facilities was identified as an important incentive for outward investment (for more than one-half of the sample). Since economic integration (and liberalization) usually stimulates efficiency-seeking investment, we can expect thisto grow after Slovenia joins the EU.

Despite the quite substantial upswing of outward FDI in 1999 and 2000, particularly in the states that emerged from former Yugoslavia, the motivation has almost not changed after two years (Table 8.1, Figure 9.6). Market-related motives remained by far the most important for outward investments, while labour costs remained the least important. Other cost-related motives and strategic-asset-acquisition motives were of similar importance. Many companies simultaneously regarded two or three motives as being equally important.

Table 8.1 Motivation for outward FDI

	N	Min.	Max.	Mean	Std. Dev.	Variance	Skewness	Kurtosis
Market-related motives	36	2	5	4.6	0.8	0.6	-1.9	3.0
Labour costs	35	1	5	2.8	1.2	1.4	0.1	-0.9
Cost-related motives	35	1	5	3.2	1.1	1.3	-0.5	-0.3
Asset acquisition	35	1	5	3.2	1.0	1.1	-0.2	-0.4

Source: Survey 2001.

Note:
Five-grade scale, 1 = not important, 5 = very important.

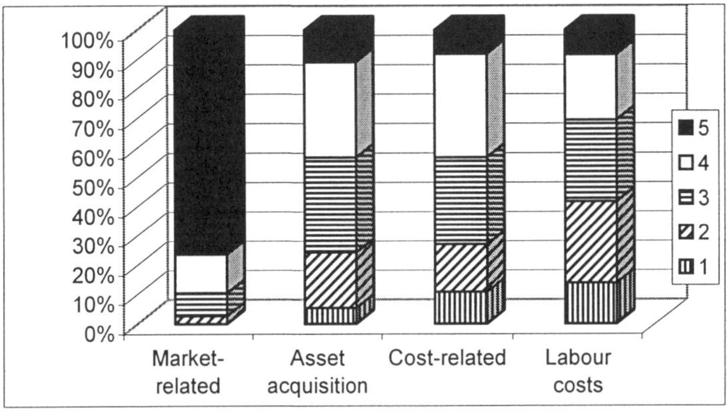

Figure 8.6 Motivations for outward FDI

Source: Survey 2001.

Note:
Five-grade scale, 1 = not important, 5 = very important.

Companies without any experience in outward FDI evaluate motivation types almost alike. The motivations of potential outward investors analyzed in 1999 on a sample of the largest exporters and fastest growing firms were very similar (more than fifty per cent of the sample actually planned outward FDI at that time)[6]. The ranking of the four motivation groups was actually the same, while the intensity of the importance differed slightly between the two samples (in favour of investors). Market-seeking motives were considered the most important, followed by strategic-asset-seeking, efficiency-seeking and resource-seeking ones. However, in the sample of exporters and the fastest growing firms the significance of the last three motivation groups was very close and much higher than in the sample of companies with outward FDI. Non-investors probably see outward FDI as a 'broader' tool, not only as a way of acquiring market shares.

The only difference worth mentioning was in the perception of resource- and strategic-asset-seeking motives. Lower labour costs, foreign experts and new technology and knowledge were assessed as being much more important for exporters and the fastest growing firms than for firms that already have outward FDI. This might also be the result of a less realistic conception of would-be investors abroad. The next important difference was the attributing of greater importance to the efficiency-seeking motives. The largest exporters and the fastest growing firms considered specialization, economies of scale, and restructuring, to be more important than investors.

Competitive advantages

Competitive advantages can serve as a proxy for ownership-specific advantages which, according to Dunning's OLI framework, are a necessary condition for outward investment. The assessment is based on companies' perception of their position in comparison to their close competitors. The grade reflects the position of a sample company according to its competitors in domestic as well as in the host-countries' market(s). When interpreting the results, we have to take into account the geographical concentration of Slovenian outward FDI (see Chapters 5 and 6). As much as 65 per cent of FDI outward stocks is located in the states of former SFRY, about 12 per cent in other European transition economies, 17 per cent in EU countries and about three per cent in the USA.

Surprisingly, the analysis of competitive advantage according to the location of outward FDI found no statistically significant differences in competitive advantages between those firms that invest exclusively in the region of former Yugoslavia, those that invest in former Yugoslavia and elsewhere, and those investing exclusively elsewhere (Figure 8.7)[7]. Although the results are statistically insignificant, we concluded that their industrial structure influences the competitive position of a company. The insignificant results might be the consequence of the similar 'geographical diversification' of foreign affiliates of the sample companies[8].

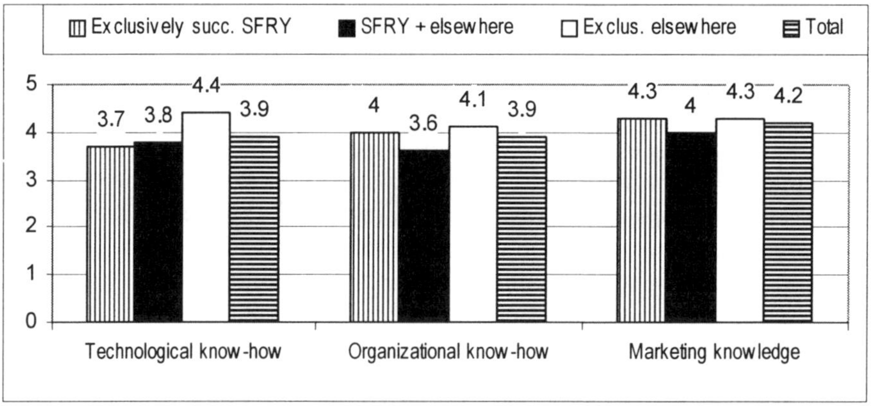

Figure 8.7 Evaluation of investors' competitive advantages according to the location of their investments

Source: Survey 2001.

Note:

1 = not important, 5 = very important.

Generally, the sample companies felt quite confident in all three areas of competitive advantages that were tested (see Table 8.2). All three, namely technological know-how, organizational know-how as well as marketing know-how were assessed above grade 3 – medium importance. They assessed marketing knowledge as their strongest competitive advantage. They feel a little weaker in technological know-how and the weakest in organizational know-how.

Table 8.2 Evaluation of competitive advantages

	N	Min.	Max.	Mean	Std. Dev.	Skewness	Kurtosis
Technological know-how	38	1	5	3.9	0.96	-0.79	1.16
Organizational know-how	38	1	5	3.8	1.05	-0.78	0.36
Marketing know-how	39	1	5	4.2	0.97	-1.28	2.10

Source: Survey 2001.

Note: 1 = not important, 5 = very important.

Different competitive advantages of investors are inter-related (see correlation Table 8.3). Companies with high marketing know-how very likely also possess competitive advantages in organizational know-how, while simultaneous competitive advantages in technological know-how are less likely. Firms with a high technological advantage most likely lack marketing knowledge, while substantial organizational know-how is very likely also their competitive strength.

Table 8.3 Correlation between competitive advantages

	Tech. know-how	Organiz. know-how	Marketing know-how
Tech. know-how	1		
Organiz. know-how	0.35[i]	1	
Marketing knowledge	-0.05	0.54[ii]	1

Source: Survey 2001.

Notes:
i Correlation is significant at the 0.05 level (2-tailed).
ii Correlation is significant at the 0.01 level (2-tailed).
Valid N=34.

Interestingly, the competitive advantage in technological know-how was assessed much higher by Slovenian companies (so-called direct investors) than by companies also owned by foreigners (so-called indirect investors[9]). Indirect investors (foreign-owned affiliations) on the other hand attributed higher competitive advantages to marketing and organizational know-how (although the differences were not significant).

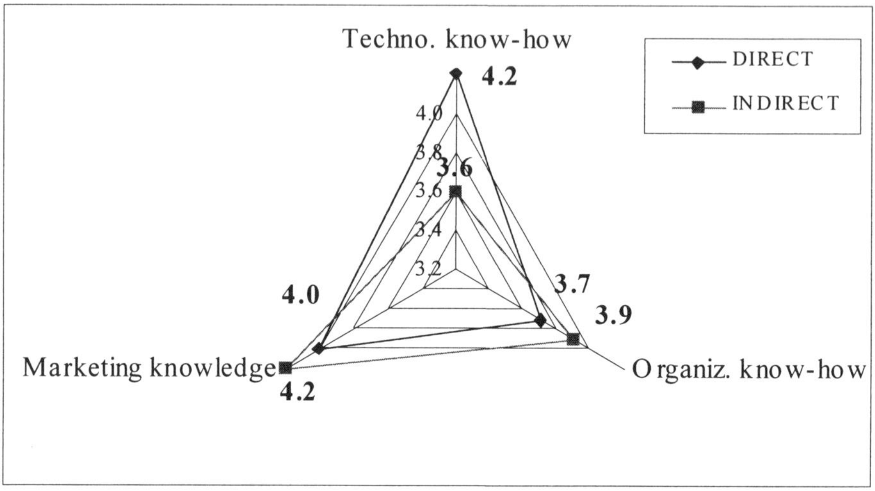

Figure 8.8 Differences in competitive advantages between direct and indirect investors

Source: Survey 2001.

Notes:

1 = not important, 5 = very important.

Indirect signifies foreign-owned firms, direct signifies firms without foreign capital.

The difference in technological advantage between direct and indirect investors was quite large and statistically significant. Spill-over effects of inward FDI (the knowledge transfer of foreign investors) is larger in the field of marketing and organizational skills than in technological know-how. The pattern we found was expected, since marketing and organizational knowledge is usually much easier to transfer and is the first to be transferred.

When analyzing competitive advantages in technological know-how, we must also consider that investors on average had much larger R&D expenditures (measured as a share of sales revenues) than the average Slovenian company. Also, the growth of R&D expenditures is higher than the growth of the average Slovenian company. According to Survey 2001, Slovenian investors increased their R&D expenditures from 3.6 to 4 per cent from 1997 to 2000 as well as the share of university-educated employees.

Does a competitive advantage influence the motive for outward investment?

In order to find out whether the competitive advantage(s) of firms influence the motivation for outward investment, a correlation analysis was performed on the Survey 2001 sample. According to our expectations, cross-tabs analysis mostly revealed a positive association between competitive advantages and motives. However, the correlations were often weak and not statistically significant, also due to the small sample size (Valid N=33).

Except for the labour-cost motive, stronger competitive advantages generally increase the importance of motives for outward investment. The strongest correlations were found for marketing knowledge. The higher the competitive advantage in marketing knowledge, the more important the market-related motives are. This expected correlation proved to be statistically significant. Investors who have a marketing knowledge advantage are also motivated to materialize it abroad through outward FDI. An advantage in marketing knowledge also enhanced cost-related motives and asset acquisitions.

Table 8.4 Correlation between motives and competitive advantages

	Technological know-how	Organizational know-how	Marketing know-how
Market-related motives	0.05 (.273)	0.24 (1.374)	0.50 (3.281)[i]
Labour costs	0.03 (.183)	-0.11 (-.617)	-0.12 (-.630)
Cost-related motives	0.35 (2.20)[i]	0.04 (.190)	0.26 (1.517)
Asset acquisition	0.14 (.828)	0.02 (.130)	0.23 (1.308)

Source: Survey 2001.

Notes:

Pearson's correlation coefficient, t-value in parenthesis, Valid N=33.

i Statistically significant correlation.

While market-related motives are stimulated by all kinds of competitive advantages, labour-cost motives only originate from technological know-how. Companies with high competitive advantage in organizational and marketing knowledge did not invest abroad to exploit lower labour costs (a negative, albeit insignificant correlation was found). These advantages are not based on low labour costs but rather on highly skilled labour and non-cost competitiveness.

Summary

Slovenian multinational companies pursue a range of motives when investing abroad, but they are primarily market-seekers. Competition in domestic and foreign markets is increasing and Slovenian companies cannot keep pace via mere export internationalization. For keeping and enlarging their foreign market shares, they have had to enter through outward investment. They have followed their competitors and their customers, but have also sought to exploit the first-mover advantage in those markets where their trademarks are well established. A direct presence was also needed to keep pace with product adaptation/differentiation and after-sales services.

Some companies also invest abroad for a strategic-assets-seeking purpose. Growth and strengthening an overall competitive position is part of their long-term strategy that can only be realized in foreign markets. Efficiency-seeking and resource-seeking motives are less important. Foreign affiliates at this stage serve in export promotion rather than international production by combining resources internationally and exploiting factor abundance differences. Although labour costs are high and cost competitiveness is low compared to other transition economies, the relocation of production is more of an exception. The motivation for outward investments did not change from 1999 to 2001, although the significant increase of FDI outflows to more risky destinations promoted the role of host-country factors like risks.

'Small country effects' often include poor resource availability and a lack of domestic demand that prevents domestic firms exploiting standardized, mass production, low costs and economies of scale, but also prevents them developing the skills and advantages needed to exploit such resources or the advantages of mass production abroad. Slovenian firms are used to looking for market niches. The small country effect, on the other hand, also enhances internationalization if investors have the necessary competitive advantages. Slovenian multinational companies feel the strongest competitive advantage in marketing knowledge, although they also feel confident in technological and organizational know-how. The prevailing motivation for outward investing is a reflection of their current competitive advantages (due to export experience, knowledge of markets and trademarks). For manufacturing firms that dominate among Slovenian MNCs, gaining, keeping and enlarging their foreign market shares is top priority. For many Slovenian companies, becoming a multinational company facilitates not only survival in foreign markets but also their survival in general.

Notes

1 This question was discussed with the sample companies in various ways; with open-type questions, interviews and evaluations of particular motives on a three-grade scale. Likert's method was used to group the individual motives listed in the questionnaire (see Figure 8.1). Secondly, each motivation group is analyzed in greater detail (Figures 8.2-8.5).
2 Also for countries like the Netherlands, Switzerland, Sweden, Finland and Portugal.
3 The availability of resources helped explain American investments in petroleum and mining, the position of Swedish MNCs producing iron ore or forest products or, for example, the position of a Swiss MNC in the dairy products industry.
4 For a comparison of labour costs, see endnote 5 (Chapter 2).
5 More that eighty-five per cent of foreign affiliates of the 1999 survey sample companies were established as a greenfield type, 11.7 per cent were through acquisitions and 2.9 per cent through mergers. See Chapter 6.
6 Motivation was tested with the same structure of questionnaire as for the sample of investing companies in 1999.
7 Means were compared using the Post Hoc Test, Bonfferoni method.
8 The three selected groups of investors (namely in the region of former Yugoslavia, those that invest in the region of former Yugoslavia and elsewhere and those investing exclusively elsewhere), might be too similar to reveal differences in competitive advantages. Another limit might be the relatively small sample (Valid N= 34).
9 The share of indirect investors in the sample was 43 per cent.

Chapter 9

Investing Firms and Foreign Affiliates

Introduction

To a large extent internationalization capabilities are a reflection of companies' characteristics and experience. Investing firms were described in great detail in Chapter 7 when their importance and performance was analyzed. This chapter concentrates on some other features of investing firms and, above all, on the characteristics of foreign affiliates. The size and age structure of investors and their experience with other internationalization modes are important for recognizing a company's propensity to undertake outward FDI. Also essential for understanding the internationalization pattern is information on foreign affiliates such as ownership structure, type of establishment, activity and their functional orientation. Much of this information is beyond the reach of official statistics[1], therefore the analysis of investing companies and their affiliates is largely based on survey data.

A short outline of investing firms' characteristics and their foreign affiliates paints a background to the findings on the Slovenian internationalization pattern presented in the previous and following chapters and will help understand the subsequent analysis of the motives for, barriers to and effects of outward FDI.

Investing firms

Size, age and experience with entry modes are all explanatory variables in internationalization when taken as an evolutionary and knowledge-accumulating process; the size of a company as an indicator of its potential resources, the age of a firm as an indicator of experience and knowledge of foreign entry modes as a direct measure of international involvement and gradualism in the internationalization process.

Size

Companies can be forced into internationalization regardless of their size. It is often argued that a firm's size can be an important factor in determining the selection of entry mode, although the empirical evidence here is still inconclusive (Ali and Camp 1993; Tyebjee 1994). Size determines a company's capital (financial, physical or human), capabilities or other resources. Larger firms are supposed to be in a better position to expand internationally than smaller ones as they have better access to financial and other resources and possess a greater 'stock' of human capital (knowledge) which is crucial in the internationalization process. Many empirical studies clearly indicate that smaller firms have internationalized less, more slowly and more passively than larger firms due to resource constraints (see Luostarinnen, 1994; p. 23, Zafarullah et al., 1998). Moreover, empirical studies have also demonstrated higher probabilities of ownership-specific advantages existing within big firms and a positive correlation between company size and internalization capability (Dunning, 1993; p. 85). Some authors have even regarded company size as the most important explanatory variable for outward investments (Horst, 1972) and predicted that a firm's size and its propensity to internationalize are correlated[2].

Findings for Slovenia do not confirm size as a dominant factor in the selection of a foreign entry mode. Internationalization through outward FDI is simply not found solely in the domain of large firms. The analysis of the size structure of Slovenian investors performed in 1997 showed that micro-, small- and medium-sized companies dominated and together represented 65% of companies. Only 15% of all investors have more than 500 employees (see Table 9.1). The size structure of investing companies did not change significantly in 1999. Companies with 500 or more employees still represented only 16%. A significant part, as high as 44%, was represented by medium-sized companies with 51 to 499 employees and, lastly, small and micro companies (each with 20%). These findings are in line with the size structure of the overall Slovenian corporate structure, where small- and medium-sized firms prevail.

Table 9.1 Slovenian firms with outward FDI by size (in per cent)[3]

Company size by no. of employees	1997	1999
Micro (0-9)	22	20
Small (10-50)	22	20
Medium (51-499)	41	44
Big (over 500)	15	16

Source: CIR database.

Although big companies represent the smallest share among investors, they are the most influential and are faster in their international expansion than smaller ones. They have experienced the most rapid growth and expanded their network of foreign affiliates.

Apart from this, one very surprising finding was that the difference in the average value of outward FDI between bigger (medium and big) and smaller (micro and small) companies is relatively small and not statistically significant[4]. On this basis, we therefore cannot say that smaller and bigger companies significantly differ in entry mode choice nor in the volume of their outward direct investments. Outward FDI propensity therefore does not seem completely tied to company size. Despite being limited in their resources, small and medium enterprises are increasingly involved in internationalization, including through outward FDI.

Further qualitative analysis based on surveys, case studies and interviews also did not yield any rule that company size significantly influences the pattern in internationalization, neither in terms of market choice and entry mode selection nor in product selection[5]. The only difference identified was the speed of foreign affiliates' expansion. An additional argument running against the conclusion that company size determines the internationalization pattern lies in experience. Small companies, although young, may employ experienced management especially those established as spin-offs. Management's experiences and knowledge have a significant influences on the internationalization process.

Age

The next most significant internationalization variable is the age of a company. According to theoretical predictions, older, i.e. more experienced firms have a greater propensity to internationalize through outward FDI. Slovenian investing firms confirmed such expectations. In 1999 the surveyed companies were prevailingly older; six per cent had existed for over 60 years, 44 per cent for between 30 and 60 years, 19 per cent for between 10 and 30 years, while less than one-third (31 per cent) were less than 10 years old. The average age was almost 34 years, while the youngest sample company was 6 years old. The age structure in the 2001 sample was very similar (Figure 9.1). Companies established in the pre-transition period largely dominated (70 per cent) and the average age of company was between 35 and 36 years. The youngest sample company was 5 years old, whereas the oldest was 105 years old.

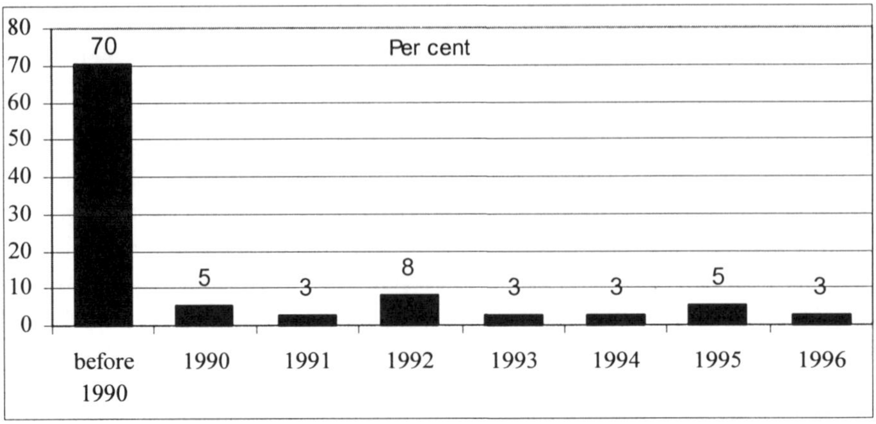

Figure 9.1 Companies with outward FDI by year of establishment (in per cent)

Source: Survey 2001.

These basic parameters indicate that outward investment lies mainly in the domain of older companies established in the previous regime. Companies originating from before the transition period underwent a substantial restructuring process and experienced many changes in their organizational and legal forms. From organizations of associated labour they were transformed into other legal forms comparable with those in developed Europe. Today, the majority of investing companies are organized as joint-stock companies (53 per cent) or as limited liability companies (45 per cent). A small proportion (two per cent) of companies uses other legal forms (for example, different forms of public company).

Age is a very good indicator of experience and knowledge despite the significant changes and restructuring undergone by investing companies and the fact that not all of their operating experience was useful or valuable in the internationalization process. Among the most important reflections of age are branding history, product development and company image, all of which are very important factors in internationalization.

Internationalization experience

Most commonly, companies enter international markets gradually by starting with exports. The aggregate data revealed (see Chapter 7) that the great majority of investing companies (above 80 per cent) gained preliminary international experience by exporting. Many non-exporting firms were established as (disintegrated) parts of the former larger exporting companies, which also reflects export experiences.

According to the surveys all investing companies are exporters. Internationalization is carefully planned; in 1999 as much as 90.7 per cent of sample firms had a developed internationalization strategy, especially as regards advanced entry modes. Companies investing abroad pursue internationalization gradually. They mostly have long experiences with participation in foreign markets, with their export activities in foreign markets on average exceeding 23 years (Survey 1999). Half the sample companies has been actively exporting for more than 20 years. The other half has been present in foreign markets for a shorter time, the majority for about 10 years. The shortest presence abroad was 2 years, while the longest was 97 years.

In the period studied from 1992-1998, the value of exports exceeded the value of imports. Sample companies were very export-oriented; in 1998 they created more than 17 per cent of total exports of all Slovenian companies (and 9 per cent of imports), although in number they represent just 0.8 per cent of the Slovenian corporate sector. Survey 2001 also confirmed the strong export orientation of the sample investors. The average export value increased 2.3 times in the 1997-2000 period. Exports are geographically quite spread out; more than two-thirds of the sample companies exported to over 10 countries. The most important export region is the European Union, followed by the successor states to the former SFRY, other regions, then the CIS and CEECs (see also Chapter 5).

In both surveys, the sample companies rarely mentioned any other market entry strategy than exporting and outward foreign direct investment. As the most frequently used of other foreign business operations they mentioned franchising and licensing. Among others, they cited indirect exporting, exporting through an agency, representative offices, production co-operation, outward processing, and the sale of know-how.

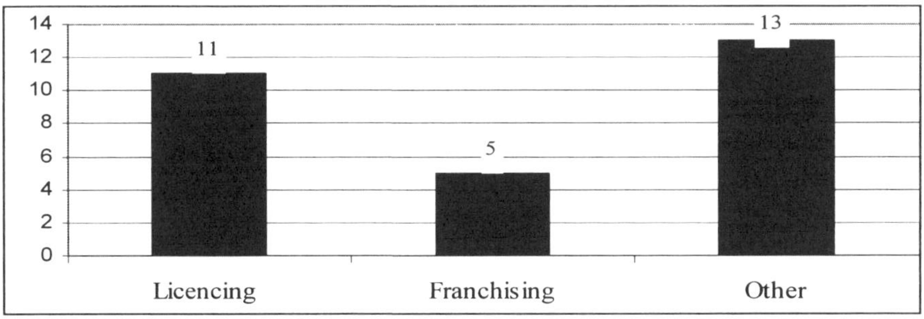

Figure 9.2 Other modes of foreign business operations used by sample firms (in per cent)

Source: Survey 2001.

The reason for the relatively low use of other, contract-based entry modes was not researched. Contractor (1981) found in his study a wide range of motives for such entry modes; the most important was when regulations or political risk were against FDI, while the second motive was when transport or tariff barriers made exporting difficult. In the case of Slovenia none of these factors provide strong incentives.

Another possible reason for the low use of other entry modes is the protection of intellectual property (intangible assets such as patents, copyrights, brand names, trademarks and designs). Intellectual property rights along with knowledge are the principal components of most licensing and franchising agreements, but they can be unlawfully exploited in an environment where the rule of law is inadequately upheld. Yet, the global economy is strengthening intellectual property rights and therefore changing the status of licensing and franchising (Cross, 2000; pp. 403-404). However, the simultaneously reduced barriers to trade and FDI are offering firms with strong intangible assets ever better possibilities for maximizing their returns on such created assets. Slovenian investing firms have a relatively high level of intangible assets since their R&D expenditures and skilled labour intensity are much above the Slovenian average and are also increasing at an above-average rate (Table 9.2). Not surprisingly they prefer outward FDI over other entry modes.

Table 9.2 R&D expenditures as a per cent of sales revenues and the share of university-educated employees as a per cent of all personnel in 1997 and 2000

	N	Minimum	Maximum	Mean	Std. Deviation
R&D 1997	21	0	13.4	3.5	3.8
R&D 2000	24	0	13.9	4.1	3.8
University-educated employees 1997	28	0.7	45.0	12.3	13.3
University-educated employees 2000	30	0	51.5	15.0	15.2

Source: Survey 2001.

In less developed markets (with lower protection of intellectual property rights), Slovenian firms prefer internalized, affiliate transactions between firms than arm's length transactions (see Chapter 5). Weak intellectual property rights encourage investors to engage in outward FDI rather than to use any other contractual form as expected by sequential internationalization. Developed markets with greater intellectual property protection are close and open enough (in terms of transport and tariff barriers) on the other hand to serve them through exports.

The experience of Slovenian investors confirmed the basic assumptions of evolutionary models that knowledge of foreign markets and business operations is an important determinant of the development of one's international operations. The knowledge needed was mainly acquired by doing such operations abroad. This applies to internationalization in the form of a firm's increasing involvement in an individual foreign country as well as the successive establishment of operations in new countries (Johanson and Vahlne, 1977, p. 23). In the internationalization process, firms gradually increase their international involvement by acquiring, integrating and using knowledge about foreign markets and operations. The case studies and interviews showed that the first step in the internationalization process (the first foreign affiliate) is the most difficult. The setting up of following foreign affiliates is usually easier.

Foreign affiliates

Some characteristics such as age and the location of foreign affiliates were described in detail in Chapter 4 (see Figure 4.1) and Chapter 5. Here, we address issues like entry strategy (greenfield or takeover), ownership structure, foreign affiliates' activities, functional orientation and the growth of foreign affiliates.

Ownership structure

The ownership structure of foreign affiliates reveals that Slovenian investors abroad generally want to actively control their investments and participate in the related decision-making process. Slovenian investors are mostly total or majority owners (about 80 per cent). Figure 7 gives evidence of the concentration of Slovenian outward investment according to five groups of ownership shares: portfolio share (less than a 10% share in a foreign affiliate, minority share (10%-49.99%), 50% share, majority share (50.01%-99.99%) and total (100%) share. The ownership structure was analyzed on the basis of the number of outward investments (left side of Figure 9.3) as well as on the basis of the volume of outward investments (right side of Figure 9.3) made in 1997.

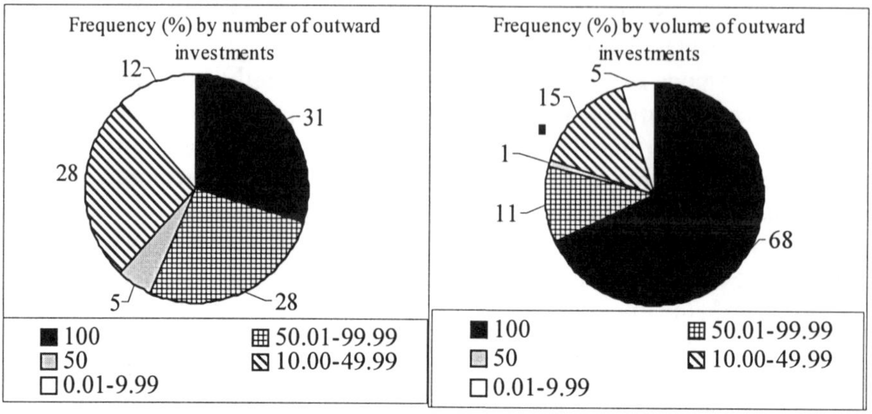

Figure 9.3 Slovenian outward FDI by size of ownership share in 1997

Source: The Bank of Slovenia, CIR database, own calculations.

Concentration is very high if we consider the number of investments, but even higher if we consider the invested volume since more than 82% of direct investment value exists in majority-owned or wholly-owned subsidiaries[6]. Testing with a Gini coefficient revealed a 0.7 concentration (the value ranges between 0 and 1, indicating no or total concentration, respectively).

The survey data confirm foreign affiliates' overall ownership structure. Wholly-owned subsidiaries are the most strongly represented foreign affiliates (Table 9.3), followed by majority-owned affiliates. While the share of wholly-owned affiliates fell, the share of majority-owned affiliates rose.

Table 9.3 Foreign affiliates by ownership structure in 1998 (share of Slovenian investors)

	Total (100%)	Majority (50.1-99.9%)	Half (50%)	Minority (10.0%-49.9%)	Together with a Slovenian partner
Share of foreign affiliates in total (1999), in %	60	22	2	16	5
Share of foreign affiliates in total (2001), in %	48	34	3	15	6

Sources: Survey 1999 and Survey 2001.

Joint ventures are very rare not only with foreign firms but also with other Slovenian companies[7]. The majority of investing companies knew their foreign partner very well before deciding to have a foreign partner. Foreign partners are mostly small in size, and are often private individuals. Partnerships with big and well-known multinational corporations are exceptional[8]. The ownership share of a local partner serves as an incentive for the locals. This helps the investor overcome barriers to and difficulties with establishment, local administration, language problems and marketing.

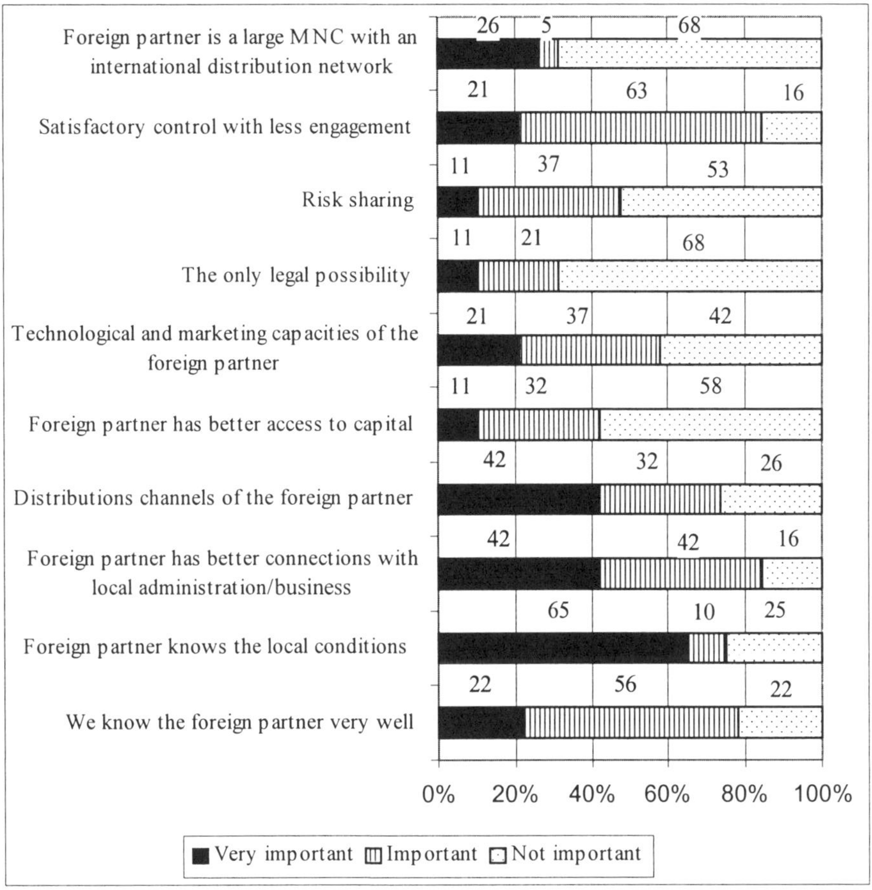

Figure 9.4 Factors influencing decisions to engage a foreign partner

Source: Survey 1999.

The decision to choose a foreign partner is chiefly motivated by the fact that the foreign local partner knows the local conditions (Figure 9.4). The next most important factors influencing a decision for a partnership are the partner's better connections with the local administration and distribution channels.

The last factor is not surprising since many Slovenian companies are aware that whoever 'owns' distribution channels 'owns' the buyers/customers, and consequently 'owns' the market share. Many sample companies evaluated foreign partnership as a form of satisfactory control with less engagement.

A foreign partner's technological and marketing capabilities, its access to capital and the possibility of risk-sharing were less important incentives for choosing a foreign partner. This is probably a reflection of the prevailing geographical concentration of Slovenian outward FDI. Firms in Croatia, BiH, Serbia, Macedonia or some other CEECs rarely have better access to capital or a higher level of technological or marketing knowledge (except where influenced by other inward FDI) than Slovenian firms' headquarters.

The tendency towards majority ownership arises from:

- Long-standing exports to the countries of penetration and good knowledge of the local conditions. Outward FDI has usually followed exports. Rich experience, knowledge of language and culture, and long-lasting business relationships due to historical ties allow Slovenian investors to enter foreign markets independently, without foreign partners.
- The early stage of internationalization; wholly- or majority-owned foreign affiliations show a low level of internationalization.
- The weak rather than strong competitive position of investors. They fear vulnerability due to a lack of control. They are simply still unprepared to co-operate with foreign partners, which could imply an asymmetrical position between them.
- The size of Slovenian investing firms. Most of them are SMEs. It is difficult to enter a partnership when the partners greatly differ in size and consequently in strength and power. Smaller companies can hardly achieve the desired position.
- The wish for control and active decision-making. This includes the control of supplies and conditions of purchase of inputs, a need to protect the quality of intermediate or final products, and the ability to engage in cross-subsidization or transfer pricing.
- The lack of suitable local partners (due to privatization not being finished, for instance).
- Protection of firm-specific assets or ownership advantages in less developed markets where the majority of Slovenian outward investment is concentrated. Competitors might easily profit from their advantages by imitating technology, skills, know-how and new products. Wholly-owned subsidiaries are more convenient to protect intangible assets.
- Lack of experience with M&A. Mergers and/or acquisitions only started within national borders in the second half of the nineties (let alone when

going international) and are yet to become a more common praxis. For smaller firms, M&A are difficult to carry out.

The lack of co-operation with foreign partners or local firms might slow down the inflow of knowledge, experience and information, perception of the current market situation, consumer behaviour and thus prevent adaptation to local needs. In the long run therefore it might become a barrier. Empirical studies have yielded no reliable evidence on the relationship between the ownership structure of foreign affiliations and knowledge (Eriksson, 1997), while several studies (Davidson and McFetridge, 1985; Hedlund and Kverneland, 1985; Millington and Bayliss, 1990; Buckley, Mirza and Sparkes, 1985; Newbould, Buckley and Thurwell, 1978) have indicated that the internationalization of ownership increases with the accumulation of knowledge and experience[9]. The early stage of internationalization of Slovenian firms correspondingly explains why firms prefer hundred-per-cent ownership. It is also expected that the advancement of the internationalization process is likely to bring other forms of business co-operation (joint ventures, mergers, strategic partnerships) parallel to the upgrading of ownership-specific advantages.

Type of establishment

Similar arguments as for ownership structure also apply to the type of establishment where greenfield investments are preferred (Table 9.4). Mergers and acquisitions are relatively exceptional (in about 17 per cent of foreign affiliates), which appears contrary to the prevailing FDI trends seen around the world in general. With increasing knowledge of how to invest abroad, more M&A are expected in the future. Already in the 1998-2000 period the share of M&A had increased. The register at the Ministry of Finance indicated an increasing share of acquisitions among investment announcements made in 2000 and 2001. The beginning of the privatization process in successors to the SFRY has also made M&A more attractive because it has increased the 'supply of potential target companies' for a reasonable price (see Chapter 6). The ownership structure connected with the type of establishment suggests the starting phase of outward FDI.

Table 9.4 Foreign affiliates by type of establishment in 1998 and 2000

	Greenfield	Acquisitions	Mergers
Foreign affiliates as a per cent of total 1998	85.4	11.7	2.9
Foreign affiliates as a per cent of total 2000	79.4	13.8	3.7

Sources: Survey 1999 and Survey 2001.

The majority of foreign affiliates (up to 89 per cent of 2001 sample affiliates) are established as companies with limited liability. About 11 percent of foreign affiliates use the form of a joint-stock company.

The activities of foreign affiliates

Affiliates abroad are most frequently involved in trade, although investors are prevailingly manufacturing firms indicating that the activities of investing firms often differ from the activities of foreign affiliates[10] (see Chapter 5). In 1999, almost two-thirds of foreign affiliates were registered in wholesale and retail trade and repair (Table 9.5). The share of trade affiliates fell slightly up until 2000. Most frequently, affiliates abroad are involved in a single activity, where there are more activities then trade is the second activity. In 2001 approximately 10 per cent of foreign affiliates was involved in trade and manufacturing at the same time. The share of affiliates involved in manufacturing rose from 1998 to 2000 demonstrating progress in the internationalization process. A considerable increase was also found in services; finance and insurance and real estate and other business services.

Table 9.5 Foreign affiliates by activity (as a per cent of all foreign affiliates)[i]

Activities (NACE classification)	1998	2000
Manufacturing industries	11.6	31.8
Wholesale and retail trade, repair services	72.2	69.9
Transport, warehousing, communications	2.9	12.5
Finance, insurance	0.7	2.8
Real estate, business services	2.2	9.7
Other	15.9	14.3

Sources: Survey 1999 and Survey 2001.

Note:

i A foreign affiliate may perform more than one activity, so the total of the percentage shares exceeds 100.

The valid percentage is taken into account.

The functional orientation of foreign affiliates

The functional orientation of foreign affiliates also confirms the sequential internationalization approach. The sales and marketing function is the first to be internationalized. In 1998 as much as 95 per cent of foreign affiliates were related to the sales and marketing function, 56 per cent to the purchasing and logistic function and approximately 50 per cent to the accounting, financial and fiscal function. Affiliates related to the research and development function are very few (Table 9.6).

Table 9.6 The functional orientation of foreign affiliates in 1998

Functional orientation of foreign affiliates	No. of investors transferring the function	No. of affiliates providing the function	As a per cent of all foreign affiliates[i]
Affiliate(s) related to production (production, assembly)	11	15	10.9
Affiliate(s) related to sales and marketing	29	130	94.9
Affiliate(s) related to R&D	2	3	2.2
Affiliate(s) related to administration	11	70	51.1
Affiliate(s) related to purchasing and logistics	14	78	56.9
Affiliate(s) related to accounting, financial and fiscal functions	12	67	48.9

Source: Survey 1999.

Note:
i The combined total of the shares exceeds 100 since each foreign affiliate can perform more than one function.

Survey 2001[11] revealed a similar dominant functional orientation of foreign affiliates, 72.1 per cent of foreign affiliates were related principally to sales and marketing, affiliates related mainly to production represented 9.3 per cent, while affiliates related to other business functions represented 22.6 percent of all foreign affiliates. Among other functions, companies specified R&D (3 per cent), design (3 per cent), setting up and repair (4.1 percent), financial and accounting function, and logistics.

Within more complex MNC systems, functions transferred vary greatly according to locations. Less industrialized locations are assigned simpler tasks like assembly and packaging, while more skill- and technology-intensive functions are allocated to industrially more advanced locations[12]. This is especially valid for industries where MNCs have set up integrated international production systems as part of an intra-firm and international division of labour. The strong centralization of business functions limits the growth possibilities of a firm. New organizational methods (aided by new technologies) allow more efficient management of global operations and encourage a greater relocation of business functions.

In general we can detect the slow progress in the decentralization of business functions among Slovenian MNCs at the end of the nineties. According to the interviews a greater spread of all business functions is however expected in the future. Formerly strongly centralized business functions such as design, R&D and financial management will become increasingly internationalized to optimize costs, efficiency and enhance flexibility. Decentralization of business functions and a flexible organizational structure have become the preconditions of a successful response to market needs and demand for local-customer-adjusted goods and services. The decline in mass production demands the localization of all business functions.

Growth of foreign affiliates

The growth of foreign affiliates has been substantial in recent years, not only in their number but also in terms of their size (see Chapter 4). Several business indicators of foreign affiliates were recorded in our surveys to examine their qualitative growth[13]. The aggregate picture of all foreign affiliates and average affiliate values are presented in Tables 9.7 and 9.8. They confirm not only the numerical growth of foreign affiliates but also growth in terms of the size of the average foreign affiliate, especially significant at the end of the past decade.

Employment increased in the 1992-1998 period, although most affiliates abroad were small and employed fewer than 50 employees. For multinational companies from all transition economies a low level of foreign employment is typical. Since the relocation of production is not common, the internationalization of employment is slower than the internationalization of sales and/or assets[14]. The 1999 Slovenian sample on average showed quite the opposite; foreign employment per affiliate increased considerably while foreign assets and foreign sales revenues per affiliate fell in the 1992-1998 period. Foreign affiliates mostly operated profitably. On average, operating profit was increasing although net sales revenues per affiliate were falling. The average equity value per foreign affiliate also dropped. Foreign affiliates are thus growing in number and employment, yet are falling in their ‘capital size’.

Table 9.7 Selected data on foreign affiliates in 1992-1998[i]

	1992	1995	1998
Employment			
No. of investors that reported data	15	21	27
Total of all employees of foreign affiliates (all sample investors)	1049	1801	2953
Average no. of employees per foreign affiliate	15.6	19.8	21.6
Average no. of employees abroad per investor	42	62	92
Sales			
No. of investors that reported data	11	17	21
Total of all sales of foreign affiliates	661.1	828.7	999.1
Sales per foreign affiliate	9.86	9.11	7.29
Assets			
No. of investors that reported data	10	14	19
Total of all assets of foreign affiliates	263.8	457.2	503.0
Assets per foreign affiliate	3.94	5.03	3.67
Equity			
No. of investors that reported data	12	18	25
Total of all equity of foreign affiliates	68.33	90.16	102.61
Equity per foreign affiliate	1.02	0.99	0.75
Exports			
No. of investors that reported data	6	9	13
Total of all exports of foreign affiliates	110,511	168,547	202,006
Exports per foreign affiliate	1,649	1,852	1,474
Exports as % of sales of foreign affiliate	16.7	20.3	20.2
Imports			
No. of investors that reported data	6	10	16
Total of all imports of foreign affiliates	237.14	284.5	378.2
Imports per foreign affiliate	3.54	3.13	2.76
Profit/loss			
No. of investors that reported data	11	17	22
Total of all profit of foreign affiliates	0.786	1.596	4.788
Profit per foreign affiliate	0.011	0.018	0.035

Source: Survey 1999.

Note:
i Except for employment and figures expressed in per cent, all values are in US$ million.

Foreign affiliates' locations have mostly been chosen to serve a local market and not as a springboard to third markets. More than 80 per cent of 1999 sample affiliates made sales mainly in the local market, while more than 65 per cent of foreign affiliates made sales exclusively in the local market. The average affiliate in 1998 realized about 80 per cent of its sales revenues in the local market. About 15 per cent of foreign affiliates also exported to third (other neighbouring) markets. As a rule, foreign affiliates do not export back to their parent companies in Slovenia[15]. Very rarely they have also exported to CEEC markets or former Soviet Union markets. On average, foreign affiliates realized about 20 per cent of total revenues with exports in 1998. The share of export revenues of foreign affiliates increased from 1992. On average, foreign affiliates were net importers. Outward FDI therefore enhanced the export capacity of the investing (parent) companies (see Chapter 11)[16].

Table 9.8 Selected data on foreign affiliates in 1997 and 2000 (US$ million)

	1997			2000		
	N	Sum – all affiliates	Average per affiliate	N	Sum – all affiliates	Average per affiliate
Fixed assets	59	96	1.62	82	182.56	2.23
Equity capital	59	229	3.88	82	241.81	2.95
No. of employees	57	1826	32	83	3338	40
Sales	56	4711	84.13	78	3012	38.62
Exports	34	3117	91.68	40	2035	50.88
Exports to parent co.	42	2613	62.22	51	1176	23.06
Imports	35	1708	48.80	36	1861	50.70
Imports from parent co.	43	1605	37.32	58	1835	31.64

Note:
N = number of affiliates recorded, Sum = total value for all recorded affiliates.

Source: Survey 2001.

The end of the nineties (1997-2000 period) on average saw further growth of foreign affiliates in terms of employment and in equity and fixed assets (Table 9.8). Due to the substantial rise of new foreign affiliates, average sales and exports per affiliate fell in that period, while imports per affiliate rose.

Summary

The identified characteristics of investors confirm the sequential internationalization pattern of Slovenian firms. Though big and old companies are the fastest and most important players in internationalization, the dominant share of small and medium enterprises of a younger age illustrate the economy's increasing and widening internationalization process. Companies give a strong emphasis to sequential entry to foreign markets. Export experience is very important, outward FDI usually follows and complements exporting, while other entry modes are very rare.

The evolutionary pattern was also confirmed by the foreign affiliates' analysis. Wholly- and majority-owned foreign affiliates established as greenfield ventures dominate. They frequently serve to promote trade and very rarely to relocate production. The end of the decade however witnessed progress in the internationalization process, since it was accompanied by an improvement in most indicators; the internationalization of ownership increased, mergers and acquisitions activity revived and decentralization of business functions continued. Foreign affiliates have experienced substantial growth in recent years not only in their number, but also in their size and functional orientation. These trends are expected to continue.

Notes

1 The official statistics do not keep a track of the foreign affiliates of Slovenian firms. What is recorded is only the number of investments, which does not correspond to affiliate numbers and does not allow one to distinguish between outward investments in newly established affiliates from an investment in an already existing affiliate.
2 These predictions were not always confirmed empirically. There seems to be more support for the notion that exporting is the most favoured entry mode by firms of all sizes.
3 Survey samples were not completely representative in terms of size structure.
4 By comparing the means, we could not confirm the difference between these two groups of companies at the 0.05 level of significance.
5 A small service company with an information technology product for example might start the direction of internationalisation towards West or South-east or both, depending on the niche product (firm-specific advantage) it possesses. The same applies for a big manufacturing company that might combine its firm-specific advantage with a location-specific advantage in different countries. Again this depends largely on the product.
6 This is partly a result of the fact that the size of the share correlates highly with the value, but irrespective of value concentration was clearly confirmed given the number of investments.
7 Such form of co-operation was found only recently in the successors to the SFRY (see Chapter 6).
8 Exceptions are strategic partnerships established before joint ventures or strategic alliances in high-tech industries (see, for example, Box 8.2: Hermes Soft Lab).
9 Research on US direct investments in Europe (Stopford, Wells, 1972, in Eriksson, 1997, p. 342) indicated that three-quarters of US foreign affiliates in Europe were wholly-owned at the beginning.
10 Since the official statistics do not collect data on foreign affiliate activity, but only on the activity of an investor, the survey is the only source of this information. Yet due to the level of missing data the activities of foreign affiliates are only approximations.
11 In Survey 2001, the dominant business function of a foreign affiliate was only noted.
12 A good example among Slovenian investors is Hermes Soft Lab (see Box 8.2) and Prevent (see Chapter 14).
13 Since the sample companies with outward FDI often returned partial answers, an average per foreign affiliate was the only indicator possible to calculate.

14 Foreign employment is most important for keeping the transnationality index of multinational companies from transition economies low. Foreign sales and foreign assets should increase much more quickly. The transnationality index is a composite internationalisation measure – an arithmetic mean that includes foreign sales revenues as a share of total revenues, foreign assets as a share of total assets and foreign employment in total employment (UNCTAD, 1998).

15 In the sample only two such cases were found, but even in these two cases exports to Slovenia represent a small part of total sales.

16 The structure of intra-firm trade revealed that foreign affiliates mostly import final products (see Chapter 11). More than three-quarters of the sample companies exported final products to their foreign affiliates in 1998 (46 per cent of them exported final goods exclusively), almost 22 per cent of investors exported intermediary goods, about 16 per cent raw materials and about 34.4 per cent services.

Chapter 10

Barriers to Internationalization

Introduction

Studies show that, irrespective of the development level of a country and company size, firms usually find the internationalization process difficult and accompanied by many barriers (see OECD, 1997). Expansion of a firm by outward FDI is more demanding than growth within the domestic setting only, as it involves more funds, more demanding management, organization and control. Pioneering steps of internationalization imply additional difficulties which are not uniform, but vary depending on a firm's size, sector and external factors such as industrial structures and the direction of outward FDI.

Although international business experience and accumulated knowledge do reduce barriers, 'born global' companies, newcomers and 'multinationals with some tradition' may face similar problems. In practice, the same factor can be either a strength or a barrier.

The main aim of this chapter is to assess the type, diversity and extent of determinants that prevent the faster internationalization of Slovenian companies. Firstly, by highlighting the conceptual classification of barriers and, secondly, by interpreting the empirical results based on surveys on how Slovenian companies investing abroad themselves evaluate the significance of particular barriers.

Conceptual framework

Barriers can be divided into two groups; external ones (or those originating from the external environment) and internal or those stemming from companies' internal characteristics (see Table 10.1). External barriers include impediments in the home as well as the host economy. This division of barriers is largely in accordance with a company's influence and the possibilities to overcome them. While overcoming internal barriers is mostly within the domain of a firm's management, external ones are often out of their reach and should also be the subject of policy concerns.

Host-country barriers refer to legislation, regulation, especially tariffs and customs regulations, institutions, the political situation, stability and country risk, corruption, immigration restrictions, approval procedures, the cost of establishing a legal entity, the protection of brand names and intellectual property and so on. In principle, these barriers are no different for companies from transition countries than for firms from other economies. However, companies from transition economies with (often) limited ownership-specific advantages are limited in their strategy of market choice. Hence, their alternatives are more limited. Currently, the predominant locations of outward FDI from transition economies (less-developed transition countries) are by definition less stable, less predictable and transparent, and can therefore be regarded as a macroeconomic barrier.

Home-country environment, degree of openness and internationalization can also be barriers to internationalization. The first one is a low level of general development. The development level of financial and capital markets, the level of institutional development – supporting institutions, public administration, transparency, regulation and the liberalization of capital flows, internationalization promotion programmes of the countries concerned significantly influence internationalization through (outward) FDI. Since human resources are an important factor of outward internationalization, the cultural environment, cosmopolitanism, or nationalism have an important impact on managers' attitudes.

External home-country barriers can have a strong impact on the internal company environment. They can create additional *internal barriers*. Several of them are transition-specific. One of the most important is the privatization model. Transition to a market economy depends on successful privatization. Studies on company restructuring demonstrate that privatized companies restructure faster than non-privatized ones. Besides, the speed of the process and the privatization model applied strongly influence corporate governance, decision-making, strategy-setting and a company's efficiency. Corporate governance approaches and corporate control systems are likely to affect the way firms deal with internationalization (Ferner, 1997).

Barriers that typically interrupt the internationalization process within a firm involve management, organization and knowledge. After realizing the ownership advantages (and their transferability), internationalization at first instance is a managerial and organizational challenge. The most frequently cited problems during the internationalization process identified in the case studies representing international business praxis involve the (de)centralization of business functions, organizational structure, organizational climate and culture, and international human resource management.

Table 10.1 Barriers to outward internationalization

INTERNAL	EXTERNAL
ADVANTAGE TYPES	HOME-COUNTRY ENVIRONMENT
Lack of advantage	Cultural
Non-transferability of advantages	Attitude of managers, cosmopolitanism
Non-adaptable product	Structural
	Legal system: foreign exchange law
	Privatization model
CORPORATE GOVERNANCE	Competition
Decision-making process	Underdeveloped supporting institutions
Risk aversion	Underdeveloped financial and capital markets
Ownership structure	No promotion policies
Lack of a global strategy/mindset	Economic
	Low degree of internationalization (level of inward FDI)
ORGANIZATIONAL PROBLEMS	Structure of industry
(In)efficiency	
Organizational structure	
(De)centralization of business functions	HOST-COUNTRY ENVIRONMENT
	Structural
Organizational culture & climate	Political instability
	Underdeveloped legal system (company law, competition, tax & accounting, labour, intellectual property, advertising, double taxation agreements)
FINANCIAL SOURCES	
(Un)availability	Rigid, inefficient institutions (non-existence of institutions)
High cost	
	Underdeveloped financial system and distribution system
HUMAN RESOURCES	
National-oriented attitude	Corruption
Lack of skilled labour	Trade & investment
Lack of international management knowledge	Tariff barriers, customs duties
	Non-tariff barriers: administrative standards, investment barriers, administrative procedures
Lack of knowledge of foreign languages	Foreign entry barriers
	Approval procedures, cost of establishing legal entity
	Cultural
	Different languages, history, religion, education, climate, life styles, tastes, habits

The studies show that companies frequently found internal barriers more difficult to overcome than external barriers[1]. It is often hard to decide what to keep and what to change within a company. Overcoming internal barriers usually significantly determines the speed and success of the internationalization process. Especially since host-country barriers are similar for all competitors in a potential market.

Empirical evaluation of barriers to outward FDI by Slovenian companies

The barriers to internationalization were evaluated on two samples of Slovenian companies that involve outward FDI. The structure of both questionnaires followed the conceptual framework presented, although the samples (about 80 per cent of companies are the same in both samples), formulation of questions and scale of grades were not completely identical.

Barriers to internationalization vary according to different variables such as host markets, a firm's size, industry etc. that create specific barriers. We analyze barriers to Slovenian enterprises in general, neglecting a firm's characteristics (size, industry, market concentration) or host-country characteristics (Table 10.2). Companies were asked to rank a given set of barriers according to their importance. The interpretation of results is supplemented by answers to open-type questions and interviews with managers.

The first survey (1999) mainly included manufacturing companies (68 per cent, 31 per cent in services) that are predominantly old i.e. experienced (the average age is above 33 years, 50 per cent of firms are older than 30 years, 30 per cent are less than ten years[2]) and bigger companies. Also similar were the characteristics of sample companies in the second survey (2001), prevalent companies were older (70 per cent were established before Slovenia's independence, the average age was about 35 years), mostly bigger (medium-sized and big) and mainly manufacturing firms (62 per cent).

The common feature of firms' evaluations of the barriers in the 1999 survey is consistent with theory and international praxis; internal barriers play a more important role than external barriers.

The biggest barriers to internationalization (as stated in an open-type question) were a lack of experience, high risks and a lack of knowledge and information on how to invest abroad. Companies lack knowledge of administrative procedures as well as international business operations, foreign market entry, international marketing and international management. General economic instability, systemic changes and the legal regulation of some former Yugoslav republics were mentioned as less important barriers.

The ranking of impediments was similar when companies assessed the importance of particular impediments stated in the questionnaire (see Table 10.2). Lack of personnel able to undertake outward investment was estimated as the most important impediment followed by high risk, difficulties with insurance (reinsurance), and a lack of both information and knowledge.

Table 10.2 The importance of individual barriers to outward FDI (in per cent)

	Very important	Important	Not important
Cultural differences	3.2	32.3	64.5
Nationalist attitudes of customers, public authorities	6.7	26.7	66.7
Corruption in the host country	10.0	46.7	43.3
Low margins, setting price	10.0	66.7	23.3
Lack of help of Slovenian diplomatic mission	13.8	48.3	37.9
Limited control possibilities	16.1	54.9	29.0
First contact with foreign companies	18.8	34.4	46.9
Unfavourable legislation/climate in Slovenia	19.4	35.5	45.2
Unfavourable legislation/climate in host country	23.3	56.7	20.0
Lack of governmental help	25.0	46.9	28.1
Delivery and distribution problems	26.7	46.7	26.7
Lack of own funds	30.0	36.7	33.3
Lack of access to/high price of financing	31.0	34.5	34.5
Lack of knowledge	32.3	41.9	25.8
Lack of co-financing	34.4	31.3	34.4
Lack of information	35.5	54.8	9.7
Difficulties with insurance/reinsurance	46.7	26.7	26.7
High risk	48.4	41.9	9.7
Lack of personnel	51.6	45.2	3.2

Source: Survey on Outward FDI of Slovenian Companies, June to October 1999.

Not surprisingly, the lack of personnel is at the forefront of *internal barriers*. International human resources management is almost unknown, undeveloped and not used. Even top Slovenian multinational companies often carry out ad hoc international human resource management. Internationalization is knowledge-intensive and calls for extensive international business related training. Formal business education available in Slovenia has not given enough attention to holistic internationalization issues. Lack of international experience is also one of the highest barriers.

Lack of knowledge and experience remained a significant barrier in spite of the considerable experience of managers gained as part of the sequential internationalization pattern. Most sample firms namely first entered foreign markets by exporting (94 per cent), 40 per cent did so through industrial co-production arrangements, nine per cent through licence agreements and 12 per cent through other forms, including investing abroad. This clearly indicates that firms have followed a certain stage development and have not leapfrogged within the gradual internationalization process by starting with investing abroad for instance. Only recently have we observed firms that were in fact 'born globals', for whom investing abroad is their first international operation. Here, the experience of managers is even more important.

The long experience of most of the respondent firms is also reflected in their training records (Table 10.3). Out of 29 firms that responded to this question, almost 50 per cent have already participated in a specialized programme on internationalization. Also impressive is their record in terms of international experiences in terms of both training and experiences abroad. In spite of such impressive records, they all point to the need for additional training on internationalization issues.

Table 10.3 Training and other experiences of managers

Question	Yes (%)
1. Have you ever attended an internationalization course?	48.4
2. Have you ever lived abroad?	25.8
3. Have you been educated abroad?	61.3
4. Have you been employed abroad?	38.7
5. Do you need additional training in internationalization?	93.5

Source: Survey 2000.

Note: Valid N = 31.

The survey results really exceeded our expectations, including their knowledge of foreign languages. The results showed (Table 10.4) that the average manager in the sample speaks at least two foreign languages. Almost all speak English, followed by Croatian/Serb and German. Very few speak Russian, which is a consequence of the fact that Russian is rarely taught in Slovenian schools. Today, it is becoming a barrier to doing business with Russia or the CIS.

Our results are in line with Walsh and Whelan's finding (2000) that privatized companies with experience in Western markets exceed in every respect the performance of companies operating in ex-socialist markets. Competition pressures in developed markets have forced them to improve their performance. Training and experience in internationalization cannot guarantee results but can minimize failures. Only learning-by-doing might prove to be too expensive, although it is a necessary tool for upgrading formal training.

Table 10.4 Knowledge of foreign languages

	Frequency	%
English	29	93.5
German	23	74.2
Italian	13	41.9
French	8	25.8
Spanish	2	6.5
Russian	5	16.1
Croatian/Serbian	24	77.4

Source: Own survey 2000.

Note: Valid N = 31, Missing = 1.

Companies also lacked funds; either they did not have easy access to outside finance or the costs (interest rates) were too high. A lack of financial resources for operations abroad used to be the most important barriers for CMEA countries (McMillan, 1987; p. 63). Despite losing its importance among several other barriers, it remains a serious hurdle for Slovenian companies, especially smaller ones. It is typical of the Slovenian banking sector that short-term deposits strongly outweigh long-term deposits (Bole, 1999). Consequently, long-term financial sources from Slovenian banks are limited and relatively expensive. For small and medium enterprises they are in fact inaccessible.

Besides a shallow money market, the capital market in Slovenia is still undeveloped. It is ineffective, small, affected by insider-trading and limited liquidity. With the chosen voucher privatization model, it was the secondary market that (artificially) developed first and not the primary market as is usual in capitalist market economies. The primary capital market has actually remained undeveloped and new share capital is rarely raised in Slovenia.

Thus, both main sources of external finance – the capital and the money market – limit the financial possibilities of firms in Slovenia. Companies have to rely on their own resources (see Table 10.5). Research studies of Slovenian firms show that their investment activity is mainly limited to sources gained within companies (Domadenik et al., 2000; p. 63) and the same applies for investments abroad. Outward direct investment capability depends on internal financial funds. Given the current external financial possibilities, internal funds are also the cheapest financial source. In particular, that involves the equity capital of non-active owners that is available in the context of dispersed ownership and the existing inefficient corporate governance in Slovenian companies (Cirman and Koniè, 2000; p. 93).

Table 10.5 Financing outward investments

Source of finance	% of sample companies
Own funds	67.6
Retained earnings	37.8
Bank loans	45.9
Loans/refinancing through export promotion agencies	21.6
Issuing securities	16.2
Other	2.7

Source: Survey 2001.

Since outward investment is largely financed with own funds this could pose a barrier for SMEs and firms that do not have enough of their own funds and/or when loans are expensive, like in Slovenia. In fact, firms can get loans abroad but SMEs or newly-established firms do not have strong enough creditworthiness to be able to raise such funds internationally. Raising capital in foreign capital markets or money markets is also not very common for bigger Slovenian firms. The survey results also showed that the lack of financing is a significantly greater barrier for companies without foreign capital than for foreign-owned companies that have better access to financial sources. The structure of capital sources within companies has only recently been approaching the capital structure typical of developed markets.

In evaluating *external barriers*, companies firstly assessed governmental support as insufficient. Legislation and the general climate at home and in the host country were also considered unfriendly. As regards *home-country barriers*, one of the most important was the slow privatization that seriously held back the internationalization of companies, especially during the early years of transition. The privatization model chosen did not bring about the capital necessary for the restructuring and further expansion of companies. Besides, it left behind very ineffective corporate governance[3]. The heritage of socialism; limited integration into the international economy, lack of experience in international markets, and the lack of specialization made the barriers to firms from transition economies very specific. All of this can be treated as external home barriers to outward FDI from the firm's point of view.

Among host-country barriers, the most important in the first survey was instability and high political and economic risk. The majority of Slovenian outward FDI is, namely, located in the ex Yugoslav republics. Host-country legislation, in fact the lack of a legal framework, and slow administrative procedures were also assessed as unfriendly, while the unfinished privatization process de-stimulated outward FDI.

Corruption in a host country was declared a relatively less important obstacle to outward investment, although Croatia, which is the most important receiver of Slovenian outward FDI, was regarded as quite a corrupt country (see Feige and Ott, 2000). One explanation for this view is that companies dislike discussing this issue, and/or have developed a capacity to handle it.

The least important investment impediments were assessed as being cultural differences and the nationalist attitudes of customers and public authorities, which is certainly a reflection of the concentration of Slovenian outward FDI in Croatia and, lately, also in Bosnia and Herzegovina. Attitudes of customers and public authorities and the general cultural vicinity to former Yugoslav markets are well known to Slovenian managers and do not represent a barrier. This and the initial stage of internationalization through outward FDI are the reasons why cultural differences are not considered important compared to many other barriers. In contrast, case studies of global/multinational companies place this issue among the top barriers. Cultural barriers will become of greater importance when more distant locations and increasing numbers of business functions move abroad (especially the production function). The former and the latter are not yet highly spread among Slovenian companies with outward FDI.

Two years later, in the 2001 survey[4], the most important change compared to the 1999 survey was the perception of external barriers (Table10.6). On one hand, host-country specific factors substantially gained in importance in 2001 in comparison to the 1999 ranking, while home-country-specific factors were treated as much less important than in 1999. Internal barriers that were tested such as lack of personnel, information and financing retained their importance. The somewhat different methodology and particularly the upswing of outward FDI in much more risky and unstable former Yugoslav republics explains some of the differences in weighting the different barriers to internationalization. Another explanation is the low diversification of the sample firms' outward investments.

Table 10.6 Difficulties in investing abroad

	N Valid	Mean	Mode	Std. Dev	Min.	Max.
Host-country specifics	36	3.75	5.00	1.16	1	5
Lack of personnel	37	3.54	4.00	1.07	1	5
Lack of financing	37	3.08	3.00	1.32	1	5
Lack of information	37	3.03	3.00	0.99	1	5
Home-country specifics	37	2.81	2.00	0.91	1	5

Source: Survey 2001. Classification of firms.

Note: 1 = not important, 5 = very important.

The differences noted in ranking reflect changes that occurred. The home-country environment, especially government orientation and institutional services in this field, have improved. Programmes for stimulating outward internationalization were introduced in 2000 and 2001 (see Chapter 20). In the future, Slovenian investors may face a new barrier, a current account surplus with each state in the region of former Yugoslavia, which will trigger off a restrictive (protectionist) macroeconomic response to balance the trade and current accounts etc. Although such a policy could limit further exports to these markets, it may enhance Slovenian investments. By investing, firms gain local status and thereby circumvent many of the restrictions. A less friendly environment for Slovenian outward FDI could be created, even involving anti-Slovenian sentiments, since they contributed a significant share of total FDI stock in respective countries and particularly in the privatization of local firms. It could create hostility since all privatizations are very sensitive from a nationalist point of view. They are also not so equitable as the general public imagined.

Summary

Slovenian companies face many barriers in their outward internationalization. Transition on one hand has accelerated the process of outward internationalization but, at the same time, introduced several barriers which are transition-specific. Many of them arise from the privatization model chosen, the slow progress of privatization or are a legacy of the former socialist system. They especially influence the efficiency of corporate governance, decision-making processes and readiness to take on risk. Even without them, internationalization through outward FDI is considered a difficult process and accompanied by many barriers, particularly for newcomer outward investors. Companies from transition economies therefore face additional barriers and greater challenges in coping with international competition and than, for instance, competing OECD firms.

In general, internal barriers were evaluated as being more important than external barriers in 1999. After the increase of outward investment in the states of former Yugoslavia, host-country-specific factors in the 2001 survey became quite understandable since those countries are still unstable, risky, and more impeding, while home-country factors are less hindering. Despite the strong significance of external barriers, the most important one is the awareness that companies should concentrate on internal barriers. These are the only ones that can be reduced by the management of a firm itself and are therefore the first key to success. The most evident is the need for skilled personnel and knowledge, international experience, information and a somewhat more risk-accepting attitude. The relatively high quality of life in Slovenia makes even higher wages as an incentive to go abroad ineffective. Companies can hardly find more experienced experts willing to go abroad for a few years. The high rate of employed women who do not want to discontinue their professional careers adds to this limitation. In short, in the long run human capital seems to be the biggest barrier to internationalization.

Notes

1 See, for example, the S.A. Chupa Chups; managing international expansion case study, written by S. Kilfoyle, 1996.

2 Although the average age is high, the beginning of the nineties brought about substantial changes and the restructuring of firms. Therefore, the formal age of a company is greater than the real age of these restructured 'new' old firms.

3 See more on the corporate governance of Slovenian firms in Gregorič, Prašnikar, Ribnikar, 2000, and Simoneti et al., 2001.

4 The barriers were tested within larger groups; namely home-country-specific factors and host-country-specific factors (as external factors), and three internal barriers – lack of personnel, lack of information and lack of financing. A five-grade scale was used in assessing the importance of a particular barrier.

Chapter 11

Effects of Outward Investment

Introduction

Unlike the impacts of FDI on a host country that have attracted much research[1], the home-country effects of outward FDI have received much less attention, both empirically and theoretically[2]. Small countries' aspects have been particularly neglected[3], one reason being that the modest volume of outward FDI makes it difficult to identify the direct impacts of such flows in the short run. In any case, the effects of outward FDI take place only after a certain time has elapsed and after a certain volume threshold has been reached, as generally applies to any investment. It is much easier to detect impacts of such investment at the firm level, whereas sectoral and macroeconomic effects are more difficult not only to detect but especially to distinguish from several other influences.

Particularly relevant impacts of outward FDI from the transition economies' point of view are those of restructuring, growth and development in general. Restructuring and the development impact of outward FDI on a home country and parent firm involve many aspects. The most frequently mentioned are effects on trade and competitiveness, domestic production and employment. Other aspects relate to the impact on technology, industrial structure, the structure of production, government revenue (tax effects), portfolio diversification (and risk reduction) and other socio-political impacts of all FDI linkages[4]. Generally, FDI theories along with the new trade theories predict positive net effects of outward FDI. The same also arises from internationalization theories. The results of empirical studies vary somewhat, but the authors agree that they are difficult to measure econometrically. The lack of any detailed data makes it difficult or even impossible to make any solid generalizations.

Public opinion and trade unions on the other hand often see outward FDI merely as an outflow of capital, which reduces the wealth of the home country and increases domestic unemployment by exporting jobs. The relatively hostile opinion encountered at the beginning of the nineties in Slovenia (Svetlièiè et al., 1994, see also Chapter 4) has recently, along with the emerging success of certain Slovenian multinational companies, been replaced by a more neutral and approving body of opinion that regards a firm's success abroad as more of a national success.

In Slovenia, larger outward investments have occurred only in the last two years which is too short a time to assess their macroeconomic impact, particularly in view of the still modest value of such flows. Such deficiencies seriously hamper the empirical analysis. Therefore, we will evaluate the effects of outward FDI mostly at the firm level based on firms' own perceptions. Since the trade effect on the investing (parent) firm proved to be the most important one, the link between exports and outward foreign direct investment will be specially emphasised. In spite of these difficulties, we shall nevertheless also attempt to shortly evaluate the development impact of outward FDI and externalities on the national economy.

Effects of outward FDI on investing firms

The experience of Slovenian direct investors abroad is generally good, which provides a sound basis for the continuing intensification of internationalization. According to Survey 1999, 85 per cent of sample companies assessed the success of outward FDI to have been in line with their expectations, while for 10 per cent the results even outperformed their expectations. Only 6 per cent were negatively surprised (Figure 11.1). The results were somewhat less enthusiastic two years later (Survey 2001), which may easily be explained by the many new investments made in successors to the SFRY in that period, which cannot yet yield results and are by definition more risky as they involve a region that features uncertainty. Nevertheless, even for the great majority of these investors in an unstable and unpredictable environment the outcome of outward FDI is still in line with their expectations. However, in this survey no investor found outward FDI to have been more successful than expected, while 19 per cent realized a less successful outcome than expected.

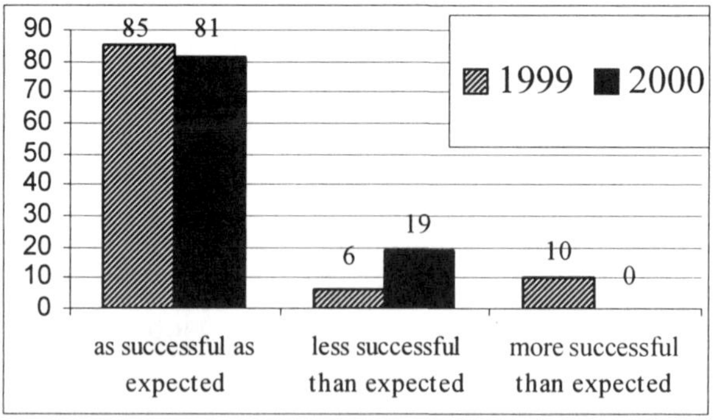

Figure 11.1 The success of outward FDI (percentage of investing firms)

Source: Surveys 1999 and 2001.

From the policy point of view, it is crucial to understand why some investors produced results that were below their expectations. The failure of outward FDI was most commonly attributed to failures of management; particularly an unsuitable choice of personnel and a lack of information. This is

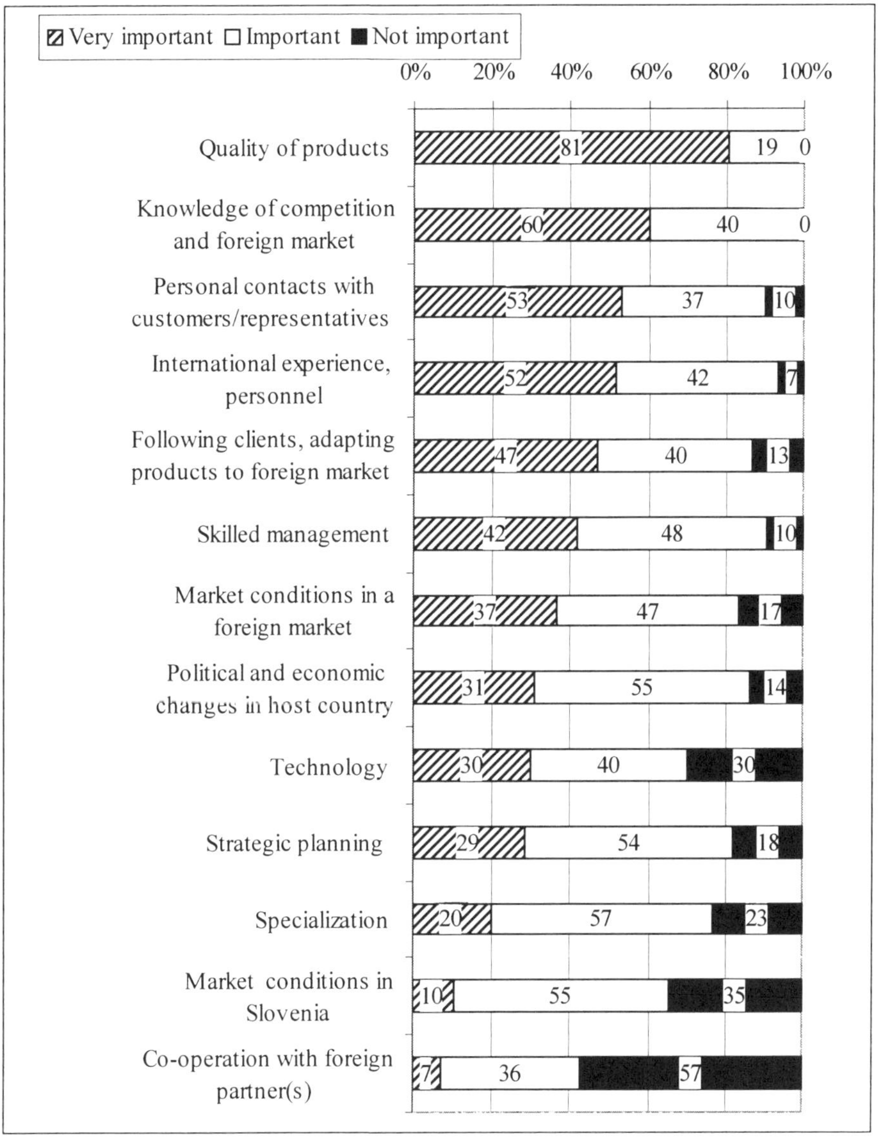

Figure 11.2 Factors influencing the success of outward FDI

Source: Survey 1999.

encouraging since such deficiencies are not too difficult to overcome. The lack of capital (in the case of SMEs) and an unfavourable political climate or unforeseen political changes were indicated as the two following barriers or reasons why some outward FDI failed.

For Slovenian firms the key determinants of outward FDI's success (ranked by importance) are ownership-specific advantages that create non-price competitiveness, i.e. the quality of products, knowledge about the competition and foreign markets, personal contacts, international experience, skilled personnel, especially management (see Figure 11.2). The common denominator of all these factors is their human resource or skill intensity. Skills and knowledge have proved to be the most important precondition for the success of outward investments.

Apart from these firm-specific factors, location-specific determinants like foreign market conditions and political and economic changes in a host country (i.e.) have also played an important role. The role of co-operation with foreign partner(s) has been relatively less important for a foreign investment's success[5]. The investor's ownership-specific advantages cannot be substituted by a partner's advantages. The partner can only enhance and complement them.

The effects of outward FDI on parent companies largely reflect the initial motives for such an investment that also explains the high degree of realization of expectations. The success of an investment basically corresponds with the expectations; investors have mostly realized what they wanted when they started the investment. As a reflection of the prevailing market-seeking-motivated investment (see Chapter 8) also supported by case studies (Chapters 12-19), sample firms in both of our surveys particularly stressed the trade and competitiveness effects (see Figure 11.3 and Table 11.1). The effects on improving strategic assets, like a better international image and higher quality, increased product variety and efficiency, that were motivated by strategic-asset-seeking and efficiency-seeking aims follow as the second most important group of impacts. In line with the finding that resource-seeking investments were considered the least important, most companies investing abroad have not improved their access to cheaper imports (inputs) due to outward investment, while the employment effect was also not significant. Lower labour costs are obviously not among the biggest considerations when firms start investing abroad. This came as a certain surprise given the high share of the textiles and footwear industry that remains in Slovenia.

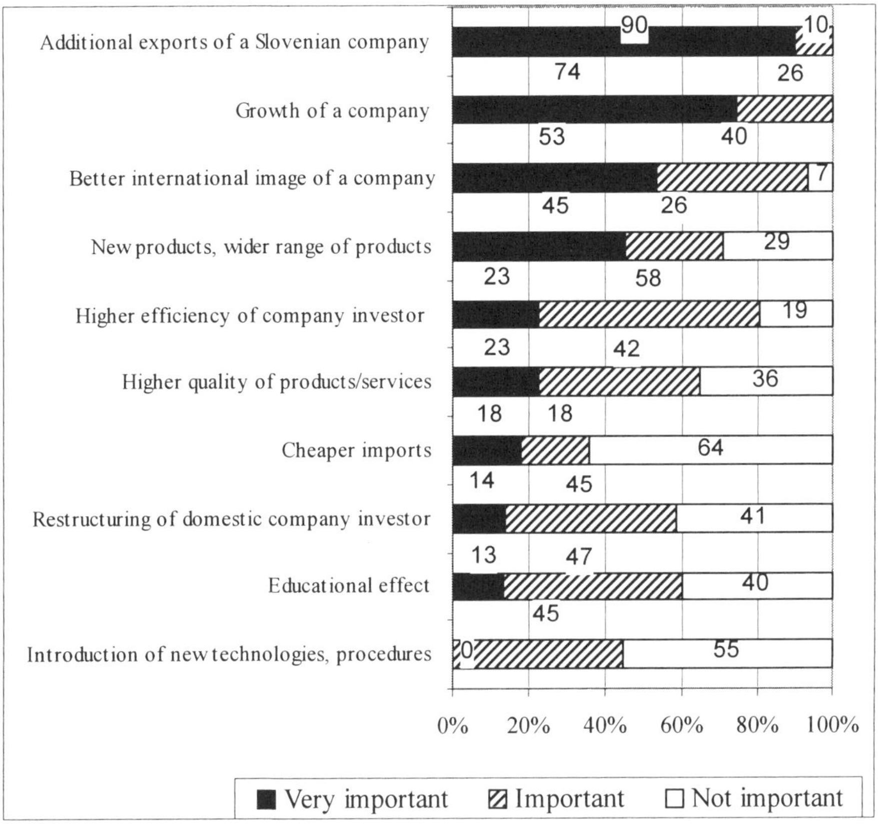

Figure 11.3 The importance of outward FDI's effects on a parent company

Source: Survey 1999.

Table 11.1 Effects of foreign affiliates on the parent company (per cent of investors)

Effects on ...	Strong increase	Increase	Unchanged	Decrease	Strong decrease
Market share	26	53	18	3	0
No. of employees	0	24	59	12	6
Exports	9	74	18	0	0
Imports	0	29	53	6	12
Production volume	9	68	24	0	0

Source: Survey 2001.

Trade, competitiveness and home production effects

The net impact of outward FDI on trade is the result of many complex and interrelated phenomena; changes in exports, imports, the international division of labour, competition and market structure. The issue of the interlinkage between trade and FDI has been discussed in several theories[6] and often empirically studied. While Mundel's model (1957), once the assumption of limited factor mobility was loosened, regarded trade and investments as substitutes, subsequent theoretical and empirical work has clearly established that viewing investment and trade as substitutes (anchored in narrow assumptions of the neoclassical framework) is unrealistic. In the mid-80s, Markusen described these relationships consensually as complementary; 'Trade in factors as well as trade in goods may be necessary to exhaust the gains from trade and introducing factor trade may increase the volume of commodity trade in a wide variety of circumstances. In both welfare and in a volume of trade sense, trade in goods and factors may be complements' (1997, p. 1).

Empirical evidence and the theory now prevailingly support a complementary relationship between outward FDI and exports, although it has not been agreed yet how this causality works – does outward FDI depend on exports or does the opposite apply? In the past, outward FDI used to be most frequently the dependent variable since it chronologically followed exports (see Vernon, 1966). Today, exports have more frequently started to be regarded as a dependant variable and the result of investing abroad is often a strong additional push for exports to the destination country/partner depending of course on the type of investment and industry. The transfer of production facilities abroad could reduce domestic sales as well as exports (if exports of inputs do not increase) and stimulate a substitute relationship, while trade-oriented outward FDI might support exports and develop a complementary relationship. The new theories of trade, that introduced product differentiation and economies of scale into the issue of multinational companies and international trade (Krugman 1983; Helpman 1985), explain that a substitutive or complementary relationship between outward FDI and trade is not defined a priori, but depends on a number of additional presumptions (vertical or horizontal FDI, income level of a host country, the type of intra-firm transactions).

For Slovenia, by far the most important effects of outward FDI have been the increase of exports and foreign market shares. Seventy-nine per cent of investing companies increased their foreign market share(s) and 83 per cent increased their exports. Such substantial effects on exports were anticipated since almost 40 per cent of all exports from the Slovenian corporate sector provided firms with outward FDI (see Chapter 7).

To a large extent this was the result of substantially increased intra-firm trade. From 1992 to 1998, intra-firm exports doubled on average and amounted to 28 per cent of total exports. The modest impact on imports, on the other hand, also indicates that Slovenian investors abroad are not motivated by lower costs abroad. Most investments abroad did not have any impact on imports whatsoever; imports remained the same in 53 per cent of cases. When it did happen, intra-firm imports increased only modestly. Foreign affiliates have therefore not been a significant vehicle for gaining access to cheaper inputs. Foreign affiliates were on average net importers, mostly sourcing domestic market goods. Their sales were also realized in the local market. Sales units, which dominate among foreign affiliates, operate as export promoters (see also Chapter 9). Outward FDI therefore enhanced the export capacity and positive trade balance of the parent companies which has already started to be a problem in some countries where regular trade has by now created huge trade surpluses (see Mrak et al., 2001).

Table 11.2 Intra-firm trade 1992-1998

	1992	1995	1998
Intra-export (as a per cent of total exports)	14.6	23.3	28.2
Intra-import (as a per cent of total imports)	7.8	10.3	13.6

Source: Survey 1999.

The structure of intra-firm trade revealed that foreign affiliates mostly import final products from their parents (Table 11.3). 46 per cent of them exported exclusively final goods. Imports from foreign affiliates to investors were smaller and also increased more slowly in the period studied.

Table 11.3 The structure of intra-firm trade in 1998

	Raw materials	Semi-manufactures	Finished products	Other (services, knowledge)
INTRA-FIRM EXPORTS				
% of investors	15.6	21.9	78.1	34.4
INTRA-FIRM IMPORTS				
% of investors	15.6	3.1	25.0	12.5

Source: Survey 1999.

Note: The average share by end-use of products.

Since the main result of outward FDI in a parent company was induced exports of mainly final products, exports and outward FDI do not seem to be substitutes but complementary. There are few investments aimed at least partly at substituting earlier exports with local production as predicted by the theory of the product life cycle. The structure of intra-firm trade showed that the production process is still mostly kept in the parent firms.

Among advantages of the investment entry mode over the export mode, the vicinity to customers, adaptation to local market, personal 'touch' and contacts with local authorities and administration that make export operations easier proved to be the most important. Factors like possibilities of avoiding high entry costs, cheaper local labour and materials, getting subsidies, tax exemptions etc. to start up operations etc. were less important. Eighty-four per cent of investors claimed customer feedback had improved as a result of foreign affiliates' activities, and 60 per cent increased the number of products (production range). Consequently, the production volume of parent companies (in size and variety) increased after establishing foreign affiliates (for 77 per cent of investors). With the improved access to foreign markets investing firms produce more output, which pushes down their average cost and also improves cost competitiveness. Thus, outward FDI has created economies of scale for home production and increased efficiency, even though most investment was not the efficiency-seeking type (see Chapter 8). The increased efficiency seen was more the result of scale economies, rationalizing and competitive pressures.

In the case of production-oriented foreign affiliates, the most expected effect on a parent firm following the theory could have been a relocation. Firstly, since it can reduce domestic production and consequently reduce the export of final goods. As a consequence, the foreign trade structure changes (lower exports of final products and more exports of intermediary products, services and knowledge) which is instrumental for parent firms' efforts to restructure in the direction of higher value-added activities (restructuring impact). According to the interviews and survey, existing production affiliates have not (yet) influenced home production, but have above all been a way to raise foreign sales mostly by establishing sales affiliates. Production facilities at this stage were established mainly as an instrument of growth and diversification of a company's activities and less as the relocation of production to cheaper locations. They mostly complement existing home production facilities, especially when local conditions improve competitiveness. No respondent company reduced the level of its production as a result of outward FDI. Greater changes and reorganization is expected with the advancement of internationalization, when investments could become more efficiency- than market-seeking.

However, the complementary relationship between outward FDI and exports can also run in the other direction; that is, an increase in exports may lead to an increase in outward FDI. For instance, after increased exports have established a certain level of demand for a product in a foreign market, firms may decide to invest abroad in order to retain and secure a stable level of demand in that market (Kim et al., 1997; p. 41). Investment in the successors to the SFRY certainly had such a character since sales (and later exports) there were big enough to guarantee a stable level of demand. Also similar was the situation in other CEECs and CIS, where local production at lower prices filled the growing local (and neighbouring countries') demand. On the basis of such arguments, outward investment can also be expected in the future in the important current export markets, especially if we take into account the future investment plans of Slovenian exporters. Exports (at least exports of final products) are expected to drop in the long run, or at least increase at slower rates.

Since export growth was evaluated as the most significant impact on the investing (parent) firm, the linkage between exports and outward foreign direct investment was also analyzed at the aggregate level (for all exporting Slovenian outward investors). The relationship between exports and outward FDI was analyzed on the basis of regression analysis[7], firstly within the same year and, secondly, with a one-year time lag for outward FDI to test the proposition that an increase in exports comes about a year later. The unavailability of data made it impossible to test for any longer time lag.

The regression coefficients were positive and statistically significant, proving a complementary relationship, albeit the values were low (see Table 11.4).

Outward FDI has obviously not substituted exports but served as a complementary foreign market penetration mode.

Table 11.4 Results of the linearized regression equation/model

Model	1997		1998 (one-year time lag)	
	Coeff.	Std. Error	Coeff.	Std. Error
Constant	4.33[i]	1.54	4.06[i]	1.48
LnASS	-0.25[i]	0.08	-0.10	0.08
LnCOST	0.89[i]	0.10	0.86[i]	0.10
LnEMP	0.16	0.19	-0.06	0.17
ln(FDI/ASS)	0.09[iii]	0.05	0.12[ii]	0.05
ACT1(trade)	-1.75[i]	0.28	-1.95[i]	0.27
ACT2 (other)	-1.48[i]	0.24	-1.58[i]	0.24
SIZ1 (micro)	-1.20	0.95	-1.22	0.87
SIZ2 (small)	-0.98	0.62	-1.26[ii]	0.57
SIZ3 (medium)	-0.83[ii]	0.36	-0.94[i]	0.34
N	285		274	
R^2	0.64		0.64	

Source: Calculations made on the basis of data from the Bank of Slovenia and AP.

Notes:

See the explanation of the variables in endnote 7! Data for 1997 used in all equations.

i Coefficient is statistically significant at the level of 0.01.

ii A 5% significance level.

iii A 10% significance level.

Otherwise, the coefficient is not statistically significant.

Asset creation, learning effects and technology transfer

In the knowledge economy which has become the major long-term development objective of all countries including Slovenia, the impacts of outward FDI on asset creation, learning effects and knowledge and technology transfer are becoming the most important. A better international image of the parent company (i.e. the creation of an intangible asset) was regarded as an important consideration when investing abroad (Figure 11.3). The image of being or becoming a multinational company helped them in improving sales opportunities (in foreign and domestic markets) and in stabilizing sales revenues. Companies gained valuable market information and improved the ability and speed to respond to customers' needs. Better sales possibilities and an improved image resulted in a better financial position and greater solvency. In Survey 2001 up to 90 per cent of investors evaluated that outward FDI had contributed positively to the parent company's financial position (although financing investments abroad is a financial burden). This often also resulted in a better credit rating.

As a result of outward FDI, the majority of sample companies introduced new products, adaptations or a wider range of products as well as improved their quality (Figure 11.3). These reflect the ability of investors to differentiate their product and adapt it to local tastes and needs. The improved quality of products and services is a sign of technological restructuring. According to the interviews, many firms increased investments in R&D for process, product and quality improvement simply as a result of a direct presence in a foreign market (see Table 9.2). International competition thus motivated a parent company to strengthen its firm-specific advantages by investing abroad. This confirms Dunning and Narula's thesis that today companies invest abroad not only to utilize the existing advantages but also to strengthen or even obtain them. Nowadays, firms start investing abroad not only because they possess firm-specific advantages but also 'from a position of weakness' (Dunning and Narula, 1996; p. 15); that is, because they seek to obtain advantages they do not currently have but which are available abroad to bolster existing competitive advantages or to speed up the process of catching up to their competitors.

This was also the case in the past as demonstrated by the eclectic paradigm. Firms were strong in one area (firm-specific advantages), but weak in terms of local factor conditions. By investing abroad, companies benefited from the factor endowments available abroad and thereby strengthened their factor conditions (see Rugman's critique of Porter's 'diamond'; 1991). Therefore, they went abroad to benefit from the 'foreign diamond'. Since natural assets are nowadays losing their relative importance and human resources (created assets) are becoming crucial, knowledge-seeking outward FDI is gaining in importance. Firms also tend to start investing abroad much earlier than they used to (see Tolentino, 1993) in order to acquire assets abroad.

In the survey, companies regarded learning effects as relatively less important (see Figure 11.3). It seems however that a knowledge spillover occurs only at the level of products (product adaptation and product innovation), but not yet in the production process. The introduction of new technologies or processes was namely evaluated as not having an important effect for most investing companies. Knowledge acquired in the field of technology was assessed as the lowest compared to other fields (Table 11.5). The most significant was knowledge transfer in the field of marketing; some knowledge was also acquired in the field of management and organizational capacity. Among other types of acquired knowledge stemming from direct investing abroad, companies mentioned financial knowledge and improving cash flow management.

The modest technological learning is a result of the geographical distribution of outward FDI and its concentration in countries less developed than Slovenia (see Chapter 5). Slovenian firms are technologically more developed than most host-country firms. Another explanation might be the short time lag involved which does not allow companies to realize potential technological effects that are long term by definition. Investors have also not been motivated to invest abroad to achieve certain technological results (see Chapter 8). Such results do not fully correspond with the results of previous studies (Blomström and Kokko, 1994; Borgensztein, De Gregorio and Wha-Le, 1995), which suggest that positive FDI spillovers on home firms are only generated if the technology gap between the foreign and domestic firm is not too large and if there is a certain threshold of human capital in the investing country. The gap between Slovenia and major countries of destination, the successors to the SFRY, has not been too wide therefore stronger technology spillovers could have been expected according to this theory. But the gap has widened during the transition and become more like that seen between Slovenia and developed countries on the other hand. If Slovenian outward investments in industrialized countries increase, the function of acquiring foreign (created) assets not only in product innovation but also production processes and technology (innovation) will also grow in importance.

Table 11.5 Knowledge acquired as a result of outward FDI

	Technology	Marketing	Management	Organization
Average	2.2	4.0	3.6	3.3
Modus	3	4	4	3
Std. dev.	0.9	0.7	0.9	0.7
Minimum	1	3	2	2
Maximum	4	5	5	4

Source: Survey 2000.

Note: 1 – no transfer, 5 – very large knowledge transfer.

Employment effects

The employment effect of outward FDI is probably the most controversial and therefore the most discussed aspect in the literature on outward FDI. The general belief of trade unions, albeit not empirically proved, is that investing abroad means the exporting of jobs and thus reduces domestic employment. Theoretically, foreign production can substitute or complement domestic production and employment. More often, the growth of a company and increased foreign production require increased employment by the parent company, which may be the result of a need to provide supervision and services to foreign operations and particularly due to greater production of intermediary products made at home for export to the affiliation abroad for final assembling and the like. Apart from that, it has to be taken into account what would have happened if such outward FDI had not taken place. In many cases of labour-intensive production, a potential investor abroad could face the danger of closing down its activity as a consequence of the erosion of comparative advantages of his country manifested by increasing labour costs. Frequently 'it couldn't have stood the competition or would have been driven out from the market causing job and export loss' (Blomström and Kokko, 2000). Competitive pressures, rationalizing and restructuring could reduce employment or even force a company to close down.

The overall picture seen in Chapter 7 showed that the share of investors in the entire Slovenian corporate sector's employment in the 1994-1999 period fell slightly, parallel to increasing shares in exports and sales. However, the loss of jobs cannot be attributed to investing abroad but more to the general restructuring process accompanying transition. It suggests that a restructuring process was underway (value added and profits namely rising) parallel to investing abroad.

Survey 2001 basically confirmed such aggregate tendencies by indicating that only 18 per cent of investing firms reduced the parent firm's employment, 24 per cent increased home employment, while employment did not change in the majority of investors (59 per cent) as a result of outward FDI (Table 11.1). The employment effect was therefore quantitatively relatively less important compared to other effects. In qualitative terms it was however more important. The employment of skilled labour in investing firms rose from 1997 to 2000 (see the increased average share of university-educated employees in Table 9.2).

Macroeconomic effects

All evolutionary models[8] predict a strong dynamic link between economic development and FDI. The relationship between FDI (inward or outward) is two-way; a higher development level increases FDI flows and *vice versa*, increased FDI stimulates growth spillovers with an important development implication. Although there is possibility of asymmetry between the micro interests of investing firms and their home economy macro interests, the number of investing companies might also be a measure of national competitiveness (Jones, 1996; p. 212). For a long time national economies do not compete only through traditional exports (Quinlan and Chandler, 2001).

Investing firms assist in economic restructuring, influence a country's trading performance, the level and structure of domestic production, investment and employment. The effects on a home economy are stronger the more investing firms have established linkages with other home firms[9]. FDI studies, so far deeply tied to viewing outward FDI as the transfer of resources from home to other economies, mostly neglect the other impacts of outward FDI. They see only an outflow of resources on one hand and no positive impact on a home country's income of earned dividends, royalties and incomes generated abroad. They tend to forget that such investments contribute to the asset creation, technology and knowledge transfer that was described for the firm level.

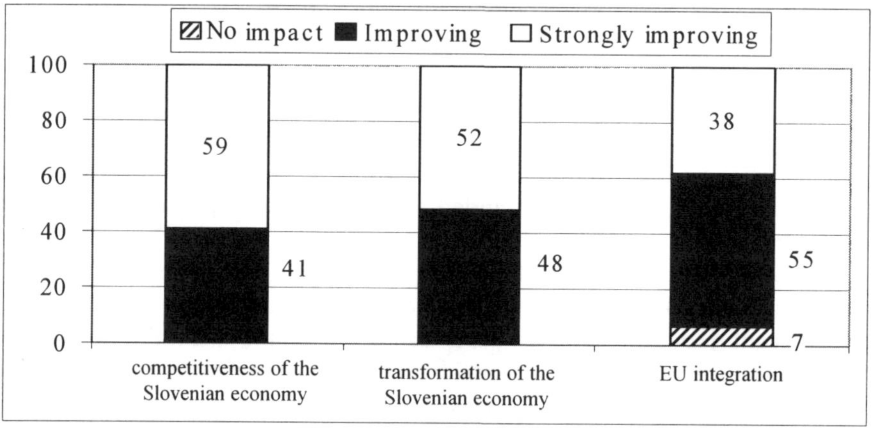

Figure 11.4 Impact of outward FDI on the Slovenian economy (managers' opinions)

Source: Survey 2000.

Note: Grade 1 – no impact; 2 – hindering; 3 – improving; 4 – strongly improving.

Slovenian managers believe that internationalization through outward FDI strongly influences the domestic economy, improving its competitiveness and transformation (Figure 11.4). Restructuring and the competitiveness impact of outward investing was also seen as a significant contribution to the EU integration process. FDI linkages are an effective long-term method of linking the countries economically, socially and politically (Lall, 1996)[10].

Although Slovenian companies investing abroad represent a very modest (approximately 1%) share of the total business sector, they have the highest growth potential and therefore a significant influence on the total corporate sector and may be regarded as a significant qualitative growth pole (see

Chapter 7). Improved exports, sales and efficiency are the next three elements where investing companies performed better than non-investing ones. Investors currently provide almost 40 per cent of Slovenian exports which indicates their competitiveness. This reflected in the national economy's positive trade balance. Exports alone can no longer ensure efficient market access nor the keeping of foreign market shares. Outward FDI significantly improves market penetration and the stability of foreign market shares. In countries which have regular trade deficits with Slovenia, outward FDI may be regarded as a way to reduce the danger of protectionist measures taken by deficit countries to reduce imports while simultaneously inviting inward FDI for other reasons (see Mrak et al., 2001). Investing abroad can thus be regarded as a macroeconomic remedy for reducing trade deficits of host countries, at least in final goods, since some intermediate goods would nevertheless also be exported in the case of investing in such a country.

As a vital part of the Slovenian economy, investors largely influence domestic industrial production in terms of both volume and structure. So far production volume has increased, although significant changes to the structure were not found. Investing abroad in areas of the core competencies of firms has proved to be too small to have an important effect on the overall economic structure.

Investing companies have better possibilities to reduce their tax burden but, since they are on average more profitable than non-investing firms, they also remain important taxpayers in the Slovenian economy.

Investment abroad has also not crowded out domestic investment activity as some have feared[11]. Investment activity is stimulated above all by access to foreign markets. This stimulates investment at home and abroad. Even more important than the quantitative changes found in production volume and domestic investment (that might turn from increasing trends to decreasing trends in the longer run) are qualitative changes. These companies are the most exposed to competitive pressures in both the domestic and foreign markets; therefore they have to constantly improve their efficiency and productivity. They learn to improve their flexibility and develop capabilities to swiftly adapt to changes. Especially important effects are the ongoing improvement in quality, product differentiation and adaptation as a response to closer links with the customers which a direct presence in foreign markets by investing there provides. In the long run this means technological restructuring.

The educational effects of outward investment are significant (see Table 11.5) not only for investing firms but also for the rest of the economy, although firms were not primarily motivated to invest abroad for this reason. Investing companies' growing demand for higher skills in the domestic labour market is slowly building up an awareness of the need to improve the knowledge and skills of labour. The surveys demonstrated the above-average and growing R&D activity of investing firms, which stimulates innovatory capacity. Since companies investing abroad are often domestic market leaders, they also introduce higher quality standards to the domestic economy and stimulate other companies to follow. Investing firms enhance competition, including in the home market. Outward FDI enables firms to exploit the advantages of globalization and to draw on factor endowments found abroad. All these changes influence the industrial structure of the home economy and help bring about changes which better reflect what the international division of labour under globalization pressures shows to be the optimal allocation of resources. Low value-added activities might be shifted abroad (to improve cost competitiveness), while higher value-added activities might be retained in the home country. Chapter 7 demonstrated that those companies which invested abroad did indeed increase the average value added per employee in the nineties. Accordingly, investing companies play a very important role in a home economy's innovatory activity, knowledge transfer and restructuring.

Outward FDI is therefore growth instrumental. As endogenous growth theory (Romer, 1986; Lucas, 1988) predicts, welfare depends much more on innovation, knowledge creation and the accumulation of human capital than the accumulation of physical capital. The development impact could be stronger if, instead of a small group of 'national champions' who invest abroad, there is a number of firms at a similar internationalization level. Such capabilities are key to the appropriate absorbing potential of firms, industries and the economy in general. This absorption potential depends on the development of related industries or a suppliers' network in the home economy. With an increasing number and volume of outward investment, the potential to absorb will also be enhanced and hence the positive growth effects of outward FDI.

Internationalization and exposure to foreign competition has substantially increased the economy's restructuring and transformation. Outward FDI has thus stimulated the transition process and helped close the gaps existing between Slovenia and developed industrial countries[12]. While differences in development levels remain, investing abroad might be treated as a catching up tool since it helps to narrow the gap in productivity, efficiency, knowledge (above all marketing, organizational, and management) and information. The most successful Slovenian investors can already compete in the world market with multinationals from developed economies which is not the case for all or most companies that do not invest abroad or those still shielded from international competition in sectors that do not trade (non-tradables).

Summary

Investing companies have generally experienced a positive net effect of outward FDI and the related success was mostly in line with the expectations. Trade and competitiveness effects were far more important than any other effects. Market-seeking investments resulted in increased market shares, growth of exports and domestic production levels. Consequently, outward FDI enhances efficiency and restructuring, although these were not the initial motives. Investing companies introduce new products, product differentiation and increased quality. Direct presence in a foreign market has helped them respond to customers' needs more rapidly. By investing abroad, firms also achieved other positive asset-creation effects. They have improved their image and enhanced and broadened their marketing, management and organizational skills. Technological learning has been modest since the majority of host countries are less developed than Slovenia. Therefore, they have benefited from the investing companies' technological expertise. In addition, the employment effect was less important, with the majority of firms seeing no changes here as a result of outward FDI.

Firm-level effects spill over to the whole domestic economy and influence the trade balance, the level and structure of industrial production, investment and employment, with all related development implications. Outward FDI was found to be a mode complementary to exports. It has not crowded out domestic investment. Investing firms have the highest growth potential, while exposure to foreign competition forces them to pursue high quality, adaptations and innovations, which are also introduced in the home economy. As welfare depends much more on innovation and knowledge creation than the accumulation of physical capital (according to the endogenous growth theory), outward FDI is also growth and development instrumental. Investing firms are those that speed up the transition process and reduce the gap between transition and developed industrial countries. The restructuring and development benefits of outward FDI can be seen more in the long term, and in the increasing number of investing firms. The effects on the home economy are stronger if investing firms develop more links with other domestic firms.

Notes

1 See, among others, those evaluating the effects on transition economies: Hunya 1999; Rojec, 2000b, for Slovenia; Zemplinerova, 1997; Djankov and Hoekman, 1998 for Czech Republic; Éltető and Antaloczy, 1998 for Hungary, etc.

2 The amount of research undertaken on the impact of MNCs on a home economy is surprisingly small (Jones, 1996; p. 214). Some authors who have addressed this issue are:

Blomström and Kokko, 1994; Borgensztein, De Gregorio and Wha-Le, 1995; Lall S., 1996, Aitkin, Brian and Harrison, 1999; Blomström, M. and Sjoholm, F., 1999; Konings, 1999. Increasing attention to the home-country effects has been seen recently i.e. Konings, Murphy, 2001; Kokko, 2000; Lall 2000.

3 Except for Sweden which has extremely good research in this area (Blomström and Kokko, 1994; Braunerhjelm and Ekholm, 1998).

4 See the more detailed explanation in Lall S., 1996.

5 This is in line with the ownership structure of foreign affiliates that are usually wholly- or majority-owned by Slovenian investors (see Chapter 9).

6 See Mundell (1957), Vernon's product life cycle (1966) and, more recently, Krugman (1983), Krugman and Helpman (1985).

7 The Cobb-Douglass production function was transformed to a linear function:
$lnEXP_i = b_1 + b_2 lnASS_i + b_3 lnCOSTR_i + b_4 lnEMP_i + b_5 ln(FDI/SRE)_i + ACT1_i + ACTJ2_i + SIZ1_i + SIZ2_i + SIZ3_i$
Index i stands for company i while variables mark the logarithmic value of export (lnEXP), assets (lnASS), material expenses (lnCOST), employees (lnEMP), and the share of outward FDI (as stocks) in assets (ln(FDI/ASS)). Variables ACT1 and ACTJ2 represent dummy variables for the activity of a company (sectors or activities are divided into three categories: manufacturing as a reference group, trade and the rest), while SIZ1, SIZ2 and SIZ3 are dummy variables for the mentioned size categories of companies (the reference being large companies).

8 For example, the investment development path (Dunning, 1981), product life-cycle model (Vernon, 1966), 'flying geese' model (Akamatsu, 1961), Ozawa's dynamic paradigm (1997), the Uppsala model (Johanson and Vahlne, 1977, 1990).

9 These linkages are strongly industry-specific and vary by the activity of the investor.

10 Outward FDI in the successors to the SFRY clearly demonstrate that FDI has stimulated and speeded up the normalization of political relations and can also be an instrument for solving some trade-related problems (trade deficits) and for accelerating its liberalisation (see Chapters 6 and 20).

11 Regression analysis showed a positive and statistically significant correlation between outward FDI and investment in a parent firm (Jakliè, 2001, see also Chapter 4).

12 According to Kraljiè (1990, pp. 14-19), these gaps are: system gap, productivity gap, capital gap, infrastructure gap, democracy gap, technology gap, marketing, environment, motivation and legislative gaps.

PART IV
CASE STUDIES

Chapter 12

Characteristics and Lessons of Cases

Why case studies?

This part of the book offers a selection of case studies of Slovenian multinational firms. Why are case studies at all necessary? By concealing many details, the aggregate evaluation may not tell the whole story. Those seeking more in-depth knowledge of what is truly going on in business activities at the firm level claim that only real-life cases are important. We combine the benefits of both approaches in the belief that cases are the only way to illustrate some general tendencies, to put some flesh on the bones of generality.

The case studies are used to complement the many lags found in the still modest macro- and micro-economic data available on outward FDI in Slovenia and to provide the necessary qualitative insights into our survey results. The cases show the process of Slovenian outward internationalization from the firm or manager's perspective. They describe a firm's competitive advantages, its strategies, its motivation and timing of outward investment, the role of human capital, the impacts of outward investing and the barriers to and problems of the multi-nationalization process by different types of firms (endogenous firms or foreign-owned), and, finally, whether outward FDI was pushed by internal factors or pulled by external ones. Although using the same methodology, the objective of each case was to highlight selected relevant aspects.

The case studies present an account of what happened to firms over several years in the decade of transition and the origins of their internationalization dating back for old companies to socialist times. Although firms experienced identical macro-environmental trends, each industry and each firm faced additional specific factors effecting demand, supply and the competitive environment. The underlying premise of all case studies is that ambitious visions and strategic planning do help overcome the barriers to internationalization. The cases reveal that many different companies facing the same problems and difficulties have responded in different ways.

Most of the material in the cases has been collected from annual reports and financial statements, combined by necessity with opinions and beliefs gathered from interviews, questionnaires, press clippings and web pages. While the selected cases differ by scope and focus, they generally share a common structure.

The selection of cases

Our primary criteria in selecting cases was to choose a representative set of Slovenian investors, to include different types of outward internationalization, to cover the major sectors and types of activities but also to reflect differences in types of firms by ownership, size and regional orientation of activities. In line with aggregate industrial distribution, we selected six manufacturing firms and one trading company. We excluded banks even though some are also quite internationalized as this is such a special area that it deserves particular attention.

The first criterion for selecting cases was their degree of multinationalization and the role of firms in international markets. Global firms, but also more regionally-oriented ones, were thereby included in order to present different firms' strategies. Including the major investors meant concentrating on large firms. Small firms are not included this time. Some are fully Slovenian-owned (Gorenje, Prevent, Mercator, Iskraemeco), others have a substantial foreign equity partner (Kolektor), while others involve some foreign (basically) portfolio foreign participation (Krka, Lek). Most firms are production-oriented; one is a trading company (Mercator). Some operate in high-tech activities (Lek, Krka), whereas two are involved in more traditional standardized products (Prevent, Iskraemeco). We have thus collected cases with different origins, experiences, activities and characteristics, which better allows us to make generalizations in the conclusions, albeit the sample can be accused of being large-firm biased. However, these firms do represent a very important part of the Slovenian economy.

Table 12.1 General characteristics of selected cases

Case	Industry	Key arguments for selection
Gorenje	Electric domestic appliances	The biggest, oldest and most internationalized Slovenian multinational company
Prevent	Mfr. of made-up textiles	Vertical integration in the global car industry, a true leapfrogging global, efficiency-seeker
Iskraemeco	Electro	Early internationalization starter, efficiency-seeker
Krka	Pharmaceutical	Knowledge-intensive, regional/global player in highly concentrated pharmaceutical industry
Lek	Pharmaceutical	Knowledge-intensive, regional/global player in highly concentrated pharmaceutical industry
Kolektor	Mfr. of electrical motors, generators	Inward-outward experience, global niche, intermediate product
Mercator	Trade	Regional player, first-mover advantage

Who are the investors?

With the exception of one case, all firms are very old and mostly large by Slovenian standards, established in the socialist era but privatized recently. Most started internationalizing many years ago but privatization and particularly the fact that they started to operate in a much smaller market after the disintegration of Yugoslavia simply forced them to look for larger markets – to internationalize. They have long traditions and have accumulated significant past experience by exporting, but also by transforming themselves from social to private firms which can be also instrumental when investing abroad in other transition economies. Some may be considered global multinationals (Gorenje, Iskraemeco, Kolektor, Prevent), while others are more regional multinationals (Mercator, Lek, Krka).

Most Slovenian investors abroad are indigenous Slovenian firms. Only in one case inward investment was a crucial basis for outward internationalization (Kolektor). For some, long-term co-operation with foreign partners was important yet remained mostly an instrument to enhance their own abilities to later internationalize since Slovenian firms are basically not driven by a foreign owner as in other countries (Hungary, for instance, where foreign firms are the major agents of outward FDI).

The common characteristic of almost all the cases included in the book is their non-central location. With the exception of Mercator and Lek, all firms analyzed are located in relatively small towns of Slovenia. The question immediately arises as to why companies located in Ljubljana, the capital of Slovenia, are not as internationalized as those included in the case studies? One explanation may be that firms located outside the centre had to rely, even in the socialist system, much more on their own capabilities while those in the centre had strengthened their competitiveness by networking with politicians and banks (crony socialism). Another explanation is the commitment of the management and those employed in such companies. They are much more committed to the company since it is often the lifeblood of the place where they live. In some cases, it is the only firm or at least a significant firm in the region. Among other things, this brings about higher employment stability and improved management, which has been demonstrated to be a key success factor.

Factors driving internationalization

Despite the differences in the cases, we can still generalize that more investments have been pulled by external factors of international environment and globalization pressures than pushed by ownership or firm-specific advantages, although the two factors are ultimately closely interlinked. Both proved to have played an important role. Nevertheless, it does seem that pull factors somehow played a more important role. Pressures from the global economy involving tougher competition and the need to reduce prices to a minimum forced firms to grow and to raise efficiency by employing economies of size and scope, which was impossible in Slovenia's small market alone.

The sample comprises firms expanding their activities globally and those only present in certain regions, wanting to become regional multinational. They basically look for new markets or to retain existing markets, while those relocating production search for cheaper labour to bolster their competitiveness by cutting costs and by being close to their customers who are either end-consumers or firms. In some cases the institutional environment has played a very important role. Some firms' internationalization has been particularly regulation-driven. Generic brand pharmaceutical producers locate their production in countries with large market potential but also where the legislation is more permissively enforced, or where other market characteristics stimulate a local presence.

Firms seem to realize that without growth there is no development and without development the company cannot survive. Therefore, if the Slovenian market is increasingly too small they simply have to internationalize their activity. Contrary to the many who believe that niche producers must stay at home, many have started to believe that it is precisely in a niche where a globalization strategy is a must. The smaller the niche the more global you have to be (see Box 12.1). Only by becoming a global producer can such a niche prove to be profitable. In short, globalization has stimulated outward internationalization provided that firms actually had the required capabilities.

In terms of the aims or reasons (Chapter 8) keeping and/or enhancing market shares is by far the most important consideration of managers when starting their company's internationalization. One case emphasizes the importance of transport costs, which is a very sector-specific consideration (Prevent). Firms that internationalized within the successor states to former Yugoslavia, or in other transition economies, have sought a first-mover advantage (most obviously Mercator). The regional destination of most outward FDI cases involves countries with a similar or lower level of development, similar cultures or common histories.

The cases also show that expansion and diversification at home is closely interrelated with expansion abroad. Firms started growing locally, mostly through acquisitions but globalization has pushed them to simultaneously internationalize since there is no time for gradual growth first at home and then internationally. Internationally, however, they generally invested greenfield, and only recently more through acquisitions. Acquisitions are seen as more demanding and not as suitable given the types of ownership advantages Slovenian investors possess. Investors abroad also try to reduce risks by complementing one sector's internationalization abroad with greater diversification in other activities in the home market.

In some cases the domestic market structure can also stimulate internationalization. The two cases of pharmaceutical firms are examples. They are active in similar fields. They are both basically generic producers of drugs. Under globalization pressures, they have to grow yet their similar programmes make it difficult for them to merge (excessive social costs due to the need for lay-offs) on top of the very different corporate cultures. Therefore, internationalization emerged as a possible strategic response.

Gradual or leapfrogging internationalization?

Although all the cases demonstrate a certain gradualism in their internationalization, most can be characterized as leapfrogging global firms. They started their internationalization some years ago, some even a few decades ago, but all of them have only recently really jumped on the 'fast train of internationalization'. In the last few years, they have become more international than before. They are not born globals because they all started internationalizing by exporting first and many years later by investing abroad. Nevertheless, their commitment to internationalization in many markets and by investing abroad only has a recent origin, after they became private firms. Gorenje may be an exception here since it was very internationalized even before it became private.

Competitive advantages

Most firms claim their advantages lie in superior technology, marketing and management skills compared to local firms. Firms have accumulated specific advantages in their markets of penetration, which more than compensate their weaknesses compared to large multinational firms. Yet some of these advantages are temporary, therefore they have to be exploited rapidly before other competitors enter the market. They are enjoying a certain extra 'time out' before foreign 'players' join the game. First-mover advantages have proved to play a much more important role compared to the experiences of investors abroad from industrial countries.

Management of companies have played crucial roles in outward FDI.

Without the clear and ambitious visions of firm managers, such successful internationalization would have been impossible. A realistic strategy, good management with excellent training, adapted technology and own R&D efforts have proved to be the key success factors in most cases. In addition, some managers have developed a very specific management style based on personal contacts, and highly assimilated to the cultures of the destinations of outward FDI.

Box 12.1 Key success factors in a small firm's internationalization

Japec Jakopin, the owner of the Seaway company (Slovenia), a major designer of sailing (and motor) boats in Europe, claims that small firms/ countries can turn their weaknesses into strengths if they follow the right policy, accompanied by:

1. a good knowledge of foreign languages;
2. good education;
3. familiarity with the partner's culture;
4. no superiority complex; and
5. flexibility.

If you are small, you must adapt, learn from others' experiences and try to assimilate productively the best practices of others when creating your own solutions. This is only possible if you know foreign languages well since you cannot otherwise adapt to other cultures and assimilate their knowledge. By listening you learn, by applying the best practices of many countries/firms in creating your own solutions you can outperform those who are larger and stronger, while by not claiming you are the best you do not threaten the superiority complex of traditional, established and large players. We have thereby created what we call a European sailing boat, which is appealing to the French, British, Swedes and most other tastes. See also: Podjetnik, December 2001; p. 7.

Cases like Seaway and Kolektor clearly demonstrate that a firm can become global and successful in a relatively small niche. It also seems that it is somewhat easier to become an important player if you specialize in an intermediate and not a final product if you are a SME or you come from a small country. Final-product orientation or consumer goods production and marketing is financially much more demanding, more threatened by changes in technology, and is brand and advertizing intensive. You must also have an already established global network in order to exploit your advantages in the shortest time possible.

It is also safer to be in an intermediate sector since you can become a major producer for many large multinationals and thus reduce your dependence on any one purchaser or market. Through such diversification you also gain economies of scale and bolster your competitiveness.

Problems, weaknesses and threats

The main reasons for problems and some failures (albeit almost all cases were generally successful[1]) were poor preparations, limited or inexperienced personnel, not enough or inadequate information which all contributed to internationalization sometimes being too early or not the best project choice in terms of the available investor capabilities or country location. Obviously, internal factors proved to be decisive. Of external institutional ones, firms emphasized the late liberalization of outward FDI regulations, inadequate coverage of risks, the absence of intergovernmental agreements and a lack of information support.

The case studies confirmed the earlier conclusions that today firms also start to invest abroad in order to gain and not only to materialize firm-specific advantages, that they invest abroad not only out of strengths but also out of the weaknesses that need to be complemented by partners' capabilities. Somewhat weaker ownership advantages compared to large multinationals make them internationalize earlier than would otherwise be the case just to gain complementary advantages and to buy time to enhance existing limited ones before other multinationals join the game (first-mover advantage). Types of advantages like knowing how to do business in particular markets also make them internationalize earlier.

Two major challenges face firms in the future. First, how to enhance firms' capabilities given the limitations SMEs face in the context of the increasing oligopolization and concentration of global markets? The response to the first challenge has been selective strengthening of own capabilities by concentrating on core strengths. Internationalization has been precisely the answer to the limits (small size) of firms and markets. Nevertheless, they are aware of the fact that, in the future, longer-term strategic or equity inward co-operation can be a strategic response to the growing challenges of globalization. The second challenge has been how to handle increasing vulnerability and the turbulent external environment. One strategy applied here is diversification. In some cases, firms adhere to their core business niche when going international but diversify at home. Others also try to diversify internationally. The prime dilemma here involves the trade-off between the benefits of specialization and the costs of diversification compared to the reduced risks.

Last but not least, firms complain they are too alone in their efforts to create or strengthen their technological capabilities. Government support is considered insufficient. Both pharmaceutical firms claim very strongly that fundamental research in Slovenia should be directed more to targeted pre-competitive R&D projects in the areas of Slovenian firms' competitive advantages. For them, this means research in the fields of biomedicine, pharmacy, chemistry and biotechnology.

Summary

The cases of Slovenian firms' successful internationalization clearly demonstrate that firms are already multinationals and have succeeded in internationalizing their businesses despite the many difficulties encountered along the road. Perhaps the most salient lesson is that many in fact resolved some of the major problems and crises precisely by turning even more to international markets, by intensifying their international operations and not withdrawing from them. The second lesson is that firms succeeded in doing this because they have local capabilities, most through the initially strong inward international co-operation via imports of technology, and licences in some by inward FDI. Yet such co-operation was at all times only part of an ambitious strategy to build up own capacities. Inward internationalization was instrumental in strengthening a firm's ownership-specific advantages, for enriching them on the basis of own R&D efforts and innovative organizational or strategic responses.

Times have changed and, although gradualism has the advantage of the unhurried accumulation of knowledge and experience – of gradual learning-by-doing, today there is frequently no time available for such a step-by-step approach. Firms have to jump into the 'global deep end' much faster, sometimes even without much previous export experience. Increased risks are therefore unavoidable. Mistakes and failures are more frequent than before. The issue is, however, not to eliminate mistakes or failures but to minimize them in efforts to leapfrog internationalization stages.

The cases of Slovenian firms included here are really examples of leapfrogging. They became multinational on the basis of specific ownership advantages, some were more product-quality based, whereas others were more know-how or established-network based. Some of their advantages have a limited time duration and therefore they have to exploit such first-mover advantages very fast in order to reduce the many weaknesses of Slovenian firms relative to large foreign multinationals when trying to sustain the initial competitive advantages over Western multinationals that have stronger ownership advantages.

The case studies show that outward FDI is set to strengthen in the future and that other forms of international linkages, including enhanced inward FDI, are becoming necessary if firms want to survive the ever-tougher competitive battles for market shares.

Note

1 Although the selection of cases includes mostly successful firms, it is not biased since it is generally too early to evaluate outward FDI which has only been initiated and whose results are hence still expected. Some early failures are included as part of the cases of Slovenian multinational firms which later compensated for such failures, learned on their bases and are more successfully continuing their internationalization.

Chapter 13

Gorenje

gorenje

Consolidated financial statements for 2001[1]:

Number of employees:	8,236
Assets:	€ 562 million (0.6% intangible assets)
Total revenues:	€ 739 million
Net profit:	€ 15 million
Value added per employee:	€ 22.6 million

Activity: Mfr. of electric domestic appliances
Number of companies within the same business activity: 24
Type of organisation: Joint-stock company d.d.
http://www.gorenje.si

Introduction

Gorenje is Slovenia's largest multinational manufacturing company with the production of household appliances lying at the core of its business activity. It started its internationalization very early and has achieved a high degree of multinationality. Unlike many other multinationals from transition economies, it is not typical since it is a completely endogenous Slovenian company, with no foreign equity partners involved. Other forms of long-term co-operation with foreign partners have played a more supplementary role in Gorenje's development. Its internationalization through outward investing started in 1965 and in 1978 with the acquisition of the German firm Körting. This was a highly surprising strategic move by a socialist enterprise for that time. Gorenje is not a typical case of gradual internationalization but is more of an example of fast moving internationalization with some downturns as well. This has helped the company consolidate and emerge from crises stronger and better prepared for future challenges.

It is a case that also demonstrates the very strong influence of both the environment in which a company operates as well as the crucial influence of a company's management, its determination, vision and courage to introduce a market-based mentality in a firm still deeply rooted in the socialist system. Today's challenges confronting the company are formidable. Faced with growing competitive pressures in domestic and global markets, the company must decide whether to develop into a real global company and compete with much larger players in its core business alone, or to enter into certain co-operative equity or contractual strategic arrangements with a competitor in the field.

History[2]

The history of Gorenje is marked by four turning points. The first was the setting up of a company that made agricultural machinery in 1950 in a village called Gorenje. The second was when the factory moved to the rapidly growing town of Velenje. The third stage came with the building its own large manufacturing premises in 1963 producing stoves, then washing machines (from 1967) and refrigerators (in a new factory built in 1970). Lastly, it diversified into kitchen furniture, ceramics, medical equipment, telecommunications, entertainment electronics and TV sets as part of an export-oriented strategy initiated in 1967. Gorenje grew from a local micro company employing 150 people into the leading Yugoslav domestic appliances producer employing 22,000 people in 1978, becoming an important exporter and innovation-driven firm.

Gorenje started its successful growth by entering the domestic appliances sector late in the fifties. During the first half of the sixties, Gorenje succeeded to manage all main programmes of domestic appliances. The number of employees jumped to about 7,000 in 1970. In the early sixties it started exporting Germany, which soon made up some 40 per cent of Gorenje's total sales. In the seventies Gorenje started to open up companies in Germany and France. In this decade, the value of the Gorenje group's exports climbed towards 60 per cent of its total sales.

In the 1980s Gorenje went through a serious crisis. As a result, the company had to restructure and recovery measures had to be introduced. Crisis management was initiated. A number of consultant companies also participated. By applying a number of market-oriented, managerial, strategic and technological norms, the Gorenje group took a huge stride forward towards greater internationalization and competitiveness. The many companies involved abroad were put into the centre of Gorenje's activities. The Gorenje group succeeded to considerably cut its costs while it improved the performance of its products and services. As a result, productivity in 1984 alone grew by 30 per cent. In the period of Yugoslavia's disintegration, the financial blockade on Slovenian companies was complete and over 700 Slovenian companies were confiscated. Gorenje as a Yugoslav group practically disappeared. It lost more than 40 per cent of its former domestic markets. The battle for survival had to start again.

Gorenje employed some 9,000 people when Slovenia declared its independence. The domestic market then contracted to about five per cent of total production. Two main factors kept the Gorenje group afloat. The first was the extremely high level of homogeneity, and consensus as one of the linchpins of the group's culture. The second reason appeared to be its successful management, which took advantage of the advanced level of the group's internationalization.

Company profile

Presently the Gorenje group employs 8,236 people[3] and is the largest manufacturing corporation in Slovenia, with consolidated annual revenues of SIT 160,531 million in 2001. Sales of the Gorenje group have been increasing by 11 per cent annually, while profits grew approximately four-fold in the 1995-2001 period. In the 1997-2000 period alone, investments amounted to € 254 million cumulatively. The group comprises 41 companies, 12 in Slovenia and 29 abroad. Value added per employee grew from 1997 to 2001 from € 10,000 to over € 11,346. In 1998 Gorenje became a public company limited by shares. The ownership share of management and employees (including retired workers) exceeds one-third.

Gorenje divides its product range into four major sectors, namely household appliances (83 per cent), machine construction tools (0.6 per cent), furniture (five per cent), and services (11 per cent). The production of household appliances (produced by Gorenje d.d. Velenje) is the core activity of the Gorenje group. It now sells annually over 2.2 million appliances (refrigerators, freezers, cookers, ovens, hobs, washing machines and dryers). Gorenje has been increasing its market share in its main markets. The current market share in Europe is almost four per cent. The share of compatible 'home programme' activities is growing within total sales of the corporation.

After the collapse of Yugoslavia, the Gorenje programme returned predominantly to the domestic appliances sector. In order to survive, Gorenje had to export close to 95 per cent of its total sales during the nineties. Such a transformation was very demanding due to the high level of market saturation in Europe, which recently was at 97 per cent for refrigerator products (Slovenia 93 per cent), 90 per cent for washers (Slovenia also 90 per cent), and nearly 100 per cent for cookers (Slovenia 97 per cent). This was one reason underlying recent efforts to diversify its production outside of its core to related business in order to achieve necessary synergies and production, logistic and marketing optimization.

In the last decade, domestic appliance companies have been improving their competitiveness through three main approaches: by cutting costs, by raising quality and performance, and through M&A. Gorenje has been trying to do the same. In such a way it has gradually transformed itself from a mostly labour-intensive producer of a mature product to a modern global corporation increasing value added by modernizing mature products and making them more user- and environmentally-friendly.

Internationalization

Gorenje's internationalization has followed certain stages; first by exporting to the main export destination countries, later by establishing sales units abroad and much later production units including in more distant countries. This process was speeded up and even reveals leapfrogging over some stages. Gorenje exports approximately 93 per cent of its total production, 80 per cent of which goes to the EU. Gorenje's products are sold in 60 international markets. The biggest customers are in Germany, Croatia, Austria and the Scandinavian countries.

This high degree of internationalization has not been achieved overnight. Up until 1965 Gorenje only sold its household appliances in Slovenia. In 1961 Gorenje exported its first 200 cookers to Germany. By 1970 exports had increased already to one-third of total production to climb to approximately 50 percent in the 1980s. Since then, exporting has been the major engine of Gorenje's growth.

Initially, exports were driven by the need to acquire foreign exchange to buy raw materials and parts from Western Europe. At that time, Gorenje was arranging exports via large Slovenian trading companies (see Vitežnik, 2000; p. 2). Obviously Gorenje started exporting not only to get foreign exchange but also to be permanently in contact with up-to-date technologies and innovation, and with market needs and norms. In the 1970s Eastern markets became a major export destination, later overseas markets like the USA and Australia followed. In order to overcome its low price competitiveness, co-operation with the Italian company Rex-Zanussi, which provided the basis for technology, know-how and innovation, started in the early period of Gorenje's growth.

The main markets are in Northern and Central Europe, with a 30 per cent share (in 2001). The share of Slovenia's market is very modest but, together with the recovering markets of successor states to the former Yugoslavia, still represent an important part of total sales (27 per cent). South-west Europe (France, Italy etc.) has gradually increased its share from ten to 12 per cent (1999-2001), Eastern Europe increased its share in 2001 to 12 per cent, while overseas markets hold a six per cent share.

Real internationalization in terms of establishing firms abroad started in the 1970-80 period when Gorenje was still a socially-owned company. In order to hide its socialist origins and resulting poor image, the firm started to establish subsidiaries in the countries of highest importance for its exports. The first one was established in France in 1965, the year of a major market-oriented reform in the then Yugoslavia, following by a second in West Germany (1971). Today, Gorenje has 29 subsidiaries located in 18 countries and six agents (located in Greece, Ukraine, Russia, Hungary, BiH, Czech Republic) involving over 600 employees or eight per cent of Gorenje's total employment.

Gorenje's subsidiaries abroad are registered trade companies with sophisticated sales networks, warehouses, and transport and product maintenance facilities. Most foreign affiliates are supervised by the Vienna-based Gorenje Beteiligungs GmbH which took on this role in 1986.

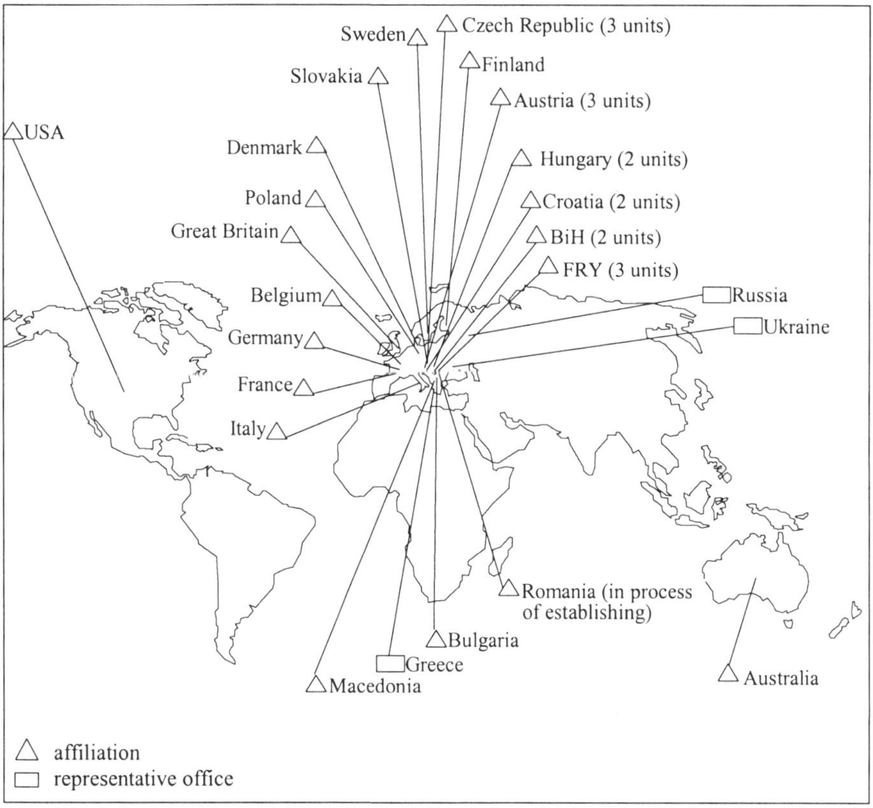

Figure 13.1 International business network of Gorenje group in 2002

There are three primary reasons for outward FDI: (i) market potential; (ii) improving buyer-seller relations and gaining access to new technological solutions; and (iii) responding to the very restrictive foreign trade and foreign exchange regulations of the then Yugoslavia (see also Vitežnik, 2000; p. 29) in order to overcome the many foreign exchange limitations and achieve a certain freedom in business operations.

After the first firm was established in Munich, the real push came with the establishment of the holding company Gorenje Beteilingungs GmbH in Vienna. Equity shares of all Gorenje's firms abroad were transferred to this firm, which became the centre for Gorenje's international operations. Initially, the role of this holding was very different to today. At that time, it was to ensure the financial stability of Gorenje within the volatile regulatory framework of the SFRY, whereas today it is managing and financing all of Gorenje's investments abroad, including optimizing organization and tax burdens (see Vitežnik, 2001; p. 29).

Table 13.1 Dynamics of Gorenje's international network by year of establishment

Country	Year	Name
France	1965	Gorenje France S.A.
Austria	1975	Gorenje Austria Handelsgesellschaft GmbH
Germany	1971	Gorenje Vertriebs GmbH
Italy	1976	Gorenje Körting Italia S.r.l.
Denmark	1976	Gorenje Skandinavien A/S
Australia	1976	Gorenje Pacific Pty. Ltd.
Austria	1986	Gorenje Beteilungsgesellschaft GmbH
Belgium	1988	Gorenje Belux S.a.r.l.
United Kingdom	1988	Gorenje UK Ltd.
Czech Republic (CZ)	1991	Gorenje Spol s.r.o.
Hungary	1991	Gorenje Budapest Kft.
Poland	1991	Gorenje Polska Sp.zo.o.
Croatia	1991	Gorenje Zagreb d.o.o.
Croatia	1991	Gorenje Split d.o.o.
FR Yugoslavia	1991	Gorenje Novi Sad d.o.o.
Macedonia	1991	Gorenje Skopje d.o.o.
FRY	1991	Gorenje Novi Sad
CZ	1991	Gorenje Spol s.r.o.
Bulgaria	1992	Gorenje Bulgaria EOOD
Slovakia	1993	Gorenje Slovakia Spol s.r.o.
United States	1994	Gorenje USA Inc.
CZ	1995	Gorenje Kuchyne Spol s.r.o.
FRY	1995	Gorenje Podgorica d.o.o.
Sweden	1996	Gorenje Sverige S.A.

FRY	1996	Goretrade d.o.o.
BiH	1998	Gorenje Commerce d.o.o.
Croatia	1999	Hyundai Auto d.o.o.
Austria	2001	Gorenje Küchen GmbH
Hungary	2001	Gorenje Real Kft.
BiH	2001	Dukanpromet, d.d. Sarajevo
Finland	2001	Gorenje OY, Finland
Austria	2001	Gorenje Freistadt GmbH
Finland	2001	Fingoren OY, Helsinki

In order to reduce costs and the role of labour-intensive programmes as well as to invest and technologically upgrade its programmes, in 1978 Gorenje's management decided to buy the troubled Bavarian electronics company – Körting. The idea was to concentrate technological and research efforts and information technologies within Körting. Targets were not met largely due to strong opposition to the reduction of unqualified labour by trade unions. In such an environment it was impossible to organize and install the planned high-technology centre to generate, acquire and transfer strategic technologies for the Gorenje group, or to create an efficient globally-oriented information system (see Soèan, 2001; p. 21).

The collapse of Körting resulted in Gorenje's most serious development crisis thus far, manifested finally in the resignation of Gorenje's General Manager, Mr. Ateljšek, after having led the firm for 28 years.

Box 13.1 Gorenje Körting Electronics

Gorenje's acquisition of the entertainment electronics company Körting from Bavaria in 1978 was for a long time a hot political and business issue in Slovenia. From one point of view, that decision seemed quite reasonable since signs of the broader use of electronics in domestic appliances were then clear enough.

Gorenje acquired Körting just at the time this company, like many others in Europe and the US, collapsed in entertainment electronics under the weight of Japanese competition. Gorenje's own potential was too weak for a quick shift of its production programme away from entertainment electronics to some more advanced segments of electronics, or to quickly adapt Körting to its own strategic needs. Ultimately, it also did not heavily reduce the number of mostly unqualified workers. As a result, losses quickly piled up and after some years started to threaten the whole Gorenje group. Therefore, Gorenje sold Körting in 1983.

Based on: Soèan, 2001; p. 22.

On the basis of financial support from the Slovenian government, Gorenje succeeded to decentralize its system, reduce its wages, improve its information system, streamline its management, and enhance the role of its R&D. During the second half of the eighties, Gorenje's management strengthened strategic relations with large production and trading multinational companies in Europe and the USA.

In the 13-year period (1987 to 1999) over € 46 million was invested abroad.

Table 13.2 Affiliates abroad by number of employees and turnover in 2002

Company/Country	No. of employees	Company/Country	Turnover in €
1. Gorenje Austria Handels GmbH	138	1. Gorenje Vertriebs GmbH Germany	180,477,222
2. Gorenje Zagreb d.o.o. Croatia	114	2. Gorenje Zagreb d.o.o. Croatia	68,196,789
3. Gorenje Spol s.r.o. CZ	93	3. Gorenje Austria Handels GmbH	54,403,814
4. Gorenje Vertriebs GmbH Germany	64	4. Gorenje France S.A.	53,945,710
5. Gorenje Commerce d.l.j. BiH	32	5. Gorenje Skandinavien A/S Denmark	35,154,103
6. Hyundai Auto Croatia	30	6. Gorenje Commerce d.l.j. BiH	30,350,748
7. Gorenje Polska Sp. z.o.o.	30	7. Hyundai Auto Croatia	30,015,783
8. Gorenje Skandinavien A/S Denmark	29	8. Gorenje Spol s.r.o. CZ	25,621,345
9. Gorenje France S.A.	24	9. Gorenje Körting Italia S.r.l.	24,948,299
10. Gorenje Slovakia Spol s.r.o.	18	10. Gorenje Polska Sp. z.o.o.	13,241,631
11. Gorenje Skopje, d.o.o. Macedonia	12	11. Gorenje UK Ltd.	8,927,014
12. Gorenje Budapest Kft. Hungary	10	12. Gorenje Slovakia Spol S.r.o.	8,247,113
13. Goretrade d.o.o. Yugoslavia	9	13. Gorenje Skopje, d.o.o. Makedonia	7,362,155
14. Gorenje Körting Italia S.r.l.	7	14. Gorenje Budapest Kft. Hungary	5,817,451
15. Gorenje Beteiligungs GmbH Austria	4	15. Gorenje Bulgaria EOOD	4,026,829
16. Gorenje Bulgaria EOOD	4	16. Gorenje Sverige S.A.	3,816,523
17. Gorenje Sverige S.A.	3	17. Gorenje Belux S.a.r.l. Belgium	1,859,747
18. Gorenje UK Ltd.	2	18. Gorenje Beteiligungs GmbH Austria	1,109,300
19. Gorenej Belux S.a.r.l. Belgium	2	19. Goretrade d.o.o. Yugoslavia	523,204
20. Gorenje USA Inc.	1	20. Gorenje USA Inc.	31,889
21. Gorenje Pacific Pty. Ltd. Australia	0	21. Gorenje Pacific Pty. Ltd. Australia	0

Source: Quoted from Duris, 2002.

Gorenje still sees room to expand, based on further cost cuts and improved performance, and regaining its market share in the new countries emerging from former Yugoslavia. The saturation level of domestic appliances in these countries is low. The long-running business experience in these markets coupled by a very positive brand image, familiarity with their business culture, languages, buying psychology and other factors are Gorenje's advantages. Units in these countries could serve as a springboard for expansion to other countries in the region as well.

The roles of most affiliations abroad are to promote sales of household appliances and provide service to customers. Recently however, as part of the diversification strategy, some other sectors have moved to the fore. Furniture production started abroad in 1977 in Austria. The main goal is to produce complete kitchens and kitchen elements paying attention to the individual needs of consumers and the environmental friendliness of the production process combined with the highest quality products. Initially, kitchen parts were imported from Slovenia and assembled in Austria. Gorenje Freistadt now produces 350 kitchen parts a day or 7,000 kitchens a year, realizing a net sales revenue of € 14.5 million which makes Gorenje the sixth biggest producer of furniture in Austria by the number of products sold (see Duris, 2002; p. 17).

Gorenje's other production site abroad is Gorenje Kuchyne CZ, which produces kitchen furniture. Its production amounts to about 2.5 per cent of the Czech market, generating net sales revenue of € 2.31 million and selling 85 per cent of production in the domestic market and exporting the rest mainly to Slovakia.

While Gorenje Freistadt is practically not involved in export activities, it was involved in the process of setting up Gorenje Kuchyne CZ. Gorenje Freistadt provided the production system, information technology solutions, know-how and personnel. Gorenje Kuchyne produces kitchen furniture in lower price segments for the home market and exports some 15 per cent of its output, mainly to Slovakia.

Why did Gorenje locate this low value-added production of furniture in a 'more developed economy' and higher value-added production of white goods in a less developed economy (Slovenia)? The explanation of this value-added paradox is the new idea of combining the production of household appliances with kitchen furniture. Production started in 1977 and quickly substituted the initial low value-added assembling. In both cases, Gorenje produces household appliances in Slovenia and furniture in Austria with relatively high value-added levels (see Duris, 2002; p. 20).

In addition to its own network of companies abroad, Gorenje has also been developing high quality business relations with some large international distributors. Gorenje has developed a co-operative network with about ten technologically leading global producers in order to link its supply programme to the needs of specific markets. In 2000 a joint venture with the Italian design studio Pininfarina was born. In 1999 new offices in Moscow were opened, while the construction of a logistics centre in Prague started (which opened in 2000) as well as a warehouse facility in Sarajevo.

Through the above network of own companies, Gorenje has succeeded to expand its exports and increase its market share, to observe consumption trends, quality characteristics of these markets, and to stay in touch with their technical standards and logistics. The network of foreign companies has played an important role in achieving Gorenje's strategic targets: during the seventies to expand exports and upgrade technologies, during the eighties to internationalize, and during the nineties to enable growth, improve competitiveness, and diversify risk.

In view of the maturity seen in household appliances, higher growth is planned till 2002 for related activities (76 per cent compared to 23 per cent for household appliances). Regionally speaking, highest sales growth is planned for Eastern Europe (44 per cent). In terms of internationalization new acquisitions are planned there. The target market share in Europe is 3.5 per cent. Although concentrating on Europe, new opportunities will also be sought in the emerging Asian and Latin American markets.

Competitive advantages

Gorenje's competitiveness is reflected by its high market shares: three per cent of the European market, in Germany up to 29 per cent, Croatia 14 per cent, France 10 per cent, BiH 5 per cent, Austria 4.9 per cent, Denmark 3.6 per cent, and the USA 3.2 per cent. This has not been achieved without difficulty. At first, low wages were an advantage yet this is losing its importance given the gradual wage convergence between Slovenia and other more developed countries. What is perhaps the most distinctive characteristic of Gorenje is that it emerged from crises stronger, that its response was not defensive but offensive leading to creating and enhancing competitive advantages and not just concentrating on cost cutting. The crises in the 1980s was overcome thanks to high quality products appreciated by customers and which are friendly to the environment and, secondly, by the already high internationalization with well-organized distribution networks abroad which was instrumental in promoting sales globally. All of this could not have been achieved without highly trained people, good management and dedication to the company. The company started its life as 'a family' and is continuing its successful business mission as one of the larger multinationals in the domestic appliances industry with the highest possible 'consensus' in the corporation. The above business culture has created a constant and intense feeling of belonging to Gorenje during both good and bad times (see Sočan, 2001; p. 12). There have been no strikes at all during the whole half-century history of this company.

Another very unique approach or strategy of the Gorenje group in times of concentration on core business and outsourcing trends is the main strategy: 'Everything for the home'. This means not only the continuation and expansion in white goods production but also an expansion to all related areas (see Duris, 2001; p. 22).

Unlike many other companies that downsized R&D efforts in times of crisis, Gorenje has been constantly strengthening these efforts in-house and also in co-operation with institutes and universities in Slovenia and abroad. Early on the company started its own R&D institute. It thereby gradually transformed from a labour-intensive producer into an innovation-based firm. The result was the development of its own trademarks. Today, 70 per cent of Gorenje's total production is sold under its own trademarks – Gorenje, Sidex, Korting (Italy, Greece) and Gorenje Pacific – and the rest under intermediary buyers' trademarks. Gorenje is the dominant brand employed in the main Gorenje markets: Germany, Austria, Northern Europe, and CEECs, Slovenia and the countries of former Yugoslavia. Sidex has been used first of all in retail chains in France, while the brand Körting is applied in 'German image' countries like Italy and Greece, and partly Germany. Another brand name being used in Germany is Galant. That is chiefly used for the distribution of cooking studios. Gorenje earmarks some two per cent of its revenues to promote its brand names. The share of sales through its own brands has been constantly growing, and presently encompasses more than 80 per cent of Gorenje's total sales. The identity of Gorenje's brands has recently focused on the corporation's image, 'simple and logical', 'Pininfarina design' etc. In such way, Gorenje is succeeding to climb the ladder of relative prices in relation to its main competitors.

The company's high quality orientation was sparked off very early on. In 1974 a Quality Control system was introduced. The ISO 90001 certificate, which guarantees that Gorenje's appliances sold in the market place meet their design and performance specifications, was acquired in 1995. The company's 'user-friendly' strategy has also paid off. In 1997 Gorenje's washing machines Simple and Logical were declared the most user-friendly ones in Europe (Milestones, 2000; p. 64). A year earlier, an Excellence Award was received from Icograda.

This was enabled by extensive training (languages, computer skills, marketing and management). In 1999, close to three-quarters of all employees underwent various types of training. Gorenje spent close to ten times more than the average company in Slovenia on training. Gorenje has recently turned from the external towards the internal organization of its human-resource upgrading in order to bring training closer to the corporation's needs (Sočan, 2001; p. 23).

The strengthening of ecological awareness and environmentally-friendly production and products has become a competitive advantage in this otherwise mature industry. Gorenje therefore decided in 1996 that by 2000 at least in the parent company the environment management system should be adapted to the requirements of the ISO 14001 standard (the certificate was awarded to it in 2000) so as to minimize environmental risks and to improve the firm's image.

Gorenje identifies its advantages in the following areas:

- Flexibility and ability to adapt to market requirements.
- Well-positioned and developed sales network in Europe.
- Recognized brand name in key markets, particularly in South-east Europe.
- Good relations with customers.
- Skilled staff with strong corporate loyalty.
- Strong internationalization.

Most companies from former socialist countries, and today's transition economies, can hardly escape the image of an enterprise from a low-wage economy. Gorenje has succeeded in considerably reducing or even eliminating its image of a low-wage company through its successful long-term process of internationalization. This was the way it escaped any bad image as a socialist firm.

One very important factor of Gorenje's success is the combination of kitchen furniture and household appliances. There is no single player in the Austrian market that offers and markets this integrated solution. Just-in-time supplies and production are also part of Gorenje's policy of minimizing storage time.

Problems, weaknesses and threats

The first problem yet simultaneous 'blessing' a company like Gorenje faces is the very tough competition seen in the household appliances industry which is a relatively standardized, mature industry dominated by a few large multinationals. The only way to survive in such a tough market is to reduce costs, to offer better, more friendly and appealing products; in short, to innovate products and technologies and to become more customer-friendly, to come in to consumers' homes. Although Gorenje is giving a lot of attention to innovations, management is aware that efforts to draw closer to its competitors in terms of knowledge, consumer satisfaction and managerial efficiency are still insufficient. Gorenje's position in the global market is weaker than it should be also because of the lack of state support for internationalized companies compared to other countries.

Globalization is introducing many additional problems involving risk management. Gorenje's response was, after deciding for a core business in household appliances in order to reduce costs, to also diversify to some related fields like marketing Polish Zetor tractors (since 1993) in Slovenia and BiH, producing tools for the automotive industry (Volkswagen, Revoz/Renault and Mercedes-Benz in particular)[4] and producing furniture. Diversification in services is another effort to reduce risks. Gorenje GTI trade and agency services has become the exclusive importer of Hyundai automobiles in Croatia. Diversification has been going on at home and abroad. In Slovenia, several companies were acquired. The most important diversification involves acquisition of the furniture factory Marles and the establishing of furniture production in Austria and in CZ, which later became integrated with Gorenje Interieri (1999).

The high level of Gorenje's internationalization means this corporation has already done most of its adaptation 'homework' regarding accession to the European Union. And yet the new 'domestic' market will impose additional competitive pressures on Gorenje as a much smaller producer of 'white goods' than its competitors.

One possible source of problems for Gorenje could stem from the common price policy within the EU, where goods have to be sold at the same prices across the whole market. This might cause difficulties in adjusting the price policy and could negatively effect sales especially in regions with lower purchasing power (see Duris, 2002; p. 22).

In spite of the very high emphasis on R&D and training, Gorenje still faces difficulties in acquiring suitable personal for firms located abroad. Slovenian expertise, no matter how able, has to be supplemented by local experts since this is a must in such highly demanding international business operations. Secondly, the relatively good standard of living and high quality of life in Slovenia makes even younger experts reluctant to work abroad in spite of the higher pay offered. Problems with schooling of children or jobs for partners also hinder such internationalization.

The main challenge ahead is whether to grow as an independent company, or to form a strategic alliance with one of the largest players in the industry in the world or to find an equity partner. Being a public joint-stock company, all options are naturally open but the firm's emphasis is to remain an independent player with strong international contractual international co-operation.

Summary

Today, Gorenje is a global producer that has achieved a relatively high level of technological expertise and innovation. By exporting more than 93 per cent of its total production, Gorenje competes more through its innovation and brands within a 'simple and logical' design.

After a long, not always trouble-free, development Gorenje has become a flexible, dynamic and modern European, even global, corporation. This has been achieved largely thanks to restructuring as a response to the crises it met in the past. Unlike many companies that in times of crisis seek to reduce R&D and training, Gorenje sought a solution in greater internationalization and a stronger reliance on its own innovations and capabilities. This orientation has been facilitated by its business philosophy and culture based on a consensus-supported decision-making process, high respect of its customers, the market, and its own employees.

The very early internationalization helped Gorenje overcome two major crises and enhanced its capabilities to face up to global challenges. Firms it established abroad have played a pivotal role in transforming the company from a small labour-intensive producer to a large and modern multinational company.

The evolution of Gorenje's marketing confirms its mature internationalization. It started to penetrate Western European markets through retail chains, continued through its own network of companies abroad and is today also trying to seize the advantages of the Internet.

Future priorities are to enhance internationalization by focusing on household appliances and business with the highest growth potential (like machine construction and tool-making) and integration with Gorenje's core activities to produce synergetic effects and continuing its long-term orientation of maximizing consumer satisfaction and environment-friendly products.

Notes

1 Just for Gorenje d.d., not for the whole consolidated group.

2 In preparing this chapter we relied heavily on Milestones, 2000. A paper prepared by Sočan (2000) was also intensively used throughout this case study.

3 If not otherwise stated, figures are taken from Gorenje's Annual Report 2000 and 2001.

4 At the international Forma Tool 99 exhibition, Gorenje orodjarna received the Gold Medal award for a tool manufactured for Mercedes-Benz (Milestones, 2000; p. 72).

Chapter 14

Prevent

Financial statements for 2000[1]:

Number of employees:	252
Assets:	€ 153 million
Shareholders' funds:	€ 15 million
Total revenues:	€ 368.7 million
Net sales abroad:	68.5%
Net profit:	€ 5.8 million
Value added per employee:	€ 50,435

Activity: Mfr. of made-up textiles, excl. apparel
Number of companies within the same business activity: 62
Type of organization: Joint-stock company d.d.
http://www.prevent.si/

Introduction

The Prevent group is one of the fastest growing companies in Slovenia. It has become the third largest exporter thanks to its intensive internationalization coupled with offensive company restructuring. Internationalization and diversification (at home and abroad) was not only seen as a way to grow but also to reduce vulnerability and excessive dependence on any one core product. Internationalization was also facilitated and induced by external factors. Firstly, by strategic partnerships with large foreign partners, secondly by the type of product demanding close vicinity to customers, namely car producers, thirdly by high labour intensity which makes production inefficient if labour costs are rising and, finally, by the local regulatory framework.

History

The birth of the Prevent group can be traced to the production of protective gloves in Slovenj Gradec in 1952. The name Prevent appeared for the first time in 1969. In 1995, two companies emerged out of Tovarna Usnja Slovenj

Gradec TUS (Leather Factory Slovenj Gradec) as part of its privatization plan. One was Prevent d.d. Today, Prevent d.d. is a private joint-stock company, 84 per cent owned by private individuals and 16 per cent by legal entities from Slovenia. The production of car-seat covers started in 1976.

The Prevent group is one of the most rapidly growing companies in Slovenia. In the period since 1996 alone, its employment level has increased more than six times. The production of car-seat covers has increased nearly six-fold (almost three million sets in 2001). Sales in 2001 amounted to € 257 million, a 26 per cent increase over 1999, with 96 per cent of the production being exported. Imports amount to about 60 per cent of its export levels.

In the last four years, the Prevent group has grown from a medium-sized exporter (taking 284th place among Slovenian firms) to the third largest exporter in Slovenia. Its really rapid growth can best be illustrated by the fact that for the first million car-seat covers it needed 12 years, for the next million it took five years and in 2001 they produced almost three million of them (Tkalec, 2001; p. 17).

Development of the company was not without its own problems. On the contrary, it was precisely the problems which the firm faced when automobile production was in a crisis in 1993 and after the collapse of the Yugoslav market that the Prevent group harnessed for its offensive and not defensive restructuring. An important factor facilitating this strategy included the very high unemployment rate in the region where the Prevent group is situated. Many companies went into liquidation and therefore a lot of qualified labour was available. After 1994, there was not enough labour in the region therefore Prevent started to open new facilities in other places around Slovenia. Another significant impact on the internationalization orientation that started then was the contribution of N. Hastor, a Bosnian businessman who was for many years a representative of UNIS (a large Bosnian firm) in Wolfsburg and is now Executive Director of Prevent's subsidiary in Germany.

A partnership with Volkswagen started back in 1976 and has developed into a strategic partnership. Today, the Prevent group is the largest single supplier to Volkswagen.

Company profile

The Prevent group consists of 30 firms, all legal entities, eight of them located abroad. It now employs 7,200 people. Turnover in 2001 was € 330 million, and its exports were worth € 322 million. Their activity extends from the production of automotive parts through to construction, work clothes and gloves, metals, wood-processing and protection materials. At the top of the group structure is Prevent d.d., which concentrates on strategic development.

The Prevent group is the largest European manufacturer of passenger car-seat covers. They are produced under the Prevent group trademark as are work gloves (excluding gloves made in Brazil sold under the Previlon trademark) and special protective garments. Its European market share is 17 per cent, while the world share is six per cent. Its customers are VW, Ford, Peugeot, Renault and Citroen. Production is in line with ISO/TS 16949 standards.

By acquiring a number of companies in Slovenia (see p. 212), the Prevent group broadened its core business to include construction materials, wood and metal industry, which have since become an important export item as well. In the production of inner doors and jambs, the market share in Macedonia and Kosovo is as high as 80 per cent, in Bosnia 5 per cent.

Internationalization

The Prevent group has grown from a predominantly local company with growing exports to a highly internationalized company. The domestic market now constitutes only eight per cent of total turnover.

The internationalization strategy is a combination of an endogenous decision based on the need to locate production of its core product close to the customer (car producers) and a concerted decision taken together with its long-term partners[2]. Finally, it also involved a reaction and adaptation to the demands of regulators. The then Yugoslav legislation prescribed that if cars were to be sold in the domestic market as having been locally produced then a certain proportion had to be produced domestically. This was why the production of car-seat covers started since it was one of the easiest components to produce locally so as to comply with the local content requirements.

There are two directions of the internationalization strategy; growth by establishing greenfield operations abroad in the firm's core business and diversification into related activities in order to improve the firm's positioning in unstable and volatile automotive industry markets mostly by acquisitions.

Although internationalization was strong when measured by the share of exports in turnover, it was very modest in terms of the internationalization of production that started only a few years ago. The Prevent group is an example of a firm that turned into a multinational almost overnight. There was no time to move step by step like the Scandinavian School would have predicted. The leap from the exporting stage to a global production network happened in only a few years.

Today, the Prevent group has affiliations in Slovenia, BiH, Moldova, Croatia, Spain and Brazil. The main motive for internationalization is to set up manufacturing close to the customer so as to improve, enhance and shorten the response time to their needs. Increasingly expanding production means constructing new facilities in their vicinity since seat covers as the chief product of the Prevent group are transport-cost intensive. Lastly, production simply has to be organized in the era of globalization in locations that are, apart from being in close vicinity to car manufacturers, also cost efficient. Slovenia has become too expensive in terms of labour costs, which reduces the profitability of the labour-intensive production involved in car-seat covers. The only solution is therefore to concentrate higher value-added activities in locations where labour costs are higher and to decentralize labour-intensive parts of production to lower-cost locations. This is precisely the advantage of organizing businesses globally. The Prevent group is at the moment expanding more through internationalizing but, due to recessionary trends in the world, it is already under pressure to reduce employment in Slovenia and relocate certain lower echelons of value-added activities abroad and to start the abovementioned dynamic restructuring through internationalization.

The first investment made abroad was Prevent Sarajevo, only three years after the war in BiH had ended. The key objective was to produce car-seat covers for first installation for the reopened Volkswagen factory there. Lower labour costs were in fact just a second motive. The first was the promising growth potential after the reopening of Volkswagen production in BiH since Volkswagen is expected to aim at achieving the production levels seen in Vogušče near Sarajevo before the war. This investment was the first step in the strategy of expanding production to locations where labour costs are lower. The objectives of this outward FDI were therefore four-fold:

- to create new markets;
- to increase market shares;
- to boost sales, exports and profits; and
- to reduce labour and transport costs.

Initially, the factory employed only 50 people, 180 were employed when the factory was opened in 2001 and, in 2002, Prevent Sarajevo already employs 600 people. In 2001, Prevent Sarajevo realized € 51million in exports. All production was exported. The profit rate was four to five per cent. Revenue increased in 2001 compared to 2000 by 40 per cent. Production increased to today's levels of 1100 sets of car seat covers and over 1100 covers for spring mattresses. For Volkswagen, Prevent Sarajevo is producing leather covers, for Peugeot and Renault textile covers and for BMW leather covers for hand brakes. For the Slovenian firm Šepič, it produces covers for spring mattresses which the Slovenian firm chiefly exports to the German market.

Although considered a very risky business at the time, it has turned out to be a very successful operation. Investment was made by companies using their own resources in times when there were no investment protection agreements between the governments of the two countries. The Prevent group did not even insure the business against political risks since in those days such insurance was not available.

Internationalization has not stopped there. Prevent Sarajevo is a co-owner of the financial management company Blago. In January 2001, it acquired permission to establish the privatization investment fund Prevent Invest with initial capital of DM 200 million.

The Prevent group also became an owner[3] with a 42 per cent share in Volkswagen Sarajevo (October 2001) which it bought for DM 2.1 million from UNIS Holding Sarajevo amidst the tough bidding of the Privatization Agency of BiH. Suppliers and customers were thereby integrated under the one roof. The objective of this acquisition is to increase the production of cars there from the present 3,000 annually to 30,000 annually. Future plans are to invest an additional DM 18 million, with DM three million invested in 2001 in the future development of car manufacturing and parts and in acquisitions of related car industry firms in BiH[4]. Plans are also to diversify to areas other than car-seat cover production.

The most recent expansion (July 2001) involved establishment of a new factory valued at € 4 million near Sao Paolo Prevent Thierry Brazil. It has started producing approximately 400 car cover seats per day with the objective to reach 1000 soon.

The Prevent group is becoming a truly global company. Although strategic decisions relating to development and marketing are centralized, many are decentralized. Design is undertaken in the vicinity of the major customers. Therefore, a special unit Prevent DEV GmbH was established near the Volkswagen factory with the objective of being close to the manufacturer and thus in a position to respond to its demand in the shortest time possible. The same function to be close to French customers is filfilled by Thierry Prevent Development Paris SA. AD Plastik, a firm acquired in Croatia, was for instance given the responsibility to run the Zagreb firm RIS, which was bought just before the process of its liquidation started.

Prevent Zlatar, was established in 2000 by buying the premises of the firm SKIM in liquidation. The objective was to strengthen co-operation with French customers and to enhance competitiveness thanks to lower costs of local labour and expected increase of sales of French cars in the Croatian market. The Croatian venture presently employs 350 people. The company produces car-seat covers for the French market (Citroen and Peugeot).

Prevent Moldova was also established in 2000 since labour costs in Moldava are much lower than in Slovenia and qualified labour with experience in the textile industry is readily available. It employs 200 people.

Prevent Vigo SA, Spain was established a year later, in 2001 as the result of fruitful previous co-operation with the PSA Group. It employs 80 people producing car-seat covers for Peugeot Partner, Citroen Berlingo, and the C15 pick-up. By locating production there, Prevent is able to serve customers better. In addition, there are chances to broaden the production programme to supply the whole PSA Group in Spain with car-seat covers.

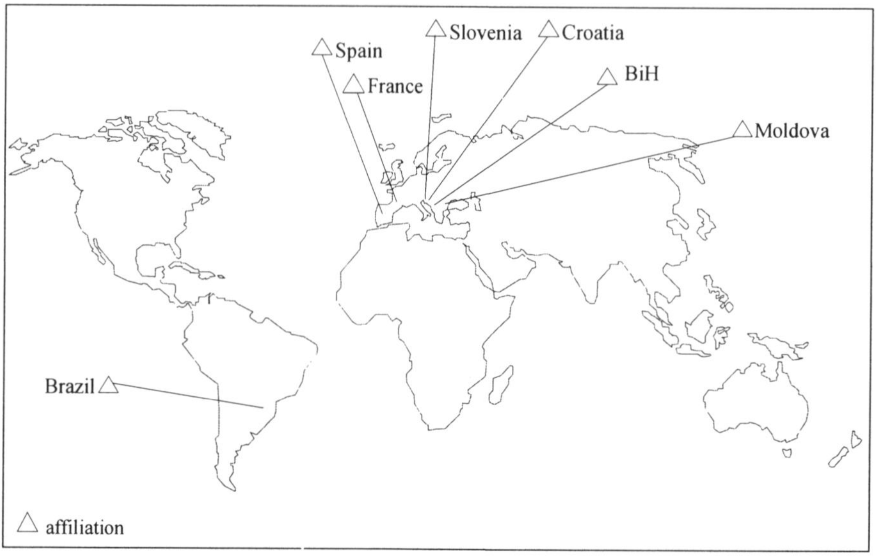

Figure 14.1 International business network of Prevent group in 2002

Competitive advantages

The core competitive advantage is the high and standardized quality of Prevent group products, which has also been achieved thanks to the initial long-term co-operation with foreign partners. The automotive industry generally has very high standards and only those producers that can satisfy such demands can stay in business. In 1996, the Prevent group received the ISO 9002 certificate and a year later the ISO 9001 certificate. In 1998, the automotive standard VDA 6.1 and in 1999 the QS 9000 were gained. In January 2001, the Prevent group received an award for best international company in BiH, which is not surprising since it is second most profitable manufacturing company in BiH. Manager of the company Prevent Sarajevo also received the award for the manager of the year 2001 in BiH. Volkswagen recognized the Prevent group twice with a value to the customer award. Jože Kozmus,

President of the Prevent group Management Board received an award from the Slovenian Chamber of Commerce and Industry for excellent economic results. Prevent Sarajevo has received the ISO 9001 certificate, the VDA 6.1 from the German automotive industry and the QS 9000 standard of the American automotive industry and ISO/TS 16949. Perhaps the most important recognition of quality is the fact that the protective gloves produced by the Prevent group have almost become the trademark for such glove types also produced by other manufacturers, who simply copy such gloves.

The standardized quality of products is achieved by a new system of control involving a self-elimination method for products not meeting the demanded quality standards. In order to implement this method, it was necessary to supplement it also with a system of pre-qualification and/or additional training of those workers who cannot keep up such quality standards.

This has all been possible due to highly qualified employees. Strategic competitive advantages, according to the Prevent group's management, are in fact its highly trained human capital. In order to strengthen this in the future, the firm is trying to create and enhance the corporate culture (see Pavlin, 2001; p. 24).

The second advantage lies in the Group's rapid reaction and adaptation to trends in the world economy, particularly in the car industry. It tries to detect trends ex ante and strategically respond before changes really happen. Another way of doing this has been the long-term strategic partnership contracts it has with many multinational companies.

Competitive advantages have been created and are maintained by modern electronic communication systems and management. Since 1997 production has been computerized, employing CAD-CAM for cutting. An information system (SAP/R3 introduced in 2000) is in use, which enables fast, reliable and simple management with all the data needed without any delay. The firm is customer-oriented. The satisfaction of customers is measured through annual surveys, which are seen as an instrument for improving the quality of production. An important element of reliability and the high quality of the products is 24-hour service guarantee.

Competitive advantages result from the Group's own research and development efforts. The Prevent group invests in R&D approximately three per cent of annual sales. The development and design of car-seat covers is its own.

Speed is a must in modern business. Therefore, the Prevent group uses in addition to its own 150 trucks its own plane to transport its products[5]. More importantly, customs procedures are performed at the factory premises in order to facilitate foreign trade operations and enable 24-hour operation.

Adaptation to the new environment is also considered an important competitive advantage. Each firm has to try to adapt to the prevailing local production and habits and to find a way to match the local and prevailing corporate culture. Imposing your own at the expense of local culture can prove to be a very expensive strategy. In order to do this, the Prevent group's strategy is to employ local managerial staff as much as possible. Only in the very initiation of a new company does a small number of top managers from the Prevent group help in organizing production.

Adaptations cannot of course be compromised in product quality terms but only in the way it is achieved. In order to bring about the standardized quality of its products, the ongoing transfer of knowledge from parent to subsidiary and appropriate training has become crucial. Training is extensive and usually starts in Prevent, Slovenia. The Prevent group has also decided that not only middle but also top management should undergo the training process.

Clearly another not unimportant advantage is knowing how to live with inflation. This has proved to be an advantage when investing in Brazil with its still high inflation rate. The rate of inflation is no longer high in Slovenia but it used to be in the socialist period. Therefore, the Prevent group has the know-how to handle it, giving it a competitive edge over firms from low inflation, OECD countries.

Weaknesses and threats

Initially, the Prevent group's core business almost entirely involved automotive-industry-related products. The firm was therefore highly dependant on the business cycles of just one industry. Crises experienced by the car industry in 1993 made diversification a must in order to reduce excessive dependence and high risk exposure. Diversification aimed at achieving 30 per cent of turnover realized in business other than the automotive industry (Tkalec, 2001,p. 18) is oriented to five sectors:

- car-related industry (AD Plastic[6], Unis-umico, Težanj, BiH);
- rubber industry (AD Plastic, Split, ACM, Ris Zagreb, Croatia);
- metal industry (acquisition of Tovarna rezalnega orodja Prevalje);
- wood industry (Lesna, Slovenj Gradec);
- construction industry[7] (Stavbar IGM, Hoče, Rudarska gradbena družba (RGD), Trbovlje, Gradis nizke gradnje, Maribor[8]).

Diversification and rapid adaptation and assimilation, combined with internationalization within a complex strategy is very demanding and creates problems when highly skilled staff with some international experience are hard to find. This is a problem in Slovenia, let alone when it comes to sending experts abroad. Even much higher wages can hardly attract people to go abroad, particularly to some risky location like BiH was when the affiliation was established. The Prevent group is trying to overcome this difficulty by intensifying training and thereby broadening the human capital base and through acquisitions through which it also gains access to local personnel.

The second difficulty seems to be a quality problem since labour in newly acquired firms is not used to the quality standards demanded by customers and gradually accumulated in the Slovenian location. Intensive training is therefore undertaken to overcome such problems not only of workers in production, but also of managers at all levels to keep up with customers' high demands and to stay in line with Prevent group quality standards and management and production methods, let alone according to the Prevent group's corporate culture. The time for such restructuring is short since the tough demands of global markets do not allow more than two years for an affiliation to become profitable.

There are already signs the Prevent group will face ever stronger local pressure to keep production at home[9] since globalization's cost minimization focus forces firms to relocate parts of their production to cheaper locations. Trade union voices will mount as will local political pressure given the prevailing public opinion that investing abroad also means losing jobs at home.

The biggest threat stems, however, from the fact that it is no longer the car producers which are the customers of Prevent but the producers of car seats. Being a supplier to a supplier puts the first one in a much more vulnerable position. In order to reduce such risks Prevent initially wanted to develop the production of whole car seats but failed. The second strategic answer was diversification to other car parts production.

Summary

The Prevent group is a typical case of pulled or induced internationalization. External circumstances 'forced' the firm to begin thinking internationally. Co-operation with foreign partners actually forced the Prevent group to go international. Firstly, to respond quickly to multinational companies' demands and, secondly, to locate production close to car production due to the prohibitive transport costs for a voluminous product like car-seat covers. Internationalization was also induced by too high a dependence on one product and one industry. The Prevent group's response was diversification, which was again only possible on a global scale.

Notes

1 Financial statement for the Prevent joint-stock parent company Slovenj Gradec and not for the whole consolidated group.
2 Expansion in Brazil was, for instance, taken on together with Volkswagen.
3 The investor was the subsidiary company Prevent Sarajevo.
4 In March 2002 producer of car filters Unis-umico was acquired by Prevent Sarajevo (51 per cent share). Prevent plans to invest all profits earned there in the next five years for tripling production in the next three years.
5 The idea is also to acquire the second largest airport in Slovenia in Maribor, not far from the location of Prevent d.d.
6 This was not a classic acquisition. The Prevent group acquired a 26 per cent share (the Prevent Zlatar, Croatia, part was 9.65 per cent). The Prevent group provided a loan to employees with which they were able to buy the company out. The idea was to stimulate the future owners to become interested in the destiny of the company they owned.
7 The idea is to embrace three pillars; production of construction materials, building constructions, particularly apartment houses and, finally, infrastructure like roads, bridges etc.
8 The Prevent group is not the owner of these firms but controls them indirectly instead. All these firms are not yet part of the Prevent group's consolidated balance, but they will be next year according to Jože Kozmus, the General Manager of Prevent. The idea is to merge RGD Trbovlje and Gradis nizke gradnje.
9 Today approximately 65 per cent of car-seat covers are produced in Slovenia.

Chapter 15

Iskraemeco

ISKRAEMECO

Energy Measurement and Management

Financial statements for 2000[1] :

Number of employees:	2,075	Value added per employee: € 20,129
Assets:	€ 72.6 million	Activity: Mfr. of instruments for measuring etc.
Shareholders' funds:	€ 45.3 million	Number of companies within the same business activity: 82
Total revenues:	€ 99.3 million	
Net sales abroad:	93.7% of revenues	Type of organization: Joint-stock company (d.d.)
Net profit:	€ 3.1 million	http//www.iskraemeco.si/

Introduction

Among firms included in our case studies, Iskraemeco is one of the first to have started internationalization and today it has truly internationalized its activities in many countries across almost all continents. It is a typical case of a firm that experienced internationalization step by step: first by exporting, then by licensing production to partners, followed by the establishment of sales units and finally production units abroad. Gradualism also describes the regional orientation of such internationalization. The main export markets were the early targets of internationalization, followed by more distant countries as a response to different national regulations and partly increasing relevance of differences in labour costs under the pressures of globalization. Internationalization was regarded as a strategic way of staying in business, keeping market shares, and growing and enhancing competitiveness. It is one of just a handful of Slovenian firms that relocate production abroad due to the lower labour costs available there.

History

Iskraemeco is a relatively old firm. It grew out of pre-World War II textile and machine industrial plants located where Iskraemeco stands today. In 1945 the plants were renamed *Strojne tovarne* and electricity meters were introduced into the production programme. In 1946 *Strojne tovarne* was renamed Iskra, later developing into one of the largest companies in both Slovenia and the then Yugoslavia. Only three years later the regular production of single-phase meters commenced. In 1958 the production of three-phase meters started. In the seventies, the first electronic precision meters and ripple control receivers were developed by Iskra's specialists.

In the 1990s Iskra as a large conglomerate, the largest exporter in former Yugoslavia disintegrated into a number of individual companies. Most of them are now very successful firms in their core business[2]. The common denominator of these firms was strong internal technological/know-how capabilities. Other firms not exporting to Western markets but mainly relying on the then Yugoslav market and/or basing their production on foreign licences without many domestic R&D inputs were in difficulty and not performing well. Iskra Števci became an independent company in 1990. The production of monolithic meters, in which some of Iskra's patented devices were built in, started in 1992. In 1994 the privatization of Iskra Števci was carried out and Iskraemeco d.d. (a joint-stock company) was founded. At that time, the employees owned 60 per cent of the joint-stock company.

Company profile

Iskraemeco's sphere of activity is the measurement, registration and management of energy in order to facilitate the efficient use of electrical energy. The company produces electricity meters for industry, households and for distribution and transmission of electrical energy companies. Separation of distribution of electricity from electrical meters was crucial for first entry to markets where otherwise large electrical meters producers would dominate. Its core business is equipment and systems for energy measurement and management segmentation (by energy and customers). In product terms, the industry is generally relatively mature[3] although production technologies have been constantly modernized. With the introduction of electronics in the electricity meters industry it is starting to climb the ladder of value-added activities, transforming in more technology intensive than at the start.

Today's ownership structure is still dominated by internal owners. Employees of Iskraemeco established their own Investment Company (similar to an Employee Stock Ownership Plan) which owns 47 per cent, followed by the Slovenian Pension Fund (24 per cent), the Slovenian Indemnity Fund (10 per cent), similar shares held by small shareholders (seven per cent), while the Slovenian Agriculture Bank and the internal shares fund each have six per cent of shares.

Today, Iskraemeco employs some 2,100 people in Slovenia and approximately 800 abroad. In 2000, revenue reached SIT 20.4 billion (€ 99.5 million). Net profit constituted 3.1 per cent of revenues and seven per cent of capital, some 15 per cent above the level of the previous year. Sales are constantly but not spectacularly increasing. In 2000 Iskraemeco increased sales in its electronic products programme by more than 50 per cent.

In 2001 Iskraemeco produced all together approximately 2.5 million electricity meters and other electricity measuring instruments. Its market share is constantly increasing. It is among the leading producers in the world in meter manufacturing, together with Siemens, Actaris, ABB and General Electric. The European market share is 12 per cent (only Siemens with 28 per cent and Actaris with 27 per cent have larger market shares).

Internationalization

Internationalization also finds its genesis in Iskraemeco's predecessor Iskra that internationalized its activities far back in the socialist era. Iskra established a number of firms abroad, some as early as in the 1960s (see endnote 11 Chapter 3). For that period and for a socialist firm, this was a very revolutionary approach. The major internationalisation driving factor was small domestic, then still medium-sized Yugoslav market. With independence, the need to acquire new markets was even more pressing. Technology simply demands large production volumes, becoming profitable only after a certain size threshold is reached. Another reason is the fact that the industry as such is very competitive, demanding on one hand permanent and ongoing technological improvements which then forced firms to co-operate internationally. It also demanded very close contact with customers because of differences in national standards and regulations among countries. Enhancing capabilities was a must in the industry. This is also why Iskra very early on embraced what is today called the knowledge economy. Special in-house training programmes were organized and later transformed into a special school already in 1980 in co-operation with the Faculty of Economics from Ljubljana[4].

The first steps in the direction of more long-term international co-operation involved licensed production abroad, which started already in the 1970s. This was subsequently expanded to long-term co-production agreements, also stimulated by the then foreign trade and foreign exchange regime that allowed large parts of the foreign exchange earned to be kept.

Iskraemeco has therefore also built and strengthened its internationalization based on the experience and knowledge accumulated by its predecessor. Human capital was thereby trained and picked up internationalization experiences.

The company is highly internationalized and sells its products in 80 countries. The Slovenian market constitutes just one per cent of all its revenues from sales. The EU and other parts of Western Europe make up a major export market (51 per cent), followed by Asia and Oceania with 23 per cent, and CEECs with 20 per cent in 2000. Recently, sales have increased especially in India, Hong Kong, Saudi Arabia and Hungary. Libya and Poland became Iskraemeco's new markets in 2000.

Equity types of internationalization started in the 1990s. The first company abroad founded was Iskra GmbH, Bamberg, Germany in 1993 (in 1995 renamed Iskraemeco GmbH). The key objective of this company was the promotion of sales of electricity meters and the acquisition of permits and certifications for such products and related equipment for measuring and managing energy there. By 1996 Iskraemeco already had seven companies abroad. At first the main motive was getting a market share, whereas now it is enhancing competitiveness by gaining access to cheaper labour and other inputs.

Today, the company has eight production firms located abroad (Russia, Portugal, Spain, Croatia, BiH, Romania, Malaysia and India) and four trade ones (Great Britain, Germany, Sweden and Austria).

Total invested capital in all firms abroad was € 3.9 million by 2001, with plans to increase it by € 10 million by 2005. Units established abroad produced 8.6 billion tolars of sales revenues in 2000.

The firm has employed as many as 800 workers abroad.

The objectives of sales and production units differ. Production abroad is basically a way to keep already achieved market shares. These are markets to which Iskraemeco was originally exporting its products but, upon reaching a certain export level, the need arises to make the product local and thereby overcome tariff barriers to keep the market share also by adapting products to customers' demands given the still very different national standards and local certifications needed in this industry. If production units had not been established, markets would have been lost. The second reason is simply the need to grow. In order to do this, the company needs new markets. 'There are many countries in our business' said Nikolaj Bevk, Chairman of the company's Management Board 'where you cannot enter the market if you do not produce locally. Such markets are, for instance, Saudi Arabia to which you just can't export. The third reason is to make production cheaper due to the three to six times lower labour costs available abroad compared to Slovenia. By moving production abroad you increase the profitability of those parts of production which remain in Slovenia' (see Bevk, 2000).

The main objective of establishing trading firms abroad is to promote sales by making sales distribution cheaper. Dealers want to get a 20-30 per cent markup on sales. By establishing your own firm, part of this can be earned by the new firms. The second reason is to be able to better promote sales where dealers have not performed well enough. When Iskraemeco reaches a 10 per cent market share of a certain market, the establishment of its own sales unit there can lead to 10 to 20 per cent cost reductions.

Four companies are producing electricity meters under an Iskraemeco licence (Colombia, Argentina, Saudi Arabia, and Tunisia).

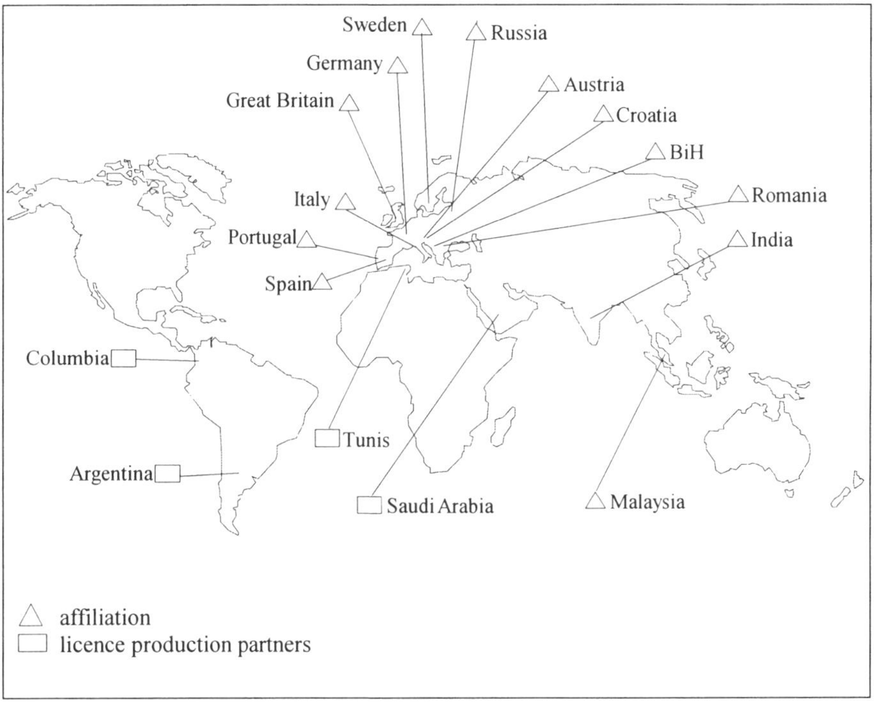

Figure 15.1 International business network of Iskraemeco in 2002

The degree of internationalization can also be measured by the share of the production of induction electricity meters abroad in their total production. This was approximately 17 per cent in 2000. In the next few years the share of electricity meters produced abroad is planned to increase parallel to the overall growth of Iskraemeco in order to stay in the market, said Nikolaj Bevk (see Bertoncelj, 2002; p. 21). A major expansion is planned abroad.

Iskraemeco's strategy is to have a controlling share in its firms abroad. The reasons are to 'get control over the distribution of profits'. The company is involved in strong development efforts therefore it does not want to pay too many dividends and prefers to invest them instead in its development. The second reason is that 'we are moving more and more phases of production abroad and therefore control over the quality of the products produced everywhere is becoming increasingly more important' added Nikolaj Bevk (see Bertoncelj, 2002; p. 21). Iskraemeco is still entering into co-production agreements but without parallel licence agreements in order to avoid creating its own competitors. This was one reason why it acquired a former licensing partner in Spain.

One of the latest international expansions was the establishment of a company together with the Romanian partner Contor Zenner Romania S.A. in Arad in 2001. The objective was to become a local supplier for the complete range of products and systems, enabling efficient metering and billing of electricity energy sales and the assembling of mechanical meters for residential customers.

In order to increase the market share in India's growing market, in 2002 Iskraemeco acquired one of the largest Indian firms producing electricity meters. The idea is to increase market share by introducing its own modern technology, restructuring the acquired firm, and improving the quality of electricity meters produced. It is also thinking of upgrading the present co-operation agreements with firms in Columbia and Argentina with an equity arrangement.

In January 2002 Iskraemeco organized the first conference of the whole group of associated companies in Slovenia[5]. Besides the parent company, four trading companies and seven production companies participated at the conference. A common strategy of Iskraemeco's associated companies was adopted. Directors of the companies presented their companies' operations, position in the market, and expectations for the next medium-term period. The Iskraemeco strategy is to strengthen the internationalization of sales and production. Current operations in 80 countries around the world are still planned to expand. In the next five years, the number of markets and share of production outside of Kranj in Slovenia are to be increased. The importance of organization and teamwork within the Group has been highlighted. Such meetings will become a regular practice in pursuing the Iskraemeco Group's strategic targets.

Competitive advantages

Iskraemeco grew out of the large firm Iskra that highly prioritized in-house R&D and training. The firm's knowledge has been developed and manifested in many patents. The most intensive years in terms of technological transformation were between 1995 and 1997, i.e. after its successful privatization. R&D has been successful. A number of new products have been developed in-house; in 2000 for instance a new meter and new tariff-switching clock.

Quality has always been at the forefront, lately even more so. In order to achieve standardized quality, the company adjusted its production and organization to ISO 9001 international standards back in 1991. Therefore, it has not been difficult selling its products under its own recognized brand name of Iskra around the world. In some countries, local producers also wanted to add to this global trademark the names of their own companies in order to localize the products.

In spite of having good products with well-recognized brand names, Iskraemeco has to permanently reduce its costs. Internationalization has proved to be instrumental here. Therefore, the highly and very early developed international network of production, co-production and sales units abroad has become one of Iskraemeco's main competitive advantages. Without such a direct presence in major markets it would be impossible to achieve such high market shares.

Training has become one of the major strategic components of the company's development. One reason for this is the rapid technological changes seen in the industry, which call for the permanent prior qualification of employees. A specific reason for such intensive pre-qualifications was the transition from the production of mechanical to electronic meters. The number of participants in training programmes has been increasing. In 2000 up to 1,000 people participated in different training programmes.

The company pays special attention to the environment with the aim of achieving high environmental production standards. In 1999 the firm also obtained the ISO 14001 certificate for environmental standards.

Problems, weaknesses and threats

Iskraemeco's impressive results have been achieved in a very turbulent international environment, when accelerating globalization has forced all companies to reduce their costs to the minimum. Competition continues to be tougher every day with resulting pressure on prices, especially in the EU markets. The German mark's exchange rate, lagging behind the inflation rate in Slovenia, had a negative effect on Iskraemeco's business operations by lowering its price competitiveness. On the other hand, strengthening of the US dollar produced a positive effect.

Sometimes there is a problem with local workers abroad, but only for more qualified jobs like technology supervisors, managers and similar jobs calling for a university or higher education. Therefore, for such highly skilled tasks Iskraemeco temporarily employs its own experts abroad at least. Employing one's own people for longer times abroad would be too costly since it is not only the salary but also the related costs of housing, schooling etc. that are involved. The policy is therefore to employ local engineers as much as possible. Otherwise, Iskraemeco predominantly employs local workers without any problems. Skills necessary for the production of electricity meters can be learned in the parent company.

Internationalization is also legally a very demanding business. It is not only knowledge about laws but particularly their implementation which can vary greatly in different countries. One cannot be too careful in this regard but at the same time if you are too careful 'you cannot establish a unit abroad because of the many administrative barriers and long procedures. You just do it and try to shorten the pay-off period as much as possible' (Bevk, 2000).

One future challenge involves the further diversification of production; on top of the ongoing transition from mechanical to electronic meters. Since the firm now produces parts for mechanical meters in Slovenia, pressure will be growing to reduce employment in Slovenia. Components used for the production of electronic meters are not being produced by Iskraemeco nor in Slovenia. They are from global component producers that are competitive and whose products are then assembled into the final product according to Iskraemeco's specifications, quality standards and designs.

The transition from mechanical to electronic electricity meters is a historic turning point for this industry. Many of present technologies and skills will become obsolete and make some traditionally skilled workers redundant. Core competencies are dramatically changing. The company is and will be addressing this issue in three ways; firstly by giving even more emphasis on marketing and acquisition of new markets. Secondly by pre-qualifying workers, training them for more demanding higher value-added activities and, thirdly, by limited diversification of activities in related fields. In view of growing electricity demand in the future, also due to the fact that some two billion people are still without electricity in the world and that electricity is environmentally one of the cleanest energies, there seems no threat to Iskraemeco's core business which will continue to be its future main strategic orientation.

Iskraemeco is a successful company. Therefore, it may become a target for a takeover although management is not planning to sell the company since there is no need for a strategic partner. The company is successful as it is, with good products and growing sales. It wants to remain mostly owned by its employees.

Summary

Iskraemeco is one company for which internationalization is really a way of keeping and enhancing its competitiveness not only by gaining economies of size but also by reducing labour costs by moving production to low-cost countries. The high degree of internationalization would have been unfeasible without the step-by-step accumulation of knowledge throughout the long history of the company and its predecessor. Investing abroad has been based on firm-specific advantages, its own products and brand name.

The volatility accompanying intensified globalization trends poses management additional challenges. The response has so far been to bolster R&D, emphasize the development of new products and technologies as well as stepping up internationalization in order to reduce costs and strengthen competitiveness. Another response involves modest steps in the direction of diversification, which could reduce dependence on only a narrow set of products in a single industry.

Notes

1 This refers only to Iskraemeco's joint-stock company at Kranj in Slovenia and not to the whole consolidated group.

2 Apart from Iskraemeco, also Iskra Avtoelektrika Šempeter pri Gorici, Iskratel Kranj, Domel Železniki and Rotomatika Idrija. They are all some of the major exporters of Slovenia; with Iskra Avtoelektrika assuming 14th place, Iskratel 18th, Iskraemeco 22nd, Domel 42nd and Rotomatika which, as part of the Hidria Group, is the 11th biggest exporter.

3 The method of measuring electricity had basically not changed in the last 100 years before introduction of the electronic way of measuring recently. Electronic meters involve a new way of measuring electricity.

4 The programme was running for about 15 years. It was obligatory for all experts supposed to work in international network of ISKRA and all executives including managers of factories. It was a 3-month residential programme. It can be claimed that this was in fact the first managerial school in then Yugoslavia. The example of ISKRA was followed by some other large firms like Jugotekstil and Slovenijales.

5 This is somewhat of a continuation of the same practice introduced back in 1972 by the predecessor firm Iskra. It became a regular annual event at which all managers and representatives abroad participated. It was in fact a strategic conference designing a long-term strategy of the firm. At that time it was a very original and novel approach demonstrating the high priority the firm gave to international operations and long-range planning.

Chapter 16

Krka

Financial statements for 2000[1] :

Number of employees: 2,864 and 271 abroad		Activity: Manufacturing of pharmaceutical preparations
Assets:	€ 498 million	Number of companies within the same business activity: 13
Shareholders' capital:	€ 334 million	Type of organization: Joint-stock company d.d.
Total revenues:	€ 320 million	http://www.krka.si
Net sales abroad:	77% of revenues	
Net profit:	€ 34.7 million	
Value added per employee:	€ 56,468	

Introduction

Krka from Novo mesto is one of two relatively large pharmaceutical companies in Slovenia given the size of its economy. It was formally established after Lek and has become the other major drug maker in the country. Its internationalization started very early, not only with exports and under licensing and similar long-term co-operation contracts with major drug producers in the world, but also by establishing a joint venture to make drugs in Kenya as early as in the 1970s. Today, the biggest target countries, besides Slovenia, are the Russian Federation, Poland and other CEECs where Krka has over 40 years of market experience. In spite of the not particularly happy experiences with its pioneering venture in Kenya, it can now be claimed that the episode was highly instrumental in creating self-confidence and helped create internal internationalization capabilities for later outward FDI expansion. Nevertheless, Krka may still be considered a leapfrogging globalizer. Apart from its own branded generic drugs, Krka's specific competitive advantage is its emphasis on close relations with immediate customers, doctors, pharmacists, and drug distributors. Management has developed a very personal style of developing such contacts, also based on excellent knowledge of the Russian language and familiarity with Russian and other (Polish, Croatian) cultures.

History

The earliest beginnings of Krka can be traced back to 1954 when the first pharmaceutical laboratory was established[2] out of the private chemist's shop of Mr. Adrijaniè, established before the Second World War. That was followed by the plant which later moved to the present location in Novo mesto, registering of the first patent, and the start of producing and exporting cosmetics in the period before 1964. Investments in new plants and the start of processing of medical herbs (the so-called green programme supported by a 'back to nature' slogan) and health resort facilities marked the next ten years of development. The 1975-1984 period may be regarded as a time of deepening development by registering antibiotics with the American Food and Drug Administration (FDA) of the USA and also taking the first steps in production outward internationalization with the establishment of Dawa Kenya.

The next few decades were marked by the intensification of internationalization through the opening of representative offices in many countries, also made possible due to substantial investment in its own R&D. By 2001, Krka had positioned itself among the leading pharmaceutical companies in CEE based on strengthening its own generic drugs programme, emphasizing quality and maintaining close contacts with its customers. In 2002 Notol, a major new plant for the production of solid-dosage forms, the largest and most important investment (€ 66.8 million) in Krka's history, was officially opened. It extends over 23,000 square metres with a planned production target of 2.5 billion tablets, coated tablets and capsules annually.

Company profile

Krka is the largest joint-stock company listed on the Ljubljana Stock Exchange with a current market capitalization of SIT 132 billion (€ 588 million) and is mostly Slovenian owned. Foreign shareholders currently hold 9.6 per cent of its shares. Their share has been slowly increasing. The company is classified among the top Slovenian companies regarding turnover and export (it is the largest exporter), certainly among the few important exporters of hi-tech products. It also generated the highest profit of industrial companies in Slovenia in 2000 (profit increased by 58 per cent compared to 1999). At the end of 2001 it employed 3,520 employees, 570 abroad. The share of highly-educated staff is constantly rising and exceeded 30 per cent at the close of 2001.

Krka's mission of 'Living the healthy life' is realized through its rich range of products and services that improve the quality of life. This orientation substitutes the earlier one aimed at curing diseases, whereby the production of antibiotics constituted almost 40 per cent of the production programme (today it is just 20 per cent).

Krka's core efforts are centred on pharmaceutical-chemical activities which, in addition to the production and sale of drugs for human use, also include the production of self-medication and cosmetic products. It is mainly a producer of generic drugs with added value. Krka's capacities are directed toward the development of modern, mainly generic, drugs that already constitute some 75 per cent of today's production levels. Its remaining drugs are the fruit of co-operation with world leading multinational pharmaceutical companies. About 15 years ago, such licensed drugs made up almost 80 per cent of Krka's total sales.

In order to enhance its own capabilities and cope with the ever more pressing need for ongoing education, Krka set up a special education centre in which each employee participates on average more than twice in various forms of training (approximately 45 training hours). Special emphasis is given to management training. In 2000 more than 500 of Krka's leading personnel took part in training sessions on modern management methods.

In the 1996-2000 period, sales increased from below € 236 to € 297.5 million. Prescription pharmaceuticals constitute the lion's share of these sales[3] (74 per cent in 2001), followed by OTC drugs (13 per cent), veterinary products (seven per cent) and cosmetics with five per cent.

Krka's regional orientation of exports and internationalization is generally diversified yet somewhat balanced since Eastern Europe, Slovenia and South-east Europe constitute almost the same shares.

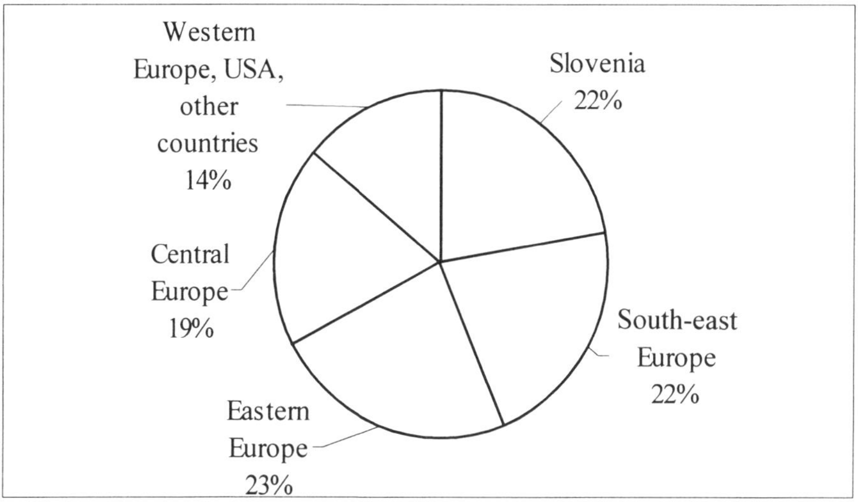

Figure 16.1 Sales by regions in 2000 (in per cent)

Slovenia remains a key market although its relative importance is shrinking (see Box 5.1); the share of sales in 2001 fell compared to 1999 from 26 per cent to 21 per cent. This was not a reflection of reduced sales in Slovenia but of the substantial relative growth of sales in other regions, particularly South-east Europe[4]. In Eastern Europe, Russia is the biggest partner experiencing a doubling of sales since its crisis in 1998. In Central Europe, Poland is the main market. The EU is constantly expanding its share (Krka is one of the leading generic producers of enalapril in tablet form), while the US has only recently become a more important destination for Krka's exports[5] and is not regarded as a long-term strategic market. The very strong competition from generic producers there is making this market ever less attractive.

Internationalization

Krka markets its products today in more than 70 countries around the world. The high degree of internationalization is manifested in a small share of the domestic market in total production (only one-fifth is sold in Slovenia). The network of firms abroad currently involves 38 companies and representative offices (13 companies and 25 representative offices in 24 countries).

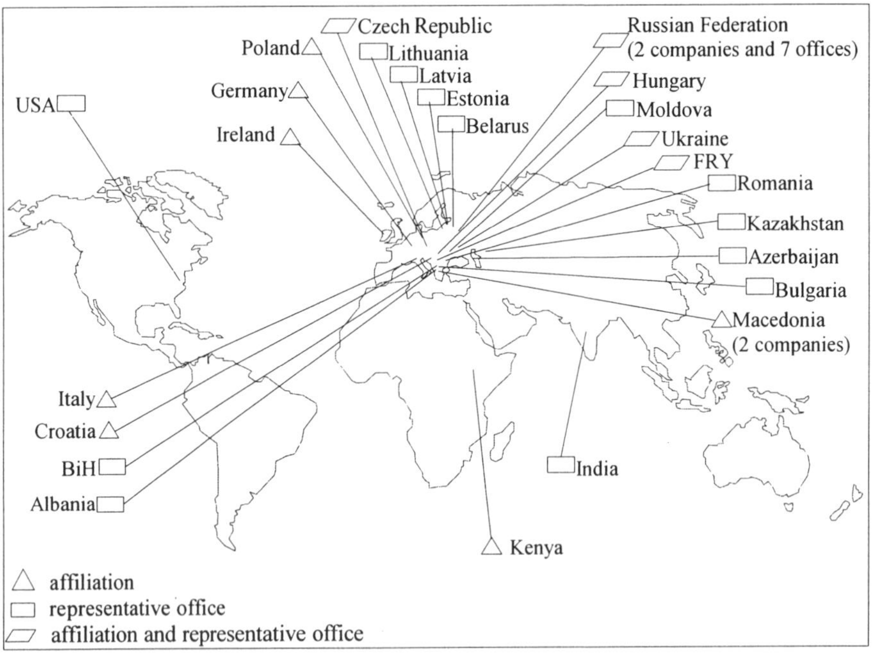

Figure 16.2 International business network of Krka, end 2001

Internationalization has particularly strengthened in the last few years. In 1996, the number of companies abroad was much smaller, namely 16 companies abroad and 16 representative offices in 13 countries.

Outward investment is also becoming more and more important in employment terms since almost one-seventh of its employees work abroad. Three investments abroad (Russia, Croatia and Poland) amounted, according to M. Kovačič the President of the Management Board of Krka, to more than € 70 million.

There are several reasons for undertaking outward investment. The first is the small domestic market that pushes one to internationalize. Secondly, there is a trend towards more restrictive legislation for generic pharmaceuticals and, thirdly, it allows the gaining of domestic producer status since all countries favour local production.

Regionally speaking, the chief orientation of both production and marketing is the former socialist countries of Eastern Europe. Krka has established only a few companies in EU countries; in 1992 in Italy, in 1996 in Germany, and in 2000 in Ireland. Among representative offices, the only additional Western country is the USA.

The internationalization strategy is based on the so-called five pillars, with each pillar representing one region. In the long run, each should attract a similar share of Krka's sales. This regional diversification strategy was designed to reduce risks due to potential economic difficulties in one or other region. The significant emphasis given to the Russian market is reflected in its widespread network there (seven representative offices in different locations), on top of two production facilities that are being finalized near Moscow.

This internationalization strategy is strongly anchored to Krka's long-term strategy as a mainly a producer of generic drugs with added value, i.e. based on familiar substances but with improved methods and state-of-the-art chemical synthesis and biosynthesis of pharmaceutical raw materials incorporated in final drugs sold under its own trademarks. It is believed that generic drugs are gaining in world importance since their quality, safety and efficacy mean they provide an equivalent, and in cost terms more acceptable, alternative to treatment than innovatory medicines.

Krka started to internationalize its production in the 1970s by establishing Dawa, the then second largest pharmaceutical factory in sub-Saharan Africa near Nairobi, Kenya with local shareholders in 1976 (construction started in 1974). The share of Krka was 33 per cent. The basic idea was to produce medicines for local consumption. The Kenyan pharmaceutical drug market was at the time quite liberal yet it was thought and discussed with the authorities that, once local production had been established, the government would start protecting local production. It was also planned that the factory would become a major supplier for the whole East African Economic Community. This did not transpire due to political changes in Kenya and the collapse of the East African Community in 1977. Therefore, Dawa encountered many problems in operating in such a liberal environment. Nevertheless, Dawa was a fruitful experience and the 'price' paid was relatively low for such an early internationalization venture[6].

Krka may still be regarded as a leapfrogging global firm meaning that its intensive international production activity is of a relatively recent origin, and was also achieved quite fast only in more recent times. In 1997 Krka expanded its business network abroad by three new units. The same year Krka started constructing the first production-distribution centre abroad in Warsaw (Poland) with the aim to become a business operations, storage and production facility also involving a high-bay warehouse with 2000 pallet positions (the most modern automated warehouse in Poland). Its trading operations started in 1999 while production was launched in 2001. Sales in 2001 amounted to almost € 38 million. The production and distribution centre in Warsaw, spreading over 7,000 square meters, was officially opened in October 2001 by the presidents of the two republics. Now Krka has a 1.63 per cent share of the Polish pharmaceutical market with a target of 2.5 per cent, according to the firm's director (see Finance, 2 November 2001; p. 5). Employment is also planned to increase from 141 in 2001 to over 170 in the next few years.

Russia is nevertheless Krka's main market. Therefore, it also has there, besides a representative office in Moscow and six offices around the country, two companies. In Moscow and Zagreb (Croatia) preparatory work for a unit similar to that in Warsaw also started in 1999. In 1999 Krka was in ninth place among all pharmaceutical producers in Russia while in 2002 it became, according to the local Farmacevtski vestnik, already the third biggest foreign producer and the third biggest importer of drugs with a two per cent market share.

Despite the crisis in Russia in 1998 Krka did not withdraw from this market but in fact the same year acquired a site to build the abovementioned production-distribution centre which is now expected to start production in 2003. With its factory in Podmoskovie (an investment worth USD 25 million) aiming to produce mainly solid-form drugs (capsules, coated tablets and tablets), Krka is set to become a regional producer. Establishing a development unit there is also planned so as to employ experts from both the Russian Federation and abroad.

In Croatia a factory in Jastrebarsko will start up production in 2003. This production and distribution centre is similarly under the one roof. The warehouse started to operate in 2001. Increasingly important are the Baltic markets where Krka's market share is seven per cent. Initially, this market was handled from the representative office in Riga, which has now moved to Vilnius.

So far, the outward FDI strategy has predominantly been to enter markets through greenfield investments. It has not been necessary to acquire market shares through acquisitions. According to a more proactive future strategy, a smaller factory-distribution centre in Germany is also anticipated. One explanation is that the EU is still not a unified market in this industry. Therefore, having a local presence in individual countries is still necessary.

Competitive advantages

Krka is known in its traditional export markets for its high quality, wide range and reliable supply of products to customers. Its key competitive advantage is the high quality generic drug products according to international standards[7] reflected in the fact that 90 per cent of Krka's trade stems from its own production of drugs and chemicals. They are based on Krka's research and development[8] focusing on the development of new and modern technologies for chemical synthesis, biosynthesis of pharmaceutical raw materials and further pharmaceutical formulation to final forms of drugs. It also performs extensive research into quality control (analysis, stability), safety (pre-clinical use) and efficiency (clinical use). The research is carried out in accordance with very demanding and rigorous technical regulations such as good management practice (GMP), good laboratory practice (GLP) and in line with the United States Food and Drug Administration (FDA), the European Community, and other requirements for the registration of drugs in the developed world. The successful, safe, environmentally-friendly and almost traditional industrial chemical synthesis and biosynthesis of pharmaceutical raw materials, incorporated into the final drugs, lies at the heart of Krka's development. Many pharmaceutical, chemical and biochemical technologies have been developed and patented. In the field of generic drugs, Krka can only be competitive with fast and professional interdisciplinary development and the efficient elaboration of professional documentation for product registration in both Slovenia and abroad. The strong export orientation namely requires rapid and effective registration activities. Krka's patent policy is straightforward: respect the rights of others and, at the same time, protect your own rights. In past years, Krka has applied for a patent for 50 inventions and submitted 405 patent applications in over 20 countries. Recently, more emphasis has been paid to the protection of its own knowledge in the area of pharmaceutical formulations (see Japelj, 1998; pp. 12-16).

Its long-term objective involves the production and sale of the company's trademark-protected products, the building up of relations with customers and strengthening and synergetic collaboration among R&D, marketing, production and other divisions. It main competitive strength is in the introduction of new techniques based on research studies on the morphology of active substances by which the quality, safety and efficacy of products is ensured. As a result, the share of own products in total sales is constantly increasing (from 62 per cent to 74 per cent in the 1996-2000 period). Newly-developed drugs are also substantially increasing their share (from 21 to almost 27 per cent in the same period).

Flexibility and innovativeness in launching new forms of drugs is also regarded as a specific advantage of Krka. R&D efforts are oriented to finding new ways of more efficiently using known drugs in new concentrations or strengths, aiming at more immediate effects and prolonged action. The key direction in the veterinary field is the ever increasing movement towards healthy food production.

Since quality is a must in the pharmaceutical industry, Krka places high importance on the quality of its products. 'The philosophy of total quality control is a key element in Krka's development strategy facilitated by the acquisition of the ISO 9001 Quality System Certificate for the design, production and sale of pharmaceutical and chemical substances, enzymes and feed-grade products in 1996' (Japelj, 1998; p. 15).

Only highly trained personnel can achieve this objective. The relatively strong pharmaceutical industry in Slovenia sometimes makes it difficult to recruit new personnel. Therefore, already in 1971 Krka established so-called Krka awards[9], which encourage young researchers to work in the field of pharmaceutical and chemistry diplomas, Master's and Ph.D. degrees but also in related fields like economics and law. Awarded students' research works have been realized in the framework of Krka's R&D projects, under the supervision of well-known professors, scientists and experts from both universities and Krka. In addition, a number of scholarships are awarded every year. Reflecting the awareness of the importance of R&D, the reconstruction and building of a new development and control centre started in 2000.

Perhaps the most important way of materializing competitive advantages in producing high quality drugs is based in management's skills. Krka has accumulated many years of experience in dealing with Eastern European markets, and developed know-how for doing business in these markets which is very complicated in the pharmaceutical industry. One cannot deal with 23,000 chemist's shops (for instance, only 176 in Slovenia) just by exporting. One cannot learn this overnight. The company has accumulated 40 years of business experience, claims Miloš Kovačič, President of the Management

Board of Krka (Pavlin, 2001; p. 25). Krka is therefore well placed to exploit a first-mover advantage in such markets only opened to Western competition since the fall of the Berlin Wall.

The long tradition and accumulated experience in Eastern markets is a specific competitive advantage accumulated during the Cold War period when Western firms were not allowed to export to Eastern markets. This has been strongly enhanced by the very special personal management style of Miloš Kovačič and his team's excellent knowledge of Russian history, speaking Russian fluently and having a special ability to negotiate business not only with business counterparts but also with state leaders[10]. According to him, developing personal contacts is a must. You have to do good business with your partners but also have a friendship relationship (see Pavlin, 2001b; p. 439). It has to be pointed out, however, that such advantages have been losing importance since the opening up of Eastern markets to Western companies after 1990 and parallel to the elimination of the state monopoly in foreign trade (before only one, and now many buyers). In order to facilitate business with business leaders, a lot of business with partners from Eastern Europe is conducted in Vienna to save time and make it easier for them in travel terms.

Although Krka is diversifying its product range, a specialization in cardiovascular drugs is obvious since they constitute almost 40 per cent of the company's sales in 2000, followed by drugs for gastrointestinal and metabolic diseases (approximately 20 per cent). Although much less important in terms of shares, OTC products, a rapidly growing market segment around the world, are also gaining in importance in Krka's production programme. Krka has successfully launched a number of its own brands in this area. In spite of the emphasis on the own development of generic drugs and self-medication products, Krka is continuing its production in innovation products based on co-operation agreements with leading multinational pharmaceutical companies.

Krka's second most important specific competitive advantage is perhaps what they call in the 2000 Annual Report 'swiftness in responding to market needs'[11]. 'Our goal is to be the first not only in sales, but also in discerning new market needs. This means: effective shortening of the development process, swift acquisition of the registration documents, and harmonized production and distribution' (Annual Report 2000; p. 34).

Last but not least, the firm has to pay special attention to environmental standards not only because of the growing awareness of the environment following increasing support for sustainable development around the world, particularly in Europe, but also from the internal needs of a small country and the region in which it is located. The system of environmental management was introduced in 2001 in accordance with the ISO 14001 standard.

The type of competitive advantages also influences the type of foreign market entry and the degree of ownership. Factories in Russia, Croatia and Poland are 100 per cent owned by Krka. This is not so much a reflection of ownership-specific innovation advantages created in the production of generic drugs. Krka's types of advantages call for a high level of control over production facilities abroad in order to achieve the demanded quality. In order to create high and standardized quality there can be no production mistakes. Differences in corporate cultures and different working habits in different cultures therefore demand very strong quality and managerial control.

Problems, weaknesses and threats

The domination of large multinationals in the industry is the biggest challenge a relatively small producer, by world standards, is currently facing. A generic producer encounters additional challenges of how to handle the ever more complicated and ever less transparent networks of new patents by which the originators try to prolong the patent protection even after the expiration of their monopoly position on innovative drugs[12]. The challenge is twofold. The first aspect is how to strengthen innovativeness in terms of finding new drugs (which is very difficult, time consuming and often goes beyond the financial possibilities of mid-sized firms[13]) and innovativeness in trying to find new methods for producing old drugs or active substances. The second aspect of almost the same importance is the legal challenge or strengthening the firm's capabilities to obtain market authorizations[14] as well as to find ways through the increasingly less transparent patent registrations of innovating firms. This is a relatively new area for lawyers in Slovenia and hence expertise is lacking.

Apart from the huge amount of funds needed to develop new drugs, there are three different types of entrance barriers: patents and other types of industrial property; control over the quality system in the development process; and the registration of drugs which is becoming as important as development of the product itself. Krka's R&D Division deals with all three barriers systematically. The Regulatory Affairs Department within the R&D Division is responsible for the preparation of documentation and obtaining registration approvals. Its biggest challenge in the last few years was harmonization with the EU's standards since obtaining marketing authorization for new drugs not only in an EU country but also in Slovenia or another Central European country means following the European registration guidelines precisely. The registration documents need to be in compliance with all European requirements.

The importance of staying in touch with consumers makes local production more and more a must in this industry. An additional factor stimulating internationalization is the differences seen in regulations among countries for generic drugs which increasingly make the production and marketing of such products more complicated in some countries, and more attractive for production and R&D facilities in countries with more liberal legislation[15]. Therefore, continuing relocation of such activities is expected in the future. Other EU non-candidate-countries (for instance Russia) or later-round candidate-countries of Central Europe could become more important in the future. This will certainly bring about criticism in Slovenia based on the 'export of jobs' argument that is so often heard when outward FDI is being discussed. Negotiations with trade unions could become tougher. Relations with the trade unions are currently very good since salaries are the highest in the region and the general climate in the company is very good.

Given the fact that the generic drug market is smaller in the world (12 per cent of the entire drug market) than the originators' market, generic production cannot stay the only long-term strategy for ever, although the changes in attitudes to generic drugs could make its life span longer. Under the pressing problems of developing countries, a new 'wind' is starting to blow in the WTO according to which access to cheaper generic drugs should be facilitated for those in need, particularly in developing countries. National health insurance agencies also tend to favour generic drugs since they are much cheaper. Enormous possibilities for generic producers still exist in Europe, particularly if the development of drugs starts to be permitted during patent protection, as is the case in the USA.

Being aware of the challenges globalization is bringing about, Krka hired McKinsey to study how to cope with such challenges. One of the key conclusions was that human capital is the main strength of the company but, due to the small market, a deficiency is already growing in Slovenia in absolute and relative terms. Slovenians are still unaware of the need to internationalize and are too emotionally tied to their homeland. It is very difficult to get Slovenians to work abroad. Additionally, it is hard to find experts with industrial and economic expertise who also know a few foreign languages. Even offering much higher pay[16] is not attractive enough. An even greater challenge is to transform the company from being primarily a Slovenian to a real multinational company with a new mentality, corporate culture and organization. McKinsey said that Krka is still a 'romantic' firm.

Lastly, the very personal style of the management, involving the nursing of interpersonal contacts which was very efficient during the Cold War and in the first years of the transition will gradually lose its importance alongside the decentralization of purchasing and changes to the management teams.

The company will have to start building new types of competencies in order to compensate for such advantages that are becoming less important.

Summary

Krka, ranked 14th out of the largest non-financial transnationals in Central and Eastern Europe (UNCTAD, 2001; p. 115), has gradually developed into a true multinational. It is a leapfrogging global company having internationalized itself in a relatively short time despite one much earlier attempt. Nevertheless, it also reveals a gradual internationalization, initially starting with exports. The firm can and must build on its experiences gained by exporting and jump over other stages faster than was usually done in the past under external pressures and facilitated by internal advantages. Such jumping over of stages is necessary partly due to the changing external legal and economic environment (globalization pressures). However, not all firms can be successful when so leapfrogging. Previous experiences with early internationalization have proved to be highly instrumental in facilitating later stages of outward FDI. Confidence and experiences have been accumulated and later transformed into benefits that far outweigh some of the losses such early internationalization created.

Krka is a typical case of dual-driven internationalization. Firstly, it was pushed by internal advantages necessitating a direct presence in foreign markets in order to keep such advantages (knowing how to do business, personal contacts with customers). Secondly, it was also pulled by changes in the environment which make foreign locations more attractive.

The types of determinants of internationalization by outward FDI also influenced the mode of market entry; the greenfield approach has been preferred. By entering new markets with ever tougher competition, acquisitions may become more important. Modes of entry are in fact the result of the interplay between internal and external factors whose roles are changing all the time.

Perhaps the biggest lesson of this case is the importance of developing a firm's specific advantages not only in terms of new products or technologies, but also in terms of introducing a specific management style and good personal relations with partners and customers which proved to be very efficient and rewarding at a particular time and in given circumstances but which may not always remain so.

Notes

1 The financial statement of Krka d.d., Novo mesto, and not the consolidated statement for the whole group.
2 If not otherwise stated, data is taken from Krka's Annual Report 2000.
3 Such a production orientation makes it difficult to penetrate markets where drugs are sold through shop distribution, as in the US market.
4 Former Yugoslavia, Albania, Bulgaria and Romania.
5 In August 2000 enalapril tablets started to be sold and already achieved a considerable share among generic producers in this market.
6 Investment was based on a loan under preferential conditions provided by then special Yugoslav Fund for the Promotion of Co-operation with Developing and Non-aligned Countries.
7 They are directed at market-appealing generic products with high added value to know-how (technologies for synthesis and formulations) and to quality and efficacy demonstration based on fast and professional interdisciplinary development (see Japelj, 1998; p. 13). It has been recognized in the industry that, together with another Slovenian drug maker Lek, they are the best generic firms in the world.
8 As early as the 1960s, Krka founded a Research Institute that today operates as part of the Research and Development Division. It employs 250 people, 120 experts with university education, 14 Ph.D.s and 27 Master's of Science in a variety of fields including biotechnology, industrial property and patent law. The company has built a new, modern Development and Control Centre over an area of 4,000 square meters (Japelj, 1998; p. 14). In the 1992-1997 period, Krka invested over US$ 20 million in infrastructure for research and development.
9 In 31 years, 1,760 graduate and postgraduate students from universities in Slovenia and some foreign countries (like Croatia, Russia, Czech Republic, Poland), as well as from secondary schools located in the region of Dolenjska where Krka is located, were awarded Krka prizes.
10 It has been manifested for instance in the opening of the new factory in Warsaw by the presidents of the two countries, by the fact that he has already met the Emperor of Japan and has developed good relations with the patriarch of Russia.
11 To illustrate: in 2000 Krka achieved a significant market share with its own generic drug enalapril (which substituted vazotec patented by Merck) by being the first to offer a generic drug substitute. Now the competition has already strengthened (11 new producers entered the same market) and sales are falling (see Pavlin, 2001; p. 25).
12 The result has been a number of lawsuits against generic producers in general and also against Krka. All companies filing lawsuits against Krka have so far lost their cases, which demonstrates that the related allegations have all proved to be unwarranted.
13 Some US$ 500 million is estimated to be necessary for the development of a new drug.
14 To illustrate: in 2000 alone Krka renewed market authorizations for 254 prescription pharmaceuticals in 472 forms, for 77 OTC products in 77 forms, and for 59 veterinary products in 69 forms.
15 Initially, the main driving force behind internationalization to the East was the existence of a process and not a product patent system there. Some countries have even inherited non-protection of the patent system from socialist times which remained even after transition had started.

16 Higher compared to local wages but still lagging well behind the competitors located abroad. In the future, Krka will have to gradually level out the salaries of its expatriates working abroad with those the competitors are offering, otherwise a major 'competitive advantage' will move to the competitors.

Chapter 17

Lek

Financial statements for 2000[1]:

Number of employees:	2,370 (Lek d.d.)
Assets:	€ 352.1 million
Shareholders' funds:	€ 262.3 million
Total revenues:	€ 289 million
Net sales abroad:	75.1% of revenues
Net profit:	€ 38 million

Activity: Manufacturing of pharmaceutical products
Number of companies within the same business activity: 13
Type of organisation: Joint-stock company d.d.
http://www.lek.si

Introduction

Lek is one of two pharmaceutical firms in Slovenia responsible for the country's large share of high technology exports. After the collapse of the SFRY, Lek faced an enormous market loss that provided a strong push to internationalization, starting in the form of a joint venture with Bayer in 1972. The number of companies it has had abroad increased from six in 1991 to 17 in 2002. In the same period, as an important producer of generic drugs and parallel to Slovenia's accession to the EU, the company has been encountering substantial changes in both the Slovenian legal environment and in its target markets. In the domestic pharmaceutical market, Lek faces strong competitive pressures as medicine imports continue to grow and its domestic market share consequently falls. These three fundamental changes have pushed Lek to internationalize its activities faster than otherwise in order to acquire the status of a local producer in countries where the legal environment still allows the production and sale of generic drugs. Simultaneously, its own innovative efforts are being bolstered in order to upgrade the company from a dominantly generic brand to a more innovative producer of drugs. Internationalization by establishing affiliates abroad and sales units has taken off as part of this transformation. It has been more induced by market trends and less by its own specific advantages.

History

Lek was established in 1946 to locally produce certain drugs and chemical products. It developed from a small locally-oriented firm to one of the largest drug producers in former Yugoslavia when its production orientation was the result of a certain division of labour among many drug producers. An important turning point came in the mid-seventies when a new factory was built in Ljubljana and another in 1998 when a development laboratory was created for traditional biotechnology. In 1991 Lek transformed into a joint-stock company with its shares being quoted on the Ljubljana Stock Exchange in 1992. In 1995 it became the first pharmaceutical company from CEE to enter the US market with a finished pharmaceutical product.

Relatively early on the company realized that the initial very strong reliance on producing licensed drugs and later also cosmetics had to be supplemented with longer and deeper co-operation with foreign partners. Therefore, a joint-venture agreement with Bayer was signed in 1972. Its key objective was to facilitate sales of Bayer products in Slovenia. Thus, no real synergies between the two companies developed. Bayer Pharma is even not consolidated in Lek's balance sheet, as the decision-making bases rests on the consensus of both partners. It was soon realized that too strong a reliance on foreign licensed drugs alone could not form a sound basis for any long-term global strategy in an industry dominated by a few large multinational firms. The strategy of a generic brand producer was born.

Initial internationalization steps were taken in the early sixties when exports started to become an important part of overall sales. In the seventies, Lek established its first sales offices abroad. The first step in internationalizing its production came with the establishment of a production unit in Poland in the early nineties.

Company profile

Lek is one of the largest companies in Slovenia and, together with the other main pharmaceutical producer Krka from Novo mesto, plus Bayer Pharma, it accounts for somewhat less than 40 per cent of Slovenian drug sales. Although large by Slovenia standards, it is a mid-sized pharmaceutical company ranking 104th among the leading companies in the world's pharmaceutical industry (Scrip's Pharmaceutical League Tables 2000). It is predominantly Slovenian-owned.

Altogether, in 2001 the Lek group employed 3,611 people – 2,411 in Slovenia and 1,200 or almost one-third abroad. The group's consolidated sales increased from € 227.05 million in 1994 to € 288.95 million in 2000[2]. Lek is the fifth largest Slovenian exporter, particularly of high-tech exports. Net profits almost doubled in the 1996-2000 period. Growth in R&D costs was slower, increasing in the same period by 40 per cent. Earnings per share also almost doubled (1996-2000).

While production of finished pharmaceutical products dominates (over 74 per cent in 2000) and is rising, Lek also produces active pharmaceutical ingredients (8.9 per cent, and the share is shrinking), over-the-counter drugs (OTC, 7.7 per cent), cosmetics (3.7 per cent), animal health and medical devices. The main and fastest growing product is its own antibiotic Amoksiklav, which in 2000 accounted for nearly 21 per cent of total sales. Amoksiklav was also given marketing authorization for part of the EU in 2000. Lek is one of the leaders in antibiotics in CEE.

Slovenia has traditionally been the primary market. In 2000 it accounted for nearly 25 per cent, followed by CEE, which in 2001 became Lek's number one regional market.

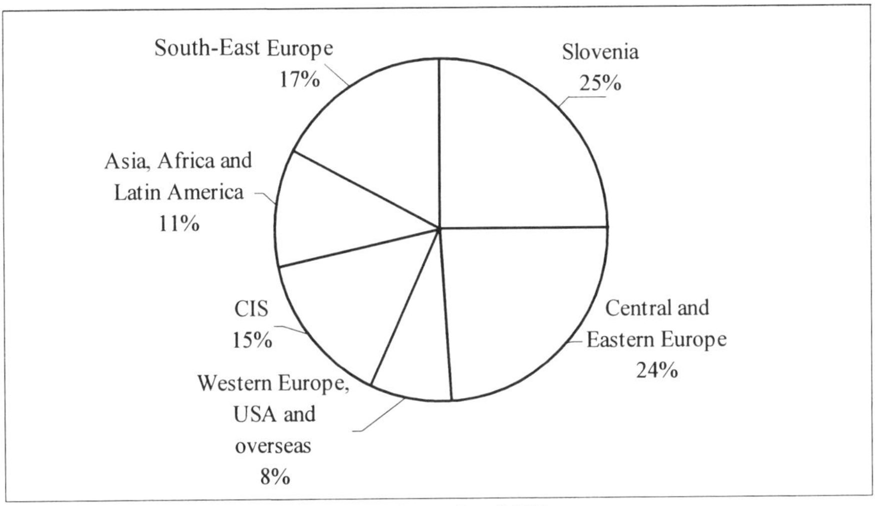

Figure 17.1 Lek's sales by regions in 2002

Source: Annual Report 2000, p. 6

Since 2001 Slovenia has lost its position of being Lek's leading sales market to Poland. Still, Lek's basic strategy is to strengthen its market share in Slovenia, to become an even more prominent player in the sales of antibiotics and cardiovascular medicines in CEE, and to win increased recognition in the most demanding international generic drug markets. The US market is regarded as the most important one. The market position in the EU also has to be boosted given that Slovenia will soon become a member of the EU.

Lek's domestic market is Slovenia, which by its size can be grouped into small pharmaceutical markets. Most other generic producers make a much larger share of their sales in their domestic markets – also because those markets are much bigger.

Internationalization

Lek has traditionally been an export-oriented company. In order to support its development, first inward internationalization started with Bayer which, in 1972, was expanded by establishing a joint venture Bayer Pharma in which Lek has a 51 per cent share. Many licence agreements were signed with almost all the major pharmaceutical companies. Recently, such co-operation was upgraded with some partnership contracts (like those with Sanofi-Synthélabo[3] or Pliva in Croatia[4]). One objective of such alliances was to optimize purchasing as well as to share information and know-how in order to better exploit its competitive advantages.

The biggest factors of outward internationalization were:

- loss of the Yugoslav market[5];
- a small domestic market;
- changes to the institutional environment;
- increased competition from foreign drug producers in the domestic market; and
- production of generic drugs that demands localization.

Internationalization was obviously triggered by a combination of push and pull factors. Specialization in generic products as the firm's prime specific advantage demanded expansion for three reasons. First, because the growth imperative called for increasing capacities that were no longer feasible in Slovenia. Second, generic drugs demand localization supported by a marketing strategy. Lastly, generic drug markets are not all regulated in the same way. With the reduction of possibilities to expand sales further in Slovenia, less regulated markets[6] and the future 'domestic' markets of the EU (parallel to Slovenia's accession to the EU) are becoming attractive targets for generic producers.

In terms of those employed abroad (almost one-third of total employment in 2001), Lek can be considered a very internationalized company. The company's internationalization has increased substantially since Slovenia became independent. The number of companies it has abroad increased from six in 1991 to 23 in 2001 (16 of which are active) and representative offices from four to 13. They are represented in 20 countries around the world. Including its representative offices, Lek now has 27 units abroad, mostly in CEECs. The year 2000 can be marked as the starting year of the new strategy cycle enhancing the company's international position by establishing own units in all strategic markets, including through acquisitions.

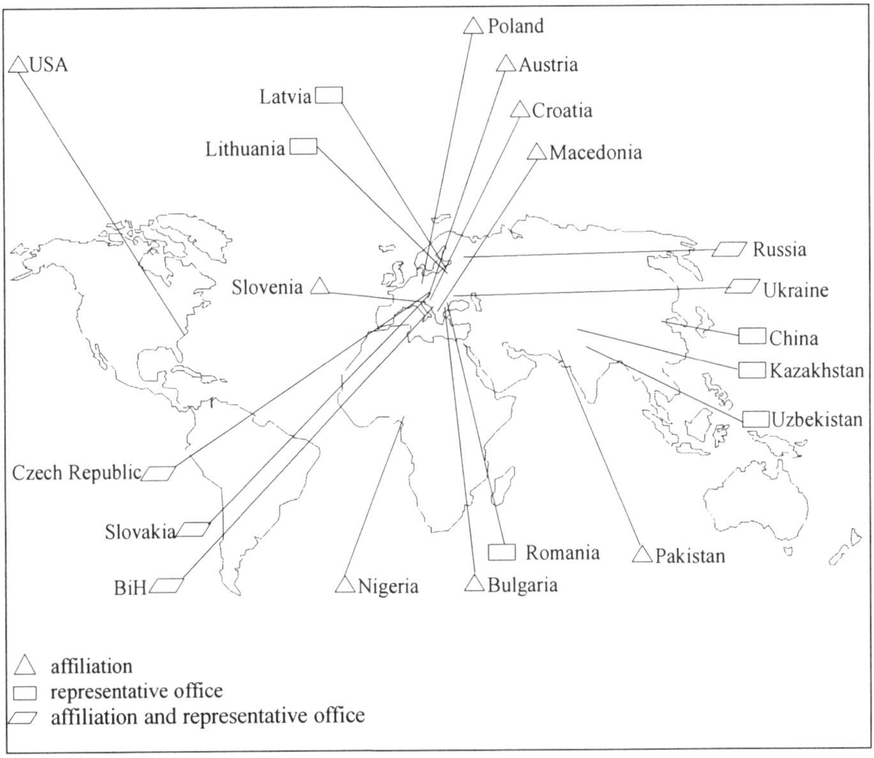

Figure 17.2 Lek's international business network in 2002

The strategic long-term orientation to Central and Eastern European markets is based on the expectation that these markets' growing medical consumption have great potential. Per capita consumption of drugs is still very low, competition is still not too fierce and firms with long experience in these markets still enjoy strong competitive advantages in terms of knowing how to do business there.

Since Poland has developed to become the biggest single national market outside Slovenia, it has naturally become the most important target for outward internationalization in the form of outward investment. It is generally among the fastest growing markets. In 2001 Lek increased its sales there by 30 per cent. It is also not surprising that in Pruszkow near Warsaw already in 1991 Lek established one of the first foreign pharmaceutical factories, Lek Polska. Its sales in 2001 were worth € 61 million. In 1999 Lek sought to acquire the Polish pharmaceutical firm Polfa Krakow from Krakow but its tender was not selected (Pliva of Croatia was successful). Therefore, in February 2001 it acquired an 89.45 per cent share of another company, Argon SA (Lodz), a complementary local producer of cardiovascular medicines. The main aim was to strengthen its market position in this fast growing market. Today, Lek employs over 310 people in Poland (including Lek Polska and Argon). The final idea is to merge the two companies into one legal entity and to increase the market share from the existing 1.8 per cent to over two per cent.

Russia is the second most important market for Lek in which loyalty to certain older products is much stronger and the share of non-prescribed drugs is much higher. After the crises in 1998, sales in Russia almost doubled. Lek succeeded in increasing its market share there also because it upgraded exports with other forms of long-term co-operation. Here Lek has established its own subsidiary to market Lek's products to local distributors. Besides, Lek is co-operating with a few local manufacturers in the production of selected Lek products and in developing a network of partners for R&D aiming at establishing its own R&D centres in Russia.

The new strategy pays special attention to South-Eastern European markets. In line with this, Lek has invested in new units in Macedonia and Romania. A new business-manufacturing centre was opened in Skopje in Macedonia in 2000 to strengthen not only the market position in Macedonia, but also in neighbouring markets so as to become a regional distribution and logistics hub. During the war in Serbia, it was also a springboard for exports to the FRY. Now a direct expansion to the FRY is planned through the acquisition of a 40 per cent share in Jugoremedija from Zrenjanin.

In January 2001, the 90 per cent acquisition of the Romanian company PharmaTech was concluded. The objective was not only to upgrade exports by gaining the position of a domestic producer, but also to acquire a local producer of products complementary to Lek's production programme in antibiotics allowing it to take the leading role (at least among the top ten) in the Romanian market.

The new representative office in Beijing in the People's Republic of China also reflects the emphasis given to the company's international expansion. China is one of its future strategic markets where even in 2001 USD 5.5 million of sales was achieved. Therefore, future plans include the possible building of its own factory in co-operation with a local partner in this fast growing market.

While CEECs are a major strategic orientation, Lek also has two companies in the USA. The first was established in 1995, the other in 2001 followed by the division of the American operations into two businesses – sales with distribution and services. The US market is Lek's most important market in the West. The expansion there started in the 1970s through the exporting of active ingredients. Its key aim is to facilitate sales in the specific US market, which makes it necessary to be physically present there. Significant amounts of drugs are sold in distribution and not by prescription. Two years ago, the strategy was upgraded from sales through other pharmaceutical firms' trade names to sales under Lek's own brand name directly through distribution channels. The creation of its own brand name there became a strategic orientation.

Competitive advantages

In response to the dramatic changes seen in the world's pharmaceutical industry in recent years, Lek has developed its long-term strategy specializing as a (innovative) generic brand drug producer[7], a value-added generic producer with generic yet differentiated products[8]. Being customer-friendly is its major competitive advantage. It demands own innovative efforts and speed in particular. Although this generic brand producer orientation has its limitations, it is now seen as a response to the currently more friendly attitudes to such drugs by the WTO and national social security authorities. Generic drugs are much less expensive, but in terms of quality and safety provide equivalent alternatives to the otherwise much more expensive innovative drugs. This is increasingly important in the face of rising health insurance costs in the ageing Europe in particular. Another specialization is know-how technology in producing active ingredients (fermentation, organic synthesis) and in biotechnology.

Positioning in such a niche is only possible thanks to substantial investments in R&D, which have supported such a strategy. The share of R&D investments in sales revenues in the last five years has been around 12.5 per cent. This is a precondition of success in the pharmaceutical industry. Therefore, a new R&D centre was constructed so as to be fully operative in early 2002. Aware that having only a generic drug orientation is unsustainable in the very long term, Lek is also gradually trying to boost its strategy in the direction of innovative drugs in order to achieve more balanced strategies between the price minimization one (generic) and the innovative-based one. This 'middle of the road' dual strategy is, however, difficult to follow.

As a mid-sized company, its R&D efforts have to be concentrated in specific areas to give tangible results. The main priorities are pharmaceutical ingredients and shortening development times in general. A large part of R&D activities is devoted to patent protection. This involves defending its own patents and filing new patent applications for original solutions in synthesising pharmaceutical ingredients and in pharmaceutical formulations. Despite these efforts, the share of new product sales resulting from its own R&D is still only 7.8 per cent (2000).

Keeping pace with competitors is only possible by strengthening the human capital base. Training and upgrading skills is therefore one of the company's strategic orientations. The company now employs 134 highly trained professionals with Ph.D.s and Master's degrees. The share of unskilled and semi-skilled workers fell from 1995 to 2000 by 41 to 30 per cent, while the share of those with a university education rose from 33 to 43 per cent. Investment in education and training reached 0.7 per cent of total sales in 2000.

The competitive advantages of generic producers are based mostly on two factors. First, on the development of one's own knowledge to start producing a known or established drug after the related patent's expiration and, second, on the speed of such development. The procedures for registering drugs is long (up to 24 months) which, when one includes the preparatory stages (filing of applications), altogether makes up some five years before a product enters the market. Therefore, human capital and expertise is crucial, alongside the legal capacity to defend such development from 'attacks' by the originators trying to keep their patent-supported monopoly position in a range of different ways even after their patent rights have expired.

Most of Lek's products are the result of its own R&D activities, supplemented with various licensing agreements and other co-operative ventures with partner firms. Having its own active pharmaceutical ingredients for its own production, based on Lek's innovative solutions and technological expertise, are one of Lek's main competitive advantages. They are used in many Lek products and also sold successfully as an intermediate product, primarily to Western markets (63 per cent in 2000).

Lek is a very environmentally conscious firm that follows the ISO 14001 international standard for environmental management. In 1999 it was awarded a licence to carry out waste elimination at its own incineration plant.

Problems, weaknesses and threats

Uncertainty and the increasingly tougher competition are generally the biggest challenges for all pharmaceutical firms in the world. Although sales are made in many markets, some markets still account for a very high share, which increases risk exposure. Better management of risk exposure has become one of the key managerial challenges. Risks in the pharmaceutical industry are enormous. One way of handling them is to diversify. Limits on a small firm's diversification potential however hinders application of such strategies. The most important one nevertheless seems to be how to transform the company from a multi-domestic firm into a truly global corporation. It seems that the 'body' of the company is already internationalized, while the corporate mentality remains prevailingly domestic. There is a need to more quickly develop the global mindset of the company at all levels if the company wants to transform itself into a real multinational.

Apart from the general challenge posed by the industry's high level of concentration facing all generic drug producers, there is the challenge of the growing exploitation of the dominant position held in global markets by the main pharmaceutical multinational firms. They control global competition and work hard to keep their dominant position as long as possible. Complementary to patent protection, and imposing new patents that are really more an extension of old ones or patenting something which is almost common knowledge, supplementary product protection and data exclusivity[9] are also tools used to this end. Patent systems are, according to the President of the Management Board of Lek, Metod Dragonja, thereby becoming less transparent (Delo, 14 February 2002; p. 11). Consequently, legislation is becoming stricter in many countries thus limiting the expansion potential of generic producers.

The pharmaceutical industry's concentration in the increasingly integrated European market and at the global level (see Box 5.1) are a great challenge for Lek. There are three strategic response options. First, a stand-alone strategy that can satisfy shareholders (by maximizing short-term profits) but does not offer much potential for growth. The second is a merger or strategic alliance of equals (at home or abroad), which is viable but probably not a really long-term solution. The third option is an equity or strategic alliance with one of the main pharmaceutical firms in the world. All three options have been on the table for some time and no final solution has been made yet. However, the parallel programmes of Lek and Krka, their different corporate cultures and the need for lay-offs flowing from any merger make such a 'domestic' merger less viable. Long-term contractual or equity arrangements may be the future strategic option if endogenous 'stand-alone' growth, the current priority, does not make the firm competitive enough in this highly concentrated industry.

In general, human capital is a fundamental advantage of Lek. But local potential is limited. Foreign firms attract young experts with better salaries, albeit with less career development potential. Another problem is having experts trained only in one discipline, while interdisciplinary knowledge (pharmaceutical, economic, legal) is increasingly needed. Lastly, Slovenians become relatively homesick and do not like to work abroad despite higher wages. All of these factors could hinder future requisite internationalization efforts.

A few years ago the USA represented a much more important market for Lek. Its share has dropped away substantially after legal problems arose there[10]. The biggest challenge for the future, in terms of regional orientation, is nevertheless the EU market where Lek's market shares are still low and where a possibility remains for the expansion of generic producers. In some European countries generic markets are still underdeveloped and Directives not applied equally. The EU is therefore still not a fully harmonized market like the USA.

Facing up to these many challenges also requires changes to the company's organization involving a more flexible and project basis instead of the more traditional divisional organizational structure. In the last few years, Lek has undergone several reorganizations; with the recent one introducing programme scheme responsibility towards the more profitable business performance of programmes as profit centres, which is also instrumental for its internationalization strategy.

Summary

Although Lek's internationalization started back in the socialist era, the real take-off of outward FDI in both its regional spread and the deepening of internationalization came with Slovenia's independence. As in many earlier cases, the real push stemmed not so much from the company's internal advantages but was induced more by external pressures on the company. Firstly, the shrinking of the domestic market from 23 to just two million inhabitants coupled by the changing institutional/legal environment (greater restrictions imposed on generic producers in more and more countries) forced the company to seek out global markets and upgrade its exports by acquiring the status of a local producer in less legally protected markets. The relatively rapid outward investment internationalization involved makes Lek a leapfrogging global firm. This is not to say that there was no stage-growth of internationalization. There was but the shift from exports to international production was very rapid.

Today, Lek faces two fundamental challenges. The first is to achieve balanced organic growth at home and internationally by enhancing its innovative capabilities in the core pharmaceutical business (and by disinvesting in other activities or keeping the existing share) in order to ensure the production of generic drugs as the first follower of originators and to expand the share of drugs resulting from its own R&D. Increasing competition in generic drug markets makes it necessary to enhance rapid internationalization and to simultaneously stress the production priority of enhancing its own innovation-based drug-making capabilities. The second challenge is to ensure continuing growth. The present stand-alone priority strategy and mergers of equal strategies have their limitations. In the long run, some form of long-term equity as part of strategic co-operation with key players in the industry may ultimately emerge as a realistic option[11].

Notes

1 From the non-consolidated financial statement of Lek d.d. only.
2 If not otherwise stated, all data are taken from the Annual Report 2000 or calculated on its basis.
3 The objective of the mixed company was to introduce new therapeutic products and to market the main products of Sanofi-Synthelabo. Realization exceeded the expectations. The share of this co-operation grew to 4.6 per cent of total sales of Lek's pharmaceutical products and active pharmaceutical ingredient sales in Slovenia.
4 To market Lek's chief antibiotic, Amoksiklav.
5 Sales fell by 32 per cent in 1992.
6 Those where legal enforcement is not as strict, or where supplementary patent protection is not widely applied.
7 As opposed to a straight generic producer making drugs 'essentially similar' to the original drugs (as the major obligation of a generic producer).
8 For instance, Amoksiklav has been improved in terms of therapeutical use compared to the original drug; for instance, instead of three times a day it can now be taken just twice a day.
9 The marketing of generic drugs can therefore be postponed for up to six years after the patent protection expires, as the data on the clinical trials of the originators cannot be used when registering a generic drug.
10 The renewed registration of Cimetidine tablets after the end of the legislative difficulties opened up the doors for a return to the US market, which is also important in view of the local laws permitting the development of generic drugs during patent protection unlike in many other countries.
11 This prognosis was made when the manuscript was submitted to the publisher and proved to be accurate months later when the book was printed. In November 2002 Novartis acquired an almost 100% share in Lek, becoming the largest FDI transaction in Slovenia so far.

Chapter 18

Kolektor[1]

KOLEKTOR

Financial statements for 2000:

Number of employees:	929	Activity: Mfr. of elec. motors, generators etc.
Assets:	€ 70.9 million	Number of companies within the same business activity: 46
Shareholders' funds:	€ 38.5 million	Type of organization:
Total revenues:	€ 86.6 million	Limited liability company d.o.o.
Net sales abroad:	82.8%	http://www.kolektor.si/
Net profit:	€ 7.8 million	
Value added per employee:	€ 41,923	

Introduction

Kolektor is not a typical case of indirect outward FDI. It is an example where through a very ambitious strategy a Slovenian company acquired, via a joint venture with a German company, enough technological, marketing and other knowledge to develop its own firm-specific advantages and started to internationalize its activities globally. Today, it is becoming a global company with its production and developmental market functions being organized in some of the world's most strategically significant locations, all of which are managed and directed from the one place – Idrija (Kolektor, 2001). Industry product and market characteristics facilitated such a transition from 'dependent' to 'independent' internationalization and was possible thanks to the ambitious management team being able to grasp the chance offered.

History of the company

The Idrija municipality established Kolektor in 1963. The main reason was to provide employment for women who could not find a job in the very old mercury mine there. Initially, the company employed only 20 employees (see more in Svetličič and Rojec, 1998; p. 5).

In order to modernize itself, Kolektor started to look for ways and means to modernize production. The solution was found in 1968, with the entrance into a long-term contract on investment and co-operation with the German company Kautt & Bux, then a leading European producer of commutators. Kautt & Bux took 49 per cent and Kolektor 51 per cent share in the joint venture. After the formation of the joint venture, Kolektor started exporting under the Kautt & Bux trademark through its European sales network.

The crucial period in the company's development was 1980-84 when Kolektor began its own development of technologies for wrap-strip commutators and starter commutators, invested in their production and acquired its first patent. In the late 1980s, Kautt & Bux ran into difficulties. To improve its creditworthiness position, Kautt & Bux wanted to incorporate Kolektor in its own consolidated financial statements, which was only possible by becoming the majority owner of Kolektor. In 1990, Kolektor agreed that Kautt & Bux should become a 51 per cent owner of the company. However, this did not save Kautt & Bux. In 1993 it was taken over by the US firm Kirkwood and has continued to operate under the Kautt & Bux firm name. Thus, Kirkwood is today a 50.01 per cent owner of Kolektor.

Negotiating the increase of the Kautt & Bux share from 49 per cent to 51 per cent was a strategic opportunity for Kolektor's management to materialize its strategic aspirations to gain more autonomy. Under the new contract, Kolektor gained marketing independence and a high level of managerial independence. Namely, a precondition of Kolektor to allow Kautt & Bux to acquire the majority share was to conclude a new partnership agreement, whereby a 75 per cent share would be necessary to take all major decisions. If a 75 per cent majority was not achieved then it would be the management of Kolektor that would decide. The management of Kolektor thereby in fact achieved managerial independence. Majority ownership really matters only in terms of distributing profits. Kautt & Bux did accept the position of a portfolio investor. This was of key importance for further independent[2] internationalization.

In 1993, US multinational company Kirkwood bought out Kautt & Bux and hence also acquired a 51 per cent equity share in Kolektor. Kolektor offered to Kirkwood to co-operate as equal partners, especially in marketing and product development. However, the strong position of management in all decisions, inherited from Kolektor's contract with Kautt & Bux, enabled Kolektor to persist with its own business strategy, even though Kirkwood's idea was to take over control over the sales of commutators in Europe. In 1994, Kolektor began to build up its own marketing and supply network and to market commutators under its own trademark only (Jaklič M., 2000; p. 170). Gradually, it launched an ambitious internationalization programme and in 1997 it became the leading producer of commutators in Europe, while in 2000 it set up two major production subsidiaries abroad.

Company profile and product characteristics

Kolektor has grown from a local supplier of commutators, the firm's main product[3], to the domestic market into a global strategic supplier to partners around the world. Now it is the largest manufacturer of commutators in Europe and the second largest in the world. In 2000, Kolektor was the 55th largest company in Slovenia in terms of turnover (GZS, 2001).

Kolektor is a fast growing, export-oriented company (87.7 per cent of its sales are exported), which is constantly developing its production techniques and enhancing its export orientation. In 1994-99, due to ongoing changes the company achieved impressive growth and performance; net profits more than doubled, while return on equity and revenues per employee almost doubled. Return on equity in 1999 was 14.5 per cent. Added value per employee increased from € 14,000 in 1993 to an impressive € 40,000 in 2000[4]. In 1993-2000, Kolektor's turnover increased from € 31.6 million to € 86.6 million, i.e. by 2.7 times, and is expected to increase further to more than € 90 million by 2002. Even more obvious is the increase in turnover per employee from € 32,000 in 1993 to € 94,000 in 2000.

Globally, Kolektor's market share in 2000 was 14.55 per cent[5]. Easily the most important share of Kolektor's sales goes to the automotive industry (approximately 60 per cent), followed by the electric power tools industry (20 per cent), and the household appliances industry (12 per cent). Europe is its main export market (65 per cent of Kolektor's sales), 17.7 per cent is sold in Slovenia, 10.8 per cent in America, 6.4 per cent in Asia and 0.1 per cent in Africa. The highest, 60 per cent market share is found in Europe in electric power tools, followed by 30 per cent in the automotive industry, 10 per cent in household appliances and 25 per cent in commutators for other purposes.

The chief customers in 2000 were Robert Bosch (23 per cent) and Black & Decker (9.7 per cent), followed by Valeo, Delco Remy, Johnson, Domel Slovenia, and Siemens.

Commutator is less of a technology and more of a process sophisticated product, which requires close and permanent interactions with predominantly known customers. The buyer of a particular commutator is forced to stay with a particular producer until the buyer changes his own product technologically.

A firm gets a competitive edge firstly by recognizing the new demands of buyers and, secondly, by speeding up the process of development of a new product, testing it and launching mass production. This is impossible without one's own R&D sector and tool-manufacturing facilities. At the beginning of the 1990s, R&D expenditures in Kolektor represented two per cent of sales, and today are running at approximately 3.5-4 per cent. Without in-house facilities and capabilities the lead-time would be too long to become or remain competitive in the sector. By developing its own products using high-tech solutions and quality materials, Kolektor helps influence world trends in commutator development, assisting it to maintain its position as a leading producer in the world market. The production of commutators is an extremely competitive industry, especially in Europe where there are four significant producers: Kolektor (Slovenia), MAM (Italy), Kautt & Bux-Kirkwood (Germany) and Nettlehoff (Germany).

Producers of commutators are faced with the danger of a substitute, i.e. a motor with electronic commutation, which would replace a commutator motor. The producers of commutators are attempting to improve their position on both sides of the chain by establishing longer-term partner relationships (Jaklič M., 2000) and by diversifying into electronics and telecommunications. Therefore, in 2000 Kolektor acquired the Slovenian electronics company Synatec and Iskra Feriti (telecommunications).

Today, Kolektor's technology is better than that of Kirkwood, and equal or better than that used by Kautt & Bux (Petrič, 1995). In cold-forging of copper and in shell commutators Kolektor is probably the best in Europe. The joint-venture contract was instrumental for the technological and business modernization of the company. Yet it would also have been impossible without the company's own developmental efforts.

The company's R&D department was established in 1976-77. In the early 1980s, Kolektor filed its first patent application. The joint venture with Kautt & Bux was instrumental for learning and gradually improved its position in the partnership. By 1988, Kolektor already outpaced Kautt & Bux by the number of patents taken out. Up until 1988, knowledge was flowing from Kautt & Bux to Kolektor, while after 1988 it moved more from Kolektor to Kautt & Bux.

Kolektor's internationalization process

Kolektor's initial strategy was to acquire technology from abroad pursuant to long-term technological contracts and when allowed by a joint-venture contract with a foreign partner (called dependent internationalization by Jaklič, 2000). Since the mid-1980s, Kolektor's strategy has been to modernize technology and the production programme, to upgrade products and technology through the assimilation and adaptation of foreign technology, to gain more independence, particularly in marketing and, finally, to strengthen its overall competitive position in the world market. By 1993 these objectives had been realized to a major extent. Since then, Kolektor's vision has been to be number one in the world in the respective production programme. It was soon realized that this could only be achieved via the outward internationalization of production since a commutator is a mature product and market-share increases can only be obtained by taking over the shares of competitors. By diversifying, the firm reduces its risk exposure to technology changes in the industry. The second wing of the strategy is growth through diversification. Traditional commutators can be replaced by electronic ones, for instance. Internationalization in the industry means more the relocation of production to the countries where their customers are located and invest ('follow the customer') than relocation to countries with lower labour costs (see Jaklič A., 2000). This is why the early directions of internationalization were the USA and Asia.

The internationalization process of Kolektor can be broadly classified in three stages. The first was the inward internationalization stage of 1968-1993. The second stage began with the acquisition of Kautt & Bux by Kirkwood and with the enforcing of the new partnership contract with Kautt & Bux, which allowed Kolektor to launch its independent international activities, i.e. exports under its own trademark and the creation of its own sales network abroad (trade subsidiaries and representative offices abroad). The last stage of Kolektor's internationalization process began in 2000 by establishing majority-owned manufacturing companies in the USA and South Korea.

By entering into the joint venture with the German partner, Kolektor was able to sell abroad under the trademark and sales network of Kautt & Bux. The exceptions here were Eastern European socialist countries' markets where Kolektor was allowed to market products first through local agents. Later, Kolektor established its own sales subsidiaries and representative offices. In 1991, Kolektor's subsidiary in Austria (Comtrade[6])was set up. It later also diversified in Germany (Stuttgart), the USA (Greenville), France (Lyon) and Italy (Verona). Their biggest tasks have been to gather information on the new needs of the major customers and the marketing of Kolektor's products (Petrič, 2000).

The outward internationalization process of Kolektor underway since 1993 can be classified in four phases. The first was the initial phase characterized by foreign sales through distributors and agents. In the development phase, Kolektor established a number of trade outlets abroad (representative offices) to improve the provision of services to customers. In the growth phase, the first indirect investments in production, via contractual relations, were realized.

The growth phase was followed by the mature phase in which Kolektor established production subsidiaries in the USA and South Korea (Petrič, 2000b).

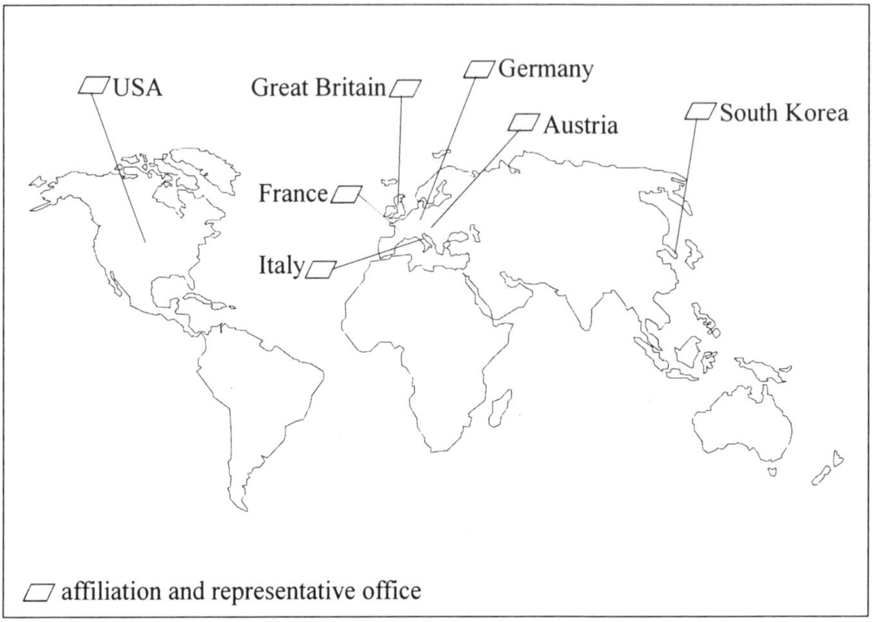

Figure 18.1 International business network of Kolektor in 2002

In accordance with the strategy of internationalization and diversification of the production programme, in 2000 Kolektor took three steps:

1. It purchased a majority equity share in the Sinyung Industrial Company in Kumi Co. Ltd., Korea[7], a manufacturer of micro commutators. This enables Kolektor to increase its production capacity at this location and to expand to other Asian markets. The marketing function of production capacities in Idrija is also carried out there.
2. It realized its interests in the NAFTA countries to accelerate all activities regarding the organization of production in Greenville, South Carolina[8], where production in the newly constructed plant started in March 2001. The original marketing function of Comtrade USA is now supplemented with production.
3. It expanded its marketing network to include a trading company in Austria (COMTRADE GmbH Klagenfurt) and representative offices in Germany (2), Great Britain, the USA, Italy and France[9].

Kolektor will only transfer production but not technology and development to the new foreign locations. It wants to retain full control over knowledge at the parent location (Jaklič M., 2000).

By far the most important motive of Kolektor in investing abroad is a market-seeking one. Labour costs, other costs and asset considerations are less important. Kolektor's foreign investments also represent a response to the strategies used by its main competitors. More precisely, why Kolektor decided to establish production to the new foreign locations involves three main factors: (i) protectionism, meaning that in some countries a company must get the status of a 'domestic producer' to be able to successfully penetrate the market there (high import barriers etc.); (ii) requests of the main customers which support the strategy of 'local production for the local market'; and (iii) the global competition and behaviour of the key competitors which follow the above trends and requests of customers.

Kolektor's strategy today is characterized by stronger internationalization and product diversification. Its objective is to become a truly international company run from its headquarters in Idrija, and to cater to the needs of the global market by organizing production at efficient locations around the world and thereby reducing potential risks.

Plans to establish or acquire new companies abroad and to expand the existing ones in the near (two-year) and mid-term (five-year) future are under consideration; one company in EU countries, as well as one in Central and Eastern European countries (probably an acquisition). Unlike a number of other Slovenian companies, Kolektor has no plans to create subsidiaries in the successor countries of the former Yugoslavia but it is interested to expand in China.

Kolektor's competitive advantages

The firm's most important competitive advantage is technological, closely followed by organizational and marketing knowledge. One could add some other competitive advantages that assist in Kolektor's internationalization, i.e. employment policy and training, customer service and a set of home-country-, micro-location-specific advantages. All of this is enhanced by the coherence of management and the long-term commitment to the company and local community shown by all employees. 'The probability of leaving Kolektor for being employed by the competitors, and in such a way to transfer the specific knowledge, is very low' (Jaklič M., 2000).

Kolektor is particularly successful in the development and creation of machinery and tools. The core abilities of Kolektor are based more on the craft skills of the employees than on patents. Such competitive advantages are difficult to imitate.

Employees are one of the key assets of Kolektor. The company attempts to develop this asset in two ways. Firstly, by improving the qualification structure (the share of semi-skilled workers fell in 1994-2000 from 44 to 19 per cent), by training and (the share of employees in vocational education rose from 33 to 53 per cent) and by increasing employees' commitment to the company.

Kolektor's most important advantage is perhaps the crucial significance of the management of the company, its stability, commitment, competence and, last but not least, vision and risk-taking attitude. The Kolektor story could have turned out very differently if management had not had the vision and courage to start travelling the 'bumpy road' of marketing its own trademark 'overnight'[10]. The right combination of managerial capabilities, serendipity, courage, and vision has proved to be a precondition for such a transition.

For Kolektor, the most important barrier to investing abroad is a lack of adequate staff with enough knowledge and experience in international business. This is followed by host-country factors (risk, investment climate) and a lack of information.

The many certificates received from its customers[11] are the result of the efforts Kolektor makes in building up partnership relations with its customers, as well the high quality of its products. Application of the Total Quality Management scheme was instrument here. Kolektor is developing a generic strategy of differentiation, based on marketing development and good relations with customers (Jaklič M., 2000).

Generally, the results of enhanced internationalization in the last four years are very positive. Kolektor's outward FDI has increased its market shares abroad, but has not brought about any major changes in the volume of its production and exports. The share of international production already constitutes approximately 20 per cent of total turnover. It is anticipated to climb to almost one-third by 2003.

Thanks to internationalization, the shares of the USA and Asian markets have increased although the biggest effects are still to come. The company successfully registered its trademark in 2001 and is now selling under it globally. Product lines were diversified and adjusted to customer needs. Internationalization was also instrumental in the accumulation of knowledge and human capital development, which also improved the production and marketing of the parent company in Slovenia. Closer contacts with customers in the global market facilitated the adaptation and diversification of products and stepped up the firm's research and development potential. Employment in Kolektor dropped a little, while imports have fallen considerably. In general, investments abroad have contributed positively to the company's financial performance.

Weaknesses and threats

In spite of a gradual transformation from a mostly local to an internationally mature company and the resulting gradual accumulation of knowledge, the lack of adequately trained local human capital is the main problem. Firstly, in Slovenia there are not enough people with international business experience. Secondly, the locally-oriented mentality discourages Slovenians from working abroad, in spite of higher pay.

Strategically, the key problem is non-diversified production, making it highly exposed to technological changes in the market. The electronic revolution will not bypass this industry. Traditional commutators could be replaced by electronic commutation. Innovation in such a direction is very R&D intensive and only very large companies can undertake it.

Kolektor is facing up to such trends through its diversification strategy, and acquisitions at home and abroad. In such a way, the firm also reduces its risk exposure and high dependence on the volatility and oscillations of a single, namely automotive, industry.

In spite of the generally very good results with internationalization, Kolektor has a negative acquisition experience in Brazil. Reasons for the failure there include: (i) differences in the acquisition terms; (ii) fear of acquisition by the management which was also the owner; (iii) the great self-confidence of local management, partly due to domestic industry's protection against imports; (iv) the postponing of decisions reduced Kolektor's interest; (v) the uncompetitive price of highly-skilled labour in Brazil compared to Slovenia; and (vi) the uncertain business environment there (see Petrič, 2000a).

Summary

Kolektor is not a typical case of indirect outward FDI. It started its outward internationalization only when and because it had succeeded in gaining an independent position vis-à-vis its majority foreign owner. In Kolektor's case, it was exactly the independent and ambitious position of management that led the company to invest abroad.

There are seven key messages of the Kolektor case. The first is that a company in its growth has to accept the challenge of internationalization. Management realized that no growth means no development and no development means death. Secondly, technologically less-developed inward FDI could be instrumental in enhancing technological and managerial/ marketing capabilities. This can only be achieved (the third lesson) on the basis of an ambitious strategy of the local partner to assimilate, adopt and develop acquired technology through its own R&D efforts. Such inward internationalization successfully paved the way to gradual outward internationalization based on the company's own knowledge (the fourth lesson). Product characteristics (the fifth lesson) together with an ambitious management strategy facilitated such transformation from inward to outward internationalization. The product namely demanded the company's own development efforts particularly in developing tools which also prevented competitors easily entering the market. The industry characteristic (the sixth lesson) requiring close links with its customers also enabled the transformation from dependant to independent marketing of its products. Finally, this transformation of the company from a small technological laggard to a product and technology leader in the industry was only possible after meeting two crucial preconditions: first because from the outset the firm was very ambitious, aiming at the development of its own high quality products and technologies and, second, because the management team was able to grasp the opportunity offered by the crisis of a foreign partner. This was a once-in-a-lifetime opportunity, which could easily have been missed[12].

Notes

1 This case study is based largely on three previous studies: Jaklič M. 2000, Petrič 2000 and 2001 and Svetličič and Rojec, 1998.

2 Jaklič M. branded such internationalisation as independent in contrast to the dependent form where a foreign partner is dominant (Jaklič M., 2000).

3 Over 30 of them are built into a car of modern design, for instance.

4 If not otherwise stated, the data comes from Kolektor, 2001.

5 Only Kirkwood Industries Cleveland has a larger share (15.45 per cent).

6 Comtrade GmbH Klagenfurt, Austria, was established as a greenfield investment, a minority-owned trading unit. Its equity capital is only € 36,000, while sales in 2000 were € 21.9 million. Its basic function is to sell Kolektor's products abroad. Comtrade Austria has subsidiaries and representative offices in Germany, Italy, France and the USA.

7 Kolektor bought the company in 2000 as a majority shareholder. The company employs 80 people, has € seven million in sales. Sixty per cent of sales goes to the local market, five per cent to EU countries and 35 per cent elsewhere. The company exports 40 per cent of its sales and imports 25 per cent of the necessary inputs. The company does not export to Slovenia, or Kolektor, or any other Central and Eastern European countries. In 2001, almost US$ one million was invested in order to increase the value of production in 2002/3 by US$ 1.5 million. In 2002, a further additional investment is planned in the new production capacities. Through Sinyung, Kolektor will expand its market and production presence in

the markets of the Far East; the plan is to at least double sales in the next five years (Jaklič, 2000). The management of Kolektor cites the following reasons for the decision to acquire Sinyung: (i) the complementary technology of Sinyung (micro commutators); (ii) direct presence; (iii) price advantage because of the Japanese competition; (iv) the advantages of Kolektor's technology for specific applications; (v) the efficiency of Korean workers; (vi) access to Sinyung's technical knowledge; (vii) comparable costs; (viii) the favourable acquisition price; and (ix) access to the East Asian market (Petrič, 2000b). Kolektor will also be able to take advantage of economies of scale and scope, and to increase the recognition and reputation of its trademark (Jaklič M., 2000). Kolektor has faced the following problems in the acquired company: (i) a different culture; (ii) different work intensity; (iii) unsettled production; and (iv) poor supply-sales logistics (Petrič, 2000b).

8 The company in Greenville, South Carolina, USA, is a greenfield investment in the majority ownership of Kolektor (a 60 per cent share), with fixed assets of € 1.4 million and equity capital of € 1.2 million. Investment in the USA was worth approximately US$ five million. The facility is planned to not only satisfy US markets but the whole NAFTA market. The company began its operations in March 2001. The intention is to supply the markets of NAFTA countries. Annual turnover of the unit is planned to be € 6 million. Kolektor's main objectives with its US subsidiary are to acquire the status of a US domestic producer (to overcome the protectionist barriers), so as to: (i) increase recognition of Kolektor's trademark in the North American market; (ii) expand the market share with a more aggressive appearance in that market; and (iii) improve contacts with customers. The investment incentives offered by South Carolina were also relevant (Jaklič, 2000).

9 Besides its investment activities abroad, Kolektor has expanded its production programme through the acquisition of a majority share in the Slovenian company Iskra Feriti. Thus, it has complemented its offer for the automotive industry with a programme of soft ferrites and wound components, and entered the field of telecommunications. Iskra Feriti is known for its quality performance and is one of the top five manufacturers in Europe. Further, Kolektor became a majority shareholder in the company Synatec Idrija, which has been Kolektor's business partner for years.

10 Such a transition was facilitated by the fact that it was not difficult for Kolektor to convince its buyers that it had already been producing commutators, sold under the K&B trademark. The situation would have been much more difficult if Kolektor had been producing for customers it did not know.

11 ITT Automotive: Liefrant des Jahres 1997, Black & Decker: Supplier of Excellence 1999, Bosch: 1995/1996, 1999/2000, United Technologies Automotive: Preferred Supplier Award 1995, Iskra Avtoelektrika; Key Supplier 1998, Valeo 1000.

12 In August 2002, i.e. after the manuscript was submitted to the publishers, the Slovene partners bought back Kirkwood's share and Kolektor then took over K&B in Germany in November 2002. Thereby, the round trip from being a totally Slovenian company and then undergoing a foreign-controlled phase came to an end in approximately 40 years. That is a relatively unique transformation, at least for a former socialist firm.

Chapter 19

Mercator

Consolidated financial statements for 2000:

Number of employees:	13,208
Number of companies in the group:	25
Sales:	€ 1,170.7 million
Net profit:	€ 20.4 million
Capital expenditure:	€ 131 million
Non-current finan. investments:	€ 28.5 million
Return on equity (in %):	6.2
Market share: (in %):	36.8
Number of companies within the same business activity in Slovenia:	761
Type of organisation:	Joint-stock company d.d.

http://www.mercator.si

Introduction

As an emerging trading multinational company, Mercator is something of a newcomer. It is an interesting case for two reasons. Firstly, because since its late start in 1999 its international operations have started to grow faster than its domestic activity and have involved clear and ambitious plans for future internationalization. Secondly, since it is a case of limited internationalization, of a clear vision to become a regional multinational. Therefore, it is interesting to see whether this regional strategy is some kind of defensive reaction to the activity of leading trading multinationals or whether this is an offensive strategy to become a regional multinational as its ultimate objective. It is also a case that shows how inherited location- and politically-based advantages (living before in the one country) can be highly instrumental in stimulating the first steps of internationalization and thereby also facilitating further internationalization steps.

History

Mercator is an old company. Its legal predecessor was 'Živila, Ljubljana', established in 1949. The Mercator name appeared for the first time in 1953.

Its subsequent development has been gradual, marked by the changing organization of the company, its local expansion, diversification of activities and improved responsiveness to changes in the political, legal and economic environments. After Slovenia's independence, there was a decade of growth transforming it into a large Slovenian trading corporation.

In 1990 the Business Group Mercator was founded. In 1993 the company was privatized. Internal reorganization and adaptation of its activities to European models of organizing trading companies and their standards of business operations began to take priority. The last two years have been years of expansion and modernization of retail trade networks, a period of consolidation through acquisitions of smaller Slovenian retailers in order to increase efficiency and optimize activities in Slovenia. The aim was to achieve economies of scale and strengthen long-term relations with suppliers in order to reduce prices for customers and enhance synergy within the growing Mercator group. In this area, Mercator learned a great deal from Interspar's system of relations with suppliers, which facilitated its joint venture. This was also a development stage when Mercator started implementing its strategic objective of expanding to new markets in Central Europe. The construction of shopping centres in Croatia and BiH started.

This strategy produced its first tangible results in 2001, for instance: (i) opening of a number of new shopping centres in Slovenia, and in Zagreb (Croatia); (ii) new acquisitions in Slovenia in retail trade and related businesses; (iii) takeover of the Croatian trading company Sloboda and its later merger in order to create a single company co-ordinating all business activities in Croatia; (iv) construction of the Mercator centre Belgrade started; and (v) diversification in the textile sector commenced. Such rapid expansion was facilitated by new long-term syndicated loans worth € 52 million , and by commercial bills amounting to € 100 million.

Company profile

Mercator is the largest trading corporation in Slovenia with 13,208 employees, and involving 23 companies. The Mercator group's core business is wholesale and retail trade in consumer goods through a wide network of shops and shopping centres (hypermarkets). The Mercator group also includes companies operating in the food-processing industry, agriculture, hotels and restaurants, and service activities. In 2000 its market share in Slovenia was almost 37 per cent (an increase from 20 per cent in 1998)[1]. In 2000, the Mercator group realized SIT 240 billion (€ 1.1 billion), sales increased by 37 per cent over 1999 and more than doubled compared to 1995. Net profits also increased by 37 per cent from SIT 1.5 million in 1998 to SIT 4.2 million in 2000. This was also achieved thanks to acquisitions of 17 (1999-2001) new trade companies in Slovenia. Return on equity also doubled from 1998-2000, from 2.9 to 6.2 per cent.

This rapid development was only possible thanks to the very ambitious plans, M&A, strong investments coupled with growing knowledge also gained through the joint venture with Interspar and the ongoing improving of services, which enabled the turning of visions into reality. The Group invested SIT 32.7 billion in 2000, SIT 5.8 billion of which was for strategic long-term equity investments as part of two medium-term development plans: 1998-2000 and 2000-2003. The priority of the first one was investment expansion and increasing the market share in the Slovenian retail industry, while the second gives special emphasis to internationalization (Marinšek, 2000). The first objective was achieved by takeovers of mainly retail companies in areas where Mercator did not have a well-established network of shops, and by the construction of large shopping complexes with a hypermarket as a centre. At the same time, the existing network of retail stores has undergone technological and other improvements. An integral part of the new investment policy also involves investment in people and their knowledge with the goal of raising the level of service quality. In 2000 Mercator started active internationalization activity involving other countries.

Mercator's key objectives in the 2000-2003 period are to become one of the top 200 trading companies in the world and an important player in Central and Eastern Europe compatible in all important elements of its supply, quality organization and business performance with the biggest global and European trading firms. Here, one of the most important strategic objectives is an expansion to the markets of former Yugoslavia, with the aim to become an important retail trade chain by establishing a number of shopping centres. Such penetration is not isolated but is also well co-ordinated with other Slovenian companies active in this area.

Outward internationalization

Mercator was the first trading company in Slovenia to enter into a joint venture with Interspar in 1989. This proved to be instrumental in accumulating the expertise that later facilitated its outward internationalization. The most important aspect was knowledge of sourcing and know-how about gaining a strategic position in relation to suppliers. The direct foreign competition in the Slovenian retail market forced all other trading companies to improve their competitiveness faster than would otherwise be the case.

Mercator's investment expansion abroad is a result of carrying out the objectives outlined in the 2000-2003 development plan. Internationalization has become a key strategic objective because expansion in Slovenia is impossible due to competition law. Its vision is to become a regional multinational, firstly in the region of former Yugoslavia and later also in other South-east European countries. In 2001 Mercator's total investments amounted to SIT 30 billion, with SIT 12.5 billion or 42 percent going abroad. Such investments will gradually increase the share of sales realized abroad to a planned 14 to 15 percent of all revenues by 2002. In 2001 they constituted seven per cent of total sales. In Croatia Mercator has achieved a 2.5 percent market share, and in BiH one percent[2] (see Križnik, 2002; p. 13).

The main reason underlying such internationalization is the saturation of the domestic market, its over-crowding and thus the limiting of possibilities for market expansion in Slovenia. Therefore, 20 per cent growth in sales, to be facilitated by outward investment, was planned.

Mercator's internationalization is only of a recent origin. It started in 1999 with the establishing of the Mercator Centre Pula (Croatia), followed in 2000 by a shopping centre in Sarajevo BiH (another one is planned in Tuzla in 2004) and the broadening of the shopping centre network in Croatia (two in Zagreb and one in Rijeka and Split) as well as the acquisition of Sloboda in Croatia. Finally, expansion to the FRY started with the construction of a shopping centre in Belgrade (the FRY) in 2002.

Mercator Pula (Croatia) was established as a joint venture with Intermercator, GmbH Austria also to avoid any nationalist attitudes and the unfriendly political climate at that time[3]. A year later, a hypermarket in Pula

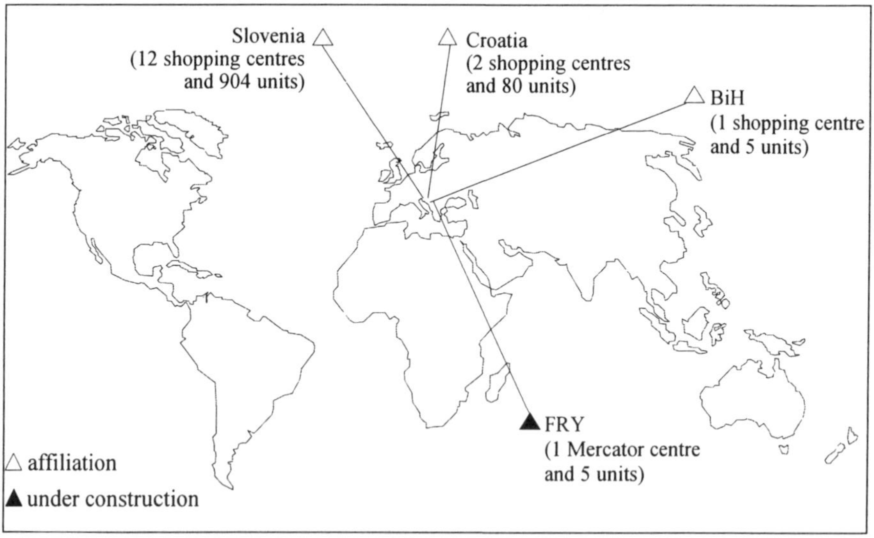

Figure 19.1 International business network of Mercator in 2002

opened. The value of the investment was € 27,313. Business is conducted through a company set up in Croatia called *Mercator – H.* The entire centre of 8,920 m^2 was built by the end of 2000 and was planned to have monthly sales worth SIT 280 million. The results have bettered the expectations.

2000 was a true milestone in internationalization with the acquisition of a 52 per cent shareholding in Mercator TC Sarajevo (BiH) through which all operations in this country are conducted. Mercator's store in BiH - *Mercator Centre Sarajevo* – opened in December 2000. The store has a surface area of 16,146 square metres, and was planned to generate monthly sales of SIT 424 million. Mercator's centre in Zagreb (Croatia) with 14,980 square metres of space opened in September 2001 becoming the second of the shopping centres the group is planning to establish in Croatia. It is larger than the one in Pula and is expected to generate monthly sales of SIT 560 million. The results achieved are according to plan. Future plans include opening a shopping centre in Belgrade[4] in 2002, a Mercator centre in Split and, by 2004, additional centres in Rijeka, another in Zagreb, and new ones in Zadar, Šibenik, Varaždin, Banja Luka, Tuzla, and Novi Sad.

All the Mercator centres are managed by its subsidiaries abroad. The type of central foreign affiliate in each market is always a limited liability company that enables efficient (less costly) and flexible operating in comparison to a joint-venture company. In every company set up abroad, Mercator is the majority shareholder. Further, everything that forms part of a project abroad – from the basic construction of a store through to the placement of goods on shelves – is designed according to Mercator's standards and technology.

Internationalization is not only taking place in the form of greenfield operations, but in 2001 also included the acquisition of the Croatian trading company Sloboda. Greenfield market entry method was in many cases the only way when privatization had still not been completed and an appropriate local partner was simply impossible to find. However, in addition to the general problems acquisitions or takeovers face in the world like opposition from local market leaders, in former Yugoslavia certain other historically-rooted factors come into play. One reason takeovers or acquisitions are a less frequently used market entry method here includes the extra attitudinal barriers a Slovenian company faces when trying to enter. A firm from a former 'neighbour' can be regarded as being more unfriendly than other foreign firms that were never part of the same economy, in spite of the many advantages they in fact have[5]. In the future, however, greenfield investments will be increasingly supplemented by local acquisitions depending primarily on the 'availability' of appropriate local partners.

A second strategic novelty which has already taken root in the FRY is a combined strategy (Makovec-Brenèiè et al. 2001; p. 372). Its first stage is the greenfield construction of a supermarket, the second is acquisition of a local retail chain under the existing name and the last is optimization of business activity within the integrated system, a greenfield shopping centre and the acquired local retail chain.

The importance of internationalization as a new strategy is best demonstrated by the fact that in 2000 investments abroad were almost twice the level of investments in trade centres and hypermarkets in Slovenia. As many as 43 per cent of all investments in 2000 were directed to foreign markets. The level of such investments in the 2000-2003 period is planned to be approximately SIT 41 billion (€ 200 million).

While internationalization is becoming important, it is less so in terms of employment since it still represented just four per cent of total employment in 2000.

These very ambitious plans are not without several difficulties. The problems Mercator faces when investing abroad vary from state to state. Those that are common and make internationalization difficult include: (i) rigidity of central and local governmental authorities and lengthy procedures involved in gathering documentation; (ii) local trade lobbies seeking to protect their own interests by attempting to prevent the entrance of any foreign competition; (iii) unfinished privatization programmes, revisions of privatization, the still strong involvement of the state in business; (iv) certain attitudinal barriers against foreign acquisitions; (v) a lack of insurance against risks; (vi) low purchasing power as reflected by low GDP per capita; and (vii) the still operating black markets in BiH and the FRY, coupled with a high share of the grey economy in both countries.

At the same time, it is precisely these types of barriers which, for a firm like Mercator, may be more easily overcome since it is a firm that used to operate in such markets before. It has more personal connections and networks compared to a newcomer international firm that does not know the market and local business culture. The key to success is therefore a selection of a reliable partner[6] and competent managerial staff.

Such regional internationalization is easier in terms of knowledge of the former market but, at the same time, more complicated due to the higher political and commercial risks involved in states which have just come out of war and are still deep in the stabilization stage of the transition process[7]. That is why any decision to invest there requires careful analysis of related legislation and its implementation, inter-state relations, and any possible insurance and guarantees.

In all of these markets there used to be and still are some macroeconomic and political problems. The first set relates to some unresolved issues relating to the succession of states. The second group of difficulties initially involved, when internationalization started, the absence of certain bilateral agreements (trade, investment, visas, administrative trade barriers to food and the lack of testing capabilities etc.[8]).

Competitive advantages

Mercator's primary competitive advantages are management, strategic position relative to local suppliers, completed and cost-efficient logistics (based on just-in-time delivery) suitable for the whole region[9], quality services in satisfying customer needs[10] and high returns on investment as part of a clear long-term strategy of internationalization. Its sales per square metre are higher than its competitors in Slovenia including multinational companies such as Interspar and E. Leclerc. The next biggest advantage is its inherited reputation built up over 55 years in former Yugoslavia. Mercator has a high reputation in these markets and, given Slovenia's faster privatization and transition compared to other parts of former Yugoslavia, such advantages have been relatively exponentially enhanced. Lately, promotion of the company has also been based on extensive social engagement. The company's philosophy is 'employing local labour, involving local suppliers and thereby increasing purchasing power and customer loyalty'.

Together with certain other Slovenian firms pioneering investing in former Yugoslavia, Mercator is building on its advantages previously gained there[11] and first-mover advantages, which could yet pay off due to psychological factors. As the saying goes 'A friend in need is a friend indeed'. The trade-off in such an investment is really between high risk and fast returns, and returns in terms of brand-name reputation built in the long run on such psychological factors like customer loyalty.

Mercator's competitive strengths in Slovenia, which are then also transplanted internationally, are: price competitiveness, own brand name development[12], up-to-date shopping centres technology and know-how, highly developed and efficient logistics, long-term relations with suppliers which improve price competitiveness, and policy of local suppliers. In foreign markets, 40 per cent of goods sold by Mercator are to be of a local origin, 40 per cent from Slovenia, and 20 per cent imported. In Slovenia, this share is even higher, i.e. 76 per cent are domestic goods and 24 per cent are imported goods. Its own credit card/ loyalty card is also the stimulating the allegiance of customers.

Two key instruments for strengthening competitiveness are training and improving quality standards. The total number of training hours rose by 29 per cent since 1999. 2000 was also a landmark year in terms of improving quality and standardization. The ISO 9001 project was successfully completed after two years of work. Some results have been detected such as simpler communications within the group, and with suppliers and business partners. Because it is an international standard, it was also regarded as an instrument to facilitate internationalization.

On top of the abovementioned general ones, the Mercator group's specific advantages enabling it to take advantage of opportunities in former Yugoslav and Balkans markets stem from:

- the poorly organized and technologically outdated retail trade there;
- good possibilities for counter-trade with raw materials, semi-manufactures and final products that are required by Slovenia's processing industry;
- reasonable conditions for logistical support;
- relatively minor language, cultural and other communications obstacles; and
- the high reputation of Slovenian trademarks and the already established Mercator trademark.

Problems, weaknesses and threats

This quick jump from a medium-sized domestic trading company to a large one predominantly through acquisitions, and from a predominantly local to a regional multinational, has brought with it many problems stemming from the company's internal organization, its culture and governance as well as from the external environment of business activities. A more ambitious and aggressive strategy in local and international markets came after a change in management of the company. It was not an easy transition and took a lot of time and changes, including in the ranks of divisions. The growing importance of international operations will demand further changes in the still divisional organization of the company in the direction of more flexible project-oriented management structures and the development of a new corporate culture anchored in a global mindset philosophy.

Expansion at home through acquisitions was also not regarded by the general public as friendly. This is a general phenomenon strongly anchored in the inherited socialist mentality for which the taking over of firms was something unthinkable. First-movers therefore have to fight such attitudinal barriers.

To increase efficiency, the company also started to introduce new measures like Sunday opening hours and extended working hours where demand supports this. The opposition of trade unions has started to strengthen not only to Mercator's policy but generally in the retail trade sector in Slovenia.

In improving its competitiveness Mercator is trying to bring its business operations in line with the best practices of leading trading companies around the world, which include:

- centralized purchasing (even together with competitors);
- Electronic Data Interchange and electronic linking with major suppliers;
- development of Internet shopping;
- permanent efforts to cut retail prices through economies of scale in purchasing;
- expansion by establishing large shopping centres;
- customer-oriented strategies involving the introduction of Customer Relationship Management;
- the introduction of Goods Category Management; and
- enhancing own trademarks and environmentally-friendly products, including the recycling of used materials.

Emphasizing this strategic orientation is one way of overcoming some of the current weaknesses compared to the world's leading trading companies.

The biggest challenge in internationalization is how to utilize 'inherited' locational and know-how advantages before competition from large multinationals arrives in the region. Authorities in all newly emerged states are declaring very liberal foreign capital policies. Foreign competition is bound to come as soon as the economy stabilizes. This is particularly the case in the FRY. Acquiring a market share before the arrival of other foreign competition with stronger brand names is therefore of strategic importance. This 'time out' before the competition arrives has to be used to strengthen market positions and upgrade them by developing new firm-specific advantages to allow Mercator to stand up to the imminent and strong international competition.

Summary

The Mercator group has an ambitious growth plan that cannot be successfully put into practice in Slovenia alone. Given that Slovenian managers better understand the local conditions in former Yugoslav states, Mercator is moving quickly into these countries. Parallel to stabilization of the economic and political situation there, these markets will also become more attractive to international retail chains. Therefore, Mercator wants to gain first-mover advantages. The organizational set-up of retail stores as well as of the sales technology which Mercator is bringing to these countries is much more advanced than the existing local versions. On the other hand, growth of its retail network helps Mercator when negotiating with suppliers for more competitive terms, both in price and payment, not only for local supply but also for supplying Slovenian markets.

This leads to the conclusion that, while outward FDI in these territories is a risky undertaking for first-comers, it is a sensible strategy for a corporation like the Mercator group given its type and size, experiences and expertise. Hence, it can be expected the company will continue to be important regional investor in the future. The lead-time before international trade chains enter these markets can be used to bolster its local market position, to organize local supply chains not only for its local shopping centres but also for exporting to Slovenia. In such a way, the Mercator group can further build on its initial more location-based advantages and firm-specific ones like knowing how to do business in the former republics of Yugoslavia, which is also linked to the character and personal style of Mercator's President of the Board, Zoran Janković.

Therefore, it seems that the mid-term objectives to become a regional multinational may prove realistic. Such a strategy is not only based on inherited advantages but every day also more on firm-specific advantages like better customer service, higher service quality and the high reputation Slovenian goods still have in markets of the new states that have sprung up in the area of former Yugoslavia. Whether it will be able to develop from its current mainly 'former Yugoslav market multinational' status to a real multinational depends on it continually strengthening its firm-specific advantages, which will be increasingly significant when more competition enters the region. This time of first-mover advantages has to be used productively to raise competitiveness in other areas, too. Such advantages can soon disappear if not supplemented by more robust long-term, firm-specific advantages. However, it remains to be seen whether Mercator's strategy will stop at the borders of Central and Eastern European markets or whether this is only a strategy of strengthening the regional position for a subsequent and more ambitious global strategy either independently one or through strategic (contractual) or equity relations with large multinational trading companies with a complementary supply of technical goods and home appliances, in particular. The very ambitious strategy is encountering some financial limitations (short- and long-term financing in 2001 amounted to € 382.2 million and improved long-term arrangements may help in overcoming these hurdles.

Notes

1 If not otherwise stated, figures are taken from the 2000 Annual Report of Mercator.
2 One problem is the remaining high share accounted for by the grey economy.
3 Unsettled political questions on sea frontiers and succession issues have caused hot debates and hostile public opinion towards Slovenia. Joint venture was a way of overcoming these attitudinal barriers through origin-hiding.
4 This will be the first shopping centre in the FRY.
5 See note 3.
6 Selecting a reliable partner is very difficult, but acquisitions are preferred over greenfield investment due to the highly underestimated values of local companies.
7 The situation in Croatia is somewhat different since the war ended, as privatisation is more advanced and the country is generally more developed.
8 Only an investment protection agreement which came into force with Macedonia (in 1999). Those with BiH, and Croatia, have been ratified in Slovenia (in 2000 and 2001, respectively) but not yet on their side. An investment treaty with Yugoslavia was initialled in February 2002 and was expected to be signed in March.
9 The completed logistics system as well as vicinity and strategic position of the chosen foreign locations helped them avoid warehousing costs (an important factor of cost competitiveness in retail trade).
10 In 2000 it was awarded the ISO 9001 certificate of quality. A customer service public opinion poll initiated for the first time in 1999 demonstrated that 80 per cent of consumers are very loyal. Almost half of the buyers visit Mercator stores every day. The highest weight among factors like location, product range, services etc was given to prices. This means that this is perhaps the major advantage although differences are very small; location was rated 4.25 out of five.
11 Mercator had a retail network in the former Yugoslavia as well, but due to the unsettled succession debate its future is still on hold.
12 This is a result of a long-term strategy of building up its image; a result of its ambitious communication strategy. Mercator won the Advertiser of the Year award in Slovenia for 2001. Part of this strategy is building up relations with the environment, including support of sports, cultural and health organizations.

PART V
LESSONS FROM SLOVENIA

Chapter 20

The Role of the Government

Introduction

As history demonstrates, companies have responded much faster and more promptly to the challenges of globalization than governments. Governments have never attached much importance to policies on outward investment compared to trade or inward FDI. Internationalization, and outward investment in particular, has been primarily considered a concern of firms themselves. The outflow of capital has often even seemed unbeneficial to a national economy. However, governments can play an important role and often dictate the tempo and direction of the process.

Although some studies (Ohmae, 1990; Reich, 1990, 1992) argued that multinational companies have recently been involved in the process of denationalization, when transforming from national to international producers, and then to global enterprises, companies do not become denationalized. Their national origins continue to have a strong influence on their investment decisions. Home governments historically support their firms in foreign investment activity, according to the size and strategic importance of the investment and the nature of the host economy (Jones, 1996; pp. 194-223). Transition economies' firms – since they lag behind in becoming multinational and in market-economy institutions – are supposed to be induced by their governments, yet these governments have not always been aware of their role in the internationalization process.

This chapter examines the role of the government in the case of Slovenia's internationalization process. It evaluates whether the government's reaction to internationalization and outward investment in the decade of transition was strategic or defensive, and reviews development of the institutional framework and promotional measures linked to outward investment. Parallel to this, we demonstrate how firms have evaluated the governmental contribution to outward internationalization. We analyze the role of the institutional framework, promotional measures and the quality of institutional services relating to outward FDI. Lastly, we reveal firms' own suggestions for what should be done by home-country governments and governmental agencies to facilitate outward investment.

The government: strategic responses or defensive reactions?

Although the strategy of an outward-oriented economy has been followed from the outset of the new state, the emphasis has been on exports as the principal form of outward internationalization. Other entry modes such as international production, capital linkages or strategic alliances or the holistic perception of internationalization of the economy have mostly been neglected. The first incentives to develop a more active attitude to outward FDI can be traced to 1993, followed by a series of development strategies[1] (Svetličič, 1993) and more developed proposals (Svetličič, 1995, 1996a, 1996b)[2]. However, only the recently elaborated strategy 'Slovenia in the next decade: sustainability, competitiveness, EU membership' (Šušteršič, Rojec and Mrak, 2001) is really based on the new internationalization paradigm. By the end of the 1990s no real implementation of incentives or institutional framework existed. There were also not many restrictions (see Chapter 4). Consequently, outward investment was driven by companies in a bottom-up fashion, rather than involving a top-down national strategy in the sense of being 'the art of implementing the adopted plans to achieve the set goals'. Not even in the sense of 'identification of the advantages and weaknesses of the economy and its companies, opportunities and threats in the business sector, as well as setting up the activities with the goal of taking the best of the opportunities and avoiding threats'[3]. Strategic means that an economy and its companies develop activities abroad as a network, whose every individual part supports the activities of the whole company/economy. This requires strong international co-operation at the macro level and intensive interaction among globally dispersed units at the company level.

Nevertheless, one cannot claim that Slovenia has in fact any clearly elaborated strategy in this field. The initial policy of mistrust of capital exports immediately after gaining independence, marked by various restrictions, began to soften and was formally transformed in 1999 (with the new Foreign Exchange Act) into an internationally compatible system of regulating international long-term capital flows. Although an unfriendly public mood towards outward FDI and fears about the exporting of jobs and capital were present (for a more detailed description, see Chapter 4) they did not translate into policies that restricted Slovenian outward FDI. The initial attitude to direct investment abroad as an unpatriotic act, since capital flows abroad, has thus changed. This form of investment gradually began to be treated as a normal, 'non-contaminated' business activity, although some remained sceptical.

Regulation

Adoption of the new, modern and relatively liberal foreign exchange legislation of 1999 was more than an element of a national internationalization strategy, part of an overall systemic change characterized by the transition from socialism and a command type of economy to market-economy capitalism. Liberalization of capital movements and the exchange regime in transactions between residents and non-residents was an important part of the whole process of accession, also spurred on by the Europe Agreement concluded with the European Union in June 1996. These agreements generally require the immediate liberalization of direct investments as the most important capital transactions for development, international co-operation and integration. Following the requirements of the Europe Agreement, the OECD Code and the EU's *acquis*, Slovenia in 1999 removed all restrictions, retaining for its foreign exchange authority only the power to monitor transactions. The legislation adopted was therefore not so much a product of autonomous beliefs in the government, but was very much the product of EU accession (harmonization with the EU and OECD standards) on one hand, and the bottom-up pressure of companies on the other.

Such liberalization, however, was initially not enhanced by the incentives for internationalization. The government assisted outward investment by building an institutional framework including bilateral investment treaties (BITs) and double taxation avoidance treaties (DTTs) as an elementary FDI institutional environment.

Bilateral investment treaties

Bilateral investment treaties are important in initial internationalization phases when the investment climate is not too favourable, or where there are different kinds of instability. The purposes for Slovenia concluding bilateral investment treaties with different countries have not been and are (still) not always the same. The main goal of concluding bilateral investment treaties with industrial countries is to promote inward investments while, for developing or capital-importing countries, the main goal is to promote and protect Slovenian outward investments in those countries. Since transition economies are net FDI receivers, bilateral investment treaties were initially and primarily stimulated by the protection of inward FDI. Later on, with the increasing importance of outward FDI, bilateral investment treaties have also been oriented to major destinations of outward FDI. The signing of a bilateral investment treaty usually follows investments and not *vice versa*. Therefore, it is hard to assert that bilateral investment treaties have played any significant role in firms' initial decisions to invest abroad.

This can also be seen in the evaluation of host-country determinants that influenced an investment location decision (see Chapter 5), where the policy framework and business facilitation programmes were assessed as being less important for an investment decision. Firms actually do complain if such agreements are not in place, but only in highly risky destinations. The importance of bilateral investment treaties increases above all after an investment decision is made or even more when an insurance or dispute settlement issues arises.

Slovenia has been entering into bilateral investment treaties since 1992[4]. By July 2001, Slovenia had signed thirty-three bilateral investment treaties, fourteen with member-countries of the EU, then with almost all of the present EU candidate-countries, with countries of former Yugoslavia, and some other countries such as Russia and China[5]. Most of the bilateral investment treaties signed have been ratified by the Slovenian parliament, and most of them have entered into force. Many agreements with developing countries entered into force only in 2000 (ten) when a substantial amount of outward FDI was made (mostly in the region of former Yugoslavia). BITs with Kuwait, Turkey, Chile and Malaysia have been initialled but not yet signed. Currently (2001/2002), BITs are also being negotiated with the United States of America, the FRY (initialled in February 2002), Belarus, and Morocco.

Table 20.1 Slovenia's Bilateral Investment Treaties (as at 5 March 2002)

Country	Date of signature (day/month/year)	Date of entering into force (day/month/year)
Albania	23.10.1997	22.3.2000
Austria	7.3.2001	3.10.2001
Belgium/Luxembourg	1.2.1999	15.2.2000
BiH	3.5.2001	25.10.2001
Bulgaria	30.6.1998	26.11.2000
China	13.9.1993	1.1.1995
Croatia	12.12.1997	31.5.2000
Czech Republic	4.5.1993	21.5.1994
Denmark	11.5.1999	3.10.2001
Egypt	28.10.1998	23.3.1999
Finland	1.6.1998	3.6.2000
France	11.2.1998	5.8.2000
Hungary	15.10.1996	9.6.2000
Germany	28.10.1993	18.7.1998
Greece	29.5.1997	11.2.2000

Italy	8.3.2000	17.7.2000
Israel	13.5.1998	2.10.1999
Lithuania	13.10.1998	22.4.1999
Macedonia	5.6.1996	21.9.1999
Malta	15.3.2001	3. 10.2001
Netherlands	24.9.1996	1.8.1998
Poland	28.6.1996	31.3.2000
Portugal	14.5.1997	4.5.2000
Romania	24.1.1996	24.11.1996
Russia	8.4.2000	8.1.2001
Singapore	25.1.1999	1.7.2000
Slovakia	28.7.1993	28.3.1996
Spain	15.7.1998	3.4.2000
Sweden	5.10.1999	9.2.2001
Switzerland	9.11.1995	20.3.1997
Thailand	18.2.2000	19.7.2000
Ukraine	30.3.1999	1.6.2000
United Kingdom	3.7.1996	12.5.1999

Source: Ministry of the Economy.

At the end of the nineties, the bulk of investments made by Slovenian companies went to countries with no bilateral investment treaties or for which agreements had not entered into force. This is especially true in the area of ex-Yugoslavia (Croatia, BiH, Macedonia, Serbia). According to managers' interviews, the information on BITs played almost no role in the past investment decisions. This is no longer the case. The perception of BITs' role among investing firms seems to be changing already.

With the expansion of outward FDI activity, the amount of invested funds and consequently the risk for companies increases. Moreover, the investing firms have more frequently confronted some unplanned events that could occur only after some years of investment. The existence of BITs also carries a weight in insurance possibilities. All these experiences stimulated Slovenian companies to change their perception of the importance of bilateral investment treaties. According to the survey by the Ministry of the Economy carried out in June 2001[6], above 70 per cent of sample companies evaluates BITs as very important, while none of them regards BITs as unimportant (see Figure 20.1). Companies are increasingly aware of the significance of such treaties and especially of the inconvenience where they do not exist.

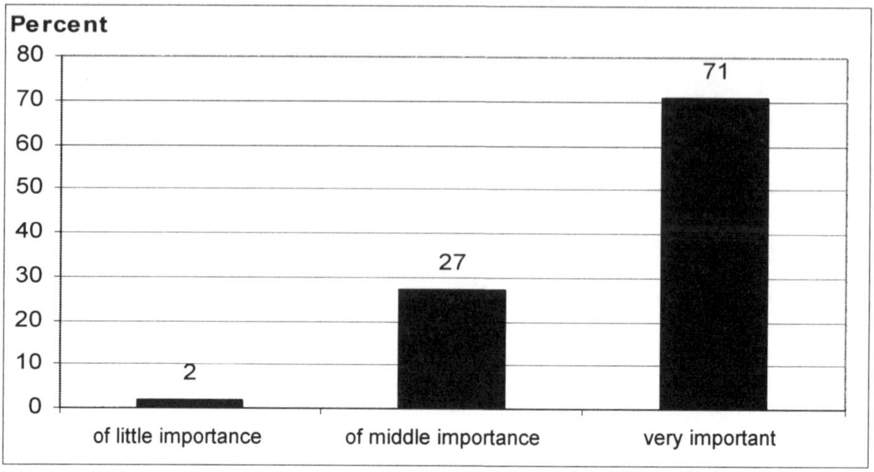

Figure 20.1 Firms' evaluation of BITs

Source: Survey by the Ministry of the Economy, July 2001.

It was therefore somewhat shocking to find that companies are not very well acquainted with BITs. Although in the abovementioned survey up to 56.4 per cent of companies already had outward FDI, only five per cent of them claimed they were very well acquainted with BITs, while 71 per cent declared themselves poorly acquainted with BITs (Figure 20.2). Ignorance of institutional environment is therefore still considerable (especially if we consider that the sample included major Slovenian exporters). For the total population of firms, one can expect even less knowledge which itself calls for additional informational support from the Ministry of the Economy.

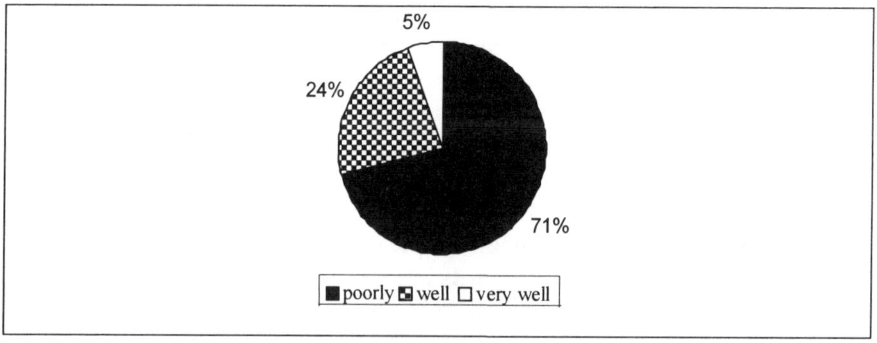

Figure 20.2 How well companies are acquainted with BITs

Source: Survey by the Ministry of the Economy, July 2001.

Consequently, companies' knowledge of BITs' contents is also very low. More than 70 per cent of the surveyed companies evaluated their knowledge about the contents of BITs as poor. Some of them were even unable to evaluate their knowledge of the BITs' contents. Only 16 per cent of them stated they know the contents well (Figure 20.3). Given this poor level of knowledge, it is unrealistic to expect that companies – in the event of difficulties such as disputes, damage or material loss – would be able to explore the possibilities offered by the agreements[7].

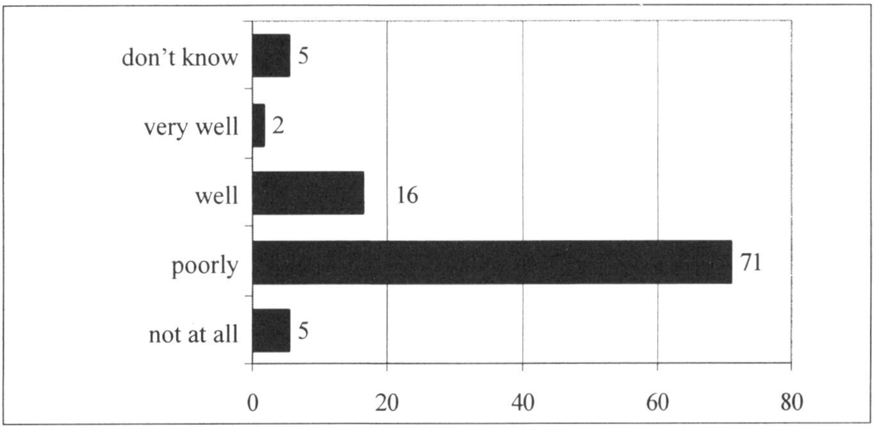

Figure 20.3 Knowledge of BITs contents: How well do you know the contents of BITs?

Source: Survey by the Ministry of the Economy, July 2001.

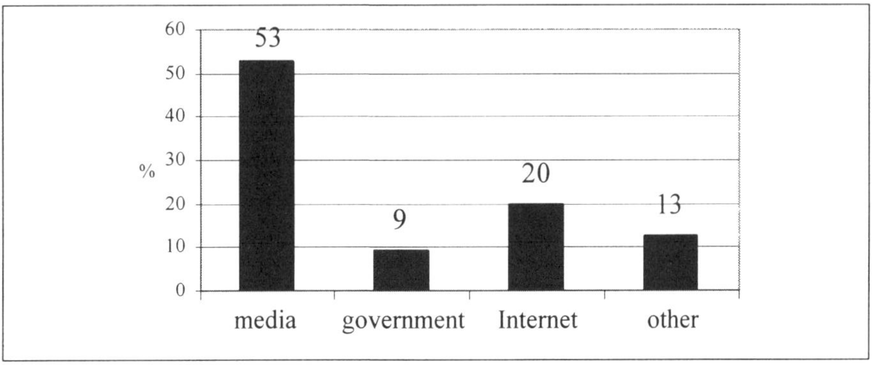

Figure 20.4 Sources of information about BITs

Source: Survey by the Ministry of the Economy, July 2001.

Poor knowledge is clearly a consequence of the availability of information, the way of dissemination and information sources. So far, companies mostly gathered the necessary information through the media (Figure 20.4), only a few gathered it from the government, namely the Ministry of the Economy (or Ministry of Economic Relations and Development as its predecessor). The main strategy of the government should be greater dissemination through the business press. About 20 per cent of companies use the Internet as their main information source on BITs, which suggests that there are easy ways to increase the awareness of BITs by improving this channel. Among other information sources, companies mentioned the Chamber of Commerce and Industry, business partners, business fairs and the Slovenian Export Corporation.

Double Taxation Conventions

The next important part of 'investment protection' infrastructure involves double taxation agreements (DTTs). In comparison to BITs, the situation with DTTs is worse, even though companies pay more attention to the latter and more DTTs were inherited from former Yugoslavia than BITs[8].

Since its independence, Slovenia has concluded double taxation agreements with five developing and three developed countries (see Box 20.1).

Box 20.1 Double taxation treaties

Country	Start of application (day/month/year)
Austria	1.1.1999
China	1.1.1996
Czech Republic	1.1.1999
Macedonia	1.1.2000
Poland	1.1.1999
Russia	1.1.1998
Switzerland	1.1.1998
United States of America	22.9.2001

Unfortunately, neither the conclusion of an agreement nor it coming into force gives any guarantee of smooth and unproblematic business. Box 20.2 discloses one example that has caused Slovenian MNCs several problems and much cost.

Box 20.2 Inefficiency of a double taxation agreement

The non-caring attitude of companies to institutional agreements might be partly a reflection of problems seen in their practical implementation. For instance, Slovenia inherited a double taxation agreement with Italy from the SFRY, signed in 1982, but even in 2002 companies with affiliates in Italy still cannot avoid the payment of double taxation due to bureaucratic procedures. Managers even claim that the DTT was never really reliable and effective. Affiliates are namely obliged to pay taxes in Italy. To be exempted from paying tax in Slovenia, the Slovenian tax authorities however request the submission of a written certificate or acknowledgement that all tax duties were paid in Italy. The Italian tax authorities never issue the required certificate and consequently Slovenian companies remain without any such evidence and are again obliged to pay taxes in Slovenia. In September 2001 a new version of a double taxation agreement was signed and the procedure of a common agreement was launched, yet the outcome is still uncertain.

Source: Interviews with sample companies and the Ministry of the Economy, 2001.

Promotional measures

Similar to bilateral investment treaties, promotional measures were also not a strong incentive for initial decisions to undertake outward FDI. Outward FDI has so far grown up much more as a bottom-up initiative than an ex ante, planned macroeconomic strategy. Push factors for outward FDI in the home-country environment originated more from competitive pressures (a small domestic market, increasing labour costs, increasing foreign competition) than governmental support. A systematic policy of promoting outward internationalization started to take shape in 2000.

All initial efforts in the field of internationalization have been devoted to inward FDI. After outward FDI started to increase, the government began to realize that a certain policy is needed, that even the promotion of internationalization seems necessary. The initial scepticism of or even hostility to outward FDI considered outward FDI only as an outflow of capital has been replaced by treating it as restructuring instrument which could contribute to boosting the competitiveness of investing companies and even facilitating integration with the European Union and the world economy.

In 2000 the state for the first time began to actively promote internationalization. In the first promotional programme launched in 2000, resources (totalling € 2.6 million) were allocated to cover some preparatory activities of firms for outward FDI (such as matchmaking, feasibility studies, training, material costs, consultancy services and experts for specific projects). The programme was mainly intended to promote the internationalization of textile and textile products companies, as well as leather- and footwear-manufacturing companies, and joint marketing in the framework of the programme for company's co-operation and the internationalization of all companies. The Ministry of the Economy approved 84 projects in a total amount of € 2.75 million. The programme was upgraded and financially strengthened in 2001[9].

Role of the Slovene Export Corporation

One of more important instruments for facilitating outward FDI is the existing export credit and insurance (guarantee) agency, the Slovene Export Corporation (SEC, Slovenska izvozna družba, d.d., SID), that has been able to provide in good time at least some of its services to outward investing[10].

The programmes offered by the SEC include a package of insurance services that enable exporters to insure themselves against commercial and non-commercial, i.e. political risks. The SEC insures against commercial risks in OECD countries for its own account (similar insurance is also provided by banks), while insurance against commercial risks in other countries and insurance against political risks is provided for on the account of the state. Besides, the SEC also provides financing possibilities (financial loans) to their clients' suppliers. Prevailingly, its activities are oriented to export promotion[11]. Since the most important outward investors are often also the most important exporters, the guarantees and loans given for export promotion also facilitate investment activities. Better conditions in financing export activities are important especially since the major source of outward FDI financing is the internal funds of investors (as described in Chapter 10) and since a large share of outward FDI stocks is based on net claims in more risky locations.

Although the financial sources devoted to investment are still low, the SEC's package of services is better than those of similar institutions in other transition economies[12]. The SEC's services were given relatively high grades ('good' in a five-grade scale) by the sample companies among the listed institutional services (Table 20.4). Most highly assessed and most widely used is the insurance against political risks. However, some complaints and suggestions for improvements were made in the surveys and interviews (see Table 20.3).

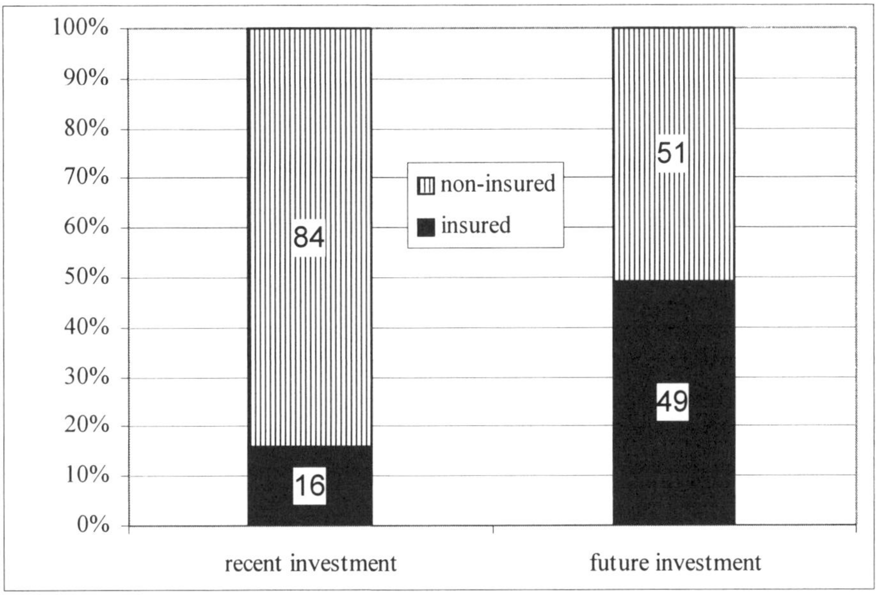

Figure 20.5 The proportion of companies recently insuring their outward investments against political risks and intentions to insure future outward FDI (in per cent)

Source: Survey 2001.

Insurance in general (against commercial or non-commercial risks) has indeed not become a common practice yet. According to the SEC's estimates, only about 3 per cent of total outward investment was insured against political risks in 2000[13]. According to the sample data, the majority of Slovenian companies did not insure their outward investments against non-commercial risks. Despite the relatively risky geographical allocation and concentration, only 16 per cent of sample companies insured their existing investments abroad against political risks. Mostly the investments that are insured against political risk are located in BiH, Croatia, Macedonia and Germany. Reasons for ignoring this type of insurance may include: (i) the fact that companies do not want to disclose information about their future investment and mergers and acquisitions activity; (ii) ignorance of the insurance possibilities; (iii) underestimated risk and/or readiness to take on risk; or (iv) the high costs of insurance (Mrak et al., 2001; p. 150).

Future intentions to insure outward investments against political risks are, according to the 2001 survey, quite different. Almost one-half of the sample companies intend to insure their future outward investments against political risk (Figure 20.5). The future insurance of direct investments abroad is planned to be realized to a great extent (94 per cent) in Slovenia, while only six per cent plan to include multilateral financial institutions (Table 20.2). The SEC has already faced increased demand at the beginning 2001. Insurance in private markets is not expected to be used.

Table 20.2 The selection of insurance (per cent)

	Of those companies that intend to insure against political risks
In Slovenia (SEC)	94
Multilateral financial institutions	6
Private market (insurance companies)	0

Source: Survey 2001.

Moreover, the weaknesses and quality of institutional services was evaluated in both surveys (1999 and 2001) firstly through open-type questions (Table 20.3) and, secondly, through a structured questionnaire (Table 20.4). On the basis of different data sources[14], three basic weaknesses of institutional services can be identified:

- the unavailability and high price of financing;
- low quality and availability of information necessary for outward internationalization; and
- non-existing or non-efficient institutional environment/agreements.

Table 20.3 summarizes the answers to the question 'What should be done by the home-country government and governmental agencies' given by the sample companies. Sixty per cent of the sample companies provided ideas for improving the activities of the home-country government and governmental agencies. Much fewer suggestions were given for 'what should be done by others' (13.5 per cent). The institution most frequently mentioned to implement some improvements was the Slovenian Export Corporation (not being viewed as a governmental institution). Suggestions called for lowering the costs of outward investments, improvement of informational support (lower costs of information), greater availability of financial resources and better bilateral investment protection treaties and double taxation treaties. The suggestions were frequently not very concrete or practical.

Table 20.3 Suggestions for improving home-country government, governmental agencies and others' support of outward FDI

Financing

- To provide financial support
- More accessible funds/loans, more accessible banking, subsidies for financing, for loans, guarantees for investments abroad, insurance
- Financial support and subsidies for initial risks, support the development of brand names
- Tax incentives, more incentive-giving regulation, profit tax relief
- Government should give greater support (financial and legislative) to the Slovenian Export Corporation for assisting outward FDI
- To improve support for companies in the business environment, to stimulate exporters in other modes

Information

- More information to be available
- To provide information as accurate as possible about possibilities of investing abroad
- Information on investment conditions by country
- Information on financial possibilities, sources of funds, insurance possibilities
- Chamber of Commerce and Industry should offer information support

Institutional environment

- To stimulate the signing of bilateral agreements: free-trade agreements, double taxation agreements, bilateral investment treaties
- To implement free-trade agreements and double taxation agreements
- Support in the territory of ex-Yugoslavia (since it involves a big and known market), the government should do more for Slovenian companies there to lower risk, enter agreements

Promotion

- To continue promoting the internationalization of Slovenian companies
- To listen to business interests and aims more, and actively support their internationalization
- To promote the Slovenian economy and its image
- The Ministry of Foreign Affairs should ensure that embassies and diplomatic missions offer better support (information, lobbying …)
- To play the role of promoter of the domestic economy

Insurance

- The Slovenian Export Corporation should insure these investments
- And upgrade the insurance limits for commercial and non-commercial insurance (not just insurance for symbolic sums), especially in the territory of Southern and Eastern Europe
- And provide non-commercial risk insurance in Serbia

Source: Survey 2001.

Table 20.4 Evaluation of selected institutional services important for outward investments

	N	Min.	Max.	Mean	Std. Deviation
Bank financing of outward FDI	26	1	5	2.8	1.0
Insurance & guarantee providing agencies financing of OFDI	26	1	5	2.6	1.2
Co-financing of (governmental) venture funds	23	1	4	1.5	0.7
Insurance of political risk	27	1	5	3.0	1.1
Information availability	28	2	5	2.9	0.9
Investment protection agreement	24	1	5	2.8	0.9
Double taxation agreement	25	1	5	3.0	1.1

Note the scale: 1 - very bad, 5 - very good.

Source: Survey 2001.

Generally speaking, the quality of institutional services was evaluated as medium. The lowest grade was given to financing possibilities. Companies on one hand criticize the existing supply of domestic banks while, on the other hand, they also miss more versatile financial possibilities, such as venture funds. Comments referred to non-flexible banks, low credit limits, high prices and short terms of financial loans. Especially SMEs were loud critics since they have been unable to get access to bank loans for outward investments while simultaneously lacking their own funds. In the area of financing possibilities, their suggestions were mostly oriented to increasing the credit limits, subsidies for interest rates and guarantees and tax incentives.

Several suggestions pointed to a lack of information, which was revealed to be one of the most important barriers to faster internationalization (see also Chapter 10). Appropriate and timely information is namely an important competitive advantage. The firms described information gathering as very costly and time consuming. Operating in a foreign market means always being in an information asymmetry with the local competitors. Responsibility for being poorly informed rests, however, only partly on the government. Their systems of disseminating information can be improved, but firms also have to do their share. Firstly, by enhancing awareness of the importance of information in general and, secondly, by improving the internal use and implementation of information.

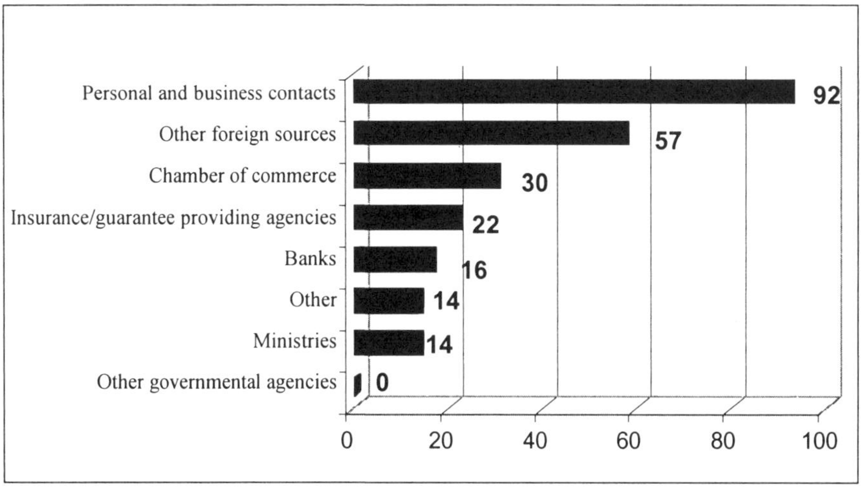

Figure 20.6 Information sources used (per cent of sample companies)

Source: Survey 2001.

The survey showed that *the sources of information used for outward investments* are not very versatile. Most commonly companies use two different data sources: personal and business contacts and foreign business sources. Companies prefer to use foreign information sources than domestic ones, which may in itself reflect the quality ranking of these two sources. Governmental agencies were not used at all.

Summary

The Slovenian internationalization process demonstrates that companies have, in comparison to the government, responded much faster and more promptly to the challenges of globalization. The growth and development of Slovenian multinational companies has, apart from the adoption of liberal legislation, not been accompanied by very effective governmental measures, since the government has lacked an appropriate strategy on outward FDI. The strategic role of FDI is only recently being realized at the macroeconomic policy level.

The liberalization of legislation was not so much a product of autonomous beliefs in the government, but more induced by external factors (harmonization with the EU and OECD standards) on one hand, and the bottom-up pressure of companies on the other. In short, first outward FDI has grown and then the government has responded by changing the institutional environment and even promoting this business activity. The state has thus reacted defensively rather than proactively in creating conditions and promoting companies to internationalize. The process could have been faster given the strategic importance of outward FDI for the transformation of the Slovenian economy and the expertise available.

The state's defensive reaction is also demonstrated by the slow pace, in companies' opinions, at which it is concluding double taxation treaties and bilateral investment treaties. Although the state has intensified activities to conclude such agreements, this has not had much impact on investment. Most capital was directly invested abroad well before treaties were concluded, while agreements with some important locations of Slovenian outward investment – like some of the states of former Yugoslavia – have still not been concluded which can be largely explained by host-state factors that have indeed hindered any more rapid conclusion of these agreements. The fact that companies described bilateral treaties as important may signify they see outward FDI as a long-term orientation that demands state infrastructure. The greater role of the institutional framework is therefore expected in the future.

Much more could also be done in the field of promotional measures. Besides broadening financing possibilities, promotion might be accompanied by tax incentives. Internal financial sources that are the prevailing source for outward investments dictate the speed of outward internationalization and put all of the burden of risk on to investors. The efforts of the Slovenian Export Corporation might be upgraded. Firms stated that 'symbolic' promotional programmes together with unsatisfactory systemic support simply cannot yield significant results. Another part of promotion is to improve the extent and quality of information sources.

Lastly, the response of education institutions is neither timely nor adequate. Not enough emphasis is paid to adequate education about the holistic process of internationalization. The government and firms should be aware that multinational companies develop on the basis of human resources. The holistic strategy on outward internationalization certainly requires an intensive interaction among governmental agencies, the education system and firms.

The first priority for future policies on promoting outward FDI is to eliminate existing barriers to outward FDI, including the elimination of attitudinal and organizational barriers. The second priority seems to be to apply the best practices used in other countries. Such best practices have proved to be: (i) the promotion of holistic internationalization, including inward and outward dimensions; (ii) the promotion of integration processes in the local economy (mergers & acquisitions); and (iii) the development of firm-specific advantages. There can be no outward FDI without certain advantages being developed by investing firms in the product or technology field. It is today difficult to develop without internationalization, and it is difficult to internationalize without development (innovation). Finally, (iv) the creation of a comprehensive macroeconomic database in line with international (OECD, IMF, and European Union EUROSTAT standards) for evaluating outward FDI is a precondition of any future more in-depth research or more ambitious outward FDI strategy.

Notes

1 The Strategy for Economic Development. Approaching Europe, Growth, Competitiveness and Integration (1995) was followed by International Economic Relations Strategies (1996) and, finally, Slovenia in the Next Decade: Sustainability, Competitiveness, EU membership (2001). On such a basis, several sectoral strategies have also been elaborated (see Svetlièiè, 1998).
2 See also Chapters 3 and 4 on the evolution of the legal regime on outward FDI.
3 See the Harper Collins Dictionary of Economics (1991).
4 The BITs signed or negotiated are based on a model BIT adopted by the government and approved by the Parliamentary Committee for Foreign Policy. The same procedure is followed when adopting a priority list of countries with which Slovenia wishes to conclude BITs.
5 Eighteen bilateral investment treaties have been concluded with OECD members.
6 The survey sample includes 55 companies that are among the major Slovenian exporters and investors.
7 For example, the possibility of dispute settlement directly between an investor and the host-country in international arbitrage.
8 Conventions with the following countries were concluded by the former SFRY and remain in force for Slovenia: Cyprus, Denmark, Egypt, Finland, France, Germany, Hungary, Italy, Malaysia, the Netherlands, Norway, the Philippines, Romania, Slovak Republic, Sri Lanka, Sweden and the United Kingdom.
9 171 companies applied for funding from the programme. The Ministry approved 116 internationalization projects, mostly focusing on the markets of former Yugoslavia.
10 Readers can find more information at http://www.sid.si.
11 In 2000, the SEC succeeded to insure almost 11 per cent of Slovenian exports (the share had doubled in a mere two years), which is substantially more than the same share in most developed countries.
12 According to First Washington Associates Ltd which evaluated the competitiveness of approximately 100 leading export credit agencies in December 2001, the Slovenian Export Corporation was ranked in fourth place, with 87 points out of a maximum 100. First place was taken by Israel's IFTRIC, second by the Australian EFIC and third by the Canadian EDC. The Slovenian Export Corporation was followed by other reputable agencies such as the Belgian OND, the German HERMES, the Jamaican EXIMBANK, the French COFACE, the Finnish FINNVERA etc.
13 The total value of investment insured against non-commercial risks by SEC (maximum sum insured) was USD 4,571,000 in 1998, USD 8,524,000 in 1999 and USD 5,209,000 in 2000 (source: internal data of the SEC).
14 Both surveys and interviews with managers.

Chapter 21

Is the Slovenian Case Relevant?

Introduction

Various international comparisons often point to Slovenia as a model of a very successful small transition economy with good prospects to join the EU soon. Such analyses usually take into account standard economic indicators such as economic growth, inflation, industrial production, and employment. As regards international integration, the studies focus on building and adapting the institutional environment, the legal framework and current account balance with a special emphasis on foreign trade trends and structure. Particular attention is paid to exports which is by far the most closely analyzed category of international economic relations. In view of all of these factors Slovenia is doing quite well. The only serious criticism Slovenia has received is directed to it lagging behind other transition economies in FDI inflows, its somewhat hesitant opening up to foreign ownership and portfolio investments of foreigners. Inward FDI with its spillover and restructuring effects has been obviously monitored with greater attention. This is understandable given the lower level of development when inward FDI is expected to be the prime engine of growth and in view of the spectacular growth of FDI seen around the world in recent decades. It has grown much faster than international trade and world manufacturing. Since 1950, it has increased by an amazing 25 times, compared to trade's 16-fold and world manufacturing's six-fold growth.

Competitiveness is today not enhanced only by promoting exports but increasingly depends on integration into the complex international production system. In spite of the temporary slowdown of FDI in 2001, from a record level of US$ 1,300 billion in 2000, we believe it will also remain the most dynamic form of international economic relations in the future. One explanation is that ever more countries, including transition ones, are joining the club of investors abroad. Middle-income countries are no longer just hosts to FDI; their firms are increasingly investing abroad. New multinationals are emerging not only in newly industrialized countries but also in transition economies.

In middle-income countries like Slovenia, outward FDI and the emergence of own multinationals should have deserved more attention since this is one of the very important tools for boosting competitiveness in contemporary international economic relations as demonstrated by our analysis of outward investment made by Slovenian firms. Globalization as a pull factor and transition as a push factor have sped up the process of internationalizing firms' activities from transition economies. Many of these are becoming real multinationals while others more regional ones in a much shorter period than in the past. The process has really accelerated in the last few years. The growth of outward FDI is faster. More and more sectors and firms are involved. The cases demonstrate that firms have been trying to escape their crises not by asking for protection as they did in the past, but by turning more to international markets by enhancing their own firm-specific advantages and transforming them into profits through international exploitation, especially if they come from small limited national markets.

Studies in the previous chapters showed the relevance of growing outward investments in the case of Slovenia. This chapter summarizes the major lessons of Slovenian internationalization through outward FDI and points out potential future challenges. To a certain extent, these lessons might be similar to lessons from small-developed European countries such as Portugal, Finland, Austria and Sweden that followed a gradual internationalization pattern by gradual accumulating knowledge and experience[1], which have been useful for Slovenia, although the time for such learning is now much shorter. Everything has to be done much faster when globalization and competition is becoming tougher every day. The Slovenian case could be relevant to all those transition economies that mostly are small in international terms and which lag behind in the internationalization process due to communism. However, the ambitious plans and quick response to opportunities on one hand, and the barriers and problems Slovenian companies faced in the transition years as well as experiences gained in less developed neighbouring countries on the other hand, might even provide universal lessons of more general application. By summing up the main characteristics of the process and comparing them to other transition and EU candidate-countries, we explain what can be learned from Slovenia's internationalization story in macro and micro points of view; what experiences may be applied to other transition economies, what are the special features of Slovenia and what is expected to be common for all transition economies.

Comparison with other transition economies

Most FDI flows take place among developed economies. Transition economies – like in other areas – lag behind although they are catching up with the developed states in their internationalization. Inward FDI is clearly more important than outward FDI. Outward FDI and emerging multinational companies from transition economies are new phenomena, which really took off only after substantial stabilization and restructuring took place in transition economies, when firms started thinking not only of their survival but also how to strengthen their position in the global economy.

The outward FDI stock of transition economies in general is slightly over 10 per cent of inward FDI stock. Although their world share is low – in 2000 their outward FDI stock (US$ 19,246 million) represented just one-third of one per cent of global world outward FDI stock (Table 21.1, UNCTAD, 2001). The share of their outflows in world outward FDI is marginal. In 2001, CEEC's share in world FDI outflows was three-fifths of one per cent, up slightly from two-fifths of one per cent in 2000. Still, outward FDI has recently increased faster than inward FDI. A number of transition countries (Russia, Estonia, Croatia, Slovenia and Slovakia) have experienced strong growth in outward FDI flows, although they started from a very low base.

Generally, transition economies can be divided into two groups, those with faster economic progress – becoming the most credible EU candidates – that started with internationalization through outward FDI already in the early nineties, and those that joined at the end of the nineties. It seems that flows of inward and outward FDI are intertwined, that they coincide not only with the development level and speed of economic transformation of these countries, but are correlated among themselves. Figure 21.1 illustrates the ranking of selected small, developed EU countries and selected first-round EU candidates in terms of all FDI flows.

In spite of its relatively low absolute figures of outward FDI, Slovenia is leading in relative indicators compared to other transition economies (Table 21.1, Figure 21.1). With US$ 401 of outward FDI stock per capita in 2000, Slovenia is ranked well ahead of Hungary, Estonia, Czech Republic, Slovakia or Poland, with US$ 199, 173, 163, 59 and 39 outward FDI stock per capita, respectively[2]. With a 4.4 per cent share of outward FDI stock in GDP, Slovenia is, together with Estonia (4.4 per cent) and Hungary (4.3 per cent), also in the leading group of transition countries, followed by Slovakia (1.7), Czech Republic (1.5) and Poland (0.9).

Table 21.1 FDI outflows from selected transition economies in 1994-2000 and outward FDI stock in 2000 in US$

	1989-1994	1995	1996	1997	1998	1999	2000	Outward FDI stock 2000
Transition economies - total								*19,246*
EU candidates - total								*9,262*
Bulgaria	–	-8	-29	-2	–	17	-2	88
Czech Republic	77	37	153	25	127	90	118	784
Estonia	3	2	40	137	6	83	157	429
Hungary	22	43	-3	431	481	249	532	2,01
Latvia	-22	-65	3	6	54	17	8	241
Lithuania	–	1	–	27	4	9	13	29
Poland	14	42	53	45	316	31	126	1,491
Romania	8	3	2		-9	16	-11	122
Slovakia	13	8	52	95	146	-372	23	320
Slovenia	-1	6	8	26	11	38	48	655
BiH	1	8	29	-2	–	–	–	40
Croatia	13	6	30	186	97	35	28	1,052
Macedonia	–	–	–	1	1	1	1	5

Source: UNCTAD, 2001.

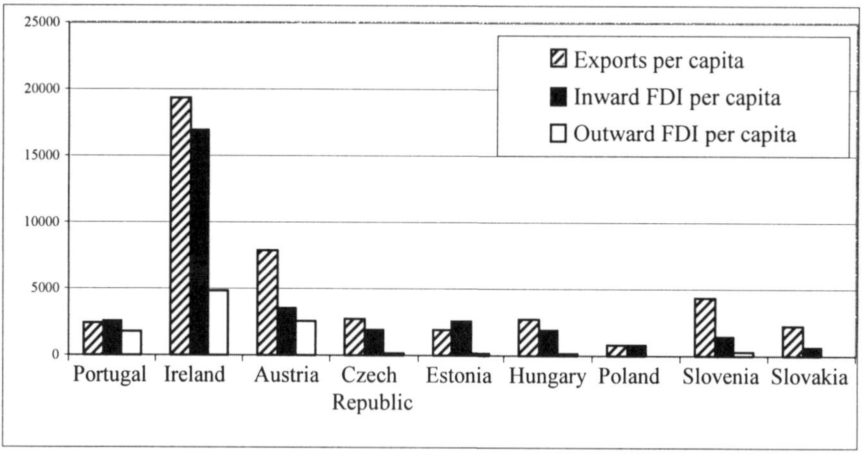

Figure 21.1 Openness and FDI in selected EU countries and EU candidates in 2000 (in US$)

Source: The IMF and national balance of payments statistics.

Similarities of transition economies

One of the greatest mistakes made by international 'parachutist' foreign advisors was to put all transition economies in one basket, as if there were no differences between them. But transition economies are not a homogenous group of countries; there are many differences. Neglecting this was an expensive mistake. We should not make the same mistake by overemphasizing similarities between them in this one aspect, in the outward FDI type of internationalization. Let us therefore simultaneously identify the differences and similarities.

The first factor distinguishing Slovenia is that it is the most developed of the transition economies (its per capita GDP is already over 70 per cent of the EU average) and has the highest productivity level. In spite of the same ideological historical legacy (socialist system) and development gap vis-à-vis developed countries, each transition economy faces a particular set of country-specific problems. Since Slovenia is a step forward in terms of general development and even in terms of internationalization (given its very early start), its experiences in outward internationalization might be applicable to many other transition economies in terms of learning from its experiences, including its mistakes.

In spite of important differences among them by the volume of outward FDI, sectoral allocation etc. transition economies face some similarities. They all are net FDI importers. Outward FDI is still a modestly used mode for entering the global economy. FDI outflows have also been fluctuating. Their importance began to increase in almost all transition economies solely after 1997, while more significant growth is visible only between 1999 and 2000, after the group of latecomers started to invest abroad, after foreign-owned firms produced results and also started to invest abroad. Slovenia and in the past many other small European states have demonstrated[3] that the internationalization of transition economies follows the evolutionary stage pattern of development reflected in different dimensions of internationalization (Trtnik, 2000, Jaklič A. and Svetličič M., 2001). These particularly refer to entry mode, type of activity and geographical location. Similarly, CEECs in early stages also invest predominantly in the neighbouring and culturally close states, countries which they know best, where they have accumulated export experiences, or where they have stronger personal ties due to a common history or a strong national minority.

While there are differences in entering foreign markets through outward FDI, greenfield investment is the prevailing form. In the last year, acquisitions of existing companies or joint ventures with host-country companies have been gaining importance almost everywhere, to a large extent depending on the progress of privatization there and consequent availability of private local partners. Investors, similar to the Slovenian ones, prefer majority ownership[4]. Their investment is most frequently market-seeking[5].

There are also no significant differences between candidates with respect to the effects of outward FDI. As a result of market-seeking investments, firms keep their foreign markets and promote exports. Investors are generally satisfied with their outward FDI and make progress in their international operations. Barriers to outward internationalization are also similar in all five transition economies that were analyzed. Host-country barriers (high risks, host-country environment, concentration of direct investment) seem more important than home-country barriers, in spite of an underdeveloped institutional framework and the fact that firms want more support from the government. In spite of some country-specific differences, the lack of knowledge, personnel and lack of financing are in most of them ranked the highest among the internal barriers to internationalization. Although firms complain a lot about the limitations imposed on them by the external environment in general and in host countries, particularly when investing in other transition economies (instability, lack of legal transparency and the like), our surveys nevertheless reveal that internal barriers are on the whole more important and should deserve more attention in future at the company level, while governments should try to reduce external barriers.

Why is Slovenia different, why is it special?

The common characteristics of the outward internationalization of the five candidate-countries should not obscure the differences that are important in terms of policy recommendations in particular but also from the theoretical point of view. The internationalization of Slovenian firms certainly has some very specific characteristics, which should be indicated before trying to generalize the relevance of its experience for other transition economies. Slovenia's case may be an instructive illustration of some of the issues to be addressed when starting to deal with outward FDI; but it is not a typical representative country of all transition economies, let alone a typical representative of CEECs.

Firstly, because Slovenian firms started their outward internationalization even before hosting inward FDI (system-escape FDI) and, secondly, because Slovenian firms enjoyed some autonomy even in socialist times. Such early experiences in exporting capital make the Slovenian case different since outward investment by other former socialist countries was much more modest and also differed in its system-escape character (see Chapter 3). However, the biggest post-transition surge of outward FDI started at almost the same time as in other transition economies. This can be regarded in a way as a second wave, a revival of the previously started outward investment activity of mostly large (previously socialist) companies. Historical experience was a good base for further expansion and also showed the way for newly established firms and firms that suffered the loss of the Yugoslav market at the start of transition. Slovenian outward FDI also demonstrates how the limitation of a small domestic market can be overcome by internationalization. Previous experiences were instrumental for two reasons: firstly by creating the necessary internationalization knowledge base and, secondly, by enhancing firms' self-confidence about their abilities to undertake this more complicated international economic activity (see the Krka case). Both factors largely explain Slovenia's considerable starting point advantage in internationalization over other transition economies.

Thirdly, Slovenia was much more 'Westernized' ideologically and economically than other former socialist countries. Co-operation with the West started already after the quarrel with Stalin in 1948. A significant share of exports was directed to the EEC when other socialist countries traded exclusively among themselves. Some market experience was accumulated due to so-called market socialism which explains why the outward internationalization of quasi-autonomous firms started so much earlier.

These reasons also influenced the fourth characteristic of Slovenia, i.e. the very prominent role of manufacturing firms while in other countries banks and trading companies used to play the dominant role. Most experiences have been accumulated by Slovenian manufacturing companies which in fact continued internationalization at a faster pace at the beginning of transition (albeit often having first been transformed and restructured). The difference in the internationalization of the manufacturing and services sectors, especially the financial (banking) sector, is larger in Slovenia than some other EU membership-candidates, e.g. Estonia (Sorg, 2001) or the Czech Republic (Bohata, 2000). An explanation of this can be found in the much slower privatization of these sectors in Slovenia. The financial sector represents important infrastructure and certainly influences the growth of outward FDI. A substantial difference in the internationalization of particular sectors of the economy may significantly influence the future development of outward FDI.

Fifthly, Slovenia is no 'champion' in the field of inward FDI. Not surprisingly, inward FDI has not been very instrumental in promoting outward FDI, as was the case in many other transition economies (for instance, Hungary). Slovenia has received less inward FDI than many other transition economies, e.g. Hungary, Estonia or the Czech Republic. Consequently, there is a big difference in the share of the so-called indirect investment abroad[6]. Unlike other transition states where outward internationalization is more or less driven by foreign-owned companies, in Slovenia it is mostly driven by indigenous, locally-owned companies. One explanation is the kind of autonomous status firms received back in socialist times (see note 2 in Chapter 3). This could make such internationalization more stable, less volatile and sustainable because it is less dependant on the internal division of labour within large multinationals. On the other hand, it can be restricted to the core competencies of Slovenian firms with all related limitations regarding possibilities to undertake higher, more capital and brand-name and value-added intensive activities.

What can be learnt from the Slovenian case?

Whereas many of the economic miracles of the 20th century (Germany, France, Japan) were primarily export-led, the falling trade barriers and different circumstances seen since the 1990s establish international production as 'superior' or at least in need of a complementary strategy for enhancing home-country competitiveness. Countries/firms can no longer rely only on export-led growth. In order to keep or even enhance global market shares they increasingly have to undertake international production abroad if they want to narrow the development gap. This is especially true of transition economies that have to do everything much faster in order to compensate for time lost during the socialist era when they were limited to mutual co-operation. The international environment has since changed so much that imitating the export-led growth model alone cannot keep and enhance competitiveness in the global economy. Today, outward investment seems a much more appropriate internationalization mode for catching-up strategies.

Confronted by the increased need for internationalization in a globalized world economy, the lack of relevant experience[7] makes such internationalization under the pressure of time a significant challenge. To cope with international competition and to benefit from globalization, transition economies have to internationalize themselves in a much shorter period. This shortness of time prevents firms from CEECs benefiting gradually from the cumulative learning process of sequential internationalization like their predecessors in developed countries once did. They have to do it in a much shorter time to keep pace. Since a lack of outward internationalization could undermine a successful transition to a market economy, this issue has especially high relevance for transition economies.

The experience and lessons from Slovenia can be divided into macro and micro aspects. Although companies are normally the first to perceive the need to invest abroad, an important message from Slovenia is that the macro point of view of outward internationalization deserves equal importance. Government and economic policy should not be defensive, but should complement spontaneous bottom-up firm activity with a more aggressive outward-looking economic strategy. Of course, when addressing the major challenges of internationalization through outward FDI, the first to address is the main barriers and problems that managers face in the early stages of such operations abroad at the micro and macro levels, alongside creating a stimulating environment for outward internationalization, supporting the spontaneous efforts of firms, particularly SMEs which lack the internal human capital to do it alone.

Macroeconomic lessons:

- High unit labour costs and high per capita incomes stimulate outward internationalization, but various countries at the same stage of their development have displayed distinctly different outward FDI propensities. The lesson is that outward FDI propensity (like outward orientation in general) does not come automatically with development, but has to be stimulated if development through international integration is the strategic objective. Liberalization of capital and firms' autonomy is a precondition for outward FDI expansion.
- The role of government is especially important in the early phases of outward internationalization, when firms start to invest abroad. Governments have to provide the initial stimulus by first reducing barriers, including attitudinal prejudices claiming that exporting capital is an unpatriotic activity. Mangers' risk-aversion at this stage is the highest, while the countries in which most outward FDI has so far been directed by investors from transition economies are also more risky (countries at a similar level of development and also in transition). Therefore, governments should try to reduce such risks by giving high priority to building the institutional framework (bilateral investment treaties, double taxation treaties, free-trade agreements etc.), and then by providing promotional measures (insurance and guarantee instruments) and making institutional services available to all, particularly to SMEs (see also Chapter 20).
- The perception that outward FDI is not a mere outflow of capital that deprives the domestic economy and lowers domestic employment must be substituted by the perception that outward FDI is an instrument of restructuring firms or economies. In such a way, outward FDI can contribute to strengthening the domestic economy, keeping and gaining foreign markets, promoting exports and competitiveness, but also to preserving and creating employment, development, growth and assets (see Chapter

11). As seen from the Slovenian experience in the mid-nineties (see Chapter 4), negative public opinion might slow down or even stymie outward FDI activity.

- Awareness-building about the importance of investing firms can create a positive attitude to outward FDI in the national economy. Countries must be aware of the role that their own multinational firms play or could play in the domestic economy and regional integrations. Although Slovenian MNCs may not be prominent at the global level, they do have weight in the regional and sometimes also international scenes. Even more important is the fact that they occupy the dominant position in the Slovenian economy (Chapters 7 and 11). Without investing abroad they would hardly remain domestic market leaders. Without internationalizing they simply could not grow. Multinational firms provide high employment and the development of wider regions (see especially the case studies, Chapters 12-19).
- In view of the analysis of the roles and consequences of outward FDI activities, countries also have to improve their statistical monitoring and coverage of outward FDI as well as foreign affiliate activity. A comprehensive and standardized macroeconomic database in line with international standards should be developed. Development strategies of outward internationalization should include research based on quality data. Sound and effective policies can only be designed if appropriate statistical data and analyses are available.
- A holistic process of internationalization should be implemented, promoting inward and outward FDI as well as other entry modes. Since outward FDI is merely the flip side of inward FDI, a comprehensive strategy has to be developed to stimulate both ways of internationalizing firms' activities. The creation of forward and backward linkages enhances the 'pull' and 'push' internationalization factors for domestic firms.
- Training is the main area in which both government and firms can do a lot. Already experienced managers indicated that they need additional specialized training regarding internationalization (Chapter 10). Existing education programmes seem insufficient. They concentrate more on the functional training of individual skills but not on what seems to be needed for a holistic approach to internationalization. There is also a lack of courses dealing particularly with FDI (including outward FDI) or more developed forms of international co-operation in general. Universities or graduate management schools have not yet really developed regular courses on international business comparable to such courses in European or American universities.
- Knowledge plays a crucial role in catching up. Therefore, the role of outward FDI is crucial to the extent that it augments knowledge and contributes

to the accumulation of human capital. It is particularly useful when a country has reached the necessary threshold of accumulated knowledge whereby it is able to absorb the knowledge available abroad. A 'policy stimulating a country's absorption capacity and the diffusion of knowledge will also generate the necessary conditions for that economy to eventually start creating new knowledge' (Aghion et al., 2000; p. 33). In this regard, outward FDI is developmentally instrumental to the extent it facilitates and enhances the absorbing capacity of the country (firm) and enhances the dissemination of knowledge thereby acquired. The fact that the principle task of the firm is 'knowledge integration' (Kogut and Zander, 1992; Grant 1991) does indicate that OFDI can improve the 'synergy capabilities' of firms. Knowledge is a precondition for firm-specific advantages.

Micro economic lessons:

- Internationalization is, in spite of different basically systemically anchored episodes, sequential, a 'path-dependant process' of expansion of the firm (Kogut and Zander, 1993; Buckley P.J. and Casson M.C., 1998; p. 38), but today the stages and steps are getting shorter and shorter, with some stages often being leapfrogged. Born globals are still rare in transition economies but leapfrogging multinationals are not so exceptional any more. Most investors developed from exporters, while other entry modes are rarely used (Chapter 9). As the case studies demonstrate, an important stimulus could also come through inward investment to the extent it creates firm-specific knowledge, which can then be exploited abroad.
- It is not only big and old firms that invest abroad, internationalization through outward FDI is also increasingly being used by SMEs. They even dominate among Slovenian investors abroad (Chapter 9), albeit only in terms of the number of investors and not by volume. Although we did not find many born globals, they are expected to be on the rise in the future. Some managers claim that the smaller the niche the more one has to be globally oriented to take advantages of the economies of scale and scope available only globally. In spite of their slower international expansion compared to big companies, SMEs are important investors and create many forward and backward linkages among domestic and foreign firms. While they are small in absolute terms, they can be large in terms of market shares and by the diversification of their co-operation with many major multinationals in their specific niche. They can also achieve higher flexibility, which is very important in these volatile times when it is not the strongest who survive but those who are most responsive to changes, to paraphrase Darwin's famous conclusion dating back to his *Origins of*

Species (1859). Smaller size might be an important advantage in comparison to other MNCs since such firms could be very flexible and adaptable. If they are able to implement efficient business models (in management, organization and marketing) that are used by MNCs they can make significant progress.

- The main source of competitive advantages involves people and their knowledge (marketing, organizational and managerial know-how; see Chapter 8). A lack of skilled human capital is therefore not surprisingly the biggest internal barrier to outward internationalization. The study's most important message to companies should be to improve human resource management, which is one of the least developed areas in Slovenian firms (see also Zupan, 1999). Special attention should be given to international human resources management, which is also undeveloped in Slovenian firms (see Chapter 10). As some case studies demonstrate, some firms started their own training for internationalization in order to overcome such a knowledge gap. More efficient human resource management should also complement such training.
- The effects of Slovenian outward FDI show that the relocation of activities abroad to lower wage countries is taking place slowly and simultaneously with the restructuring of investing firms. Investing abroad at the first stage meant growth of the company, gaining and keeping foreign markets and export promotion. The intensified international division of labour has usually stimulated increasing value-added activities in the home country, while lower value-added activities are transferred abroad. Too long and too high protection has unfortunately slowed down this restructuring process of labour-intensive activities. It shows that postponing the necessary reforms thereof are costly, that the price is higher if restructuring takes place too late.
- A very important effect of investing abroad is asset creation. Our surveys demonstrate the growth of R&D in investing firms, and also the increased share of skilled employees. Companies have also gained in their international image, knowledge and developed flexibility, enhanced responsiveness to customer needs and the capability to engage in constant improvements to their products.
- Speed is an important variable of success. Most ownership-specific advantages expire if not put into use. First-mover advantages seem to be relatively more important in the case of investors from less developed transition economies compared to large multinationals. Due to fast imitation and constantly shorter product life cycles, firms may profit more by the strategy of fast and simultaneous entry into a number of foreign countries (economies of scale) than through the constant development and adaptation

of products. Direct presence in more and bigger markets are often a precondition for sufficient sourcing for product development and differentiation. An ambitious and frequently risky strategy has often proved more advantageous than the sequence of small cumulative steps. A combination of different foreign entry modes has proved to be the most profitable strategy among Slovenian firms.

- The majority of Slovenian investing firms (60 per cent, see Chapter 11) increased the number of product varieties as a result of outward FDI. The case studies also demonstrate significant diversification and product differentiation. As known from the multinational experience (for example Nokia), this can hardly be a sustainable strategy in the long run but might be an instrumental intermediate stage of seeking the optimum global (international/regional) niche. MNCs from transition economies should be aware that contemporary global leaders underwent a similar process, which normally resulted in specialization or disintegration of the system. While diversification might be dangerous if driven too far, it is essential in the early stages of adaptation and might also bring parallel development of global product/services.
- Transition economies should especially carefully and timely take advantage of the knowledge and experience gained in previous mutual trade within the CMEA. Historical experience of the former co-operation is useful despite the rapid changes in the political and economic environments. Knowing the culture, business habits – in short knowing how to do business in such an environment – are all important variables of success in international business. Slovenia's experience in the successors to the SFRY (Chapter 6) clearly demonstrates this.
- Failures are almost unavoidable ingredients of internationalization and yet can also be instrumental as a learning process. The study demonstrated that it is better to be almost right on time than 100 per cent right and too late. Some Slovenian firms started to internationalize very early on. Although one can generally say that the problems that some ventures have been facing indicate that internationalization was undertaken too early, others say that without such ventures firms would not be able to start internationalization when the time was truly ripe. They helped in accumulating some expertise, training their personnel, creating self-confidence in their own abilities even to undertake much more sophisticated business modes later on.

Summary

The Slovenian case clearly indicates that the internationalization of activities of firms from transition economies is gaining in momentum and that they can do it in spite of all the limitations and sceptical claims that only inward FDI is relevant to them. Ricardo has proved to be right once again: you do not need absolute advantages but relative ones to compete and to benefit from international trade. Though still in an early stage, Slovenia is one of the most developed in terms of internationalization through outward FDI. Therefore, its experiences and numerous micro- and macro-economic lessons might be highly relevant and instructive for transition-country latecomers. Internationalization strategies of the selected case studies might, on the other hand, offer even more universal lessons. Internationalization patterns of transition and developing economies are namely similar in spite of the substantial differences seen in development and the degree of internationalization. Globalization as a key novelty in the external environment in which outward FDI is taking place today has modified the ways and means of outward internationalization, but not to such an extent that sequential internationalization is put in question. It has only speeded it up. Firms have to start it earlier than in the past, they have to jump over certain former early stages. Globalization has deprived firms of the time to benefit from a gradual learning process. Mistakes can therefore be expected to be more common in the future. The only way to minimize them is to improve knowledge and information about internationalization.

Both firms and governments still have a lot to learn to improve global competitiveness and progress in internationalization. The results of this analysis can be summed up in two important messages. Firstly, the effect and development implications of outward FDI are very positive at the firm and national economy levels, improving the allocation of resources, speeding up restructuring, enhancing competitiveness and, in a nutshell, for speeding up transformation. The most appropriate way to induce positive impacts is to enhance the capabilities of firms to invest abroad and thereby increase the number of multinational firms. In spite of the fact that outward FDI stock increased by 3.4 times, the analysis namely showed slow growth in the number of investing firms. Secondly, many barriers still prevent any more courageous steps in an outward internationalization direction. Those barriers found within firms outweigh the external ones, which is encouraging since firms themselves can reduce them by improving their own knowledge and organization. Above all, the many successful cases demonstrate that firms from transition economies have done it, that they can do it in spite of the many difficulties and crises. Internationalization has been one way out of crises for many firms.

Nevertheless, much help is needed from governments, particularly by SMEs. Government and firms have to co-operate in outward internationalization and intensify their efforts to reduce barriers in common efforts to promote the development and welfare of employees or the population at large.

Notes

1 For the listed countries, see Simoes, 2000, 2001; Luostarinen, 1994; Bellak, 2001; Johanson, Wiedersheim-Paul, 1975.
2 Although Slovenia holds the highest value of outward FDI per capita, this value is much lower than in e.g. the least developed EU member-state Portugal, with US$ 1,735 of outward FDI per capita.
3 E.g. Finland (Luostarinen, 1979, 1994), Portugal (Simoes, 2000) or Sweden.
4 For more on the subject, see Svetličič and Jaklič A. (2002).
5 This motive was the most important in all five EU candidate-countries included in the second ACE study.
6 Indirect investment is that made by foreign-owned companies.
7 Experiences of operating abroad accumulated in socialist times are hardly applicable due to the different rationale of the then investing state monopolies, although they did have to adapt to local conditions. Secondly, managers or those involved in such operations of old state monopolies may no longer be managing the related privatized companies.

Chapter 22

Conclusions

Transition economies in general are a group of latecomers among multinational investors. Prior to the nineties it was mostly the MNCs from large developed economies that were studied, while the former socialist economies were often mentioned amongst those left out of global integration strategies. Outward FDI from transition economies was encouraged parallel to the transition 'push' factors and intensification of the globalization 'pull' factors encountered in the past decade. Although progressing slowly and still relatively modest in volume, FDI in general and outward FDI in particular have become an integral part of an open and effective international economic system and a powerful force of global economic integration. Traditional exports do not allow efficient competition in world markets, but need to be upgraded by advanced internationalization modes in this era of globalization.

Since the global economy is characterized by oligopolistic markets with many market failures, knowledge that is becoming ever more intangible and customers who are demanding more solutions to their problems and not merely products, firms today have to select the form of international involvement that maximizes operating opportunities and profits while simultaneously reducing the risks of the free appropriation of their knowledge, assets and advantages and increasing the ability to upgrade them.

While firms from transition economies are increasingly aware of the need to engage in outward FDI, national governments are generally less responsive; they have only recently been laying greater stress on outward internationalization in their development strategies. In the future certainly both firms and governments from transition economies are expected to devote more attention to this issue. MNEs have proved to be the main facilitators of trade flows, transfers of knowledge and skills across boarders and engines of growth.

This book analyses the emergence of MNCs in Slovenia, a small Central European transition economy. It examines the origins of Slovenian firms' outward FDI and developments in the first transition decade, what are the roles and consequences of outward FDI, how does it effect the transition and how, in turn, have the transitions affected the nature of internationalization. We briefly summarize the main trends in outward FDI's evolution and then address some core issues explaining why firms have to internationalize and the pattern of their internationalization, i.e. when, how and where they undertake their international operations.

Trends and the significance of outward FDI

In spite of the early start made back in socialist times, Slovenian firms can be regarded as beginners among multinational investors. With outward FDI beginning before inward FDI, Slovenia experienced deviations from the starting phase of the investment development path, but this initial declination was so strongly system-based that did not alter the usual pattern. A cumulative learning process then started, while the transition period has actually meant the 'restart' of outward FDI. Outward FDI is therefore still a relatively new phenomenon in transition economies and conclusions are not easy to draw. Limited time series, the limited scope of data, changing methodology that is still not in full harmony with international standards and the reluctance of firms to report make such an evaluation difficult.

Pre-transition experience created the base for a quick response in the *early transition period* which caused a rapid increase in outward FDI on one hand, and restructuring and divestment on the other. Intensification of the market economy has accelerated the process of outward internationalization, although the *consolidation phase in the mid-nineties* brought slow progress in outward FDI that was mostly carried out by existing multinational companies. Deepening of the internationalization of existing internationalized firms was stronger than the widening of the process by new investors. A *new wave of internationalization* at the end of decade speeded up the outward investments of existing multinationals and newcomers in terms of broadening and strengthening their foreign affiliate networks and their rapid expansion to the former Yugoslav markets.

The volume of outward FDI by Slovenian firms is still modest by international standards, although annual flows have lately been substantially growing. In spite of the 3.4-times increase in outward FDI stocks in the 1993-2000 period, Slovenian firms have cumulatively invested € 854 million abroad, much less than Portugal, a country whose level of gross domestic product per capita is similar to Slovenia. By domestic standards, outward FDI is more important as it makes up 4.4 per cent of gross domestic product. A greater role was also found when analyzing the importance of investing firms in the entire Slovenian corporate sector, where they contribute a significant share in spite of their small number. With just a one per cent share of the corporate sector in numerical terms, they provide almost 40 per cent of exports, realize 25 per cent of sales and up to 38 per cent of value added, and give jobs to 27 per cent of employees.

Companies investing abroad perform much better than non-investing companies, and compared to the average Slovenian company. Apart from ownership-specific advantages, the differences between investing and non-investing firms were identified in six key areas that can improve performance: company size, capital intensity, value added, export intensity, skilled labour intensity and financial structure. Companies investing abroad are larger, more capital-intensive, have a better asset structure and are more export-oriented. Investing firms performed better than non-investing firms and also improved in the second half of the nineties. The growth of investing companies was much faster than that of non-investing firms. Investing abroad considerably speeded up companies' restructuring, especially as regards value added and export propensity.

The net effects of outward FDI on investing firms were generally positive. Trade and competitiveness effects outweighed any other effects. The employment effect was less important with most firms seeing no changes there as a result of outward FDI. Mainly market-seeking-driven investments resulted in increased market shares, growth in exports and in domestic production levels. Outward FDI was found to be complementary to exports. Consequently, outward FDI enhances efficiency and restructuring by introducing new products, product differentiation, increased quality and a better response to customers' needs. Investing abroad also brought about asset-creation effects by improving the image of investing firms and enhancing their marketing, management and organizational skills.

Direct investment in most cases seems sustainable since the resulting profit is used creatively to strengthen one's own capabilities, and not only to defend market positions that have been achieved. Increasing R&D expenditures, better educated staff, a strong export orientation, the beneficial effects of outward FDI on strengthening investors' competitiveness, as well as the growing share of intra-firm trade are all signs that outward FDI is forming part of a long-term internationalization strategy. For many Slovenian companies, becoming a multinational company was one way of overcoming development crises and therefore facilitates not only survival in foreign markets but also their survival in general.

While at the macroeconomic level outward FDI effects are still difficult to evaluate, firm-level effects spill over on to the domestic economy and have development implications. International growth offers much better development opportunities than growth solely within the domestic setting. 'Small country effects' often include poor resource availability and a lack of domestic demand that prevents domestic firms exploiting standardized and mass production, low costs and economies of scale, but also prevents them developing the skills and advantages needed to exploit such resources or the advantages of mass production abroad. Slovenian firms are used to looking for market niches, which can best be exploited through foreign production.

Though still in its early phase Slovenia is one of the top transition economies in outward FDI internationalization terms. Its experience and lessons can therefore be particularly relevant for transition-country latecomers, in a similar way to the instructive lessons of Finland or Portugal for Slovenia. In spite of some particularities in Slovenia's internationalization path, more similarities than differences were found in the relevant internationalization theories.

The Slovenian internationalization pattern - in theory

The complexity of international business does not show any single theory or model providing a perfect lesson even in the same period of time, but calls for broad generalizations. Relevant theories only have a partial explanatory power for the 'socialist' stage of internationalization, but can better explain its post-transition stages. There are so many system-based specific characteristics that make the application of theories based on market economies' traditions very difficult to apply to the initial stage of development of such investments. State ownership, limited integration into the international economy, and the lack of specialization make the experiences of these countries and their firms very specific. Notwithstanding the experience of small, developed countries, the evolutionary models of internationalization contain important messages for transition economies and help to explain *why, when, where* and *how* to internationalize.

Neither the different investment starting position nor the substantially changed international economic environment has altered the investment development patterns seen at the macro-economic level, albeit the evolution seems faster. Trends in Slovenian outward FDI in the nineties demonstrate the relevance of stage development or evolutionary models as regards the sequencing of entry modes, geographical orientation, type of activity and geographical concentration. Further, the position of Slovenia's outward internationalization compared to other transition economies suggests that outward FDI is a function of one's development level as predicted by the investment development path paradigm. Investors abroad are mostly indigenous Slovenian firms (the level of indirect investors is relatively low relative to some other transition economies), stimulated by increasing competition and development. They regard such moves as an efficient way of keeping their market shares and bolstering their competitiveness.

The infant internationalization phase may be considered as a reversed investment development path start. Before transition, such operations abroad by state- or socially-owned firms followed a different rationale. They were either of a system-escape type or part of the overall politics of the respective governments. Business considerations were not necessarily the only preoccupation. Their main motive was to facilitate trade and foreign currency inflows with the exception of activities in developing countries, which were production oriented. Later on, they began to fit nicely into a new version of the investment development paradigm whereby they start internationalizing earlier and individual stages are shortened. One explanation for this is globalization and integration with the European Union. Both have accelerated internationalization. Transition to a market economy, which first meant stabilization and liberalization, under the influence of globalization, European Union integration and increasing competitive pressures from global markets, has forced the now privatized companies to increase or enhance the internationalization of their activities. Today, it has been discovered that firms are starting to invest abroad much earlier than before and not only out of their strengths but also out of their weaknesses; they want to gain access to other firm advantages abroad. Outward internationalization seems more pulled than pushed.

In line with the sequential pattern, the most responsive have been firms with significant export experience. Those Slovenian firms that were once major exporters (or direct investors) in the socialist era were some of the first to start internationalizing their activities after transition started. Even in the nineties, the majority of outward investors developed from exporters. Since manufacturing has always largely depended on exports, while services suppliers have concentrated on the domestic market with its high level of protection, the manufacturing sector is far more active in outward investment activity than the services sector.

Firms firstly enter foreign markets through exports and then continue with outward FDI, initially mostly by establishing trading units abroad and later production ones. They frequently serve to promote trade and very rarely to relocate production. Other business functions are infrequently transferred to affiliates abroad, although decentralization is increasing and continuing. Also sequential is the internationalization of ownership. Wholly- and majority-owned foreign affiliates established as greenfield ventures dominate. However, the end of the decade witnessed progress in the internationalization process since it was accompanied by an improvement in most indicators; the internationalization of ownership increased, mergers and acquisitions started to be more frequent entry methods and foreign affiliates on average grew in their number, size and functional orientation.

These recent changes however have not done away with gradualism in entry modes and functional orientation, but have speeded up the internationalization process. Most investing firms abroad are what we call 'leapfrogging globals', as they became global in a very short time by jumping over some of the stages predicted by evolutionary models and investing abroad not only to exploit existing advantages, but also to create new ones. While internationalization with less gradual learning is more risky, the principle 'better too early than too late' has been applied by managers.

'Born globals' on the other hand are still very rare, even though at first glance this seems to describe some of the recently established firms. Though the main MNCs are relatively old and prevailingly large firms by national standards, SMEs dominate among investors abroad (by number but not by volume). However, their managers often came from large (socialist) companies where they acquired basic knowledge and networks of internationalization and created their own enterprises after transition started. Companies may be 'born multinational', but that does not apply to their management.

As regards the geographical location of outward FDI, evolutionary models predict internationalization first starts in culturally close, neighbouring, less demanding markets, markets with similar tastes or markets where substantial export experience has been gained. The geographical spread of activities and more distant countries lie parallel to internationalization experiences. Priority is given to those countries offering investors certain location-specific advantages which, when combined with firm-specific advantages, promise profitable business opportunities.

Slovenian firms have repeated the pattern. In spite of the wide geographical spread and diversification in terms of number of host countries, Slovenian outward FDI is concentrated in value terms in culturally and historically linked and neighbouring countries. Unlike exports, which are concentrated in developed EU markets, outward investment is mostly located in low- and middle-income countries (those less developed than Slovenia). Due to the former common market and the resulting rich knowledge and experience, particularly attractive locations for Slovenian outward investment are the successors to the former SFRY. A strategic orientation is built on brand names recognized in these markets and previous economic ties, or simply knowledge of how to do business in an environment where strong personal contacts are extremely important. Such knowledge, along with these personal contacts, is considered to be crucial to the success of outward FDI.

Developed markets are therefore mostly served by traditional exports, whereas a combination of market penetration methods is increasingly being used in less developed markets. The last decade did not bring any significant changes in the geographical distribution of outward FDI at the macro-level, despite the increase in the geographical spread at the firm level. Leading and successful companies from manufacturing have broadened their international networks of foreign affiliates around the world to become real multinationals, while internationally less experienced companies have become regional multinationals.

In addition, many exporters plan to upgrade their foreign operations from traditional exports to having a direct presence in a foreign market. The future plans of Slovenian firms reveal that firms are increasingly aware they can strengthen their competitiveness by maintaining a direct presence in foreign markets. When a firm is capable of internationalization through outward FDI it is also able to integrate into the wider economic area or, ultimately, into the global economy. The increased international competition that comes with transition accordingly motivates companies to develop firm-specific advantages with outward FDI, combine them with local specific advantages and speed up the process of catching up with the rivals. Such capabilities are a precondition for successful outward FDI. The specifically motivated starting phase of transition economies' outward FDI therefore did not change the usual internationalization pattern, although the accumulation of knowledge started earlier and contributed to the rapid development experienced in the nineties. Despite the fast changes in the international environment, internationalization remains a cumulative learning process, yet it is developing faster.

Today, it is not only business, but especially learning, that has to be more effective. Knowledge combined with the elimination of barriers and more active promotion is therefore an important tool that can convert the hitherto prevailingly pulled internationalization into pushed internationalization. Transition has enhanced and accelerated such learning. It represents a push factor of internationalization which, when combined with globalization and European Union integration as pull factors, is stimulating the outward FDI made by transition economies. With several positive effects such as increased access to market shares, higher exports and efficiency, the reverse is also true; internationalization via outward FDI enhanced transition offers one way for firms from transition economies to respond to the challenges of globalization.

Bibliography

Aghion, P., Garcia-Penalosa, C. and Howit, P. (2000), *Knowledge and Development: A Schumpeterian Approach*, paper prepared for World Bank ABCDE-Europe Conference, Paris, June 26-28, 2000.

Akamatsu, K. (1961), *A Theory of Unbalanced Growth in the World Economy*, Weltwirtshaftliches Archiv, 86, No. 2, pp. 196-217.

Ali, A.J. and Camp, R.C. (1993), 'The Relevance of Firm Size and International Business Experience to Market Entry Strategies', *Journal of Global Marketing*, Vol. 6, pp. 91-108.

Artisien, P., McMillan, C. and Rojec, M. (1992), *Yugoslav Multinationals Abroad*, Macmillan Press Ltd., London.

Artisien, P., Rojec, M. and Svetličič, M. (1991), 'Yugoslav Foreign Direct Investment in Less Developed Countries', in P.J. Buckley and J. Clegg (eds.), *Multinational Enterprises in Less Developed Countries*, Macmillan Press Ltd., London.

Artisien-Maksimenko, P. and Rojec, M. (eds.) (2001), *Foreign Direct Investment and Privatisation in Eastern Europe*, Palgrave, Basingstoke.

Bank of Slovenia (1993-2002), *Monthly Bulletin*, various issues, Bank of Slovenia, Ljubljana.

Bank of Slovenia (2000), *Direct Investment 1994-1999, 4(2)*, Bank of Slovenia, Ljubljana.

Bank of Slovenia (2001), *Direct Investment 1994-1999, 5(4)*, Bank of Slovenia, Ljubljana.

Bellak, C. (2001), 'The Austrian Investment Development Path', *Transnational Corporations*, Vol. 12, No. 2, pp. 107-134.

Bertoncelj, M. (2002), 'Iskraemeco bo rasel zunaj meja' ('Iskraemeco will Grow Abroad'), *Finance, 28 January*, Ljubljana, p. 21.

Bevk, N. (2000), *Iskraemeco*, presentation at workshop 'Slovenian FDI Abroad: Why, How and Where?', Chamber of Commerce and Industry, Ljubljana.

Bleyer, M.I. and Szapay, G. (1991), 'The "Gulliver Effect" and the "Optimal Divergence" Approach to Trade Policies; The Case of Nepal', *World Development*, Vol. 19, pp. 255-262.

Blomström, M. and Kokko, A. (1994), *Home Country Effects of Foreign Direct Investment: Sweden*, NBER working paper, No. 4639, University of Calgary Press, Calgary, pp. 341-364.

Blomström, M. and Kokko, A. (1997), *How Foreign Investment Affects Host Countries*, policy research Working Paper No. 1745, The World Bank, International Trade Division.

Blomström, M. and Kokko, A. (2000), *Outward Investment, Employment and Wages in Swedish Multinationals*, Working Paper No. 408.

Blomström, M. and Sjoholm, F., 1999, 'Technology Transfer and Spillovers: Does Local Participation with Multinationals matter?', *NBER Working Paper* No. 6816, November 1998 and European Economic Review, 43 (4-6), pp. 915-923.

Bohata, M. (2000), *Country Study Czech Republic*, paper prepared within Phare ACE project P97-8073-R, Centre of International Relations, Ljubljana.

Boillot, J. (2001), 'World Competitiveness: The Other Transition', English abstract, *Revue Elargissement*, (16).

Bojičić, M. (2001), 'Bratstvo in enotnost blagovnih znamk' ('Brotherhood and Unity of Trademarks'), *Gospodaski vestnik*, October, pp. 32-37.

Bole, V. (1999), 'The Conduct of Monetary Policy and Banking Soundness: A Slovenian Episode' in M.I. Blejer, M. Škreb (eds.), *Central Banking, Monetary Policy and the Implications for Transition Economies*, Oxford University Press, Oxford, pp. 185-212.

Bole, V. (2001), 'Ekonomsko politično obvladovanje velikih deviznih tokov' ('Economic and Political Management of Main Currency Flows'), *Bančni vestnik*, Vol. 50, Ljubljana, pp. 53-59.

Borgenzstein, E., De Gregorio, J. and Wha-Le, J. (1995), *How does Foreign Direct Investment Affect Economic Growth?*, working paper No. 5057, National Bureau of Economic Research, Cambridge.

Brandsma, A., Thumm, N. and Tübke, A. (2001), *Economic Transformation, Enlargement Future Report Series 01*, Final Report, Institute for Prospective Technological Studies.

Braunerhjelm, P and Ekholm, K. (1998), *Karolina: The Geography of Multinational Firms*, Kluwer Academic Publishers, Dordrecht.

Bučar, M. (2001), *Selected Case Studies of OFDI in Czech Republic and Slovenia*, compiled case studies prepared within Phare ACE project P97-8073-R, Centre of International Relations, Ljubljana.

Buckley, P.J. and Casson, M. (1998), 'Analysing Foreign Market Entry Strategies: Extending the Internalisation Approach', *Journal of International Business Studies*, Vol. 29, pp. 539-562.

Buckley, P.J. and Castro, B.F. (1998), *A Time Series Analysis of the Locational Determinants of OFDI in Portugal*, Academy of International Business, 25th Annual Conference, Vienna.

Buckley, P.J. and Castro, F.B. (1998), 'The Investment Development Path: The Case of Portugal', *Transnational Corporations*, Vol. 1, pp. 1-16.

Buckley, P.J. and Castro, B.F. (1999), *Outward FDI in Manufacturing from Portugal: Internationalisation Strategies from a New Foreign Investor*, European International Business Academy, Annual Conference, Manchester.

Buckley, P.J., Mirza, H. and Sparkes, J.R. (1985), 'Direct Investments in Japan as a Means of Market Entry: The case of European firms', *Journal of Marketing Management*, Vol. 2, pp. 241-258.

Business Eastern Europe, various issues.
Cantwell, J. (1994), *Transnational Corporations and Innovatory Activities*, Routledge, London.
Cantwell, J.A. and Tolentino, P.E. (1987), *Technological Accumulation and the Third World Multinationals,* paper presented at the Annual Meeting of EIBA, Antwerpen.
Centre for International Cooperation and Development (2001), *Investing in Slovenia*, Centre for International Cooperation and Development, Ljubljana.
Cirman, A. and Konič, M. (2000), 'Značilnosti delitve denarnega toka v slovenskih podjetjih' ('Characteristics of Cash Flow in Slovenian Enterprises'), in J. Prašnikar (ed.), *Internacionalizacija slovenskega podjetja*, Finance, Ljubljana, pp. 91-108.
Contractor, F.J. (1981), *International Technology Licensing: Compensation, Costs, Negotiation*, Lexington Books, Lexington.
Council Directive for the Implementation of Article 67 of the Treaty, 88/361/EEC.
Cross, A. (2000), 'Licensing and Franchising Across Borders; Theory, Management and Strategies for the 21st Century', *International Business Review*, Vol. 9, pp. 403-406.
Damijan, J.P. (1996), *Majhne države v svetovni trgovini (Small States in World Trade)*, Krt, Ljubljana.
Damijan, J.P. (2001), 'Trgovinski vs. investicijski način vstopa na trge nekdanje Jugoslavije' ('Trade vs. the Investment Entry Mode in the Former Yugoslav Markets') in J. Prašnikar (ed.), *Izivi in priložnosti na trgih nekdanje Jugoslavije (Challenges and Opportunities in the Former Yugoslav Markets*), Finance, Ljubljana.
Damijan, P.J. and Majcen, B. (2000), 'Trade Reorientation, Firm Performance and Restructuring of Slovenian Manufacturing Sector', *Emergo*, Vol. 7, pp. 24-35.
Davidson, W.H. and McFetridge, D.G. (1985), 'Key Characteristics in the Choice of International Technology Transfer Mode', *Journal of International Business Studies*, Vol. 16, pp. 5-21.
Delo, various issues, Ljubljana.
Djankov, S. and Hoekman, B. (1998), *Avenues of Technology Transfer: Foreign Direct Investment and Productivity Change in Czech Republic*, CEPR Discussion paper.
Domadenik, P., Prašnikar, J. and Svejnar, J. (2000), 'Prestrukturiranje slovenskih podjetij v razmerah nepopolno razvitih trgov' ('Restructuring of Slovenian Enterprises in the Conditions of Underdeveloped Markets'), in J. Prašnikar (ed.), *Internacionalizacija slovenskega podjetja*, Finance, Ljubljana, pp. 59-90.
Drucker, P. (1991), 'Roaches Outlive Elephants', *Forbes*, 19 August, pp. 72-74.
Dunning, J.H. (1981), 'Explaining Outward Direct Investment of Developing Countries – In Support of the Eclectic Theory of International Production', in K. Kumar, M.G. McLeod (eds.), *Multinationals from Developing Countries*, Lexington Books, Lexington, pp. 1-22.
Dunning, J.H. (1993), *Multinational Enterprises and the Global Economy*, Addison Wesley Publishing Company, Workingham.
Dunning, J.H. and Narula, R. (1996), *Foreign Direct Investment and Governments,*

Catalysts for Economic Restructuring, Routledge, London and New York.

Duris, R. (2002), Case Study Gorenje (Austria), working paper prepared within Phare ACE project P98-1162-R, Centre of International Relations, Ljubljana.

Economic Mirror, various issues, Institute of Macroeconomic Analysis and Development (IMAD), Ljubljana.

Éltető, A. and Antaloczy, K. (2002), *Outward Foreign Direct Investment in Hungary – Motives and Effects*, paper prepared within Phare ACE project P98-1162-R, Centre of International Relations, Ljubljana.

Eriksson, K., Johanson, J. and Majkgard, A. (1997), 'Experimental Knowledge and Cost in the Internationalization Process' *Journal of International Business Studies*, Vol. 28, No. 2, pp. 337-360.

European Bank for Reconstruction and Development (EBRD) (2001), *Transition Report 2001*, European Bank for Reconstruction and Development, London.

European Commission, (1997), *Capital Market Liberalisation, The Single Market Review*, Subseries III, Vol. 5.

Feige, E. and Ott, K. (2000), *Underground Economies in Transition. Unrecorded Activity, Tax Evasion, Corruption and Organised Crime*, Ashgate Publishing Ltd., Aldershot.

Ferner, A. (1997), 'Country of Origin Effects and HRM in Multinational Companies', *Human Resource Management Journal*, Vol. 7, pp. 19-31.

Financial Times (2001), 9 July 2001.

Foreign Trade Law, (1989), Official Gazette of the SFR Yugoslavia, No. 63.

Gorenje (1999), *Strategic Plan of the Gorenje Group until 2003, Summary*, Gorenje, Velenje.

Gorenje (2000), *Gorenje Group: This is Who We Are*, Gorenje, Velenje.

Gorenje (2000), Milestones on Our Path; Gorenje, Velenje 1950-2000, *Gorenje, Velenje.* Gorenje Annual Report 2000.

Gospodarska gibanja, (2001), 'Ogroženo notranje in zunanje ravnotežje' ('Threatened Internal and External Balance'), *Gospodarska gibanja* No. 323, EIPF, Ljubljana.

Gospodarska zbornica Slovenije (GZS) Chamber of Commerce and Industry (2001), *Največje in povezane družbe – v letu 2001 (The Largest Companies in 2001)*, Working Paper Vol. 8, No. 10, Chamber of Commerce and Industry, Ljubljana.

Grant, R. (1991), 'The Resource-based Theory of Competitive Advantage: Implications for Strategy Formulation', *California Management Review*, Vol. 33, No. 3, pp. 114-135.

Gregorič, A., Prašnikar, J. and Ribnikar, I. (2000), 'Corporate Governance in Slovenian Companies – A Comparison with Developed Countries', in J. Prašnikar (ed.), *Internacionalizacija slovenskega podjetja*, Časnik Finance, Ljubljana, pp. 11-36.

Guerrieri, P. (1998), *Trade Patterns, FDI, and Industrial Restructuring of Central and Eastern Europe*, working paper 124 prepared for Kreisky Forum and BRIE Policy Conference, Vienna, 1997.

Hamilton, J. (1986), *Red Multinationals or Red Herrings? The Activities of Enterprises from Socialist Countries in the West*, Frances Pinter (Publishers), London.

HarperCollins Dictionary of Economics (1991).

Hedlund, G. and Kverneland, A. (1985), 'Are Entry Strategies for Foreign Markets Changing? The Case of Swedish Investments in Japan', *International Studies of Management and Organisation*, Vol. 15, pp. 41-59.

Helpman, E. (1985), 'Multinational Corporations and Trade Structure', *Review of Economic Studies*, Vol. 52, pp. 443-457.

Horst, T. (1972), 'Firm and Industry Determinants of the Decision to Invest Abroad: An Empirical Study', *Review of Economics and Statistics*, Vol. 54, August, pp. 258-266.

Hunya, G. (1999), *Integration through Foreign Direct Investment: Making Central European Industries Competitive*, Edward Elgar, Cheltenham (UK), Northampton (MA).

Institute for Prospective Technological Studies (IPTS) (2001), *Synthesis Report*, October, Institute for Prospective Technological Studies, Seville.

Institute of Macroeconomic Analysis and Development (IMAD) (1999), *1999 Autumn Report*, Institute of Macroeconomic Analysis and Development, Ljubljana.

Institute of Macroeconomic Analysis and Development (IMAD) (2001a), *2001 Spring Report*, Institute of Macroeconomic Analysis and Development, Ljubljana.

Institute of Macroeconomic Analysis and Development (IMAD) (2001b), *Slovenija v Evropski uniji – Strategija gospodarskega razvoja Slovenije (Slovenia in the European Union – Strategy for the Economic Development of Slovenia)*, Institute of Macroeconomic Analysis and Development, Ljubljana.

Institute of Macroeconomic Analysis and Development (IMAD) (2001c), *Slovenian Economic Mirror*, Vol. 7, No. 11, Institute of Macroeconomic Analysis and Development, Ljubljana.

Institute of Macroeconomic Analysis and Development (IMAD) (2001d), *Slovenija v novem desetletju: trajnost, konkurenčnost, članstvo v EU, Strategija gospodarskega razvoja Slovenije 2001-2006 (Slovenia in a New Decade: Sustainability, Competitiveness, EU Membership; Strategy for the Economic Development of Slovenia)*, Institute of Macroeconomic Analysis and Development, Ljubljana.

International Monetary Fund (IMF) (1993), *Articles of Agreement*, International Monetary Fund, Washington DC.

International Monetary Fund (IMF) (1996), *Annual Report on Exchange Arrangements and Exchange Restrictions*, International Monetary Fund, Washington DC.

International Monetary Fund (IMF) (2001), *Article IV Consultations with the Republic of Slovenia, Public Information Notice No.01/50*, International Monetary Fund, Washington DC.

International Monetary Fund (IMF), *International Financial Statistics*, various issues.

Iskraemeco Annual Report 2000.

Jaklič, A. (2001), *Outward FDI versus Export in Economies in Transition: The Case of Slovenia*, paper presented at 27th Annual Meeting of European International Business Academy, 13-15 December, Paris.

Jaklič, A. (2001), *Outward Internationalisation by Direct Investment; The Case of Slovenia*, paper prepared within Phare ACE project P97-8073-R, Centre of International Relations, Ljubljana.

Jaklič, A. (2002), *Outward Foreign Direct Investment from Slovenia*, paper prepared within Phare ACE project P98-1162-R, Centre of International Relations, Ljubljana.

Jaklič, A., Bohata, M., Oszlay, A. and Rojec, M. (2001), *Review of Outward FDI Statistics in Czech Republic, Hungary and Slovenia and Recommendations for Improvements*, paper prepared within Phare ACE project P97-8073-R, Centre of International Relations, Ljubljana.

Jaklič, A. and Svetličič, M. (2001), 'Slovenia's Outward Direct Investment in the States of Former Yugoslavia: A Strategic or a Defensive Response?', *Economic and Business Review*, Vol. 3, No. 3-4, 2001, pp. 299-323.

Jaklič, M. (2000), 'Internacionalizacija podjetja Kolektor d.o.o.' (Internationalisation of the Company Kolektor d.o.o.), in J. Prašnikar (ed.), *Internacionalizacija slovenskega podjetja*, Finance, Ljubljana, pp. 167-195.

Japelj, M. (1998), 'Inovativne ('High-tech') tehnologije v farmacevtski industriji' ('High-tech Technologies in the Pharmaceutical Industry'), *Raziskovalec*, No. 2, pp. 12-16.

Japelj, M. (1998), *The Strategy and Development of Krka R&D*, paper presented at 14th World Congress on Project Management, 10-13 June, Ljubljana.

Johanson, J. and Mattsson, L.-G. (1986), 'International Marketing and Internationalization Processes – A Network Approach' in S. Paliwoda and P.N. Turnbull (eds.), *Research in International Marketing*, Croom Helm, London.

Johanson, J. and Vahlne, J.E. (1977), 'The Internationalisation Process of the Firm – A Model of Knowledge Development and Increasing Market Commitments', *Journal of International Business Studies*, Vol. 8, pp. 23-32.

Johanson, J. and Wiedersheim-Paul, F. (1975), 'The Internationalisation of the Firm – Four Swedish Cases', *Journal for International Business Studies*, October, pp. 305-322.

Jones, G. (1996), *The Evolution of International Business, An Introduction*, Routledge, London, p. 360.

Kalotay, K. (2002), 'Outward Foreign Direct Investment and Governments in Central and Eastern Europe: The Cases of the Russian Federation, Hungary and Slovenia', *The Journal of World Investment*, Vol. 3, No. 2, pp. 267-287.

Kilfoyle, S. (1996), *Cupa Cups S.A.; Managing International Expansion*, Case study, London Business School, London.

Kim, J.-D. and In-Soo K. (1997), 'Outward FDI and Exports: The Case of South Korea and Japan', *Journal of Asian Economics*, Vol. 8.

Knickerbocker, F.T. (1973), *Oligopolistic Reaction and the Multinational Enterprise*, Harvard University Press, Cambridge, MA.

Kogut, B. and Zander, U. (1992), 'Knowledge of the Firm, Combinative Capabilities, and the Replication of Technology', *Organization Science*, Vol. 3, pp. 383-397.

Kogut, B. and Zander, U. (1993), 'Knowledge of the Firm and the Evolutionary Theory of the Multinational Corporation', *Journal of International Business Studies*, pp. 625-646.

Kojima, K. (1977), *Japan and a New World Economic Order*, Charles E. Tuttle Company Inc., Tokyo.

Kokko, A. (2000), *FDI and the Structure of Home Country Production*, policy discussion paper No. 0018, Centre for International Economic Studies, University of Adelaide, Australia.

Kolektor Annual Report (2000).

Kolektor Annual Report (2001).

Konings, J. (1999), *The Effect of Direct Foreign Investment on Domestic Firms: Evidence from Firm Level Panel Data in Emerging Economies*, discussion paper No. 86/1999, Centre for Transition Economics and Central European Policy Research, London; LICOS Centre for Transition Economics, Katholieeke Universiteit Leuven.

Konings, J. and Murphy, A. (2001), *Do Multinational Enterprises Substitute Parent Jobs for Foreign Ones? Evidence from Firm Level Panel Data*, discussion paper No. 100/2001, LICOS Centre for Transition Economics, Katholieeke Universiteit Leuven.

Kraljič, P. (1990), 'The Economics Gaps Separating East and West', *The Columbia Journal of World Business*, Vol. 25 (4).

Kranjec, M. (1993), 'Monetary Policy of the Bank of Slovenia Since Independence' in M. Senjur (ed.), *A Small Country in the Global Economy*, Centre for International Cooperation and Development, Ljubljana, and The International Center for Economic Growth, San Francisco, pp. 203-214.

Krašovec, T. (1996), *Internacionalizacija slovenskega gospodarstva (Internationalization of the Slovenian Economy)*, Združenje Manager, Ljubljana.

Križnik, B. (2002), 'Sosed z dobički' ('Neighbour with Profit'), *Delo*, 28 February, Ljubljana.

Krka Annual Report 2000.

Krugman, P. (1983), 'The New Theories of International Trade and the Multinational Enterprises', in D.B. Audretch and C.P. Kindleberger (eds.), *The Multinational Corporation in the 1980s*, MIT Press, Cambridge, MA.

Lall, S. (1996), *Transnationals from Developing Countries; Impact on Home Economies*, Background Paper for the FIAS High Level Roundtable on the Outward Foreign Direct Investment from the Newly Industrialized Economies in Asia, Bangkok, Thailand, December 1996.

Lall, S. (2000), *FDI and Development: Research Issues in the Emerging Context*, policy discussion paper No. 0020, Centre for International Economic Studies, University of Adelaide, Australia.

Lek Annual Report 2000.

Lucas R., 1988, 'On the Mechanics of Economic Development', *Journal of Monetary Economics*, Vol. 22, pp. 3-42.

Luostarinen, R. (1979), *The Internationalisation of the Firm*, Helsinki School of

Economics and Business Administration, Helsinki.

Luostarinen, R. (1994), *Internationalisation of Finnish Firms and their Response to Global Challenges*, UNU World Institute for Development Economic Research (UNU/WIDER), Helsinki.

Makovec-Brenčič, M., Ahčan, A., Jevšnik, S., Kosi, S., Košir, I., Prosen, B. and Šturm, K. (2001), 'Analiza trgovine v Republiki Srbiji – možnosti slovenskega trgovskega podjetja Mercator, d.d. na srbski trg' ('Analysis of Trade in Republic of Serbia – Prospects of the Slovenian Trading Firm Mercator, d.d. in the Serbian Market'), in J. Prašnikar (ed.), *Slovenska podjetja na trgih nekdanje Jugoslavije*, Finance, Ljubljana.

Margan, F. (1982), *Marketing for Electrical Hand Machine-Tools of ISKRA*, VIII. Congress of JUMA, Novi Sad, p. 220.

Marinšek, M. (2000), *Mercatorjeve naložbe v tujini (Mercator's Investments Abroad)*, presentation at workshop 'Slovenian FDI Abroad: Why, How and Where?', Chamber of Commerce and Industry, Ljubljana.

Markusen, J.R. (1995), 'The Boundaries of Multinational Enterprises and the Theory of International Trade', *Journal of Economic Perspectives*, Vol. 9(2), pp. 169-189.

Markusen, J.R. (1997), *Trade versus Investment Liberalization*, Working Paper No. 6231, National Bureau of Economic Research (NBER).

Markusen, J.R. and Venables, A.J. (1995), *Multinational Firms and the New Trade Theory*, NBER working paper, No. 5036.

McMillan, H.C. (1987), *Multinationals from the Second World*, Macmillan Press, London.

Mencinger, J. (1995), *Gospodarski sistem in ekonomska politika Slovenije (Economic System and Economic Policy of Slovenia)*, Official Gazette of the Republic of Slovenia (OG RS), Ljubljana.

Mencinger, J. (2000), 'Deset let pozneje; tranzicija – uspeh, polom ali nekaj vmes' ('Ten Years Later; Transition – Success, Failure, or Something in between?'), *Gospodarska gibanja*, No. 317.

Mencinger, J. and Suppan, A., (1995), 'Slovenia', in W. Weidenfeld (ed.), *Central and Eastern Europe on the Way into the European Union*, Bertelsmann Foundation Publishers, Gütersloh.

Mercator Annual Report 2000.

Millington, A.I. and Bayliss, B.T. (1990), 'The Process of Internationalisation: UK Companies in the EC', *Management International Review*, Vol. 30, pp. 151-161.

Ministry of Finance (MF) (1999), *Poročilo o kapitalskih naložbah domačih pravnih oseb v podjetja v tujini 1995-1998 (Report on Capital Investments of Domestic Legal Entities Abroad 1995-1998)*, Ministry of Finance, Ljubljana.

More, M. (1999), *Legal Framework for Outward FDI in Slovenia*, CIS, Ljubljana.

More, M. (1999), *Uvod in komentar k Zakonu o deviznem poslovanju in podzakonskimi predpisi (Introduction and Comments on Foreign Trade Law and its By-laws)*, Oziris, Ljubljana.

More, M., Svetličič, M., Rojec, M. and Stare, M. (2000), *History of Outward Foreign Direct Investment in Slovenia*, paper prepared within Phare ACE project P97-8073-R, Centre of International Relations, Ljubljana.

Mrak, M. (1993), 'Slovenia: Creating its Own Identity in the International Financial Community', in M. Senjur (ed.), *A Small Country in the Global Economy*, Centre for International Cooperation and Development, Ljubljana, and The International Center for Economic Growth, San Francisco, 215-226.

Mrak, M., Jaklič, A. and Veselinovič, D. (2001), 'Finančni vidiki gospodarskega sodelovanja Slovenije z državami nekdanje Jugoslavije: pregled stanja in perspektive' ('Financial Aspects of Slovenian Economic Co-operation with Successor States to Yugoslavia') in J. Prašnikar (ed.), *Izzivi in priložnosti na trgih nekdanje Jugoslavije*, Finance, Ljubljana, pp. 131-160.

Mrak, M., Potočnik, J. and Rojec, M. (1998), *Strategy of the Republic of Slovenia for Accession to the European Union: Economic and Social Part*, Institute of Macroeconomic Analysis and Development, Ljubljana.

Mrak, M., Rojec, M. and Potočnik, J. (2002), 'The Transition Process in Slovenia: Transformation to an EU-Compatible Economy', *Journal of International Relations and Development*, Vol. 5, pp. 37-62.

Newbould, G.D., Buckley, P.J. and Thurwell, J. (1978), *Going International: The Experience of Smaller Firms Oversees*, Macmillan, London.

Official Gazette of the Republic of Slovenia (OG RS) (1993), *Zakon o zunanjetrgovinskem poslovanju (Foreign Trade Law)*, Official Gazette of the Republic of Slovenia (OG RS 13/93, 66/93) Ljubljana.

Official Gazette of the Republic of Slovenia (OG RS) (1994), *Zakon o zunanjetrgovinskem poslovanju (Foreign Trade Law)*, Official Gazette of the Republic of Slovenia (OG RS 7/94) Ljubljana.

Official Gazette of the Republic of Slovenia (OG RS) (1995), *Zakon o zunanjetrgovinskem poslovanju (Foreign Trade Law)*, Official Gazette of the Republic of Slovenia (OG RS 58/95) Ljubljana.

Official Gazette of the Republic of Slovenia (OG RS) (1999), *Pravilnik o vpisu v register neposrednih naložb rezidentov v tujini (Regulations on Residents' Registration of Foreign Direct Investment)*, Official Gazette of the Republic of Slovenia (OG RS 54/1999) Ljubljana.

Official Gazette of the Republic of Slovenia (OG RS) (1999), *Zakon o deviznem poslovanju (Foreign Trade Law)*, Official Gazette of the Republic of Slovenia (OG RS 23/99), Ljubljana.

Official Gazette of the Republic of Slovenia (OG RS), *various issues*, Official Gazette of the Republic of Slovenia (OG RS), Ljubljana.

Official Gazette of the SFR Yugoslavia (OG SRFY) (1960), *Decree on Certain Activities of Domestic Firms Abroad (OG SFRY, 26/60)*, Official Gazette of the SFR Yugoslavia, Belgrade.

Official Gazette of the SFR Yugoslavia (OG SRFY) (1972), *Law on Establishing Companies Abroad (OG SFRY, 39/72)*, Official Gazette of the SFR Yugoslavia,

Belgrade.
Official Gazette of the SFR Yugoslavia (OG SRFY) (1973), *Law on Establishing Companies Abroad (OG SFRY, 13/73)*, Official Gazette of the SFR Yugoslavia, Belgrade.
Official Gazette of the SFR Yugoslavia (OG SRFY) (1977), *Law on Performing Economic Activities Abroad (OG SFRY, 15/77)*, Official Gazette of the SFR Yugoslavia, Belgrade.
Official Gazette of the SFR Yugoslavia (OG SRFY) (1978), *Law on Performing Economic Activities Abroad (OG SFRY, 17/78)*, Official Gazette of the SFR Yugoslavia, Belgrade.
Official Gazette of the SFR Yugoslavia (OG SRFY) (1982), *Law on Changes and Amendments to the Law on Performing Economic Activities Abroad*, Official Gazette of the SFR Yugoslavia, Belgrade, No. 5.
Official Gazette of the SFR Yugoslavia (OG SRFY) (1982), *Law on Performing Economic Activities Abroad (OG SFRY, 5/82)*, Official Gazette of the SFR Yugoslavia, Belgrade.
Official Gazette of the SFR Yugoslavia (OG SRFY) (1985), *Law on Performing Economic Activities Abroad (OG SFRY, 71/85)*, Official Gazette of the SFR Yugoslavia, Belgrade.
Official Gazette of the SFR Yugoslavia (OG SRFY) (1989), *Zakon o zunanjetrgovinskem poslovanju (Foreign Trade Law) (OG SRFY 63/1989)*, Official Gazette of the SFR Yugoslavia, Belgrade.
Ohmae, K. (1990), *The Borderless World*, Collins, London.
Organisation for Economic Cooperation and Development (OECD) (1977), *Code of Liberalisation of Capital Movements*, Organisation for Economic Cooperation and Development, Paris.
Organisation for Economic Cooperation and Development (OECD) (1997), *Globalisation and Small and Medium Enterprises (SMEs)*, Organisation for Economic Cooperation and Development, Paris.
Ozawa, T. (1992), 'Foreign Direct Investment and Economic Development', *Transnational Corporations*, Vol. 1, pp. 27-54.
Pavlin, A. (2001), 'V Preventu želijo navdušenega kupca' ('Prevent Desires an Enthusiastic Buyer'), *Finance*, No. 127, Ljubljana, p. 24.
Pavlin, C. (2001a), 'Pred zgodovinsko reorganizacijo' ('Before the Historic Reorganization'), *Gospodarski vestnik*, No. 29, Ljubljana, pp. 24-25.
Pavlin, C. (2001b), 'Razdaja se in tudi to je poslovnost' ('Big-hearted is also Big-business'), *Gospodarski vestnik*, No. 32-33, Ljubljana, pp. 42-45.
Petrič, S. (1995), 'Včasih tudi bankrot prav pride' *(Sometimes Even a Bankruptcy Can Help), Delo, Sobotna priloga*, Ljubljana, 5 June, p. 34.
Petrič, S. (2000a), *Internacionalizacija dejavnosti slovenskih podjetij: Primer Kolektor d.o.o. (Internationalisation of the Activities of Slovenian Enterprises: The Case of Kolektor Pty. Ltd.)*, presentation at workshop 'Slovenian FDI abroad: Why, How and Where?', Chamber of Commerce and Industry, Ljubljana, Mimeo.

Petrič, S. (2000b), *Internacionalizacija slovenskega podjetja – Kolektor (Internationalization of Slovenian Enterprise – Kolektor)*, presentation at the Second Slovenian Business Conference, Portorož, Mimeo.

Pleskovič, B. and Sachs, J.D. (1992), *Political Independence and Economic Reform in Slovenia*, Mimeo.

Podjetnik (Enterpreneur), various issues, Ljubljana.

Porter, M.E., Sachs J.D., Cornelius, P.K., McArthur, J.W. and Schwab, K. (2001), *The Global Competitiveness Report 2001-2002*, World Economic Forum, Geneva.

Potočnik, J., Senjur, M. and Štiblar, F. (1995), *Approaching Europe – Growth, Competitiveness and Integration*, Institute of Macroeconomic Analysis and Development, Ljubljana, pp. 12-15.

Prevent Group Brochure 2001.

Prunk, J. (1996), *A Brief History of Slovenia*, Založba Grad, Ljubljana.

Quinlan, J. and Chandler, M. (2001), 'The U.S. Trade Deficit: A Dangerous Obsession', *Foreign Affairs*, Vol. 80, No. 3, pp. 87-97.

Reich, R.B. (1990), 'Who is Us?', *Harvard Business Review*, Vol. 68, No. 1, pp. 53-64.

Reich, R.B. (1992), *The Work of Nations*, Vintage Books, New York.

Rojec, M. (1998), 'Foreign Direct Investment's Effect on Restructuring and Efficiency Upgrading in Slovenia's Manufacturing Sector', *Journal of International Relations and Development*, Vol. 1, pp. 46-64.

Rojec, M. (2000a), *Foreign Direct Investment in Slovenia: Trends, Developments and Policy in 1997-1999*, working paper, Vol. 9, Institute of Macroeconomic Analysis and Development, Ljubljana.

Rojec, M. (2000b), 'Subsidiary Exports: A Conceptual Framework and Empirical Evidence', *Journal of International Relations and Development*, Vol. 3, pp. 128-152.

Rojec, M. (2000c), 'Restructuring and Efficiency Upgrading with FDI', in G. Hunya (ed.), *Integration Through Foreign Direct Investment*, Edward Elgar in association with The Vienna Institute for International Economic Studies (WIIW), Cheltenham, UK, Northampton, USA, pp. 130-149.

Rojec, M., More, M., Simoneti, M., Mrak, M., Svetličič, A., Močnik, M. (2001), *Slovenia: Foreign Direct Investment Review*, Faculty of Social Sciences, Ljubljana. Mimeo.

Romer, P.M., 1986, 'Increasing returns and long-run growth', *Journal of Political Economy*, 94, pp. 1002-1037.

Rugman, A. M. (1991), 'Diamond in the Rough', Business Quarterly, Winter, Ontario, Canada.

Senjur, M. (1993), 'The Viability of Economic Development of a Small State Separating from a Larger One', in M. Senjur (ed.), *A Small Country in the Global Economy, Centre for International Cooperation and Development*, Ljubljana, and The International Center for Economic Growth, San Francisco.

Senjur, M. and Štiblar, F. (1995), *Strategy for Economic Development: Approaching*

Europe – Growth, Competitiveness and Integration, Institute of Macroeconomic Analysis and Development, Ljubljana.

Simoes, V.C. (2000), *The Internationalisation of Portuguese Firms: History, Policy and Behaviour*, paper prepared within Phare ACE project P97-8073-R, Centre of International Relations, Ljubljana.

Simoes, V.C. (2001), *Outward FDI: Country Study Portugal*, paper prepared within Phare ACE project P97-8073-R, Centre of International Relations, Ljubljana.

Simoes, V.C. (2001), *The Internationalization of Portuguese Firms: What Implication for Central European Economies?*, paper prepared within Phare ACE project P97-8073-R, Centre of International Relations, Ljubljana.

Simoneti, M., Rojec, M. and Rems, M. (2001), 'Enterprise Sector Restructuring in a Small Economy: The Case of Slovenia', in D. Salvatore, M. Svetličič, J. Damijan Pavlič, (eds.), *Small Countries in a Global Economy*, Palgrave, Basingstoke and New York.

Slovenian Export Corporation (2001), *Annual Report 2001*, Slovenian Export Corporation, Ljubljana.

Sočan, L. (2001), 'Selected Case Study of OFDI; Gorenje Slovenia', in M. Bučar (ed.), *Selected Case Studies of OFDI in Czech Republic and Slovenia*, compiled case studies prepared within Phare ACE project P97-8073-R, Centre of International Relations, Ljubljana.

Sorg, M. (2001), 'The Way of Estonian Banks to the Global Market' in K. Liuhto (ed.), *East goes West – The Internationalization of Eastern Enterprises*, Lappeenranta University of Technology, Lappeenranta, pp. 315-349.

Stare, M. (2001), *Internationalisation of the Service Sector in Czech Republic, Hungary and Slovenia*, paper prepared within Phare ACE project P97-8073-R, Centre of International Relations, Ljubljana.

Stare, M. (2001), 'The Pattern of Internationalization of Services in Central European Countries', *The Services Industries Journal*, Vol. 22, No. 1, pp. 77-91.

Statistical Office of the Republic of Slovenia (SORS) (2000), *Republic of Slovenia: Statistical Yearbook*, Statistical Office of the Republic of Slovenia, Ljubljana.

Statistical Office of the Republic of Slovenia (SORS) (2001), *Slovenia in Figures*, Statistical Office of the Republic of Slovenia, Ljubljana.

Strojan Kastelec, A. (2001), *Ocena konkurenčne sposobnosti slovenskega gospodarstva, Prikazi in analize IX/1 (Evaluation of the Competitiveness of the Slovenian Economy, Surveys and Analyses IX/I)*, Banka Slovenije, Ljubljana, pp. 5-24.

Svetličič, M. (1975), *Wholly Owned and Mixed Companies in Economic Co-operation with Developing Countries in 1974*, Centre for Co-operation with Developing Countries, Ljubljana, p. 59.

Svetličič, M. (1977), *Delatnost vlastitih i mešovitih preduzeća u zemaljama u razvoju u 1977. godini (Mixed and Wholly-owned Firms Activities Abroad in 1977)*, Research Centre for Co-operation with Developing Countries, Ljubljana.

Svetličič, M. (1978), *Delatnost vlastitih i mešovitih preduzeća u zemaljama u razvoju u 1978. godini (Mixed and Wholly-owned Firms Activities Abroad in 1978)*, Research Centre for Co-operation with Developing Countries, Ljubljana.

Svetličič, M. (1979), *Proizvodnja saradnja preduzeća iz SFRJ i zemalja u razvoju (Production Co-operation between Yugoslavian and Firms from Developing Countries)*, Research Centre for Co-operation with Developing Countries, Ljubljana.

Svetličič, M. (1981), *Elementi strategije razvijenih oblika saradnje Jugoslavije sa zemaljama u razvoju kao specifičan oblik uklapanja u medjunarodnu podelu dela (Elements of the Strategy of Developed Forms of Yugoslav Co-operation with Developing Countries)*, Research Centre for Co-operation with Developing Countries, Ljubljana.

Svetličič, M. (1992), 'Izhodišča razvojne strategije Slovenije' ('Starting Points of the Development Strategy of Slovenia'), *Teorija in praksa*, Vol. 30, No. 1-2, pp. 26-37.

Svetličič, M. (1993), 'The Competitive Position of Slovenia to Attract Foreign Direct Investment', in M. Senjur (ed.), *A Small Country in the Global Economy*, Centre for International Co-operation and Development, Ljubljana, and The International Center for Economic Growth, San Francisco, pp. 155-168.

Svetličič, M. (1994), 'Foreign Direct Investment and the Transformation: Public Expectation and Results – The Case of Slovenia', in K. Fatemi (ed.), *The Globalization of Business in the 1990s: Implications for Trade and Development*, Texas A&M International University, 1369-1382.

Svetličič, M. (1995), 'Multinacionalna podjetja in razvojna strategija Slovenije. Splošni pogoji za gospodarski razvoj' ('Multinational Companies and the Development Strategy of Slovenia'), *Strategija gospodarskega razvoja*, Institute of Macroeconomic Analysis and Development, Ljubljana, pp. 65-88.

Svetličič, M. (1996a), 'Izhodna internacionalizacija dejavnosti slovenskih podjetij. Strategija ekonomskih odnosov s tujino' ('Outward Internationalization of Slovenian Firms'), *Zunanje ekonomska strategija Slovenije*, Ministry of Economic Relations and Development, Ljubljana, pp. 69-86.

Svetličič, M. (1998), *Slovenian State Strategy in the New Europe*, TKI working papers on European Integration and Regime Formation, South Jutland University Press, Esbjerg.

Svetličič, M. (2001), 'Razvojna strategija Slovenije: kritična analiza lastnih stališč' ('Slovenian Development Strategy; Critical Self-Assessment') in D. Zajc (ed.), *Slovenska država – ob desetletnici, Portorož, June 2001*, Faculty of Social Sciences, Ljubljana, pp. 151-176.

Svetličič, M. and Bellak, C. (2001), *Investment Development Path of Small Transition Countries: Conceptual Background and Empirical Evidence*, paper presented at conference 'Small states in world markets – fifteen years later', Gothenburg.

Svetličič, M. and Bellak, C. (2001), *Investment Development Path of Small Transition Countries: Conceptual Background and Empirical Evidence*, paper prepared within Phare ACE project P98-1162-R, Centre of International Relations, Ljubljana.

Svetličič, M. and Bučar, M. (1992), *The Strategy of International Economic Co-operation of Slovenia*, Development and International Co-operation, Ljubljana, Vol. 8, pp. 175-184.

Svetličič, M., Bučar, M., More, M. and Stare, M. (2000), *Promoting Outward FDI*, paper prepared within Phare ACE project P97-8073-R, Centre of International Relations, Ljubljana.

Svetličič, M. and Jaklič, A. (2002), *Comparative Evaluation of Outward FDI by Czech Republic, Hungary, Estonia, Poland and Slovenia*, paper prepared within Phare ACE project P98-1162-R, Centre of International Relations, Ljubljana.

Svetličič, M., More, M. and Rojec, M. (2001), *Development of Slovenia's Legal Policy Framework for Outward Foreign Direct Investment; Short History*, paper prepared within Phare ACE project P97-8073-R, Centre of International Relations, Ljubljana.

Svetličič, M. and Rojec, M. (1985), *New Forms of Equity Investment by Yugoslav Firms in Developing Countries*, Research Centre for Co-operation with Developing Countries, Ljubljana.

Svetličič, M. and Rojec, M. (1998), 'Kolektor: A Case Study of Foreign Direct Investment in Slovenia', *J. East-West business*, Vol. 4, No. 1-2, pp. 149-175.

Svetličič, M. and Rojec, M. (2003), *Facilitating Transition by Internationalization: Outward Direct Investment from Central European Economies*, Ashgate Publishing Ltd., Aldershot (forthcoming).

Svetličič, M., Rojec, M. and Lebar, S. (1994), 'Internationalization Strategies of Slovenian Firms: The German Market Case', in K. Obloj (ed.), *High Speed Competition in Europe*, proceedings of the 20th Annual Conference of the European International Business Association. Warsaw, International Management Center, University of Warsaw, pp. 361-385.

Svetličič, M., Rojec, M. and Trtnik, A. (2000), 'The Restructuring Role of Outward Foreign Direct Investment by Central European Firms: The Case of Slovenia', in A. Yaprak and H. Tütek (eds.), *Globalization, The Multinational Firm, and Emerging Economies*, (*Advances in International Marketing*, Vol. 10), JAI; Amsterdam, New York, An Imprint of Elsevier Science, pp. 53-88.

Svetličič, M., Simoes, V.C. and Luostarinen, R. (2001), *Selected Theories on Outward Foreign Direct Investment*, paper prepared within Phare ACE project P97-8073-R, Centre of International Relations, Ljubljana.

Svetličič, M. and Singer, H. (eds.) (1996), *The World Economy: Challenges of Globalization and Regionalization*, Macmillan, Basingstoke, St. Martin's Press, New York.

Svetličič, M. and Trtnik, A. (2002), 'Internationalisation through Outward Foreign Direct Investment; The Case of Slovenia' in M.A. Marinov (ed.), *Internationalisation in Central and Eastern Europe*, Ashgate Publishing Ltd., Aldershot.

Šušteršič, J., Rojec, M. and Mrak, M. (2001), *Slovenia in a New Decade: Sustainability, Competitiveness and EU Membership, The Strategy of Economic Development 2001-2006, Summary*, Institute of Macroeconomic Analysis and Development,

Ljubljana.
The Economist, various issues, London.
Tkalec, R. (2001), 'Kaj hoče Jože Kozmus?' ('What is it Jože Kozmus Wants?'), *Gospodarski vestnik*, No. 12, March, Ljubljana, pp. 17-19.
Tolentino, P. (1993), *Technological Innovation and Third World Multinationals*, Routledge, London.
Trtnik, A. (2000), *Internacionalizacija slovenskih podjetij z neposrednimi naložbami v tujino (Internationalization of Slovenian Companies through Foreign Direct Investment Abroad)*, Master's Thesis, Faculty of Economics, Ljubljana.
Tyebjee, T.J. (1994), 'Internationalization of High Tech Firms: Initial vs. Extended Involvement', *Journal of Global Marketing*, Vol. 7, pp. 59-80.
United Nations Conference on Trade and Development (UNCTAD) (1998), *World Investment Report 1998. Trends and Determinants*, United Nations Conference on Trade and Development, Division on Transnational Corporations and Investment, Geneva.
United Nations Conference on Trade and Development (UNCTAD) (2001), *World Investment Report 2001*, United Nations Conference on Trade and Development, Division on Transnational Corporations and Investment, Geneva.
United Nations Development Programme (UNDP) (2000), *Human Development Report 2000*, Oxford University Press, New York, Oxford.
Uvalić, M. (1996), *Economic Problems and Prospects of the Successor States of Former Yugoslavia*, presentation at Conference of the International Network Europe and the Balkans, Bologna and Forli, December 5-7.
Vahlne, J.E. and Wiedersheim-Paul, F. (1977), *Psychic Distance – An Inhibiting Factor in International Trade*, Working Paper, 1977/2, Centre for International Business Studies, University of Uppsala, Sweden.
Vernon, R. (1966), 'International Investment and International Trade in the Product Cycle', *Quarterly Journal of Economics*, 80, pp. 190-207.
Vezjak, D. (ed.) Fabinc, I., Gusel, L., Hrastelj, T., Tavčar, M. and Falatov, P. (1988), *Aktualne teme zunanje trgovine (Contemporary Foreign Trade Issues)*, Založba Obzorja, Maribor.
Vezjak, D., Falatov, P. and Hrastelj, T. (1980), *Načrtovanje skupnih vlaganj v tujini (Planning Joint Investments Abroad)*, Založba Obzorja, Maribor.
Vienna Institute for International Economic Studies (WIIW) (1999), *Countries in Transition 1999*, WIIW Handbook of Statistics, The Vienna Institute for International Economic Studies, Vienna.
Vilfan, J. (2001), 'Kako konkurenčna je Slovenija?' ('How Competitive is Slovenia?'), *Podjetnik*, June 2001, pp. 16-17.
Viteżnik, M. (2000), *Primer Gorenje d.d. (Case study of Gorenje d.d.)*, presentation at workshop 'Slovenian FDI Abroad: Why, How and Where?', Chamber of Commerce and Industry, Ljubljana.
Viteżnik, M. (2000), *The Experience of Slovenian Companies in FDI – the Case of Gorenje*, Centre of International Relations, Ljubljana.

Walsh, P. and Whelan, C. (2000), *Firm Performance and Political Economy of Corporate Governance: Evidence from Bulgaria, Hungary, Slovakia and Slovenia*, presentation at CEPR/WDI Annual International Conference on Transition Economies, Moscow, July, 2-5.

Welch, L.S. and Luostarinen, R. (1988), 'Internationalisation: Evolution of Concept', *Journal of General Management*, Vol. 14, pp. 36-64.

World Bank (WB) (1999), *Slovenia, Economic Transformation and EU Accession*, Vol. 2, Main Report, The World Bank, Washington D.C.

World Bank (WB) (2000), *Entering the 21st Century; World Development Report 1999/2000*, Oxford University Press, Oxford.

Zafarullah, M., Ali, M. and Young, S. (1998), 'The Internationalization of the Small Firm in Developing Countries – Exploratory Research from Pakistan', *Journal of Global Marketing*, Vol. 11, pp. 21-41.

Zemplinerova, A. (1997), *The Role of Foreign Enterprises in the Privatisation and Restructuring of Czech Economy*, Research Reports, No. 238, The Vienna Institute for Comparative Economic Studies (WIIW), Vienna.

Zupan, N. (1999), *Upravljanje s človeškimi viri v slovenskih podjetjih* (*Human Resource Management in Slovenian Companies*), doctoral thesis, Faculty of Economics, Ljubljana.

Name Index

Subject Index

ABPL-B

£55-00 Cl 10
ABPL-B